Buddha Nature

The Mahayana Uttaratantra Shastra

by Arya Maitreya

Arya Maitreya

Buddha Nature

The Mahayana Uttaratantra Shastra

by

Arya Maitreya

✦

written down by

Arya Asanga

commentary by

Jamgön Kongtrül Lodrö Thayé
"The Unassailable Lion's Roar"

explanations by

Khenpo Tsultrim Gyamtso Rinpoche

translated by

Rosemarie Fuchs

Snow Lion Publications
Ithaca, New York

Snow Lion Publications
P.O. Box 6483
Ithaca, New York 14851 U.S.A.
Telephone: 607-273-8519

www.snowlionpub.com

Copyright © 2000 Khenpo Tsultrim Gyamtso Rinpoche
and Rosemarie Fuchs

Illustrations by R.D. Salga

Printed in Canada on acid-free recycled paper.

ISBN 1-55939-128-6

Library of Congress Cataloging-in-Publication Data
Ratnagotravibhāga. English. Buddha Nature:
the Mahayana Uttaratantra Shastra / by Arya Maitreya;
with commentary by Jamgön Kongtrül Lodrö Thayé,
The Unassailable Lion's Roar, and explanations by
Khenpo Tsultrim Gyamtso Rinpoche; translated by Rosemarie Fuchs.
p.   cm.
Includes bibliographical references.
ISBN 1-55939-128-6 (cloth)
1. Yogācāra (Buddhism) I. Koṅ-sprul Blo-gros-mtha'-yas, 1813-1899.
II. Khenpo Tsultrim Gyamtso, 1934- III. Fuchs, Rosemarie, 1950-
BQ3022.E5 F83 2000   294.3'85--dc21
00-008017 CIP

Contents

Dedicated to
Khenpo Tsultrim Gyamtso Rinpoche
in deep gratitude and love

May your noble activity continue
as long as there is anyone in need.

✦ ✦ ✦

Namo Guru
As time goes by, with your blessing
may time itself reveal itself as timeless.
In timeless time and endless space
may truth be felt as it beholds its face.
May the lotus of compassion bloom,
fostering all beings in time and space.
May all suffering and torment be ended
and all Enlightened Ones come to rest.

Foreword

This book presents the commentary by Jamgön Kongtrül the Great, Lodrö Thayé, on Arya Maitreya's *Mahayana Uttara Tantra Shastra* (Tib. *theg pa chen po rgyud bla ma'i bstan bcos*). This is the first time an English translation of this commentary has been published. The book is the fruit of twenty years of study by Rosemarie Fuchs, a member of the Marpa Translation Committee and a devoted student of the very Venerable Khenpo Tsultrim Gyamtso Rinpoche.

This commentary has been taught by Khenpo Tsultrim Gyamtso Rinpoche to many Buddhist students around the world. In 1997, he taught it at the Rigpe Dorje winter program in Pullahari, Nepal, the main seat of His Eminence Jamgön Kongtrül Rinpoche. At the end of the teachings Khenpo Tsultrim Gyamtso Rinpoche gave the responsibility of finding ways to publish this commentary to the Jamgon Kongtrul Labrang, with his heartfelt wish that the activity of the Fourth Jamgön Kongtrül Rinpoche, Lodrö Chökyi Nyima, would flourish auspiciously.

Khenpo Tsultrim Gyamtso Rinpoche has been the spiritual advisor of Pullahari since His Eminence the Third Jamgön Kongtrül passed away in April 1992, and has clearly fulfilled the Third Jamgön Kongtrül's wish in establishing Pullahari as a place for the study and practice of Buddhadharma.

The Jamgon Kongtrul Labrang is profoundly grateful to Khenpo Tsultrim Gyamtso Rinpoche, Rosemarie Fuchs, and Snow Lion

Publications for making this teaching available to students and practitioners today and in the future. May this book benefit countless beings through the proper understanding of the ultimate Buddhist view.

Tenzin Dorjee
General Secretary to H.E. Jamgön Kongtrül Rinpoche
Pullahari Monastery, Nepal
July 16, 1999, the auspicious day of the first turning of
    the Wheel of Dharma.

Preface

This is a translation of the *Mahayana Uttara Tantra Shastra* (root text by Arya Maitreya, written down by the noble Asanga, with commentary by the first Jamgön Kongtrül Rinpoche Lodrö Thayé) as explained by Khenpo Tsultrim Gyamtso Rinpoche in 1978 in La Poujade, France, and in 1979 in Brussels, Belgium. It is the first translation of this particular commentary into a Western language. Throughout Buddhist history, the words of the Buddha and the scriptures explaining their meaning were translated when they were imported into different cultures. Though the first translation was never a final or flawless one, it constituted a basis for better ones to come in the future. I hope that this present text may continue this tradition. As it has been created at the advice and under the guidance of a truly accomplished master, there should be some virtue in it, and I wish that it may be of utmost benefit to any reader.

The introduction to Jamgön Kongtrül Rinpoche's commentary is not translated here, but can be found in S.K. Hookham's book *The Buddha Within* (Albany: State University of New York Press, 1991), pp. 263-288.

I would like to express my deep gratitude to Dzogchen Pönlop Rinpoche, Sangjä Nyenpa Rinpoche, Ringu Tulku Rinpoche, Acharya Lama Tenpa Gyaltsen, the late Acharya Tenpa Gyaltsen Negi, and Burkhard Quessel for their kind and invaluable help in the translation of passages that I found myself unable to do on my own. My further thanks go to Ani Jinpa for kindly proofreading the root text, to Lama Alaisdar MacGeaugh, and to Alexander Wilding for his incessant willingness to share his knowledge of dharma, improve my command of English, and to eliminate my old-fashioned reluctance to use computers. Special heartfelt thanks are owed to Katia Holmes who translated Khen Rinpoche's teachings on the root text in 1978 and thus made his instructions accessible for me and was my first teacher of his native language. Finally, I would like to thank Chris Hatchell for his careful and considerate help in editing the text.

The stanzas of the root text are presented in accordance with their explanation in the commentary. To stay as closely as possible to the original, the translation keeps the number of lines of the Tibetan text. As to the use of brackets, the content therein was added when it seemed necessary to facilitate understanding. In the case of the root text, these interpolations are derived from the commentary by Jamgön Kongtrül Lodrö Thayé; in the case of the commentary they are based on the explanations given by Khenpo Tsultrim Gyamtso Rinpoche.

One final point should be noted. Unlike Tibetan, the English language frequently requires the introduction of a pronoun, so a choice between "he" and "she" seemed necessary to avoid clumsiness. As buddha nature is neither male nor female, the term "he," when used for a buddha or bodhisattva, should be understood as meaning "he or she." Being a woman myself and convinced of the possibility of reaching enlightenment in female appearance, I thought it permissible to make this decision and hope it will not cause offense.

Rosemarie Fuchs
Hamburg, 23rd of July, 1999

Introduction

I.

The content of this volume is of the following essence: the teacher who explains the ground, path, and fruition of practice is the perfect Buddha, and from among all philosophies in the world his words are the highest and most genuine. The greatest commentary on their intention is the *Mahayana Uttara Tantra Shastra*, the Treatise on Buddha Nature, which is translated here.

This text can be considered as being the speech of the Buddha himself for the following two reasons: Firstly it was spoken by Maitreya, whom the Buddha empowered to be his regent in Tushita Heaven by placing his crown on Maitreya's head before he left this realm for the human world. Secondly it is stated in the *Sutra Compendium:*

> All the rivers in the world, carrying the waters that ripen flowers and fruit and cause forests to thrive, flow due to the power of the Naga King who resides in Lake Madröpa. Similarly any explanation, debate, composition, practice, and attainment of fruition achieved by his retinue of disciples depends solely on the power of the Victorious One himself.

For these reasons the *Uttara Tantra Shastra* can be considered either as the words of the Buddha spoken with his permission, or as those uttered by the power of his blessing. However, since according to Lord Maitreya's own words the *Uttara Tantra Shastra* contains a commentary on the intended meaning of the perfect speech of the capable and mighty Buddha himself, it is formally accepted as such. Furthermore, we should bring to mind that there is not the slightest difference between the pure speech of the Buddha on one hand, and that of Maitreya, the Lord of the Tenth Level, or of Manjushri, Avalokiteshvara, and Vajrapani, the Lords of the Three Families, on the other. From among all the innumerable commentators on the Buddha's words, their likes have never been seen in this world. For these reasons all the scholars and meditation masters of India and Tibet revere this great commentary called the *Uttara Tantra Shastra* and place it respectfully on the crowns of their heads.

II.

As to the question of which of the Buddha's sutras are commented upon by the *Uttara Tantra Shastra*, numerous scholars make many different assertions. The glorious Third Karmapa Rangjung Dorjé, however, clarifies that it is mainly a commentary on the Tathagatagarbha-sutras explaining buddha nature, which the Buddha expounded during his third turning of the Wheel of Dharma and which express the definitive meaning of all his teachings. Rangjung Dorjé explains that the Buddha in his omniscience saw that complete enlightenment is within all sentient beings in terms of their true nature. Yet, due to their ignorance they cannot see this and thus continue to wander through the cycle of existence. To provide the means to clear away the stains of this ignorance, the Buddha taught the Dharma, doing so in a gradual way that corresponded to his disciples' faculty of comprehending the meaning of his words. Initially the Buddha did not expressedly reveal the true nature of reality. Eventually he spoke directly of it, until finally he revealed it in full clarity, as it truly was.

The final and supreme among all the Buddha's countless teachings are those that express the definitive meaning and will ripen bodhisattvas with sharpest faculties whose mindstreams are thoroughly purified. These teachings are to be found in several sutras containing the profound and secret words of the most evolved philosophical tenet imaginable. Four of these elucidate the Chittamatra philosophy. They are the *Sutra Unraveling the Intention* (Tib. *dgong pa nge par 'grel pa'i mdo*), the *Travel to Lanka Sutra* (Tib. *lang kar gshegs pa'i mdo*), the *Sutra Taught in the Highest Pure Land "Greatly Adorned"* (Tib. *rgyan stug po bkod pa'i mdo*), and the *Flower Ornament Sutra* (Tib. *phal po chen*). Further sutras conveying the highest view are the *Sutra on Buddha Nature* (Tib. *bde gshegs snying po'i mdo*), the *Sutra of the Great Drum* (Tib. *rnga po che'i mdo*), the *Sutra For the Benefit of Angulimala* (Tib. *sor mo'i phreng wa la phen pa'i mdo*), the *Sutra Requested by the Goddess "Glorious Garland"* (Tib. *lha mo dpal phreng gis zhus pa'i mdo*), and others.

People like us, however, are of dull wits and our wrong views and lack of realization prevent us from being able to understand these sutras directly. In order to sustain the likes of us, Maitreya clearly taught their full content in the Seven Vajra Points that form the *Uttara Tantra Shastra*.

III.

Commentators on the words of the Buddha are classified by the scholars as being of three types: those of superior, middling, and faint qualifications. The author of the *Uttara Tantra Shastra* is not only renowned for possessing the highest qualities, such as profound learning in all sciences and direct vision of the truth of pure being. He is furthermore the undefiable Lord Maitreya who resides on a Dharma-cloud on the tenth bodhisattva level, who is the Buddha's great regent wielding all the powers and mastery that go along with that rank, who has infinitely excelled in the practice of the ten perfections, and who due to these achievements stands ready to become the fifth Buddha of this fortunate eon.

The one who preserved and spread these teachings of the *Uttara Tantra Shastra* within the world of humans was the master of learning Asanga. He was born as the son of the former nun Salwe Tsultrim, who out of her superior and altruistic motivation of benefitting the Dharma gave up her robes in times of a severe decline of the Buddha's teachings, married, and had two sons who she prayed would become great masters. Following his mother's wishes, Asanga first studied the Great Vehicle's teachings on "Manifest Knowledge." He found these studies incredibly difficult, however, and eventually turned to the practice of meditation on the deity Maitreya. He went into retreat and continued this practice for twelve years, during which he met with great difficulties again and again, as is related elsewhere in detail. After that time, though, Maitreya appeared to Asanga, accepted him as a disciple, and took him to Tushita Heaven. Asanga stayed there at Maitreya's feet for fifty human years, receiving many teachings, especially those now known as Maitreya's "Five Treatises." Bringing these back to the human world he wrote them down, and propagating them widely caused them to flourish. He himself wrote a commentary on the *Uttara Tantra Shastra* and, as was predicted by the Buddha in *The Root Tantra of Manjushri* (Tib. *'jam dpal rtsa rgyud*), he became one of the two most sublime proponents of the teachings of the

Great Vehicle. In view of his wondrous deeds, all true scholars and meditation masters of India and Tibet would have deepest devotion for Asanga and place him respectfully on the crowns of their heads.

IV.

There are many commentaries on the *Uttara Tantra Shastra* written in India and Tibet from the perspectives of both the Empty of Self and the Empty of Other views of the Middle Way philosophical traditions. Especially outstanding is the commentary written by Jamgön Kongtrul Lodrö Thayé. He was a saintly being prophesized by the Buddha in many sutras and tantras. His wisdom and achievement were such that he knew and assimilated every aspect of the philosophies and pith instructions of the eight practice lineages. His commentary is called the *Unassailable Lion's Roar.*

V.

In the unequaled tradition of the Dhagpo Kagyü, there are three lines of teachings on the Great Seal or Mahamudra. These are Sutra, Mantra, and Heart-Essence. Sutra-Mahamudra is the name the incomparable Dhagpo Rinpoche, Gampopa, lent to the view expressed in the *Uttara Tantra Shastra.* He did so in order to soothe the hearts of those who wanted to receive Mahamudra instructions but were not capable of fully comprehending the meaning behind them. He presented Sutra-Mahamudra as a means to guide these disciples towards the understanding of its latter two types.

In a similar way, the Venerable Jamgön Lodrö Thayé presents the *Uttara Tantra Shastra* as a background and context for the Mahamudra teachings. He explains it in the light of the Empty of Other School and makes its view quite easy to understand. Through his activity he has provided utmost benefit to all practitioners of Mahamudra. Especially nowadays, when centers for the study and practice of the teachings of the Kagyü Lineage have spread to all parts of the world, his instructions become equally important. In order to help the practitioners in these centers worldwide, Lodrö Thayé's commentary has been translated into English and been printed in this book.

✦ At the request of Khenpo Tsultrim Gyamtso Rinpoche this was written by Drupön Khenpo Acharya Lodrö Namgyal, at Pullahari Mahamudra Retreat Centre, Kathmandu, Nepal.

Arya Asanga

PART ONE

Root Text

CHAPTER ONE

Tathagatagarbha

Introduction

I bow down to all buddhas and bodhisattvas.

If condensed, the body of the entire commentary
[consists of] the following seven vajra points:
Buddha, Dharma, the Assembly, the element,
enlightenment, qualities, and then buddha activity.

In the above order, which presents them in a logical sequence,
  these [vajra points]
should be known to be derived from the *Sutra Requested by King
  Dharanishvara*.
The [first] three stem from its introductory chapter and the [latter]
  four from [its chapters]
on the properties of those who possess understanding and the
  Victorious One.

From the Buddha [stems] the Dharma, from the Dharma the
  Assembly of noble ones,
from the Assembly the attainment of buddha nature, the element of
  primordial wisdom.
This wisdom finally attained is supreme enlightenment, the powers
  and so on,
[thus] possessing the properties that fulfill the benefit of all sentient
  beings.

The First Three Vajra Points: The Three Jewels

Buddha

Buddha is without beginning, middle, or end. He is peace itself,
    fully self-awakened and self-expanded in buddhahood.
Having reached this state, he shows the indestructible, permanent
    path so that those who have no realization may realize.
Wielding the supreme sword and vajra of knowledge and
    compassionate love, he cuts the seedling of suffering
and destroys the wall of doubts along with its surrounding thicket
    of various views. I bow down to this Buddha.

Being uncreated and spontaneously present,
not a realization due to extraneous conditions,
wielding knowledge, compassionate love, and ability,
buddhahood has [the qualities of] the two benefits.

Its nature is without beginning, middle, or end;
hence [the state of a buddha] is uncreated.
Since it possesses the peaceful dharmakaya,
it is described as being "spontaneously present."
Since it must be realized through self-awareness,
it is not a realization due to extraneous conditions.
These three aspects being realized, there is knowledge.
Since the path is shown, there is compassionate love.
There is ability since the mental poisons and suffering
are relinquished by primordial wisdom and compassion.
Through the first three there is benefit for oneself.
Through the latter three there is benefit for others.

Dharma

The Dharma is neither non-existent nor existent. It is not both
    existent and non-existent, nor is it other than existent and
    non-existent.
It is inaccessible to such investigation and cannot be defined. It is
    self-aware and peace.
The Dharma is without defilement. Holding the brilliant light rays
    of primordial wisdom,
it fully defeats attachment, aversion, and dull indifference with
    regard to all objects of perception. I bow down to this sun of the
    sacred Dharma.

Inconceivable, free from the two [veils] and from thought,
being pure, clear, and playing the part of an antidote,
it is free from attachment and frees from attachment.
This is the Dharma with its features of the two truths.

Freedom from attachment [as fruit and means]
consists of the truths of cessation and path.
Accordingly these should also be known
by means of three qualities each.

Not being an object of conceptual investigation, being inexpressible,
and [only] to be known by noble ones, the Dharma is inconceivable.
Since it is peace, it is free from the two [veils] and free from thought.
In its three [aspects of] purity and so on it is similar to the sun.

Sangha
This mind being by nature clear light, they have seen the poisons to
    be essenceless
and therefore truly realize [the nature of] every being as peace, the
    ultimate non-existence of a self. They perceive that the Perfect
    Buddha pervades them all.
They possess the understanding that is free from the veils. Thus
    seeing that beings are utterly pure and that [this purity pervades]
    their limitless number,
they are endowed with the vision of primordial wisdom. I bow
    down to this [Sangha].

The assembly of those who have understanding
and thus do not fall back has unsurpassable qualities,
since their vision of inner primordial wisdom,
which knows correctly and knows completely, is pure.

Realizing beings in their state of peace
[the noble ones] know correctly,
for [the mind] is by nature utterly pure
and the poisons were always exhausted.

Their understanding, which realizes the knowable
as well as [its] ultimate condition, sees
that the state of omniscience is within all beings.
Thus the [noble ones] know completely.

Such realization is the vision of wisdom
that is self-aware. This wisdom is pure,
since it [sees] the undefiled expanse,
free from attachment and obstruction.

Their vision [of] primordial wisdom is pure
and [nears] unsurpassable buddha wisdom.
The noble ones who do not fall back
are therefore a refuge for all beings.

The Three Refuges

There being the teacher, his teaching, and his disciples
leads to respective aspirations towards three vehicles
and to three different activities [of veneration].
Viewing this, the refuge is shown as threefold.

[The Dharma] will be abandoned and is of an unsteady nature.
It is not [the ultimate quality], and [the Sangha] is still with fear.
Thus the two aspects of Dharma and the Assembly of noble ones
do not represent the supreme refuge, which is constant and stable.
In a true sense only the Buddha is beings' refuge,
since the Great Sage embodies the dharmakaya,
and the Assembly also reaches its ultimate goal
when these [qualities of dharmakaya are attained].

Their occurence is rare, they are free from defilement,
they possess power, they are the adornment of the world,
they are sublime, and they are unchanging.
Thus [they are named] "rare and sublime."

The Last Four Vajra Points

The virtuous Three Jewels, which are rare and sublime,
arise from suchness bound up with pollution, from the one free
    from pollution,
from the qualities of unpolluted buddhahood, and from the deeds of
    the Victor.
This is the object of those who see the ultimate truth.

The disposition of the Three Rare and Sublime Ones
is the object [of vision] of those who see everything.

Furthermore, these four aspects in the given order
are inconceivable, for the following four reasons:

[The buddha element] is pure and yet has affliction.
[Enlightenment] was not afflicted and yet is purified.
Qualities are totally indivisible [and yet unapparent].
[Activity] is spontaneous and yet without any thought.

Constituting what must be realized, realization,
its attributes, and the means to bring it about,
accordingly the first is the cause to be purified
and the [latter] three points are the conditions.

The Fourth Vajra Point: The Element

The perfect buddhakaya is all-embracing,
suchness cannot be differentiated,
and all beings have the disposition.
Thus they always have buddha nature.

The Buddha has said that all beings have buddha nature
"since buddha wisdom is always present within the assembly
    of beings,
since this undefiled nature is free from duality,
and since the disposition to buddhahood has been named after
    its fruit."

Essence, cause, fruit, function, endowment, manifestation,
phases, all-pervasiveness of suchness, unchangingness,
and inseparability of the qualities should be understood
as intended to describe the meaning of the absolute expanse.

Just as a jewel, the sky, and water are pure
it is by nature always free from the poisons.
From devotion to the Dharma, from highest wisdom,
and from samadhi and compassion [its realization arises].

[Wielding] power, not changing into something else,
and being a nature that has a moistening [quality]:
these [three] have properties corresponding
to those of a precious gem, the sky, and water.

Enmity towards the Dharma, a view [asserting
an existing] self, fear of samsara's suffering,
and neglect of the welfare of fellow beings
are the four veils of those with great desire,
of tirthikas, shravakas, and pratyekabuddhas.
The cause that purifies [all these veils]
consists of the four qualities [of the path],
which are outstanding devotion and so on.

Those whose seed is devotion towards the supreme vehicle,
whose mother is analytical wisdom generating the buddha qualities,
whose abode is the blissful womb of meditative stability,
and whose nurse is compassion, are heirs born to succeed
      the Muni.

The fruit is the perfection of the qualities
of purity, self, happiness, and permanence.
Weariness of suffering, longing to attain peace,
and devotion towards this aim are the function.

In brief, the fruit of these [purifying causes]
fully divides into the remedies [for the antidotes],
which [in their turn] counteract the four aspects
of wrong beliefs with regard to the dharmakaya.

The [dharmakaya] is purity, since its nature is pure
and [even] the remaining imprints are fully removed.
It is true self, since all conceptual elaboration
in terms of self and non-self is totally stilled.
It is true happiness, since [even] the aggregates
of mental nature and their causes are reversed.
It is permanence, since the cycle of existence
and the state beyond pain are realized as one.

Their analytical wisdom has cut all self-cherishing without
      exception.
Yet, cherishing beings, those possessed of compassion do not adhere
      to peace.
Relying on understanding and compassionate love, the means to
      enlightenment,
noble ones will neither [abide] in samsara nor in a [limited] nirvana.

If the buddha element were not present,
there would be no remorse over suffering.
There would be no longing for nirvana,
nor striving and devotion towards this aim.

That with regard to existence and nirvana their respective fault and
   quality are seen,
that suffering is seen as the fault of existence and happiness as the
   quality of nirvana,
stems from the presence of the disposition to buddhahood. "Why so?"
In those who are devoid of disposition, such seeing does not occur.

Like the great sea it holds qualities
immeasurable, precious, and inexhaustible.
Its essence holds indivisible properties.
Thus [the element] is similar to a lamp.

Unifying the elements of dharmakaya,
a victor's wisdom, and great compassion,
it is shown as being similar to the sea
by the vessel, the gems, and the water.

Clairvoyance, primordial wisdom, and absence of pollution
are totally indivisible and native to the unstained abode.
Thus it has properties corresponding
to the light, heat, and color of a lamp.

Based upon the manifestation of suchness dividing
into that of an ordinary being, that of a noble one,
and that of a perfect buddha, He who Sees Thatness
has explained the nature of the Victor to beings.

[It manifests as] perverted [views in] ordinary beings,
[as] the reversal [of these in] those who see the truth,
and [it manifests] as it is, in an unperverted way,
and as freedom from elaboration [in] a tathagata.

The unpurified, the both unpurified and purified,
and the utterly purified [phases]
are expressed in their given order
[by the names] "being," "bodhisattva," and "tathagata."

The element as contained
in the six topics of "essence" and so on
is explained in the light of three phases
by means of three names.

Just as space, which is by nature free from thought,
pervades everything,
the undefiled expanse, which is the nature of mind,
is all-pervading.

As the general feature [of everything], it embraces [those with]
    faults,
[those with] qualities, and [those in whom the qualities are]
    ultimate
just as space [pervades everything] visible,
be it of inferior, average, or supreme appearance.

Having faults that are adventitious
and qualities that are its nature,
it is afterwards the same as before.
This is dharmata ever unchanging.

[Though] space permeates everything,
it is never polluted, due to its subtlety.
Likewise the [dharmadhatu] in all beings
does not suffer the slightest pollution.

Just as at all times worlds arise
and disintegrate in space,
the senses arise and disintegrate
in the uncreated expanse.

Space is never burnt by fires.
Likewise this [dharmadhatu]
is not burnt by the fires
of death, sickness, and aging.

Earth rests upon water and water upon wind.
Wind fully rests on space.
Space does not rest upon any of the elements
of wind, water, or earth.

Likewise skandhas, elements, and senses
are based upon karma and mental poisons.
Karma and poisons are always based
upon improper conceptual activity.
The improper conceptual activity
fully abides on the purity of mind.
Yet, the nature of the mind itself
has no basis in all these phenomena.

The skandhas, entrances, and elements
are to be known as resembling earth.
Karma and the mental poisons of beings
should be envisaged as the water element.
Improper conceptual activity is viewed
as being similar to the element of wind.
[Mind's] nature, as the element of space,
has no ground and no place of abiding.

The improper conceptual activity
rests upon the nature of the mind.
Improper conceptual activity brings about
all the classes of karma and mental poisons.
From the water of karma and mental poisons
the skandhas, entrances, and elements arise.
As this [world] arises and disintegrates,
they will arise and disintegrate as well.

The nature of mind as the element of space
does not [depend upon] causes or conditions,
nor does it [depend on] a gathering of these.
It has neither arising, cessation, nor abiding.

This clear and luminous nature of mind
is as changeless as space. It is not afflicted
by desire and so on, the adventitious stains,
which are sprung from incorrect thoughts.

It is not brought into existence
by the water of karma, of the poisons, and so on.
Hence it is also not consumed by the cruel fires
of dying, falling sick, and aging.

The three fires of death, sickness, and aging
are to be understood in their given sequence
as resembling the fire at the end of time,
the fire of hell, and an ordinary fire.

Having realized thatness, the nature of the [dharmadhatu], just as it is,
those of understanding are released from birth, sickness, aging, and
    death.
Though free from the destitution of birth and so on, they demonstrate
    these,
since by their [insight] they have given rise to compassion for beings.

The noble have eradicated the suffering
of dying, falling ill, and aging at its root,
which is being born due to karma and poisons.
There being no such [cause], there is no such [fruit].

Since they have seen reality as it is,
they are beyond being born and so on.
Yet, as the embodiment of compassion itself
they display birth, illness, old age, and death.

After the heirs of the Victorious One
have realized this changeless state,
those who are blinded by ignorance
see them as being born and so forth.
That such seeing should occur is truly wonderful and amazing.
When they have attained the field of experience of the noble,
they show themselves as the field of experience of the children.
Hence means and compassion of the friends of beings are supreme.

Though they are beyond all worldly matters,
these [bodhisattvas] do not leave the world.
They act for the sake of all worldly beings
within the world, unblemished by its defects.
As a lotus will grow in the midst of water,
not being polluted by the water's [faults],
these [noble ones] are born in the world
unpolluted by any worldly phenomena.

Viewing the accomplishment of their task,
their understanding always blazes like fire.
And they always rest evenly balanced
in meditative stability, which is peace.

By the power of their former [prayers]
and since they are free from all ideation,
they do not exert any deliberate effort
to lead all sentient beings to maturation.
These [heirs of the Victorious One] know precisely
how and by what [method] each should be trained—
through whatever teachings, form kayas, conduct,
and ways of behavior are individually appropriate.
Always [acting] spontaneously and without hindrance
for sentient beings whose number is limitless as space,
such [bodhisattvas] who possess understanding
truly engage in the task of benefitting beings.

The way the bodhisattvas [unfold activity]
in the post-meditative phase
equals the tathagatas' [action] in the world
for beings' true liberation.
Though this is true, indeed, whatever difference lies
between the earth and an atom or else between
[the water in] the sea and in an ox's hoofprint,
is the difference between a buddha and a bodhisattva.

[The dharmakaya] does not change into something else, since it has
    inexhaustible properties.
It is the refuge of beings, since [it protects them] without any limit of
    time, until the final end.
It is always free from duality, since it is foreign to all ideation.
It is also an indestructible state, since its nature is uncreated.

It is not born, and it does not die.
It suffers no harm and does not age
since it is permanent and steadfast,
the state of peace and immutability.

It is not [even] born in a body of mental nature,
since it is permanent. Steadfast it does not die,
not [even] through the death and transmigration
that constitute an inconceivable transformation.
Since it is peace, it does not [even] suffer harm
from illnesses caused by subtle karmic imprints.
Since it is immutable, there is not [even] aging
induced by compositional factors free from stain.

[Combining] sentences from the foregoing
two by two, the uncreated expanse should be known
[as possessing] in the same sequence
the attributes of being permanent and so forth.

Since it is endowed with inexhaustible qualities, [the dharmakaya]
is unchangingness itself and thus [has] the attribute of permanence.
Equaling the uttermost end it is refuge itself
and thus [holds] the attribute of steadfastness.
Since absence of thought is its nature, it is dharmata
free from duality and thus [has] the attribute of peace.
Hosting uncreated qualities, it is immutability itself
and thus [possesses] the attribute of indestructibility.

Why is it the dharmakaya, the tathagata,
the noble truth, and the absolute nirvana?
Its qualities are inseparable, like the sun and its rays.
Thus other than buddhahood there is no nirvana.

Since the unpolluted expanse has, put briefly,
four different types of meaning,
it should be known in terms of four synonyms:
the dharmakaya and so forth.

Buddha qualities are indivisible.
The disposition is attained as it is.
The true state is [always] free from any fickleness and deceit.
Since beginningless time the nature has been peace itself.

Direct perfect enlightenment [with regard to] all aspects,
and abandonment of the stains along with their imprints
[are called] buddha and nirvana respectively.
In truth, these are not two different things.

Liberation is distinguished by indivisibility
from qualities present in all their aspects:
innumerable, inconceivable, and unpolluted.
Such liberation is [also called] "tathagata."

Suppose some painters mastered their craft,
each with respect to a different [part of the body],
so that whichever part one would know how to do,
he would not succeed with any other part.
Then the king, the ruler of the country,
hands them a canvas and gives the order:
"You all together paint my image on this!"
Having heard this [order] from the [king]
they carefully take up their painting work.
While they are well immersed in their task,
one among them leaves for another country.
Since they are incomplete
due to his travel abroad,
their painting in all its parts
does not get fully perfected.
Thus the example is given.

Who are the painters of these [parts of the image]?
They are generosity, morality, patience, and so on.
Emptiness endowed with all supreme aspects
is described as being the form [of the king].

Illuminating, radiating, and purifying,
and inseparable from each other, analytical wisdom,
primordial wisdom, and total liberation
correspond to the light, rays, and orb of the sun.

One will therefore not attain nirvana
without attaining the state of buddhahood.
Just as one could not see the sun
if one were to eliminate its light and its rays.

In this way the nature of the Victorious One
is expressed [by] the "Tenfold Presentation."

This [tathagatagarbha] abides within the shroud of the afflictions,
as should be understood through [the following nine] examples:

Just like a buddha in a decaying lotus, honey amidst bees,
a grain in its husk, gold in filth, a treasure underground,
a shoot and so on sprouting from a little fruit,
a statue of the Victorious One in a tattered rag,
a ruler of mankind in a destitute woman's womb,
and a precious image under [a layer of] clay,
this [buddha] element abides within all sentient beings,
obscured by the defilement of the adventitious poisons.

The defilements correspond to the lotus,
the insects, the husk, the filth, the earth,
the fruit, the tattered rag, the pregnant woman
direly vexed with burning suffering, and the clay.
The buddha, the honey, the grain, the gold,
the treasure, the nyagrodha tree, the precious statue,
the continents' supreme ruler, and the precious image
are similar to the supreme undefiled element.

Seeing that in the calyx of an ugly-colored lotus
a tathagata dwells ablaze with a thousand marks,
a man endowed with the immaculate divine vision
takes it from the shroud of the water-born's petals.

Likewise the Sugata with his buddha eye perceives his own true
    state even in those
who must abide in the hell of direst pain.
Endowed with compassion itself, which is unobscured and endures
    to the final end,
he relieves them from their obscurations.

Once his divine eye sees the Sugata abiding within the closed
　　ugly lotus,
the man cuts the petals. Seeing the perfect buddha nature
　　within beings,
obscured by the shroud of desire, hatred, and the other mental
　　poisons,
the Muni does likewise and through his compassion defeats all
　　their veils.

Honey is surrounded by a swarm of insects.
A skillful man in search of [honey]
[employs], upon seeing this, suitable means
to fully separate it from the host of bees.

Likewise, when his eye of omniscience
sees the honey-like element of awareness,
the Great Sage causes its bee-like veils
to be fully and radically abandoned.

Aiming to get honey that is obscured by millions and millions of
　　honeybees,
the man disperses all these bees and procures the honey, just as he
　　wishes.
The unpolluted knowledge present in all sentient beings is similar
　　to the honey,
and the Victor skilled in vanquishing the bee-like poisons resembles
　　the man.

A grain when still in its husk
is not fit to be eaten by man.
Those seeking food and sustenance
remove this [grain] from its husk.

[The nature of] the Victorious One, which is present within beings
[but] mixed with the defilement of the poisons, is similar to this.
While it is not freed from being mingled with the pollution of these
　　afflictions,
the deeds of the Victor will not be [displayed] in the three realms of
　　existence.

Unthreshed grains of rice, buckwheat, or barley, which not having
    emerged from their husks
still have husk and beard, cannot be turned into delicious food that
    is palatable for man.
Likewise the Lord of Qualities is present within all beings, but his
    body is not liberated from the shroud of the poisons.
Thus his body cannot bestow the joyous taste of Dharma upon
    sentient beings stricken by the famine of their afflictions.

While a man was traveling, gold he owned
fell into a place filled with rotting refuse.
This [gold], being of indestructible nature,
remained for many centuries just as it was.
Then a god with completely pure divine vision saw it there
and addressed a man: "Purify this supremely precious gold
lying here in this [filth], and [then convert it into something]
that is worth being made from such a precious substance!"

Likewise the Muni sees the quality [of] beings,
which is sunken in the filth-like mental poisons,
and pours his rain of sacred Dharma upon them
to purify the muddiness of their afflictions.

Once the god has seen the gold that has fallen into the place full of
    rotting refuse,
insistently he directs the man's attention to this supremely beautiful
    thing so he may completely cleanse it.
Seeing within all beings the precious perfect buddha that has fallen
    into the great filth of the mental poisons,
the Victorious One does likewise and teaches the Dharma to persuade
    them to purify it.

If an inexhaustible treasure were buried
in the ground beneath a poor man's house,
the man would not know of it, and the treasure
would not speak and tell him "I am here!"

Likewise a precious treasure is contained in each being's mind. This
    is its true state,
which is free from defilement. Nothing is to be added and nothing
    to be removed.

Nevertheless, since they do not realize this, sentient beings
continuously undergo the manifold sufferings of deprivation.

When a precious treasure is contained within [the ground beneath] a
    poor man's house,
the treasure cannot tell him "I am here!" [and] the man does not
    know of its presence.
Like the poor man, beings are [unaware] that Dharma's treasure lies
    in the house of their minds
and the great Sage truly takes birth within the world to cause them
    to attain [this treasure].

The seed contained in the fruit of a mango or similar trees
[is possessed of] the indestructible property of sprouting.
Once it gets plowed-earth, water, and the other
    [conditions],
the substance of a majestic tree will gradually come about.

The fruit consisting of the ignorance and the other defects of beings
contains in the shroud of its peel the virtuous element of the dharma[kaya].
Likewise, through relying on virtue, this [element] also
will gradually turn into the substance of a King of Munis.

By means of water, sunlight, wind, earth, time, and space, the
    necessary conditions,
the tree grows from within the narrow shroud of the fruit of a
    banana or mango.
Similarly the fertile seed of the Perfect Buddha, contained within the
    fruit-skin of the mental poisons of beings,
also grows from virtue as its necessary condition, until the [shoot of]
    Dharma is seen and augmented [towards perfection].

An image of the Victorious One made from precious material
lies by the road, wrapped in an evil-smelling tattered rag.
Upon seeing this, a god will alert the [passersby]
to its presence by the road to cause its retrieval.

Likewise, being possessed of unhindered vision
[the Buddha] sees the substance of the Sugata
wrapped in the multitude of the mental poisons,
even in animals, and teaches the means to free it.

When his eye perceives the statue of the Tathagata, which is of
    precious nature
but wrapped in a stinking rag and lying by the road, the god points
    it out to passersby, so that they retrieve it.
Likewise the Victor sees that the element, wrapped in the tattered
    garments of the poisons and lying on samsara's road,
is present even within animals, and teaches the Dharma so that it
    may be released.

A woman of miserable appearance
who is without protection and abides in a poorhouse
holds in her womb a glorious king,
not knowing that a lord of man dwells in her own body.

Birth in an existence is similar to the poorhouse.
Impure beings are like the woman bearing [a king] in her womb.
Since he is present within her, she has protection.
The undefiled element is like [the king] who dwells in her womb.

A ruler of the earth dwells in the womb of a woman who has an
    unpleasant appearance and whose body is dressed in dirty
    clothes.
Nevertheless she has [to abide] in a poorhouse and undergo the
    experience of direst suffering.
Likewise, beings deem themselves unsheltered though a protector
    resides within their own [minds].
Thus they have to abide in the ground of suffering, their minds being
    unpeaceful under the predominating drive of the mental poisons.

An artistically well-designed image of peaceful appearance,
which has been cast in gold and is [still] inside [its mold],
externally has the nature of clay. Experts, upon seeing this,
will clear away the outer layer and cleanse the gold therein.

Likewise those of supreme enlightenment
fully see that there are defilements [on] the luminous nature,
but that these stains are just adventitious,
and purify beings, who are like jewel mines, from all their veils.

Recognizing the nature of an image of peaceful appearance,
    flawless and made from shimmering gold,
while it is [still] contained in its mold, an expert removes the
    layers of clay.
Likewise the omniscient know the peaceful mind, which is
    similar to pure gold,
and remove the obscurations by teaching the Dharma, [just as
    the mold] is struck and chipped away.

The lotus, the bees, the husk, the filth,
the earth, the skin of the fruit, the tattered rag,
the woman's womb, and the shroud of clay
[exemplify the defilements], while [the pure nature]
is like the buddha, the honey, the kernel, the gold,
the treasure, the great tree, the precious statue,
the universal monarch, and the golden image.
It is said that the shroud of the mental poisons,
[which causes the veils] of the element of beings,
has had no connection with it since beginningless time,
while the nature of mind, which is devoid of stains,
[has been present within them] since beginningless time.

The nine aspects of defilement: desire, aversion,
and mental blindness, their fierce active state,
the remaining imprints [of unknowing], the defilements
to be abandoned on the paths of seeing and meditation,
and the defilements based upon the impure levels
and the pure levels respectively, are fully taught
by the shroud of the lotus and the other examples.
[When] classified, the shroud of the secondary poisons
is beyond any end. But when it is comprised concisely,
the nine defilements of desire and the other afflictions
are well explained in the given order by the nine similes
of the shroud of the lotus and the subsequent examples.

These defilements cause in their given sequence
the four impurities of children, the impurity of arhats,
the two impurities of followers of the path of training,
and the two impurities of those with understanding.

When a lotus [just] born from the mud
appears to [a beholder], it delights his mind.
Yet later it changes and becomes undelightful.
The joy born from desire is similar to this.

Bees, when extremely agitated,
will fiercely use their stings.
Similarly, hatred, once arisen,
brings suffering to the heart.

The kernel of rice and so on
is obscured by its outer husk.
Likewise the vision of the [true] meaning
is obscured by the eggshell of ignorance.

Filth is repugnant.
Being the cause for those bound up with greed
to indulge in sense pleasures,
the active state [of the poisons] resembles it.

When wealth is hidden, one is ignorant of it
and therefore does not obtain the treasure.
Likewise self-sprung [wisdom] is veiled in arhats
by the ground of remaining imprints of ignorance.

As by gradual growth from bud to shoot
the skins of the seed are cut,
the vision of thatness averts
[the stains] to be abandoned by seeing.

Through their junction with the noble path
they have overcome the essential part of the transitory collection.
What their wisdom must abandon [on] the path of meditation
is explained as being similar to tattered rags.

The stains based on the seven [impure] levels
resemble the defilements of the shrouding womb.
Concept-free primordial wisdom [is released]
like the mature [prince] from the womb's confine.

The defilements connected with the three [pure] levels
should be known as being similar to the layer of clay.
They must be overcome by the vajra-like samadhi
of [those] who are the embodiment of greatness.

Thus desire and the further of the nine defilements
correspond to the lotus and the following examples.

Its nature unifying three aspects, the element has properties
that correspond to those of the Buddha and the other similes.

Its nature is dharmakaya, suchness,
and also the disposition. These are to be
known by the [first] three examples,
the [fourth] one, and the [following] five.

The dharmakaya is to be known [in] two aspects.
These are the utterly unstained dharmadhatu
and the cause conducive to its [realization],
which is teaching in the deep and manifold way.

[The dharmakaya] being beyond the worldly,
no example for it can be found in the world.
Therefore the element and the Tathagata
are explained as being [slightly] similar.
Teaching in the deep and subtle way
is like the one single taste of honey,
while teaching through various aspects
resembles grain in its variety of husks.

Since the nature is unchanging,
full of virtue, and utterly pure,
suchness is said to correspond
to the shape and color of gold.

Similar to the treasure and the fruit of a tree,
the disposition is to be known in two aspects,
as it has existed [as] the nature since beginningless time
and has become supreme [through] right cultivation.

The attainment of the three kayas of a buddha
is seen to stem from the twofold disposition.
By the first aspect there is the first [kaya],
through the second there are the latter two.

The beautiful svabhavikakaya
is like the statue of precious material,
since [it exists] naturally, is not created,
and is a treasure of gem-like qualities.
Wielding the sublime majesty of the Great Dharma,
the sambhoga[kaya] resembles the Chakravartin.
Being of the nature of a [mere] representation,
the nirmana[kaya] is similar to the golden image.

This truth of the Self-Sprung Ones
is to be realized through faith.
The orb of the sun blazes with light,
[but] is not seen by the blind.

Nothing whatsoever is to be removed.
Not the slightest thing is to be added.
Truly looking at truth, truth is seen.
When seen, this is complete liberation.

The element is empty of the adventitious [stains],
which are featured by their total separateness.
But it is not empty of the matchless properties,
which are featured by their total inseparability.

[The sutras of the second turning of the wheel of Dharma] state in
   numerous places
that all knowable [phenomena] are in all ways empty like a cloud, a
   dream, or an illusion.
Why is it then, that in [the sutras of the third turning of the wheel of
   Dharma]
the Buddha, having said this, declared that buddha nature is present
   within beings?

With regard to faintheartedness, contempt for inferior beings,
perceiving the untrue, disparaging the true nature,

and exceeding self-cherishing, he said this to persuade those
who have any of these five to abandon their defects.

The final truth is in every respect
devoid of anything compounded.
The poisons, karma, and their product
are said to be like a cloud and so on.

The mental poisons are like a cloud.
Karma resembles a dream experience.
The skandhas produced by the poisons and karma
are similar to an illusion or a deceptive apparition.

For the time being it was thus expounded.
Additionally in this unsurpassable continuity
it was then taught: "The element is present,"
so that the five evils would be abandoned.
As long as they have not heard this,
bodhichitta will not be born in those
whose minds are feeble and fainthearted,
stirred by the evil of self-contempt.
Having engendered [a little] bodhichitta,
some proudly imagine: "I am supreme!"
Towards those who have not developed it
they are imbued with notions of inferiority.
In those who entertain such thoughts,
true understanding will not arise.
They hold the untrue [to be true]
and thus will not realize the truth.
Being artificially produced and adventitious,
these faults of beings are not truly [existent].
In truth these evils do not exist as self,
but exist as the qualities by nature pure.
While they hold the evils, which are untrue, [to be true]
and disparage the true qualities, [denying their presence,]
even those of understanding will not attain the love
that perceives the similarity of oneself and others.

Once one has heard this, joy will be born.
Respect as towards the Buddha, analytical wisdom,
primordial wisdom, and great love will arise.

Through the arising of these five qualities,
one is rid of the faults and sees similarity.
[By realizing] the absence of defects and the presence of qualities,
and through love, [seeing] the equality of oneself and [all] beings,
buddhahood will be quickly attained.

• This was the section "Tathagatagarbha," the first [chapter] of *The Commentary on the Highest Continuity of the Mahayana Dharma which Analyzes the Disposition of the Rare and Sublime Ones.*

CHAPTER TWO

The Fifth Vajra Point: Enlightenment

With its purity, attainment, freedom,
benefit for oneself and others, [their] basis,
depth, vastness, and greatness of nature,
duration, and suchness [it has eight qualities].

By [the topics] essence, cause, fruit,
function, endowment, manifestation,
permanence, and inconceivability,
the level of a buddha is presented.

[Enlightenment, of which the Buddha] said: "It is by nature clear
  light," is similar to the sun and space.
It is free from the stains of the adventitious poisons and hindrances
  to knowledge, the veils of which obscured it [like] a dense sea of
  clouds.
Buddhahood is permanent, steadfast, and immutable, possessing all
  the unpolluted buddha qualities.
It is attained on the basis of [two] primordial wisdoms: [one is] free
  from ideation with regard to phenomena, [the other is] discriminative.

Buddhahood is indivisible, yet can be divided
according to its property of [twofold] purity.
[Thus] it has two features, which are abandonment
and primordial wisdom, similar to space and the sun.

Luminous clear light is not created.
It is indivisibly manifest [in the nature of beings]
and holds all the buddha properties
outnumbering the grains of sand in the river Ganges.

By nature not existent, pervasive,
and adventitious, the veils of the poisons
and of the hindrances to knowledge
are described as being similar to a cloud.

Twofold wisdom causes release from the two veils.
Since there is the one that is free from ideation
and the one ensuing from this in post-meditation,
it is held that there are [two] primordial wisdoms.

Like a lake filled with unpolluted water gradually overspread by
    lotus flowers,
like the full moon released from Rahu's mouth and the sun liberated
    from a sea of clouds,
it is free from affliction. Being free from pollution and possessing
    qualities,
[buddhahood] is endowed with the brilliant light rays [of correct
    and complete vision].

Being similar to the [statue of the] Muni, the leader of beings,
and to the honey, the grain, the precious gold, the treasure, the
    mighty tree,
the Sugata's statue [made from] immaculate precious material,
the ruler of the earth, and the golden image, [a buddha] has gained
    victory.

Purity from the adventitious afflictions
of desire and the other mental poisons
is like the water of the lake and so forth.
When put concisely it can be fully shown
as the fruit of wisdom free from ideation.
The actual attainment of the buddhakaya,
which has all supreme aspects, is explained as the fruit
of primordial wisdom ensuing from this after meditation.

Having eliminated the silt of desire,
he lets the waters of meditative stability
flow onto the lotus[-like] disciples,
and thus resembles the lake of pure water.
Having freed himself from the Rahu of hatred,
he pervades beings with the light rays
of his great love and compassionate concern,
and thus is similar to the immaculate full moon.
Totally freed from the clouds of unknowing
and dispelling [its] darkness within beings
through the light rays of primordial wisdom,
buddhahood is similar to the unpolluted sun.

Since [enlightenment has] peerless properties,
since it bestows the taste of sacred Dharma,
and since it is free from the peel [of the veils],
it is like the Sugata, the honey, and the grain.
Since it is purified, since [beings'] poverty
is dispelled by the wealth of its qualities,
and since it grants the fruit of total liberation,
it is like the gold, the treasure, and the tree.
Representing the jewel of the dharmakaya,
and [the attainment of] the supreme lord of humans,
and [manifesting in] the likeness of a precious image,
they are like the bejeweled, the king, and the golden.

Rid of pollution [and] all-pervasive, [true buddhahood] has
    an indestructible nature
since it is steadfast, at peace, permanent, and unchanging. As
    the abode [of qualities]
a tathagata is similar to space. For the six sense-faculties of a
    saintly being
it forms the cause to experience their respective [pure] objects
    [of perception].

It is the cause for visible objects, which are non-arising, to be seen,
for good and pure speech to be heard,
for the pure scent of the moral conduct of the Sugata to be smelled,
for the flavor of sacred Dharma [of] the great noble ones to be tasted,

for the blissful touch of samadhi to be felt,
and for the mode [of the Dharma], which is by essence deep, to be
    realized.
When reflected upon in a very fine way, a sugata bestowing true bliss
is like space, devoid of any reasons.

In brief, [two kayas] are to be understood
as functions of the two primordial wisdoms:
the vimuktikaya [representing] perfection,
and the dharmakaya [representing] refinement.
Vimuktikaya and dharmakaya are to be known
in terms of two aspects and [a common] one,
as they are free from pollution and all-pervasive,
uncreated and thus embody the ground [of virtue].

Since the mental poisons along with their remaining imprints are ended,
[the vimuktikaya] is free from any pollution.
Since there is no attachment and obstruction,
[the dharmakaya] is considered as pervasive primordial wisdom.
Being of a nature forever indestructible
[neither kaya] is something that is created.
While "indestructibility" is the [concise] explanation [of uncreatedness],
it is taught in more detail through [the topic] "steadfast" and so forth.
"Destructibility" is to be understood [in terms of] four aspects,
since it constitutes the contrary of "steadfastness" and so on.
These are decay, drastic change, being cut-off, and transmigration,
which is inconceivable [and] a transformation [in various] ways.
Since [the vimuktikaya and dharmakaya] are free from these [features],
they are to be known as steadfast, peaceful, permanent, and
    unchanging.

As absence of pollution and [primordial] wisdom are the support
    for the unstained properties
[to come forth in the disciples], they are [also] the abode [of the best
    possible benefit for others].
Space is not a cause, and yet the cause
for all visible things to be seen,
for sound, odor, flavor, touch,
and phenomena to be heard and so on.
Just so, they cause the unstained qualities

to arise as objects sensed by those
[whose vision is] stable by junction
with the unveiled [seeing of] the two kayas.

Buddhahood is inconceivable, permanent, steadfast, at peace, and
  immutable.
It is utterly peaceful, pervasive, without thought, and unattached
  like space.
It is free from hindrance and coarse objects of contact are eliminated.
It cannot be seen or grasped. It is virtuous and free from pollution.

As was explained, the vimuktikaya and the dharmakaya
[accomplish] benefit for oneself and benefit for others.
These [kayas], being the support of this twofold benefit,
possess the qualities of being inconceivable and so forth.

Being the object of the omniscient primordial wisdom,
buddhahood is not an object for the three types of insight.
So even those with a wisdom body must realize
that [buddha enlightenment] is inconceivable.

Being subtle it is not an object for study.
Being absolute it cannot be reflected upon.
Dharmata is deep. Hence it is not an object
for any worldly meditation and so on.

Why [is it hard to realize]? Like the blind with regard
to the visible, the children have never seen it before.
Even noble ones [see it] as babies [would glimpse]
the sun from within the house where they are born.

Since it is free from being born, it is permanent.
Since it is without cessation, it is steadfast.
Since these two are not present, it is peaceful.
It is immutable, for the dharmata [ever] remains.

It is utter peace, since the truth of cessation [is revealed].
Since everything is realized, it pervades [all the knowable].
Since it does not dwell upon anything, it is without ideation.
Since the mental poisons are eliminated, it has no attachment.

Since the veil of the hindrances to knowledge is cleansed,
it is in all ways unobstructed [with regard to complete insight].
Being free from its two [obstacles], it is suited for [samadhi]
and thus relieved from the touch of coarse objects of contact.

Since it is not something visible, it cannot be seen.
Since it is free from features, it cannot be grasped.
It is virtuous, [the dharmadhatu] being by nature pure,
and it is free from stains, since pollution is abandoned.

What is the nature of dharmadhatu? It is without beginning, middle,
   and end.
It is totally indivisible and far away from the two [extremes],
rid of the three [veils], unpolluted, and not an object of thought.
Its realization is the vision of a Yogi who Dwells in Meditative
   Equipoise.

The unpolluted sphere of a tathagata possesses the [four] qualities
   [of realization].
It cannot be fathomed and [in number] is beyond the grains of sand
   in the river Ganges.
It is inconceivable and peerless and there is furthermore
elimination of all faults along with their remaining traces.

Through various aspects of the sacred Dharma, through bodies shot
   with light rays,
and through its readiness to accomplish the task of the total
   liberation of beings,
its deeds resemble the activity of a king of wish-fulfilling jewels.
[It appears as] a variety of things, yet is not of the nature of these.

[The nirmanakaya persuades] the worldly beings to enter the path
   towards peace.
He fully matures them and, granting prophecy, [becomes] the cause
   [of their release].
These form [kayas] remain forever in this [world]
like the realm of form within the realm of space.

The Omniscience of All the Self-Sprung Ones is given
the name of "Buddhahood." Its meaning is [also termed]:
"Most Supremely Beyond Torment," "The Inconceivable,"

"Foe-Vanquisher," and "Quintessence of Self-Awareness."
When these are categorized, they can be fully divided
into [three] properties, which are the qualities of depth,
vastness, and greatness, or the nature [kaya] and so on.
[The benefits] are fulfilled through these three kayas.

Of these, the svabhavikakaya
of the buddhas is to be known
as having five characteristics
and, if condensed, five qualities:

It is uncreated and totally indivisible.
The two extremes are completely abandoned.
It is definitively freed from the three veils—
the mental poisons and the obstructions
to knowledge and meditative equipoise.
It is unpolluted and not an [object of] thought.
Being the field of the yogis and the dharmadhatu,
being by essence pure, it is luminous clarity.

The svabhavikakaya truly has
the final and ultimate qualities
of being unfathomable, countless,
inconceivable, unequaled, and pure.
Since it is vast, not to be numbered,
not an object of reasoning, and unique,
and since the remaining traces are eliminated,
it is in the same order unfathomable and so on.

It perfectly enjoys the various aspects of Dharma
and appears [in the form] of natural qualities.
Corresponding to the pure cause of its compassion,
the benefit of sentient beings is uninterrupted.
Totally without any thought and spontaneously
it wholly grants all wishes exactly as they are
by miraculous powers, like a wish-fulfilling gem.
It therefore fully abides in Perfect Enjoyment.
Since the stream of verbal expression, display [of form],
and action [of mind] is uninterrupted and not a product,
and since it shows that it is not of the essence of these,
it is taught here in five aspects, as "various" and so on.

Due to the various colors [of its background] a gem appears [in
    manifold colors],
[but] is not a thing fulfilling their function.
Likewise the All-Pervasive [Ones] appear due to the manifold
    conditions [set by beings]
without being a thing fulfilling their function.

[The Supreme Nirmanakaya] knows the world and having gazed upon
all worldly [beings demonstrates] out of his great compassion
[twelve wondrous deeds]. Without moving away from the dharma-
    kaya
he manifests through various [aspects] of an illusory nature.
Having [first] been born spontaneously in a [divine] existence
he then leaves the realm of Tushita and passes [into this world].
He enters [his mother's] womb, takes birth, and gains perfect skill,
mastering all the various fields of handicraft, science, and art.
He mirthfully enjoys amusement among his spouse and her retinue.
Feeling weariness and renunciation he practices as an ascetic.
Then he goes to Awakening's Heart and defeats the hosts of Mara.
[He finds] perfect enlightenment and turns the wheel of Dharma.
He passes into nirvana [the state beyond any torment and pain].
Within all the [endless] fields totally infested with impurity
he shows these deeds as long as [beings] abide in existence.

With the words "impermanent," "suffering," "selfless," and "peace"
[the Buddhas] who know all means persuade sentient beings
to generate weariness with the three realms of existence
and to fully enter into the state beyond torment and pain.

Those who have perfectly followed the path of peace
believe that they have attained the state of nirvana.
By the *White Lotus of Dharma Sutra* and similar aspects
of his sacred teaching he explains the nature of phenomena.
Thus he causes them to refrain from their former belief,
to fully adopt skillful means and discriminative wisdom,
and gain maturity on the [path of the] supreme vehicle.

Then he grants them prophecy of their supreme enlightenment.

Since [these kayas] constitute depth, best possible power,
and supreme guidance in tune with the aims of the children,
they should be known in accordance with this number
as being deep, vast, and the embodiment of greatness.

Here the first is the dharmakaya,
and the latter are the form kayas.
As the visible abides in space,
the latter abide in the first.

There is permanence [since] the causes are endless and sentient
   beings inexhaustible [in number].
They have compassionate love, miraculous power, knowledge, and
   utter [bliss].
They are masters of [all] qualities. The demon of death has been
   vanquished.
Being not of the essence [of the compounded] it is the [true]
   protector of all worldly [beings].

Having offered bodies, lives, and goods
they [purely] uphold the sacred Dharma.
In order to benefit all sentient beings
they fulfill their vow as initially taken.
Buddhahood supremely expresses itself
as compassion both cleansed and purified.
Appearing on the feet of miraculous powers
they [can] act forever by means of these.
By knowledge they are freed from the belief
fixed on the duality of samsara and nirvana.
They always possess the best possible bliss
of samadhi, beyond ideation [and end].
While acting in the world [for other's good]
they are unsullied by all worldly phenomena.

Free from dying, it is the attainment of peace.
In this sphere the demon of death cannot roam.

The state of the Muni being of uncreated nature
has been fully pacified since beginningless time.
For all those who are bereft of permanent shelter
it provides the most delightful refuge, and so on.

The first seven reasons clarify
the permanence of the form kayas,
while the latter three illustrate
why the dharmakaya lasts forever.

It is not an object of speech and is embraced by the absolute.
It is not a field for ideation and is beyond any example,
unexcelled and not embraced by existence and peace.
Even the noble cannot conceive the sphere of the Victor.

It is inconceivable since it cannot be verbally expressed.
It is inexpressible since it consists of the absolute [truth].
It is absolute since it cannot be [intellectually] scrutinized.
It is inscrutable since it cannot be inferentially deduced.
It is not deducible since it is peerless, the highest of all.
It is the highest of all since it is not comprised by anything.
It is uncomprised since it does not dwell [on any extreme].
This is because there is no dualistic idea of quality and fault.

For the [first] five reasons the dharmakaya is subtle
and thus beyond the reach of thought. For the sixth
the form kayas are inconceivable. [They show appearance]
but are not something that fulfils the function of this.

Since through peerless primordial wisdom, great compassion, and
    further attributes
all qualities are finally perfected, the Victor is inconceivable.
Thus the last mode of the Self-Sprung Ones is not even seen
by those Great Sages who have received "the Empowerment [of
    Splendorous Light Rays]."

• This was the section "Enlightenment," the second chapter of *The
Commentary on the Highest Continuity of the Mahayana Dharma which
Analyzes the Disposition of the Rare and Sublime Ones.*

CHAPTER THREE

The Sixth Vajra Point: Qualities

Benefit for oneself and benefit for others are equivalent
to the ultimate kaya and the relative kayas based upon it.
Being the fruits of freedom and complete maturation
these are [endowed with] sixty-four types of qualities.

The abode adhering to [benefit] for oneself
is the kaya being [wisdom's] sacred object.
The symbolic kaya of sages is the ground
of best possible [benefit] for other beings.
The first kaya has the qualities of freedom,
which are the qualities of power and so on.
The second has those of full maturation,
which are the marks of a great being.

Power is like a vajra against the veil of unknowing.
Fearlessness acts like a lion amidst [any] assembly.
Like space are the unmixed features of the Tathagata,
like a water-moon the two facets of the Muni's teaching.

Knowing what is worthwhile and worthless,
knowing the ripening product of all action,
knowing faculties, temperaments, and wishes,
knowing the path reaching the entire range,
knowing meditative stability and so on—
when it is afflicted or without pollution—
memory of past states, divine sight, and peace
are the ten aspects of the power of knowledge.

[Knowing] the worthwhile and worthless, complete ripening, the
    various temperaments, paths, and aspirations of beings,
their manifold faculties, the defiled and the utterly pure,
    remembrance of previous states [of existence], divine sight,
and [knowing] the way in which [all] pollution is exhausted
    piercingly destroys the armor of ignorance, fells its trees
and smashes its unshakable walls, laying them in utter ruin. Such
    power, therefore, resembles an [indestructible] vajra.

Perfectly enlightened [in] all phenomena,
setting an end to [all] hindrances,
teaching the path, and showing cessation
are the four aspects of fearlessness.

Knowing and causing [others] to know all the different aspects of
    things that are to be known of oneself and others,
having abandoned and causing abandonment of all things that are
    to be abandoned, having relied on what is to be relied upon,
having attained and causing attainment of the Peerless and Stainless
    to be attained,
they relate their own truth to others. Thus the Great Sages are
    unhindered anywhere.

The lord of animals is ever fearless to the far ends of the jungle,
undauntedly roaming amongst the [other] animals.
In [any] assembly the Lord of Munis is a lion as well,
remaining at ease, independent, stable, and endowed with skill.

There is no delusion and no idle talk.
The Teacher's mindfulness is unimpaired.
Never is his mind not resting evenly.
There is no harboring of various ideas.
There is no equanimity without analysis.
His aspiration, diligence, mindfulness,
and discriminative wisdom are unimpaired,
as are total release and its eye of wisdom.
All action is preceded by primordial wisdom
and this is unobscured with regard to time.
Thus these eighteen features and others
are the unmixed qualities of the Teacher.

Delusion, idle talk, forgetfulness, mental agitation, ideation of
    duality, and indifferent equanimity:
the Sage does not have any of these. His aspiration, diligence, and
    mindfulness,
his utterly pure and unstained discriminative wisdom, his constant
    total release,
and his primordial wisdom of liberation seeing all fields of the
    knowable do not suffer any impairment.
His three activities are preceded [by primordial wisdom] and
    display themselves in its likeness.
He manifests his vast definitive knowing, always unhindered in its
    vision of the three times.
By such insight he is fearless and supremely turns the Great Wheel
    of Pure Dharma for beings.
Endowment with great compassion and quintessence of victory are
    what all buddhas will find.

The nature of any of the properties native to earth and so on is not
    the nature of space.
Any of the features of space, such as being non-obstructive and so
    on, is not a feature of the visible.
Earth, water, fire, air, and space, being equally [elements], have
    something in common in the world.
The unmixed qualities and worldly beings have nothing in common,
    not even as much as a single atom.

His perfectly even [soles] are marked with wheels.
His feet are broad and his ankles are not visible.
His fingers and toes are long and the digits
of his hands and feet are entwined by a web.
His skin is soft and his flesh remains youthful.
His body has seven elevated and rounded parts.
His calves are like those of an antelope and
his secret parts are hidden as are an elephant's.
His [mighty] torso is similar to that of a lion.
[The hollow] between his clavicles is well filled.
The curve of his shoulders is perfect and beautiful.
His hands and arms are rounded, soft, and even.
His arms are long and his utterly immaculate body
is enfolded in the mandala of an aureole of light.

His neck, unblemished [in hue], resembles a conch.
His cheeks are like those of the king of all animals.
His forty teeth are equal [in number in both his jaws].
His teeth are supremely pure and most beautifully set.
They are totally immaculate and aligned in even rows.
The eye-teeth are of supreme and excellent whiteness.
His tongue is long, his speech unlimited and inconceivable.
His sense of taste is supreme, and the Self-Sprung's voice
is like the kalavinka's call and the melody of Brahma.
His pure eyes are like blue lotuses, his eyelashes [dense]
as those of an ox. He has the stainless white urna hair
embellishing his face and the ushnisha crowning his head.
His skin is pure and delicate and of the color of gold.
Extremely fine and soft, each of the hairs on his body
curls from one pore to the right and upwards to his crown.
His immaculate hair resembles [in color] a deep-blue gem.
Well-proportioned in stature like a perfect nyagrodha tree,
the Great Sage who is all-good and without any example
has an unbreakable body possessed of Narayana's strength.
These thirty-two marks, which one cannot conceive or grasp
and which are resplendent [in their brightness and beauty],
the Teacher has described as the signs of a lord of humans.

Just as in autumn the form of the moon is seen
in a cloudless sky and in the deep blue water of a lake,
the form of the All-Embracing is seen by the Victor's heirs
in the perfect buddha mandala [and in the world].

These sixty-four qualities
each combined with its cause
should be known in their order
to follow the *Ratnadarikasutra.*

Being unchangeable and never weakened,
dissimilar and unmoving, they are taught
by the examples of the vajra, the lion,
space, and the moon in sky and water.

Of the powers, six powers, three, and one,
in this sequence, have totally dispelled

[the veils of] knowledge and meditation,
along with that of the remaining imprints.
Resembling armor, a wall, and a tree,
they were pierced, shattered, and felled.

Being firm, essential, steadfast, and unchangeable
the powers of the Great Sage are similar to a vajra.
Why are they firm? Because they are essential.
Why essential? Because they are steadfast.
Why steadfast? Because they are unchangeable.
Being unchangeable, they are like a vajra.

Since he is not intimidated, is independent,
stable, and [possessed of] best possible skill,
the Muni is like a lion. The Lion [of Mankind]
does not have fear in any assembly whatever.

Knowing everything directly, he always remains
totally fearless of anyone, no matter of whom.
Seeing that even pure beings are not his equal,
he is unimpressed and not daunted [by others].
His mind being one-pointed as to all phenomena,
[his samadhi] is the quintessence of stability.
He possesses skill, having crossed the earth
of the latencies of unknowing, ever so [subtle].

The understanding of worldly beings, of listeners,
of biased practitioners, of those who have insight,
and of self-sprung buddhas getting ever subtler
and progressively refined, there are five similes:
Sustaining the life of all worldly beings, [buddhas]
are likened to earth and water and to fire and air.
Away from the features of the worldly and of those
being beyond the world, they are similar to space.

So the dharmakaya fully divides
into these thirty-two qualities,
indivisible like a precious gem
in its light, radiance, and shape.

Granting satisfaction whenever they are seen,
the qualities called "the thirty-two [marks]"
adhere to two kayas, being the illusory kaya
and the kaya perfectly rejoicing in Dharma.

Those far from and close to purity [see them]
as the mandalas of the world and the Victor,
like the form of the moon in water and sky.
Thus these [kayas] are beheld in two ways.

♦ This was the section "Qualities," the third chapter of *The Commentary on the Highest Continuity of the Mahayana Dharma which Analyzes the Disposition of the Rare and Sublime Ones.*

CHAPTER FOUR

The Seventh Vajra Point: Activity

An All-Embracing One always has spontaneous access
to the disciples' temperaments, the means of training,
the [various] trainings that suit their temperaments,
and to seeking them wherever they are, at the right time.

Having multitudes of supremely precious qualities and the waters
    of the ocean of primordial wisdom, possessing the sunlight of
    merit and wisdom,
it is the definitive accomplishment of all vehicles without exception.
    [Enlightenment] is vast, without middle or end, and thus all-
    pervasive like space.
Fully seeing that buddhahood, the treasure of the unpolluted
    qualities, is [present] within all sentient beings without the
    slightest distinction,
the wind of the Buddhas' sublime compassion totally dispels the
    clouds of afflictions and hindrances to knowledge, which have
    spun their net about it.

For whom? How? By which training?
Where? and When? Since ideation
as to such [questions] does not occur,
the Muni always [acts] spontaneously.

The temperaments of the disciples,
which of the many means for each,
which training at what place and time:
[He is not mistaken as to any of] these.

Since, with regard to the definitive revelation of release,
its support, its fruit, those being fully sustained,
their obscurations, and the condition cutting these veils,
there is no ideation, [buddha activity is uninterrupted].

The ten levels definitively reveal release.
The two accumulations provide their cause.
Supreme enlightenment is the fruit of these.
Enlightenment in beings is fully sustained.
These are obscured by the endless afflictions,
the secondary afflictions, and the latencies.
A buddha's great compassion is the condition
that, at all times, vanquishes these [veils].

These six points: being similar
to an ocean, the sun, space,
a treasure, clouds, and wind
are to be grasped accordingly.

Holding wisdom's waters and qualities
like gems, the levels are like an ocean.
Closely sustaining all sentient beings,
the two accumulations are like the sun.
Being vast and without any middle or end,
enlightenment is like the element of space.
Genuine perfect awakening is dharmata,
hence beings' nature is like a treasure.
Adventitious, pervasive, and not existent,
its afflictions are like a host of clouds.
Always ready to dispel these [afflictions],
compassion is similar to a merciless wind.

Their release [is accomplished] for the sake of others.
They see the equality of themselves and sentient beings
and their activity is not completed to its full extent.
Thus their deeds will never cease while samsara exists.

A tathagata is similar to Indra,
to the drum [of the gods], clouds,
to Brahma, the sun, a precious gem,
to an echo, to space, and the earth.

If the surface of the ground here changed
into the nature of immaculate lapis lazuli,
because of its purity one would see in it
the [appearance of] the Lord of All Gods
with his following of many young goddesses.
One would see his sublimely beautiful palace
"the All-Victorious" and other divine abodes,
the gods' various palaces and manifold wealth.

Once the assembly of men and women
who inhabit the surface of the earth
saw this appearance, each would say:
"Before a long time passes, may I too
become like this Lord of the Gods!"
Prayers like these they would utter
and to achieve this feat would adopt
genuine virtue and remain within it.

"This is just an appearance!" There would not be
any such understanding. Still their virtuous deeds
would lead them to be reborn in a divine existence
after they departed from the surface of the earth.
These appearances are totally free from ideation
and do not involve the slightest movement at all.
There is nothing of this kind, and yet nevertheless
they are accompanied by great benefit on the earth.

Those endowed with unpolluted faith and so forth,
having cultivated the qualities of faith and so on,
will see in their own minds the Buddha's appearance,
which is perfect and has special signs and marks.
They will see the Buddha while he is walking,
while he is standing, sitting, or resting in sleep.
They will see him in manifold forms of conduct:
when explaining the teaching leading to peace,
when silently resting in meditative equipoise,
or when displaying various forms of miracles.
Possessed of great splendor and magnificence,
[the Buddha] will be seen by all sentient beings.

Once having seen this, they too will wish
to fully join what is named "buddhahood,"
and adopting its causes in a genuine way
they will attain the state they longed for.

These appearances are totally free from ideation
and do not involve the slightest movement at all.
There is nothing of this kind, and yet nevertheless
they are accompanied by great benefit in the world.
"This is the appearance of my own mind."
Worldly beings do not have such insight.
Yet, their seeing of this visible kaya
will become meaningful for these beings.
Relying on gradually beholding this form,
all those who follow the [Great] Vehicle
will see their genuine inner dharmakaya
by means of the eye of primordial wisdom.

If the whole earth became rid of fearful places
and turned into an even surface of lapis lazuli
that was flawless, radiant, and beautiful,
having a gem's qualities and unstained luster,
various divine abodes and the form of their Lord
would shine forth within it because of its purity.
Then, as the earth gradually lost these properties,
they would be invisible again and appear no more.
Yet, for their real attainment the men and women
would side with the vows of individual release,
with penitence, authentic giving, and so forth,
scattering flowers and so on with longing minds.

Likewise, to attain the state of a Lord of Munis shining forth in their
    minds, which is similar to pure lapis lazuli,
the heirs of the Victor, their vision filled with sheer delight, give rise
    to bodhichitta in the most perfect manner.

Just as mirrored by the purified lapis lazuli ground
the physical appearance of the Lord of Gods is seen,
likewise the kaya of the Lord of Munis is reflected
in the purified ground of sentient beings' minds.

Whether these reflections will rise or set in beings
owes to their own minds being sullied or unstained.
Like the form [of Lord Indra] appearing in the worlds,
they are not to be viewed as "existent" or "extinct."

By the power of the gods' former virtue
the Dharma drum [arose] among them.
Involving no effort, origin, or thought,
no vibration and no intention at all,
the drum resounds again and again
with "impermanence" and "suffering,"
"non-existence of self" and "peace,"
admonishing all the careless gods.

Likewise, though free from effort and so on,
the buddha speech of the All-Pervading Ones
permeates sentient beings without exception,
teaching Dharma to those of karmic fortune.

Just as the sound of the drum arises
among the gods from their own deeds,
the Dharma spoken by the Muni arises
in the world from beings' own deeds.
Just as the sound [of the drum] accomplishes peace
without effort, origin, visible form, or intention,
likewise the Dharma causes accomplishment of peace
without deliberate effort or any other such feature.

The sound of the drum in the city of the gods acts as the cause,
    yielding the gift of undauntedness and granting them victory
over the host of the asuras, when these, driven by their poisons,
    make war upon them, and it dispels the gods' reveling in play.
Likewise, arising in the worlds from the cause of meditative stability,
    formless dimension, and so on, it expresses the mode
of the unsurpassable path, which will fully overcome all affliction
    and suffering and thus lead all sentient beings to peace.

Universal, of benefit, bestowing bliss,
and endowed with threefold miracle,
the Muni's melody is by far superior
to the cymbals treasured by the gods.

The mighty sound of the drum in the divine realms
does not reach the ears of those dwelling on earth,
whereas the drumming sound of Buddha's [speech]
even reaches the subterranean worlds of samsara.
Millions of divine cymbals resound among the gods
to set the fire of lust ablaze and to fan its flames.
The single melody of Those of Compassionate Being
manifests to fully quench all the fires of suffering.
The beautiful and bewitching sound of the cymbals
causes among the gods increase of their distraction,
whereas the speech of the compassionate Tathagata
exhorts [us] to reflect and commits the mind to samadhi.
Any cause of happiness for earthly beings and gods
in whichever sphere of the world without exception,
briefly spoken, fully depends upon this melody
that pervades all the worlds, not forsaking one.

Without [an intact sense of] hearing
one cannot experience subtle sound,
and all [its manifold variations]
do not even reach the ears of a god.
Likewise, as the field of experience
of the very finest primordial wisdom,
the subtle Dharma only reaches the ear
of someone whose mind is rid of poison.

The monsoon clouds in summertime
continuously and without any effort
pour down their vast masses of water,
causing on earth the best possible crops.
Just so, from the cloud of compassion
the rain of the Victor's pure teaching
pours down its waters without ideation,
causing a harvest of virtue for beings.

Just as the wind-born clouds cause rain to fall
when the worldly beings follow the path of virtue,
from the buddha cloud called by compassion's wind,
pure Dharma rains to nurture the virtue of beings.

Through great knowledge and compassionate love with regard
    to existence
it abides in the midst of space unsullied by change and
    non-change.
Holding the essence of the unpolluted waters of dharani and
    samadhi,
the cloud of the Lord of Munis is the cause of the harvest of virtue.

Water that is cool, delicious, soft,
and light when it falls from the clouds
acquires on earth very many tastes
by touching salty and other grounds.
When the waters of the noble eightfold [path]
rain from the heart of the vast cloud of love,
they will also acquire many kinds of tastes
by the different grounds of beings' make-up.

Those of devotion towards the supreme vehicle,
those who are neutral, and those with animosity
are three groups [of beings] who are similar
to humans, peacocks, and craving spirits.

At the end of spring, when there are no clouds, human beings and
    the birds that rarely fly
[are unhappy or neutral, respectively]. When rain is falling in
    summertime, the craving spirits suffer.
Similar to this example, the arising and non-arising of the Dharma-
    rain from the host of clouds of compassion
also [leads to opposite reactions] in worldly beings who long for
    Dharma or are hostile to it, respectively.

When releasing a deluge of heavy drops or hurling down hailstones
    and thunderbolts,
a cloud does not heed any tiny beings or those who have sought
    shelter in the hills.
Likewise the cloud of knowledge and love does not heed whether
    its vast and subtle drops
will purify the afflictions or [increase] dormant tendencies towards
    holding the view of a self.

In this cycle of beginningless birth and death five paths are open for
    sentient beings to tread.
Just as no sweet scent is found in excrement, no happiness will be
    found among the five types of beings.
Their suffering resembles the continuous pain arising from fire and
    weapons, or [from a wound] being touched by salt, and so on.
The great rain of sacred Dharma pours down in cascades from the
    cloud of compassion, fully soothing and appeasing this [pain].

"[Even] gods have the suffering of death and transmigration, and
    man suffers from desperate strife!" Realizing this,
those endowed with discriminative wisdom have no desire for even
    the highest [state] of a lord of humans or gods.
There is wisdom [from the past] and they faithfully follow the
    sublime words of the Tathagata,
so insight makes them see: "This is suffering! This is its cause! And
    this is cessation of misery!"

In the case of disease, one needs to diagnose it, remove its cause,
attain the happy state [of health], and rely on suitable medicine;
similarly one needs to recognize suffering, remove its cause,
come in touch with its cessation, and rely on the suitable path.

Just like the way in which Brahma,
without departing from his abode,
effortlessly shows his appearance
in all the residences of the gods,
without moving from dharmakaya
the Muni effortlessly demonstrates
illusory appearances in every realm
to beings who have karmic fortune.

When Brahma, never departing from his palace, has manifested in
    the desire realm, he is seen by the gods.
This vision incites them to emulate him and to abandon their delight
    in [sensuous] objects.
Similarly, without moving from dharmakaya, the Sugata is seen in
    all spheres of this world
by beings of karmic fortune. This vision incites them to emulate him
    and to dispel all their pollution.

By his own former wishing prayers
and the power of the virtue of the gods
Brahma appears without deliberate effort.
So does the self-sprung illusory kaya.

He moves from [Tushita] and enters the womb, gets born, and goes
    to his father's palace.
He enjoys amusement and then seeks solitude, undergoes austerity,
    and defeats all evils.
[In Bodhgaya] he finds great enlightenment and shows the path to
    the citadel of peace.
The Muni, having shown [these deeds], becomes invisible to those
    of no karmic fortune.

When the sun blazes down, lotuses and so on open
while simultaneously kumuta flowers totally close.
On the benefit and fault of the water-born flowers' opening and closing
the sun does not shed any thought. The sun of the Noble acts
    likewise.

As the sun shining its own light
simultaneously and without thought
makes lotus flowers open their petals
and brings ripening to other [crops],
so the sun of the Tathagata manifests,
shedding its rays of the sacred Dharma
on the lotus-like beings to be trained
without harboring any thought or idea.

By the dharmakaya and the visible kayas
the sun of omniscience rises in the sky,
which is the very heart of enlightenment,
to shed light beams of wisdom on beings.

In all disciples, as in water vessels,
simultaneously the sun of the Sugata
is mirrored in countless reflections
owing to the purity [of these beings].

[From] within the space of dharmadhatu,
which continuously pervades everything,

the buddha sun shines on the disciples
[like] on mountains, as merited by each.

Just as the rising sun with thousands of far-reaching beams
illuminates all the worlds and then gradually sheds its light
on the highest mountains, then the medium-sized, and the small,
the buddha sun gradually shines on the assembly of beings.

The sun does not radiate to the depth of space in every field, nor
    can it show
the meaning of the knowable [to those] confined to the darkness of
    unknowing.
Appearing in clarity through a multitude of light emitting various
    colors,
Those of Compassionate Nature show the meaning of the knowable
    to beings.

When a buddha goes to the city [of the disciples], people without
    eyes become sighted.
Being freed from all meaningless things they see the meaningful and
    experience [happiness].
When blinded by delusion they fall into existence's sea and are
    wrapped in the darkness of views,
the light of the buddha sun illumines their vision and they see the
    very point they never saw before.

A wish-fulfilling gem, though free from thought,
grants all those who dwell in its field of activity
each of their desires simultaneously,
doing so in the most perfect manner.
Likewise beings of different ways of thinking,
when they rely on the wish-fulfilling Buddha,
will hear various kinds of teachings,
though he generates no ideas of these.

As a precious gem, which is free from thought, fully bestows
the desired riches on others, doing so without any effort,
the Muni always stays for others' sake, as merited by each
and as long as existences last, doing so without any effort.

The good jewel lying underground or in the ocean
is very hard to find for beings wanting it.
Likewise, one should understand that beings held in the grip of the
  poisons,
and whose karmic gifts are poor, will hardly see the Sugata in their
  minds.

Just as the sound of an echo arises
due to the perception of others,
without thought or purposeful labor
and neither abiding without or within,
so the speech of the Tathagata arises
due to the perception of others,
without thought or purposeful labor
and neither abiding without or within.

Space is nothing at all and does not appear.
It is neither an object [of the senses] nor a support.
It is totally beyond being a path for the eye.
It has no form and is not to be demonstrated.
Nevertheless it is seen as being high and low,
but it is not at all like that.
Likewise all [his appearances] are seen as Buddha,
but he is not at all like that.

Everything that grows from the earth
will increase and become firm and vast
on the support of its thought-free soil.
Likewise, relying on the Perfect Buddha,
who [like] the earth is free from thought,
every root of virtue of sentient beings
without exception will flourish and grow.

It is not obvious that one could act
without exerting deliberate effort.
Therefore nine examples are taught
to cut the doubts of the disciples.
The place where these nine examples
were explained in very great detail

is the sutra which through its very name
teaches their necessity and purpose.
Adorned with the far-reaching light
of knowledge arisen from hearing it,
those of insight will quickly enter
the field of experience of a buddha.

This point is made clear in the nine examples
of Indra's reflection in lapis lazuli and so on.
Their concise meaning, when grasped precisely,
is to [illustrate] display [of physical form],
speech, and the all-pervasiveness [of mind],
illusory emanation, radiation of wisdom,
the secret aspects of body, speech, and mind,
and the fact that compassion itself is attained.

All streams of effort being fully appeased
and the mind being free from all ideation
is similar to Indra's reflection appearing
within stainless lapis lazuli and so forth.
Appeasement of effort is the proposition;
mind free from ideation its justification.
In order to establish the meaning of this nature
the similes of Indra's form and so on are given.

Here the meaning of the chapter is as follows:
The nine aspects of physical display and so on
[show] that the Teacher has no birth and death,
and yet perfectly manifests without any effort.

Something that, similar to Indra, the drum, clouds, Brahma,
the sun, the precious king of wish-granting gems, an echo, space,
and the earth, effortlessly and as long as existence may last
fulfils others' benefit is only conceived of by [supreme] yogis.

[Kayas] are displayed like the Lord of Gods appearing [in] the gem.
Explanation being well bestowed resembles the drum of the gods.
With cloud-hosts of insight and deep concern, the All-Embracing
pervades the limitless number of beings up to existence's peak.
Like Brahma, not moving from his sphere devoid of pollution,
he perfectly displays a manifold number of illusory appearances.

Like a sun, primordial wisdom perfectly radiates its brilliance.
Buddha mind resembles a pure and precious wish-fulfilling jewel.
Buddha speech has no letters, like an echo resounding from rock.
Similar to space, his body is pervasive, formless, and permanent.
Like the earth, a buddha is the ground holding without exception
and in any way all medicinal herbs of beings' unstained qualities.

The cause for the Buddha to be seen in the mind
similar to pure lapis lazuli
is the purity of this ground,
[achieved] by a firm faculty of irreversible faith.
Since virtue arises and ceases,
the form of a buddha arises and ceases.
Like Indra, the Muni who is dharmakaya
is free from arising and ceasing.

Effortlessly, like [Indra] he manifests his deeds,
displaying [physical appearance] and so forth,
from birthless and deathless dharmakaya
for as long as samsaric existence may last.

The condensed meaning of the examples is [contained] herein.
Their order is also [not arbitrary], as they are abandoned such
that properties not in tune are eliminated
[progressing] from the former to the latter.

A buddha is like the reflection, and yet dissimilar,
since the reflection is not endowed with his melody.
He is like the drum of the gods, and yet dissimilar,
since the drum does not bring benefit everywhere.
He is similar to a vast cloud, and yet dissimilar,
since a cloud does not eliminate worthless seeds.
He is like the mighty Brahma, and yet dissimilar,
since Brahma does not continuously cause maturity.
He is like the orb of the sun, and yet dissimilar,
since the sun does not always overcome darkness.
He is like a wish-granting gem, and yet dissimilar,
since the gem's appearance is not so rarely found.
He is similar to an echo, and yet dissimilar,
since an echo arises from cause and condition.
He is similar to space, and yet dissimilar,

since space is not a ground of pure virtue.
Being the lasting basis for every goodness,
the best possible for all without exception,
for worldly beings and those beyond the world,
[activity] is similar to the mandala of earth.
Because based upon all buddhas' enlightenment,
the path beyond the world will arise, as will
the path of virtuous deeds, mental stability, and
the immeasurable and formless contemplations.

♦ This was the section "Unfolding the Activity of the Tathagata," the fourth chapter of *The Commentary on the Highest Continuity of the Mahayana Dharma which Analyzes the Disposition of the Rare and Sublime Ones.*

CHAPTER FIVE
Benefit

Buddha element, buddha awakening,
buddha qualities, and buddha activity
cannot be thought, not even by purified beings.
They are the field of experience of their guides.

Those of insight who have devotion to this buddha domain
will become vessels for the multitude of all buddha qualities,
while those truly delighting in these inconceivable properties
will exceed in merit [the good actions of] all sentient beings.

Someone striving for enlightenment may turn to the Dharma kings,
    offering golden fields adorned with gems
of equal [number] to the atoms in the buddhafields, and may
    continue doing so every day.
Another may just hear a word of this, and upon hearing it become
    filled with devotion.
He will attain merits far greater and more manifold than the virtue
    sprung from this practice of giving.

An intelligent person wishing for enlightenment may by body,
    speech, and mind
guard a flawless moral conduct and do so effortlessly, even through
    many eons.
Another may just hear a word of this, and upon hearing it become
    filled with devotion.
He will attain merits far greater and more manifold than the virtue
    sprung from this discipline.

Someone here may finally achieve the divine meditative stabilities
    and Brahma's abode, thus quenching all affliction's fire
within the three realms of existence, and may cultivate these as a means
    to reach unchanging and perfect enlightenment.
Another may just hear a word of this, and upon hearing it become
    filled with devotion.
He will attain merits far greater and more manifold than the virtue
    sprung from this meditation.

Why [is it so beneficial]? Generosity only yields wealth,
discipline leads to the higher states of existence, and meditation
    removes affliction.
Discriminative wisdom fully abandons all afflictions and
    [hindrances to] knowledge.
It is therefore supreme, and its cause is studying these.

The presence [of the element], its result,
its qualities, and the achievement of benefit
are the objects of understanding of a buddha.
When towards these four, as explained above,
one of understanding is filled with devotion
to their presence, ability, and qualities,
he will be quickly endowed with the fortune
by which one attains the state of a tathagata.

Those who realize: "This inconceivable object is present
and someone like me can attain it;
its attainment will hold such qualities and endowment"
will aspire to it, filled with faith.
Thus becoming vessels of all qualities,
such as longing, diligence, mindfulness,
meditative stability, wisdom, and so on,
bodhichitta will be ever-present in them.

[Bodhichitta] being ever-present in them
the heirs of the Victor will not fall back.
The perfection of merit will be refined
until being transformed into total purity.
Once these five perfections of merit
are not ideated in threefold division,
they will become perfect and fully pure,
as their opposite facets are abandoned.

The merit of generosity arises from giving,
that of morality arises from moral conduct.
The two aspects of patience and meditative stability
stem from meditation, and diligence accompanies all.

Whatever ideates [in terms of] the three circles
is viewed as the veil of the hindrances to knowledge.
Whatever is the impulse of avarice and so on
is to be regarded as the veil of the mental poisons.

Since apart from discriminative wisdom
there is no other cause to remove these [veils],
this discriminative wisdom is supreme.
Its ground being study, such study is supreme.

Based on the trustworthy words of the Buddha and on
    scriptures of logic,
I have explained this for the sole purpose
of purifying myself and supporting all those
whose understanding has the best of virtue and devotion.

As someone with eyes sees by relying on a lamp,
or on lightning, a jewel, the sun, or the moon,
this has been truly explained by relying on the Muni,
brilliant in meaning, words, phenomena, and power.

Whatever speech is meaningful and well connected with Dharma,
which removes all afflictions of the three realms
and shows the benefit of the [attainment] of peace,
is the speech of the Sage, while any different speech is other.

Whatever someone has explained with undistracted mind,
exclusively in the light of the Victor's teaching,
and conducive to the path of attaining release,
one should place on one's head as the words of the Sage.

There is no one in this world more skilled in Dharma than the Victor.
No other has such insight, knowing everything without exception
    [and knowing] supreme thatness the way it is.
Thus one should not distort the sutras presented by the Sage himself,
since this would destroy the Muni's manner [of teaching] and
    furthermore cause harm to the sacred Dharma.

Those blinded by poisons [and possessed of] the nature of ignorance
revile the noble ones and despise the teachings they have spoken.
Since all this stems from a fixated view, mind should not be joined
   with polluted vision.
Clean cloth is totally transformed by color, but never is cloth [to be
   treated] with oil.

Due to a feeble intellect, lack of striving for virtue, reliance on false pride,
a nature obscured by neglect of pure Dharma, taking the provisional
   for the definitive meaning—for thatness, craving for profit,
being under the sway of [inferior] views, relying on those
   disapproving [of Dharma], staying away from those who uphold
   the teachings,
and due to mean devotion, the teachings of the Foe-Vanquishers are
   abandoned.

Skillful beings must not be as deeply afraid of fire and cruel
   poisonous snakes,
of murderers or lightning, as they should be of the loss of the
   profound Dharma.
Fire, snakes, enemies, and thunderbolts [can] only separate us
   from this life,
but cannot take us to the utterly fearful states of [the hells] of
   direst pain.

Even someone who has relied on evil friends again and again and
   thus heeded harmful intentions towards a buddha,
who has committed one of the most heinous acts—killing his father,
   mother, or an arhat, or splitting the sublime Assembly—
will be quickly released from these, once genuinely reflecting the
   dharmata.
But where would liberation be for someone whose mind is hostile to
   Dharma?

Having properly explained the seven [vajra] points of the jewels, the
   utterly pure element,
flawless enlightenment, qualities, and activity, may any virtue I
   harvest from this
lead all sentient beings to see the Lord of Boundless Life who is
   endowed with Infinite Light.
Upon seeing, may their stainless Dharma-eye open and may they
   reach highest enlightenment.

On what basis, for what reason, and in what way
[this has been given], what it explains
and what cause is conducive [to understanding it]
have been taught by means of four stanzas.
Two stanzas [show] the means to purify oneself
and one [shows] the cause of deterioration.
Thereupon, by means of two further stanzas
the fruit [sprung from deterioration] is explained.
[Being born] in the mandala of a buddha's retinue,
attaining patience and [then] enlightenment:
expressing these qualities, the two aspects of fruit
are explained by the last in a summarized way.

♦ This was the section "Benefit," the fifth chapter of *The Commentary on the Highest Continuity of the Mahayana Dharma which Analyzes the Disposition of the Rare and Sublime Ones.*

Jamgön Kongtrül Lodrö Thayé

PART TWO

Commentary: *The Unassailable Lion's Roar*

Table of Contents

B.II.2.1.2.2. Explanation of the meaning of the praise presented in categories

B.II.2.1.2.3. Summary of the categories in terms of the truth of cessation and the truth of the path

B.II.2.1.2.4. Explanation of the reasons by combining the praise and its meaning

B.II.2.1.3. The essence of the Sangha whose members hold this teaching

B.II.2.1.3.1. Presentation of the subject matter by means of a praise

B.II.2.1.3.2. The Sangha is established as having two or six qualities

B.II.2.1.3.3. Detailed explanation by combining the praise and the presentation of the qualities

B.II.2.1.3.3.1. Explanation of the way they realize correctly

B.II.2.1.3.3.2. Explanation of the way they realize completely

B.II.2.1.3.3.3. Explanation of the particularity of complete purification

B.II.2.1.3.3.4. Explanation of its being a sublime refuge

B.II.2.1.4. Explanation of the three kinds of refuge

B.II.2.1.4.1. The necessity to present three types of refuge

B.II.2.1.4.2. Explanation of which is the ultimate refuge and which are not

B.II.2.1.4.3. Explanation of the meaning of the name "rare and sublime"

B.II.2.2. Detailed explanation of the last four points describing the way the Three Jewels are attained

B.II.2.2.1. General explanation of the four points considered together

B.II.2.2.1.1. Explanation of the four points as being the object of perception of a buddha

B.II.2.2.1.2. Explanation that they are inconceivable

B.II.2.2.1.3. Explanation why they are inconceivable

B.II.2.2.1.4. Summary of the way realization takes place, by presenting the four points in terms of cause and conditions

B.II.2.2.2. Specific explanation of the four points considered separately

B.II.2.2.2.1. The element is what needs to be realized

B.II.2.2.2.1.1. Short explanation of the meaning of the element

B.II.2.2.2.1.2. Detailed explanation of the intended meaning

B.II.2.2.2.1.2.1. Short explanation by means of a brief survey

B.II.2.2.2.1.2.2. Detailed classification of the meaning of the brief survey

B.II.2.2.2.1.2.2.1. Essence and cause

B.II.2.2.2.1.2.2.1.1. Joint explanation of what is to be purified and the means of purification

B.II.2.2.2.1.2.2.1.2. Separate explanation of the essence of each

B.II.2.2.2.1.2.2.1.2.1. The essence being what is to be purified

B.II.2.2.2.1.2.2.1.2.2. The cause being the means of purification

B.II.2.2.2.1.2.2.1.2.2.1. The way the four veils to be abandoned are given up

B.II.2.2.2.1.2.2.1.2.2.2. The way to become an heir of the Victorious One by means of the antidote

B.II.2.2.2.1.2.2.2. Fruit and function

B.II.2.2.2.1.2.2.2.1. Joint explanation of what is to be attained and what causes attainment

B.II.2.2.2.1.2.2.2.2. Separate explanation of the essence of each

B.II.2.2.2.1.2.2.2.2.1. The fruit being what is to be attained

B.II.2.2.2.1.2.2.2.2.1.1. The way to eliminate whatever is incorrect and thus needs to be abandoned

B.II.2.2.2.1.2.2.2.2.1.2. The way a fourfold fruit is attained by abandonment

B.II.2.2.2.1.2.2.2.2.1.3. The way this attainment liberates one from the two extremes

B.II.2.2.2.1.2.2.2.2.2. The function being what causes attainment

B.II.2.2.2.1.2.2.2.2.2.1. Explanation of the disposition's function by means of the contrary

B.II.2.2.2.1.2.2.2.2.2.2. Explanation of the particular feature being the power of the disposition by means of deduction

B.II.2.2.2.1.2.2.3. Endowment

B.II.2.2.2.1.2.2.3.1. Joint explanation of the qualities of cause and fruit

B.II.2.2.2.1.2.2.3.2. Particular explanation of the individual essence of each

B.II.2.2.2.1.2.2.3.2.1. Endowment in terms of the cause

B.II.2.2.2.1.2.2.3.2.2. Endowment in terms of the fruit

B.II.2.2.2.1.2.2.4. Manifestation

B.II.2.2.2.1.2.2.4.1. Short explanation of the reason

B.II.2.2.2.1.2.2.4.2. Detailed explanation of the reason

B.II.2.2.2.1.2.2.5. Phases

B.II.2.2.2.1.2.2.5.1. The way a name is attached to three phases

B.II.2.2.2.1.2.2.5.2. The way these three names contain six topics

B.II.2.2.2.1.2.2.6. All-pervasiveness

B.II.2.2.2.1.2.2.6.1. Explanation of the essence

B.II.2.2.2.1.2.2.6.2. Explanation of the different types

B.II.2.2.2.1.2.2.7. Unchangingness

B.II.2.2.2.1.2.2.7.1. Concise explanation of the essence

B.II.2.2.2.1.2.2.7.2. Detailed explanation of unchangingness throughout the three phases

B.II.2.2.2.1.2.2.7.2.1. Unchangingness in the unpurified phase

B.II.2.2.2.1.2.2.7.2.1.1. The way the essence is not polluted by the
defilements

B.II.2.2.2.1.2.2.7.2.1.2. The way there is appearance of arising and
disintegration as far as the subject is concerned

B.II.2.2.2.1.2.2.7.2.1.3. The way the true state is not harmed by
destruction

B.II.2.2.2.1.2.2.7.2.1.4. Detailed explanation of interdependent
origination

B.II.2.2.2.1.2.2.7.2.1.4.1. Explanation of the way generation takes
place, by combining an example and its meaning

B.II.2.2.2.1.2.2.7.2.1.4.1.1. Example

B.II.2.2.2.1.2.2.7.2.1.4.1.2. Meaning

B.II.2.2.2.1.2.2.7.2.1.4.1.3. Joint explanation of the example and its
meaning

B.II.2.2.2.1.2.2.7.2.1.4.1.4. The way generation takes place

B.II.2.2.2.1.2.2.7.2.1.4.2. Explanation that the essence is undefiled and
free from extremes

B.II.2.2.2.1.2.2.7.2.1.4.2.1. The way the essence is free from arising
and cessation

B.II.2.2.2.1.2.2.7.2.1.4.2.2. The way its purity is not touched by
defilements

B.II.2.2.2.1.2.2.7.2.1.4.3. Summary of the example and meaning of
arising and disintegration

B.II.2.2.2.1.2.2.7.2.1.4.3.1. Summary of the way the nature of mind is
free from arising and disintegration

B.II.2.2.2.1.2.2.7.2.1.4.3.2. Summary of the way disintegration takes
place

B.II.2.2.2.1.2.2.7.2.2. Unchangingness in the partly unpurified and
partly purified phase

B.II.2.2.2.1.2.2.7.2.2.1. Explanation of the fact that there is no change
through birth and so forth

B.II.2.2.2.1.2.2.7.2.2.1.1. The way bodhisattvas appear as being
subject to change although they are not

B.II.2.2.2.1.2.2.7.2.2.1.2. Detailed explanation of the foregoing
section's meaning

B.II.2.2.2.1.2.2.7.2.2.1.2.1. The way bodhisattvas are not subject to the
change caused by suffering

B.II.2.2.2.1.2.2.7.2.2.1.2.2. The way they appear as being subject to
change out of their compassion

B.II.2.2.2.2.3.2. Detailed explanation of the fruit

B.II.2.2.2.2.3.2.1. Concise explanation of freedom from stains by means of examples

B.II.2.2.2.2.3.2.1.1. The fruit of liberation from the veil of the mental poisons

B.II.2.2.2.2.3.2.1.2. The fruit of liberation from the veil of the hindrances to knowledge

B.II.2.2.2.2.3.2.2. Detailed explanation of the reason for this

B.II.2.2.2.2.3.2.2.1. The fruit attained through meditative equipoise and the post-meditative phase

B.II.2.2.2.2.3.2.2.2. The fruit of purification from the three poisons

B.II.2.2.2.2.3.2.2.3. Combination of the meaning with the nine examples

B.II.2.2.2.2.3.3. Detailed explanation of its function

B.II.2.2.2.2.3.3.1. Concise explanation of the way the two benefits are accomplished

B.II.2.2.2.2.3.3.1.1. The function of the essence

B.II.2.2.2.2.3.3.1.2. The function in terms of there being purity throughout all phenomena

B.II.2.2.2.2.3.3.2. Detailed explanation of the meaning

B.II.2.2.2.2.3.3.2.1. Explanation of the way the two benefits are accomplished, combined with their respective classification

B.II.2.2.2.2.3.3.2.2. Particular explanation of the best possible benefit for oneself

B.II.2.2.2.2.3.3.2.3. Particular explanation of the best possible benefit for others

B.II.2.2.2.2.3.4. Detailed explanation of endowment

B.II.2.2.2.2.3.4.1. Concise explanation through listing the names [of the qualities]

B.II.2.2.2.2.3.4.2. Detailed explanation of the meaning [of the qualities]

B.II.2.2.2.2.3.4.2.1. Concise explanation of who is endowed with qualities

B.II.2.2.2.2.3.4.2.2. Definition of the qualities that constitute endowment

B.II.2.2.2.2.3.4.2.2.1. Detailed explanation of the reason why they are deep

B.II.2.2.2.2.3.4.2.2.1.1. General explanation of the way they are inconceivable

B.II.2.2.2.2.3.4.2.2.1.2. Detailed explanation of the specifics

B.II.2.2.2.2.3.5.2.3. Summary of their meaning

B.II.2.2.2.2.3.5.2.3.1. Summary into three [kayas] with reference to reasons

B.II.2.2.2.2.3.5.2.3.2. Summary into two [kayas] with reference to the way they are

B.II.2.2.2.2.3.6. Detailed explanation of its permanence

B.II.2.2.2.2.3.6.1. Concise explanation of the reason

B.II.2.2.2.2.3.6.2. Detailed explanation of its meaning

B.II.2.2.2.2.3.6.2.1. The seven reasons why the visible kayas are permanent

B.II.2.2.2.2.3.6.2.2. Explanation of the three reasons why the dharmakaya is permanent

B.II.2.2.2.2.3.6.3. Summary of its general meaning

B.II.2.2.2.2.3.7. Detailed explanation of inconceivability

B.II.2.2.2.2.3.7.1. Concise illustration of the way it is inconceivable

B.II.2.2.2.2.3.7.2. Detailed explanation of the reason for this

B.II.2.2.2.2.3.7.2.1. Gradual explanation through eight logical reasonings

B.II.2.2.2.2.3.7.2.2. Summary into six causes

B.II.2.2.2.2.3.7.2.3. Explanation of the way it is difficult to realize

B.II.2.2.2.3. The qualities are the attributes [of realization]

B.II.2.2.2.3.1. Concise explanation of their number combining them with the two kayas

B.II.2.2.2.3.1.1. Explanation classifying them in terms of kaya and primordial wisdom

B.II.2.2.2.3.1.2. The qualities combined with these individually

B.II.2.2.2.3.2. Detailed explanation of the different classes of qualities

B.II.2.2.2.3.2.1. Concise explanation combining the meaning with an example

B.II.2.2.2.3.2.2. Detailed explanation presenting each individually

B.II.2.2.2.3.2.2.1. Illustration of the fruit of freedom

B.II.2.2.2.3.2.2.1.1. The ten powers

B.II.2.2.2.3.2.2.1.1.1. Depiction of the essence of the point to be demonstrated

B.II.2.2.2.3.2.2.1.1.2. Clarification through examples as the means of demonstration

B.II.2.2.2.3.2.2.1.2. The four fearlessnesses

B.II.2.2.2.3.2.2.1.2.1. Concise explanation of the essence

B.II.2.2.2.3.2.2.1.2.2. Detailed explanation of the function

B.II.2.2.2.3.2.2.1.2.3. Clarification by means of examples.

B.II.2.2.2.3.2.2.1.3. The eighteen unmixed features
B.II.2.2.2.3.2.2.1.3.1. Concise explanation of the essence
B.II.2.2.2.3.2.2.1.3.2. Detailed explanation of the function
B.II.2.2.2.3.2.2.1.3.3. Clarification by means of examples
B.II.2.2.2.3.2.2.2. Explanation of the fruit of maturation
B.II.2.2.2.3.2.2.2.1. The different kinds of signs intended to be illustrated
B.II.2.2.2.3.2.2.2.2. Summary through examples, being the means of illustration
B.II.2.2.2.3.2.3. The way these are to be realized from the words of the Teacher
B.II.2.2.2.3.2.4. Explanation by once more summarizing meaning and example
B.II.2.2.2.3.2.4.1. General teaching of the reason for the similarity of meaning and example
B.II.2.2.2.3.2.4.2. Explanation of each individually by combining [meaning and example]
B.II.2.2.2.3.2.4.2.1. Explanation of the fruit of freedom
B.II.2.2.2.3.2.4.2.1.1. Illustration of the powers by means of examples
B.II.2.2.2.3.2.4.2.1.1.1. Illustration of the individual kinds
B.II.2.2.2.3.2.4.2.1.1.2. Illustration of their common feature
B.II.2.2.2.3.2.4.2.1.2. Illustration of the fearlessnesses by means of examples
B.II.2.2.2.3.2.4.2.1.2.1. Concise teaching
B.II.2.2.2.3.2.4.2.1.2.2. Detailed explanation
B.II.2.2.2.3.2.4.2.1.3. Illustration of the unmixed features by means of examples
B.II.2.2.2.3.2.4.2.1.4. Summary of the way they are indivisible
B.II.2.2.2.3.2.4.2.2. Explanation of the fruit of maturation
B.II.2.2.2.3.2.4.2.2.1. The way the marks are based upon the two kayas
B.II.2.2.2.3.2.4.2.2.2. The way the two kayas are illustrated by the example of the moon
B.II.2.2.2.4. Activity is the action [of realization]
B.II.2.2.2.4.1. Concise teaching
B.II.2.2.2.4.1.1. Concise teaching [of activity] being spontaneous
B.II.2.2.2.4.1.2. Concise teaching [of activity] being uninterrupted
B.II.2.2.2.4.2. Detailed explanation
B.II.2.2.2.4.2.1. Teaching of the summarized meaning of spontaneity
B.II.2.2.2.4.2.1.1. Manifesting free from ideation

B.II.2.2.2.4.3.2.1.2.6. Where the power of speech does not enter and where it is unhindered

B.II.2.2.2.4.3.2.1.3. The way the mind is pervasive through knowledge and compassionate love

B.II.2.2.2.4.3.2.1.3.1. Short presentation of the example of clouds

B.II.2.2.2.4.3.2.1.3.2. Detailed explanation of the example

B.II.2.2.2.4.3.2.1.3.2.1. Presentation of the meaning and the example

B.II.2.2.2.4.3.2.1.3.2.2. Explanation of the meaning through corresponding properties

B.II.2.2.2.4.3.2.1.3.3. The way there is change in terms of the vessel

B.II.2.2.2.4.3.2.1.3.4. Effortless manifestation

B.II.2.2.2.4.3.2.1.3.4.1. Concise presentation

B.II.2.2.2.4.3.2.1.3.4.2. Detailed explanation

B.II.2.2.2.4.3.2.1.3.4.2.1. Combination of example and meaning in terms of corresponding properties

B.II.2.2.2.4.3.2.1.3.4.2.2. The way it is not discriminatory

B.II.2.2.2.4.3.2.1.3.5. Connection with the property conducive to eliminating suffering

B.II.2.2.2.4.3.2.1.3.5.1. Depiction of suffering and its elimination

B.II.2.2.2.4.3.2.1.3.5.2. Realizing in terms of change

B.II.2.2.2.4.3.2.1.3.5.3. Seeing the way of the four truths

B.II.2.2.2.4.3.2.1.4. Emitting illusory manifestations

B.II.2.2.2.4.3.2.1.4.1. Short presentation of the example and its meaning

B.II.2.2.2.4.3.2.1.4.2. Detailed explanation

B.II.2.2.2.4.3.2.1.4.3. Presentation of the cause of seeing

B.II.2.2.2.4.3.2.1.4.4. Explanation of the twelve deeds of the nirmanakaya

B.II.2.2.2.4.3.2.1.5. The way primordial wisdom manifests

B.II.2.2.2.4.3.2.1.5.1. Presentation of the manifestation and non-manifestation of primordial wisdom

B.II.2.2.2.4.3.2.1.5.2. Explanation of its manifestation's activity

B.II.2.2.2.4.3.2.1.5.3. They way primordial wisdom radiates

B.II.2.2.2.4.3.2.1.5.4. The way there is manifold manifestation

B.II.2.2.2.4.3.2.1.5.5. The gradual manifestation of primordial wisdom

B.II.2.2.2.4.3.2.1.5.5.1. Concise presentation

B.II.2.2.2.4.3.2.1.5.5.2. Detailed explanation

B.II.2.2.2.4.3.2.1.5.6. The special excellence of its function

B.II.2.2.2.4.3.2.1.5.6.1. Presentation in terms of being beyond the example

B.II.3.1.3. Explanation of its special excellence in comparison with generosity and two further [virtues]

B.II.3.1.3.1. Explanation in comparison with generosity

B.II.3.1.3.2. Explanation in comparison with moral conduct

B.II.3.1.3.3. Explanation in comparison with meditative stability

B.II.3.1.4. Presentation of the reason for this excellence

B.II.3.1.5. Very detailed explanation of the benefit

B.II.3.1.5.1. Attainment of enlightenment

B.II.3.1.5.2. Firm bodhichitta

B.II.3.1.5.3. Attainment of complete perfection

B.II.3.1.5.4. Definition of the accumulations

B.II.3.1.5.5. Elimination of the veils

B.II.3.1.5.5.1. Depiction of the veils to be abandoned

B.II.3.1.5.5.2. Explanation of wisdom being the supreme remedy

B.II.3.2. The way the commentary was composed

B.II.3.2.1. The reason for its composition

B.II.3.2.2. The basis on which it was composed

B.II.3.2.3. Definition of the words of the Buddha

B.II.3.2.4. Explanation that everything according with the Buddha's words should be accepted

B.II.3.2.5. One should not teach contradicting the Buddha's words

B.II.3.2.6. Explanation of the fault of contradiction

B.II.3.2.6.1. Defining how the Dharma is abandoned

B.II.3.2.6.1.1. Explanation of how it is abandoned due to the condition of one's stream of being

B.II.3.2.6.1.2. The ten direct causes for abandoning the Dharma

B.II.3.2.6.2. Defining how not to abandon the profound Dharma

B.II.3.2.6.3. Explanation that abandoning the Dharma is more grave than the immeasurably negative acts

B.II.3.3. Dedication and summary of the meaning

B.II.3.3.1. Meaning of the benefits combined with a dedication prayer

B.II.3.3.2. Summary

B.II.3.3.3. The way it was perfected

B.III. The way the meaning has been well presented [*not translated*]

CHAPTER ONE

Tathagatagarbha

INTRODUCTION

A. Part One: Introduction [not translated]
B. Part Two: Words and meaning of the actual text expanded in detail
B.I. Title and salutation corresponding to the meaning [not translated]
B.I.1. Title [not translated]
B.I.1.1. Combination of the two languages [not translated]
B.I.1.2. Explanation of their meaning [not translated]
B.I.2. Salutation of the translator

I bow down to all buddhas and bodhisattvas.

For the term "buddha," as he is called in his native language, in Tibetan the term *sangs rgyas* [pronounced "sanjay"] is used, which literally means "awakened and expanded." This refers to two aspects: abandonment and realization. A buddha has awoken from the sleep of ignorance just as, for example, one wakes up from ordinary sleep. This is the aspect of abandonment. Similar to a fully blossomed lotus, his understanding has expanded with regard to the knowable. This is the aspect of realization.

The Tibetan equivalent for the Sanskrit term "bodhisattva" is *byang chub sems dpa'* [pronounced "jang chub sem pa"], the three components of which can be literally translated as "enlightenment" (Tib. *byang chub*), "mind" (Tib. *sems*), and "courage" (Tib. *dpa'*). This refers to the fact that a bodhisattva has two objectives. By means of his discriminative wisdom he focuses on enlightenment, and by means of his compassion he focuses on beings [literally, "on those who have a mind"].

The term *sems dpa'* can also be understood as "courageous mind" in terms of mental steadfastness, curative capacity, inner strength, and courage, which refer to the fact that a bodhisattva is capable of enduring great hardships for the sake of enlightenment.

To all these buddhas and bodhisattvas I bow down respectfully with body, speech, and mind.

Before the great translators undertook a translation work, they first paid homage to all buddhas and bodhisattvas. Likewise, we should follow their example and also begin by bowing down to our yidam deity before we engage in an explanation or a similar task.

B.II. The actual commentary, which has supreme meaning
B.II.1. Presentation of the body of the text
B.II.1.1. Explanation of the body of the commentary as consisting of seven vajra points

> If condensed, the body of the entire commentary
> [consists of] the following seven vajra points:
> Buddha, Dharma, the Assembly, the element,
> enlightenment, qualities, and then buddha activity.

In a condensed way, the entire content or body of the commentary to be explained is taught in terms of seven vajra points. The term "vajra" is used since a precious vajra is composed of indestructible material, and the subject to be expressed is difficult to penetrate by means of the discriminative wisdoms resulting from study and reflection.

The first point contains the explanation of perfect buddhahood, which constitutes what is to be attained—this being the ultimate level of the two benefits, which are benefit for oneself and benefit for others.

The second point explains the sacred Dharma as having the characteristics of the two truths, which are free from attachment.

The third point is the Sangha of the noble ones, the assembly of those who do not fall back since they possess the two types of primordial wisdom (Skt. *jñāna*, Tib. *ye shes*).

The fourth point explains the expanse (Tib. *dbyings*) or the element of beings that is by nature completely pure. This is what needs to be truly realized, its realization constituting the way in which Buddha, Dharma, and Sangha are attained.

The fifth point is unsurpassable enlightenment, the essence of realization, the state in which this element is purified from all defilements without the slightest remainder.

The sixth point describes the qualities accompanying great enlightenment. They are the attributes of realization and consist of [two] fruits: those of freedom and complete maturation.

Finally, the seventh point explains buddha activity, which is spontaneous and uninterrupted. This is the power or ability of the qualities, the means causing others to gain realization. (See also Part Three, annotation 1.)

B.II.1.2. Reference to the sutras constituting their source

> In the above order, which presents them in a logical sequence, these [vajra points]
> should be known to be derived from the *Sutra Requested by King Dharanishvara*.
> The [first] three stem from its introductory chapter and the [latter] four from [its chapters]
> on the properties of those who possess understanding and the Victorious One.

The order in which these seven vajra points are explained here, where they are presented in a logical sequence corresponding to their essence or characteristics, is the same as given in the sutra famed as *The Explanation of the Great Compassion of the Tathagata*, or the *Sutra Requested by King Dharanishvara* (Skt. *Tathāgatamahā-karuṇānirdeśa-sūtra/ Dhāraṇiśvararājaparipṛcchā*, Tib. *de bzhin gshegs pa'i thugs rje chen po bstan pa'i mdo/ gzungs kyi dbang phyug rgyal pos zhus pa'i mdo*). In this context the first three vajra points, the explanation of the Three Jewels, should be known as being derived from the introductory chapter of this sutra. The bodhisattva Dharanishvararaja says there [in answer to a question of the Buddha]:

> O Bhagavan! He is directly and perfectly awakened and expanded within the equality of all phenomena. He faultlessly turns the wheel of Dharma. He possesses a limitless assembly of extremely well trained disciples...,

and so on.

As for the remaining four vajra points, first the buddha element is elucidated by means of "The Explanation of the Sixty Methods of Completely Purifying the Qualities or Properties of the Path of a Bodhisattva who Possesses Understanding," which follows upon the introductory chapter. In relation to this [Nagarjuna], in the *Dharmadhātustava* (Tib. *chos kyi dbyings su bstod pa*), says:

> If the element is present and one labors, pure natural gold will be
> seen. If the element is not present, no matter how much one la-
> bors, one only exhausts oneself in weariness and pain.

Since a ground to be purified from the defilements is present in the
form of the tathagatagarbha or the dharmadhatu, which is by nature
pure, it is justified to show ways of complete purification for the sake
of its direct manifestation.

The sixty methods of complete purification are the four ornaments
of a bodhisattva, the eight aspects of appearance, the sixteen kinds of
great compassion, and the thirty-two kinds of activity.

The last three vajra points should be understood as being derived
from "The Explanation of the Eighty Types of Qualities of the Victorious One." Following the explanation of the dharmadhatu, enlightenment is elucidated from the explanation of the sixteen kinds of great
compassion. After that, the qualities are clarified by means of the explanation of the ten powers, the four kinds of fearlessness, and the
eighteen exclusive or unmixed features of a buddha. Subsequently,
activity is elucidated by means of the explanation of the thirty-two
aspects of the unsurpassable activity of a tathagata. With the passage:
"O Son of Noble Family, the action of a tathagata consists of these
thirty-two!" action and actor are expressed simultaneously.

Due to the formulation in the root text [the last syllable of the stanza
(Skt. *śloka*) explained here being a particle that could either be understood as a finishing or a combining particle] some scholars hold that
the way in which the seven vajra points are explained is derived from
different sutras. According to this opinion the Three Jewels are derived from the *Sutra Teaching Higher Reflection* (Skt. *Dṛdhā-parivarta*,
Tib. *lhag pa'i bsam pa bstan pa'i mdo*). The element is derived from the
Sutra that is Free from Increase and Obscuration (Skt. *Anunatvāpūrnatvā-
nirdeśa-parivarta*, Tib. *'phel ba dang 'grib pa med pa'i mdo*). Enlightenment stems from the *Lion's Roar of Shrimaladevi Sutra* (Skt. *Śrīmālādevi-
siṃhanādasūtra*, Tib. *lha mo dpal 'phreng gi seng ge'i sgra'i mdo*), the qualities from the *Sutra that is Free from Increase and Obscuration* (Skt. *Anun-
atvāpūrnatvā-nirdeśa-parivarta*, Tib. *'phel 'grib med pa'i mdo*), and activity
from the *Sutra Showing the Realm of the Inconceivable Qualities and Wisdom of the Tathagata* (Skt. *Tathāgata-guṇa-jñānācintya-viṣayāvatāra-nirdeśa-
sūtra*, Tib. *de bzhin bshegs pa'i yon tan dang ye shes bsam gyis mi khyab pa'i
yul la 'jug pa bstan pa'i mdo*). (See also Part Three, annotation 2.)

B.II.1.3. Explanation of their sequence by means of the given order

> From the Buddha [stems] the Dharma, from the Dharma the
> Assembly of noble ones,
> from the Assembly the attainment of buddha nature, the
> element of primordial wisdom.
> This wisdom finally attained is supreme enlightenment, the
> powers and so on,
> [thus] possessing the properties that fulfill the benefit of all
> sentient beings.

From whoever is directly and perfectly awakened and expanded within the expanse of the equality of all phenomena stems the faultless turning of the wheel of Dharma. From the Dharma being practiced as it was taught stems the Assembly of the noble ones, a limitless number of extremely well trained disciples. In their streams of being, the element or buddha nature, which has become the cause of primordial wisdom, is attained in the sense that it is [apparently] present. From having become [a member of] the Sangha, this primordial wisdom of a buddha is finally attained at the end of the process in which the defilements obscuring the buddha nature are removed. This is the attainment of supreme enlightenment. This enlightenment possesses the qualities, which consist of the powers and so on. These qualities in their turn constitute the primary condition for the arising of the endowment with properties equivalent to activity, which fulfills the benefit of all sentient beings.

Acknowledging this sequence, the commentary is therefore presented in this order. (See also Part Three, annotation 3.)

THE FIRST THREE VAJRA POINTS: THE THREE JEWELS
The First Vajra Point: Buddha

B.II.2. Detailed explanation of the parts
B.II.2.1. Detailed explanation of the Three Jewels as being what is to be attained
B.II.2.1.1. The Buddha who is the teacher
B.II.2.1.1.1. Presentation of the nature of the Buddha by means of a praise

> Buddha is without beginning, middle, or end. He is peace
> itself, fully self-awakened and self-expanded in
> buddhahood.

> Having reached this state, he shows the indestructible,
> permanent path so that those who have no realization may
> realize.
> Wielding the supreme sword and vajra of knowledge and
> compassionate love, he cuts the seedling of suffering
> and destroys the wall of doubts along with its surrounding
> thicket of various views. I bow down to this Buddha.

Since buddhahood is free from an initial coming into existence, an abiding in the meantime, and a final cessation, it is uncreated. Since all thoughts and conceptual elaborations are pacified, it is spontaneously present. Since a buddha is fully self-awakened and self-expanded without a teacher by means of self-aware primordial wisdom, buddhahood is not a realization due to extraneous conditions. These are the qualities constituting one's own benefit.

Since a buddha has awoken from the sleep of ignorance and his understanding has expanded to embrace the knowable, he has gained possession of the most excellent knowledge. By means of this knowledge he shows within samsara the permanent path, the meaning of the indestructible true state (Skt. *dharmatā*, Tib. *chos nyid*). This is compassionate love. Wielding the supreme sword of knowledge and compassionate love he cuts the shoot of "name and form," which are the immediate causes of suffering. Wielding the supreme vajra of knowledge and compassionate love, he destroys the wall of doubts about the truth and about action and its fruit, which is surrounded by the thick forest of the various views that precede the formation of those views belonging to the fearful [or transitory] collection. This is ability or power. With these he possesses the qualities constituting the benefit of others.

Therefore I bow down to this Buddha with great respect. (See also Part Three, annotation 4.)

B.II.2.1.1.2. Explanation of the meaning of the praise presented in categories

> Being uncreated and spontaneously present,
> not a realization due to extraneous conditions,
> wielding knowledge, compassionate love, and ability,
> buddhahood has [the qualities of] the two benefits.

By the preceding section buddhahood is shown as having six or eight qualities:

Since it is not engendered by causes and conditions, it has the quality of being uncreated and unchanging (1). Since it is free from deliberate effort, it has the quality of being spontaneously present (2). Since it is self-aware, it has the quality of not being realized due to extraneous conditions (3).

Since a buddha possesses these three qualities, he has the quality of knowledge (4). Since he leads the other beings to also attain this knowledge, he has the quality of great compassionate love (5). Since he brings about the relinquishment of the causes of suffering of all other beings, thereby eradicating the suffering that is the fruit of these causes, he has the quality of being endowed with ability (6).

In terms of subject matter there are six different kinds of qualities. If classified according to aspects, the first three form the quality of best possible benefit for oneself, and the latter three form the quality of best possible benefit of others. Considering these as a whole, buddhahood possesses eight qualities. (See also Part Three, annotation 5.)

B.II.2.1.1.3. Detailed explanation by combining the praise and its meaning

> Its nature is without beginning, middle, or end;
> hence [the state of a buddha] is uncreated.
> Since it possesses the peaceful dharmakaya,
> it is described as being "spontaneously present."
> Since it must be realized through self-awareness,
> it is not a realization due to extraneous conditions.
> These three aspects being realized, there is knowledge.
> Since the path is shown, there is compassionate love.
> There is ability since the mental poisons and suffering
> are relinquished by primordial wisdom and compassion.
> Through the first three there is benefit for oneself.
> Through the latter three there is benefit for others.

Here buddhahood is explained in such a way that the statements made in the foregoing section on the different types of qualities are successively proven on the basis of the reasons taught in the praise:

(1) Whatever is compounded or created consists of the three aspects of beginning, middle, and end, or in other words, has the properties of coming into existence, of abiding, and then being destroyed. Since buddhahood is of a nature that is free from these, it is uncreated.

Generally speaking there are four teachings with regard to the term "uncreated." Depending upon the following criteria, the subject in question is considered as being created or uncreated: The first criterion is whether or not there is arising and cessation due to causes and conditions. The second is whether or not there is arising and cessation of karma and mental poisons. The third is whether or not arising through a body of mental nature and cessation in terms of an inconceivable death take place. The fourth is whether or not the subject in question appears to the disciples as something that arises and ceases.

In this context, Rongtönpa holds that in the light of these four criteria the dharmakaya of all buddhas is uncreated, in the sense of not appearing to the disciples as something that comes into existence and ceases.

It is therefore necessary to understand that buddhahood possesses the quality of being uncreated. Yet if one takes it as a whole as being uncreated, one needs to understand that this contradicts its having knowledge, compassionate love, and ability.

(2) Buddhahood is endowed with the dharmakaya itself, which is complete peace. It is peace in the sense of freedom from any deliberate effort in terms of the concept-bound activity of body and speech, the conceptual activity of the mind, and so on. Therefore it is described as "spontaneously present activity."

(3) Since it must be realized by means of self-sprung primordial wisdom being self-aware, it is not a realization due to outer conditions such as other people's utterances and so on.

(4) Having realized the dharmadhatu in its three aspects of qualities, which are uncreatedness and so on, a buddha [also] realizes that it is within all sentient beings alike. Thus he possesses the most excellent primordial wisdom of knowledge.

(5) In order to also lead all other beings who are to be trained to this ultimate purity, he clearly demonstrates the path beyond the world in accordance with their respective karmic fortunes. Therefore he possesses the most excellent love and compassion.

(6) By means of his primordial wisdom and his great compassion mentioned before, he is able to cause the relinquishment of the suffering of beings, eradicating their skandhas, which attract suffering, and their mental poisons, which cause these skandhas, up to their very end. Therefore he possesses the most excellent activity or ability.

In this context it is explained that by the first three qualities the best possible benefit for oneself is accomplished, while the latter three accomplish the best possible benefit of others. (See also Part Three, annotation 6.)

The Second Vajra Point: Dharma
B.II.2.1.2. The Dharma that is his teaching
B.II.2.1.2.1. Presentation of the subject matter by means of a praise

> The Dharma is neither non-existent nor existent. It is not both existent and non-existent, nor is it other than existent and non-existent.
> It is inaccessible to such investigation and cannot be defined.
> It is self-aware and peace.
> The Dharma is without defilement. Holding the brilliant light rays of primordial wisdom,
> it fully defeats attachment, aversion, and dull indifference with regard to all objects of perception. I bow down to this sun of the sacred Dharma.

(1) The sacred Dharma in terms of the truth of cessation does not fall into the extreme of nihilism, which is the belief in non-existence, since the absolute truth, or in other words, the dharmadhatu, suchness, the true nature, exists as the field of experience of self-aware primordial wisdom.

It does not fall into the extreme of eternalism, which is the belief in existence, since it has been free from arising as a relative adventitious thing since beginningless time.

It is also not the common basis of a collection of the two aspects "existent" and "non-existent," since on one hand it is neither of these, both having been refuted, and since on the other hand they contradict each other.

Since it is impossible for something to be both existent and non-existent, it cannot be investigated as their contrary either, as something other than both existent and non-existent.

For this reason the Dharma is completely liberated from the conceptual elaboration consisting of the four extreme views (Tib. *mu bzhi*).

Since it is inexpressible by means of symbols and terms and since it is truly beyond the field of experience of speech, it cannot be verbally defined.

It cannot be explained by means of examples, logical reasonings, and so on. Not being an object of experience of an other-aware perception, it must be perceived by the noble ones through self-awareness. For these reasons it is inconceivable.

Since karma and the mental poisons, the root of samsara, are pacified, it is free from these two aspects. Since their cause, improper mental activity, has come to complete peace, it is freedom from thought.

(2) The Dharma in terms of the truth of the path is utter purity, being free from the mental poisons along with their remaining imprints.

It is clarity, since it is endowed with the brilliant light rays of the direct knowledge of all aspects. This is primordial wisdom, which is free from the veil of the hindrances to knowledge.

With regard to the objects of perception, it fully overcomes desire and attachment towards agreeable objects, aversion and anger towards disagreeable objects, and the darkness of dull indifference, which is ignorance and delusion, when facing neutral objects. For this reason it acts as a remedy.

I faithfully bow down to this sacred Dharma, which in these three aspects is similar to the sun. (See also Part Three, annotation 7.)

B.II.2.1.2.2. Explanation of the meaning of the praise presented in categories

Inconceivable, free from the two [veils] and from thought,
being pure, clear, and playing the part of an antidote,
it is free from attachment and frees from attachment.
This is the Dharma with its features of the two truths.

In the preceding section the rare and sublime Dharma is shown as having six or eight qualities. In terms of subject matter the Dharma has six qualities:

The first three consist of the facts that it is inconceivable in that it cannot be grasped by a conceptual understanding (1), it is free from the two [veils] of karma and the mental poisons (2), and it is free from their cause, which is improper conceptual activity (3).

The latter three consist of the facts that it is pure, since the defilements that [obscured] the essence have been purified (4), it is clear, since it illuminates all phenomena (5), and it plays the part of the very antidote that counteracts the three poisons (6).

If classified in terms of aspects, the first three qualities constitute the fruit, the truth of cessation, which must be freed from attachment [and will then be revealed as being freedom from attachment] (7). The latter three constitute the cause, the truth of the path, which frees one from attachment (8). Thus it has the characteristics of the two truths, which comprise full purification. Together with these two aspects, in total there are eight qualities.

That which possesses these eight qualities is called the sacred Dharma. (See also Part Three, annotation 8.)

B.II.2.1.2.3. Summary of the categories in terms of the truth of cessation and the truth of the path

Freedom from attachment [as fruit and means]
consists of the truths of cessation and path.
Accordingly these should also be known
by means of three qualities each.

Freedom from attachment or desire is called the Dharma. This consists of the truth of cessation, which is the fruit—that which is free from attachment—and of the truth of the path, which is the means to free oneself from attachment. In the given order these two truths should also be known as being explained by means of three qualities each. The truth of cessation, when it has twofold purity, is explained by means of the three qualities of being inconceivable, free from the two veils, and free from thought. The truth of the path, which causes purification, is explained by means of the three qualities of being pure, clear, and an antidote. (See also Part Three, annotation 9.)

B.II.2.1.2.4. Explanation of the reasons by combining the praise and its meaning

Not being an object of conceptual investigation, being
inexpressible,
and [only] to be known by noble ones, the Dharma is
inconceivable.
Since it is peace, it is free from the two [veils] and free from
thought.
In its three [aspects of] purity and so on it is similar to the sun.

Taking the reasons from the above section, where the Dharma is explained in the form of a praise, its different categories are successively proven and explained as follows:

The Dharma to be attained, the truth of cessation, is not an object to be investigated by means of an understanding that perceives in terms of the four extreme views of existence, non-existence, and so on. It is not an object to be expressed by means of words, terms, definitions, and so forth, and it has to be known by the noble ones through self-aware primordial wisdom, which is present during meditation. For these three reasons it is inconceivable for a worldly understanding.

Since the karma bound up with pollution and the mental poisons fully raising this karma have come to peace, the truth of cessation is free from these two [veils]. It is free from thought since the improper conceptual activity that acts as their cause has been pacified.

The three aspects of purity and so on, that is, purity, clarity, and acting as an antidote, are the three qualities of the paths of seeing and meditation, which cause the attainment of this truth of cessation. These are to be understood as being like the sun in that there are three corresponding properties. Just as the orb of the sun is completely pure, the truth of the path is free from all the defilements of [even] the secondary mental poisons. In the same way as the sun illuminates the visible, the truth of the path illuminates all the aspects of the knowable, or in other words, all phenomena. Just as the sun acts as an antidote that overcomes darkness, the truth of the path acts as the antidote against all obstructions preventing the seeing of suchness. (See also Part Three, annotation 10.)

The Third Vajra Point: Sangha

B.II.2.1.3. The essence of the Sangha whose members hold this teaching
B.II.2.1.3.1. Presentation of the subject matter by means of a praise

> This mind being by nature clear light, they have seen the
>   poisons to be essenceless
> and therefore truly realize [the nature of] every being as peace,
>   the ultimate non-existence of a self. They perceive that the
>   Perfect Buddha pervades them all.
> They possess the understanding that is free from the veils.
>   Thus seeing that beings are utterly pure and that [this
>   purity pervades] their limitless number,
> they are endowed with the vision of primordial wisdom. I bow
>   down to this [Sangha].

Of the different types of Sangha, the bodhisattvas who do not fall back are an especially noble assembly. Since their own minds have directly revealed themselves as being by nature clear light and functioning as the antidote itself, they have seen that the essence of the mental poisons to be abandoned has been free from arising since beginningless time. Therefore the bodhisattvas truly realize the nature of every being just as it is. They realize it as a state of peace or as freedom from any conceptual elaboration: the ultimate selflessness of persons and of phenomena. By means of this realization they have primordial wisdom that knows correctly.

They see that the nature of a perfect buddha—the dharmakaya, the true state—has always been present within beings whose state is relative, such that it pervades them all. By means of this seeing they have the primordial wisdom that knows completely.

These two types of primordial wisdom are the quality of awareness.

In the given order, these are also an understanding that is free from the veil of attachment and one that is free from the veil of obstructions. With these understandings the bodhisattvas possess the discriminative wisdom beyond the worldly. By means of this discriminative wisdom, they have the perception that knows the utterly pure dharmadhatu of beings, and furthermore knows that this dharmadhatu pervades their limitless number. Therefore they possess the completely pure vision of primordial wisdom with regard to the entire range of the knowable.

This is the quality of liberation.

I bow down to these [bodhisattvas] with open faith. (See also Part Three, annotation 11.)

B.II.2.1.3.2. The Sangha is established as having two or six qualities

**The assembly of those who have understanding
and thus do not fall back has unsurpassable qualities,
since their vision of inner primordial wisdom,
which knows correctly and knows completely, is pure.**

(1) By the preceding section the rare and sublime Sangha is shown as having two qualities:

Focusing on the true state as their object, noble ones perceive the presence of suchness just as it is. They see this in a way that is not held in common with other beings: by means of inner self-aware primordial wisdom. This vision is purified from the veil of attachment. For this reason they have the quality of primordial wisdom that knows correctly.

Focusing on those whose state is relative as their object, noble ones perceive that the dharmadhatu is all-pervasively present within all sentient beings alike, no matter how many there are. This is also seen in a way that is not held in common with others: by means of inner self-aware primordial wisdom. This vision is purified from the veil of obstruction. For this reason they have the quality of primordial wisdom that knows completely.

Since they possess these qualities, the members of the rare and sublime Sangha, the assembly of bodhisattvas who have understanding and thus do not fall back from great perfect enlightenment, are superior to the shravakas and pratyekabuddhas. They are therefore said to possess the quality of unsurpassable primordial wisdom.

(2) Or, according to another explanation, the assembly of the bodhisattvas who have understanding, the Sangha of the noble ones who do not fall back, is presented as having eight qualities: Since they have

the visions of primordial wisdom that knows correctly, of primordial wisdom that knows completely, and of inner primordial wisdom, there are the three qualities of awareness.

Since they are purified from the two veils of attachment and obstruction, and since they have the quality of being unsurpassable, there are the three qualities of liberation.

Adding to these six qualities the two aspects of awareness and liberation that are their basis, the bodhisattvas who have understanding possess eight qualities altogether.

The first is the individual presentation as intended by the Sanskrit commentary, the latter corresponds to the usual explanation of the early Tibetan commentaries. (See also Part Three, annotation 12.)

B.II.2.1.3.3. Detailed explanation by combining the praise and the presentation of the qualities
B.II.2.1.3.3.1. Explanation of the way they realize correctly

> **Realizing beings in their state of peace**
> **[the noble ones] know correctly,**
> **for [the mind] is by nature utterly pure**
> **and the poisons were always exhausted.**

By means of their self-aware primordial wisdom the awakened noble ones realize directly that the nature of mind of all sentient beings has a state of peace beyond any conceptual elaboration. Therefore they possess the primordial wisdom that knows correctly. This is because they realize that the minds of beings are by nature utterly pure and luminous clarity, and that the adventitious mental poisons [obscuring] their minds have never arisen [or existed] and are therefore exhausted and ceased.

B.II.2.1.3.3.2. Explanation of the way they realize completely

> **Their understanding, which realizes the knowable**
> **as well as [its] ultimate condition, sees**
> **that the state of omniscience is within all beings.**
> **Thus the [noble ones] know completely.**

Their understanding, or in other words, the discriminative wisdom beyond the worldly, realizes all knowable objects and realizes suchness, their ultimate condition. By means of self-aware primordial wisdom this understanding sees directly that the state of omniscience, the tathagatagarbha, is all-pervasively present within all beings, no matter how many there are, as the nature [of their minds]. Therefore the awakened noble ones possess the primordial wisdom that knows completely—knowing all those whose state is relative.

As is stated in [Asanga's own] commentary, this seeing arises from the first bodhisattva level onwards, since the dharmadhatu is realized as being all-pervasive. (See also Part Three, annotation 13.)

B.II.2.1.3.3.3. Explanation of the particularity of complete purification

Such realization is the vision of wisdom
that is self-aware. This wisdom is pure,
since it [sees] the undefiled expanse,
free from attachment and obstruction.

Such realization is the vision of the noble ones. It is the realization of the path beyond the worldly achieved through the two types of primordial wisdom. This vision takes place in a way that is not held in common with others: through self-aware primordial wisdom. This wisdom knows correctly since it perceives that the dharmadhatu, which is by nature undefiled, pervades everything, and since it is free from the veil of the mental poisons, which are bound up with attachment. It knows completely since it realizes that this dharmadhatu pervades all knowable things, and since it is free from the veil of the hindrances to knowledge, which are bound up with obstruction. Therefore these two types of primordial wisdom are of extreme and utter purity in comparison to a seeing by means of an ephemeral primordial wisdom. (See also Part Three, annotation 14.)

B.II.2.1.3.3.4. Explanation of its being a sublime refuge

Their vision [of] primordial wisdom is pure
and [nears] unsurpassable buddha wisdom.
The noble ones who do not fall back
are therefore a refuge for all beings.

Since they have the vision of the two types of primordial wisdom, thus possessing the quality of awareness, and since they are purified from the veils of attachment and obstruction, thus possessing the quality of liberation, they are near to the unsurpassable primordial wisdom of a buddha. Therefore the noble ones who directly see the true state and thus do not fall back from perfect enlightenment have become a refuge protecting all sentient beings from having to feel suffering within samsara.

THE THREE REFUGES

B.II.2.1.4. Explanation of the three kinds of refuge
B.II.2.1.4.1. The necessity to present three types of refuge

There being the teacher, his teaching, and his disciples
leads to respective aspirations towards three vehicles
and to three different activities [of veneration].
Viewing this, the refuge is shown as threefold.

For the following reason the refuge is presented as being threefold:
The fact that the qualities of the Buddha who is the teacher are taught
entails two different reactions. On one hand there are those [individu-
als] who see the qualities of this teacher and thereupon strive for the
attainment of buddhahood. Of the three vehicles they follow the
Mahayana. On the other hand there are those who of the three types
of activities of veneration have the aspiration of venerating the Buddha as being supreme among gods and humans. Considering this,
buddhahood is presented as the first of the three refuges.

Likewise, the fact that the qualities of the sacred Dharma are taught
leads to two reactions. On one hand there are those [individuals] who
see the qualities of this teaching and thereupon wish to realize and
attain the profound Dharma of interdependent origination on their
own. They follow the Pratyekabuddhayana. On the other hand there
are those who have the aspiration of venerating the Dharma as being
supreme among that which is free from desire. Considering this, the
Dharma is presented as the second refuge.

The fact that the qualities of the Sangha, of the assembly of disciples, are taught leads to the following two reactions: On one hand
there are those [individuals] who see the qualities of these disciples
and thereupon wish to attain their state, [the state of an arhat], by
practicing the teaching [of the Buddha] as taught by others. They follow the Shravakayana. On the other hand there are those who have
the aspiration of venerating the Sangha as supreme among assemblies. Considering this, the Sangha is presented as the third refuge.

Put briefly, the refuge is presented as being threefold in consideration of the fact that the three aspects [of teacher, teaching, and dis-
ciples] result in six types of individuals. This presentation is taught in
order to enable beings to gradually gain access [to the path]. (See also
Part Three, annotation 15.)

B.II.2.1.4.2. Explanation of which is the ultimate refuge and which are not

[The Dharma] will be abandoned and is of an unsteady nature.
It is not [the ultimate quality], and [the Sangha] is still with fear.
Thus the two aspects of Dharma and the Assembly of noble ones
do not represent the supreme refuge, which is constant and stable.
In a true sense only the Buddha is beings' refuge,
since the Great Sage embodies the dharmakaya,
and the Assembly also reaches its ultimate goal
when these [qualities of dharmakaya are attained].

One may wonder whether the three kinds of refuge explained above equally represent an ultimate refuge. This is not the case. The Dharma in terms of teaching is to be abandoned like a boat is left behind once one has crossed the water. Of the two aspects of Dharma in terms of realization, the realization of those who travel the path of training proceeds from one level to the next and is therefore of an unsteady or changing nature. The truths of cessation of the lesser vehicles and of [bodhisattvas] traveling the path of training do not constitute the ultimate quality. The Sanghas of arhats of the lesser vehicles and of noble bodhisattvas who are on the path of training are still with the fear of the veils. As long as they have not arrived at the level of a buddha who is free from fear, they themselves will take refuge in the Buddha as well. For these reasons, neither the two aspects of Dharma, that is, teaching and realization, which constitute the training, nor the assemblies of the noble ones who are the trainees, are the constant and stable supreme refuge.

In a true or definitive sense only a buddha is the ultimate refuge of the limitless number of sentient beings, since the Great Sage, the Buddha, is the embodiment of the dharmakaya, which is the completion of freedom from desire and attachment, and since the members of the assembly, the Sangha, also reach their ultimate [goal] when they attain the qualities of this [dharmakaya].

Here [in the context of the *Mahayana Uttara Tantra Shastra*] the Buddha is called "the inexhaustible refuge," "the permanent refuge," "the immutable refuge" (Tib. *g.yung drung gi skyabs*), and "the absolute refuge." In the given order this explanation refers to the fact that a buddha is free from death, free from birth, free from aging, and that he is unfailing. This is also the intention of the *Aryashrimalasutra* (Tib. *'phags pa dpal phreng gi mdo*). (See also Part Three, annotation 16.)

B.II.2.1.4.3. Explanation of the meaning of the name "rare and sublime"

Their occurence is rare, they are free from defilement,
they possess power, they are the adornment of the world,
they are sublime, and they are unchanging.
Thus [they are named] "rare and sublime."

One may wonder what is the meaning of the term "rare and sublime" (Tib. *dkon mchog*). It is derived from the term "ratna" [Skt. for "jewel"] and is here defined by means of six aspects corresponding to the properties of a precious [wish-fulfilling] gem.

A [wish-fulfilling] jewel is difficult to find. Its essence is free from defilements. It possesses the power to fulfill needs and wishes. Due to its beauty it becomes an adornment. It is more sublime than an artificial gem and it does not change through being praised, blamed, and so on. Likewise, the occurrence of the three refuges is also rare, since those who have not cultivated the roots of virtue will not even meet them in the course of many kalpas or eons. The three refuges are free from the pollution of the two veils. They possess the inconceivable power of the qualities of clairvoyance and so on. Since they are the cause of all virtuous thoughts and intentions of sentient beings in the world, they have become its adornment. Since they are beyond the world, they are more sublime than anything worldly. Since they are not created by karma, mental poisons, and so on, they are unchanging. For these reasons they are similar to a precious [wish-fulfilling] gem and are therefore expressed by means of the name "rare and sublime."

THE LAST FOUR VAJRA POINTS

B.II.2.2. Detailed explanation of the last four points describing the way the Three Jewels are attained
B.II.2.2.1. General explanation of the four points considered together
B.II.2.2.1.1. Explanation of the four points as being the object of perception of a buddha

The virtuous Three Jewels, which are rare and sublime,
arise from suchness bound up with pollution, from the one
free from pollution,
from the qualities of unpolluted buddhahood, and from the
deeds of the Victor.
This is the object of those who see the ultimate truth.

In the phase of [ordinary] beings the dharmadhatu is not freed from the covering of the mental poisons. In that phase it is called "the tathagatagarbha." This is suchness bound up with pollution. In the phase of the level of buddhahood this dharmadhatu is called "the dharma-kaya of the Tathagata." The level of a buddha is characterized by a complete change or transformation of state, in that through cultivating the path this tathagatagarbha has become free from all the adventitious defilements up to their very end. This is suchness free from pollution. What is linked with this dharmakaya are the buddha properties such as the powers and so on, constituting the fruits of freedom and of complete maturation. These properties are the qualities of unpolluted buddhahood. Through the power of these qualities there is unsurpassable activity accomplishing the benefit of sentient beings, spontaneously and uninterruptedly, in ways corresponding to each individual. This activity consists of the deeds of the Victor.

These four points constitute the cause and the conditions for the arising of the fruit, of the virtuous Three Jewels, which are rare and sublime. The way in which this arising takes place is inconceivable to shravakas, pratyekabuddhas, noble ones, and so on. This is solely the object of perception of buddhas who possess the ultimate primordial wisdom that directly sees the true state of everything or the absolute truth. (See also Part Three, annotation 17.)

B.II.2.2.1.2. Explanation that they are inconceivable

> The disposition of the Three Rare and Sublime Ones
> is the object [of vision] of those who see everything.
> Furthermore, these four aspects in the given order
> are inconceivable, for the following four reasons:

The [last] four [vajra] points are the disposition bringing about the accomplishment of the Three Rare and Sublime Ones, constituting the cause and the conditions that give rise to this fruit. Their actual correct meaning is the object of perception of the primordial wisdom of buddhas alone who directly see all the aspects of the knowable. Furthermore, as for the meaning of the element and so on, these four aspects are inconceivable to ordinary beings. This is due to four reasons which will be explained in the next section according to the given sequence [of the last four vajra points].

B.II.2.2.1.3. Explanation why they are inconceivable

> [The buddha element] is pure and yet has affliction.
> [Enlightenment] was not afflicted and yet is purified.
> Qualities are totally indivisible [and yet unapparent].
> [Activity] is spontaneous and yet without any thought.

Our nature of mind has been completely pure since beginningless time, and yet at the same time it has the affliction through the adventitious defilements which are temporarily present. For this reason the meaning of the element is inconceivable.

Previously, enlightenment was not afflicted at all by the adventitious defilements, and yet later it has become utterly purified from all defilements up to their very end through the cultivation of the path. For this reason the meaning of enlightenment is inconceivable.

On one hand the absolute qualities exist in the true state, which is also completely indivisible during the phase of an ordinary being who is bound up with affliction. On the other hand, these qualities do not become apparent since their power does not unfold until buddhahood is reached. For this reason the meaning of the qualities is inconceivable.

The activity of a buddha fulfils the wishes and hopes of the disciples in correspondence to their respective karmic fortunes, and does so in a way that is free from deliberate effort, spontaneous, and at all times uninterrupted. Nevertheless it is completely free from thought and consideration, such as "this or that needs to be done" and so on. For this reason the meaning of activity is inconceivable.

These [four points] are inconceivable, as seemingly two contradictory statements are made in relation to the same basis. In fact there is no contradiction: The element is a completely pure nature empty of the essence of the defilements. Its impurity consists of the fact that it has adventitious defilements.

"Previous freedom from defilements" means that the defilements do not exist as the nature of the element. "Later purity" means that purification from the defilements is to be considered like gold being purified from the surrounding dross. Although there is an absence of purity during the phase of an ordinary being, whereas later complete purification from the defilements is achieved, this later purity is native to the true state in a completely indivisible way. For this reason there is no contradiction.

Since in the phase of an ordinary being there is no purification from the defilements, the qualities are not [apparently] present. Nevertheless, when later purification from the defilements is achieved, [it proves that] the qualities exist in the true state in such a way that they are not able to be separated from it. This is similar to the following example: Though in the phase in which gold is not purified from the surrounding dross there is no luster, later luster will manifest in an inseparable way. Therefore again there is no contradiction.

Activity will be explained below in its own chapter by means of nine examples. (See also Part Three, annotation 18.)

B.II.2.2.1.4. Summary of the way realization takes place, by presenting the four points in terms of cause and conditions

> Constituting what must be realized, realization,
> its attributes, and the means to bring it about,
> accordingly the first is the cause to be purified
> and the [latter] three points are the conditions.

Being explained in this way, these [last] four vajra points also comprise all objects of knowledge. In this context the element, bound up with pollution, constitutes what is to be realized. Enlightenment free from pollution is the very essence of realization. The qualities linked with enlightenment are the attributes of this realization. Activity is the power of these qualities causing all other [sentient beings] to realize this element as well. For this reason, the first of the four vajra points in their given sequence, that is, suchness bound up with pollution, is the cause to be purified. This is because the Three Rare and Sublime Ones arise from the fact that this suchness has been completely purified from any defilement. The last three vajra points are the conditions causing this purification. (See also Part Three, annotation 19.)

THE FOURTH VAJRA POINT: THE ELEMENT

B.II.2.2.2. Specific explanation of the four points considered separately
B.II.2.2.2.1. The element is what needs to be realized
B.II.2.2.2.1.1. Short explanation of the meaning of the element

> The perfect buddhakaya is all-embracing,
> suchness cannot be differentiated,
> and all beings have the disposition.
> Thus they always have buddha nature.
>
> The Buddha has said that all beings have buddha nature
> "since buddha wisdom is always present within the assembly
>   of beings,
> since this undefiled nature is free from duality,
> and since the disposition to buddhahood has been named after
>   its fruit."

The dharmakaya of a perfect buddha embraces and pervades all phenomena. With regard to suchness or the true state of the entirety of samsara and nirvana, there is not the slightest differentiation. The disposition of the Tathagata is present within all sentient beings in terms of the dharmadhatu being by nature pure and its veils being able to be purified. For these reasons all sentient beings have had the nature of the absolute Buddha, always and uninterruptedly, since beginningless time.

As it is said in the sutras: "The Buddha Bhaghavat has said 'all sentient beings always have the tathagatagarbha.'"

With regard to [the three reasons given above], the great translator from Ngog (Tib. rngog lo chen po, i.e. Lodän Sherab, who first translated the *Mahayana Uttara Tantra Shastra* into Tibetan) states the following:

> In the given sequence they represent the sugatagarbha in terms of the fruit, the sugatagarbha in terms of the nature, and the sugatagarbha in terms of the cause. The first is the dharmakaya. This is the real Tathagata, whereas the nature of beings is only named after it. Since it is able to be attained by beings, it is explained as being all-pervasive. The second is the real nature of both a Tathagata and beings. When merely considered from the aspect of suchness being by nature completely pure, the sugatagarbha [or tathagatagarbha] is really present within a Tathagata and beings alike. The third is the real nature of beings. Since it is the cause of the Tathagata, it has been named after it.

At this point the noble Asanga states [in his commentary]:

> In brief, there are three reasons for which all beings have the nature of the Tathagata. The Bhagavan has said: "All beings have buddha nature, since buddha wisdom is always present within the assembly of beings, since this undefiled nature is free from duality and since the disposition to buddhahood has been named after its fruit." These three reasons have been taught extensively in all the words of the Buddha. With respect to this they are explained as follows: due to the fact that the dharmakaya of the Tathagata embraces all beings, that the suchness of the Tathagata is completely indivisible and that they have the disposition of the Tathagata...

In some commenting scriptures these lines do not appear. Yet they have been quoted and explained extensively by Golo (Tib. 'gos lo), Könchön (Tib. dkon gzhon), Rongtön (Tib. rong ston), and others, and they have been explained in detail by the Great Venerable Jonangpa (Tāranātha) and others. Nevertheless they seem to have been omitted in present-day scriptures. (See also Part Three, annotation 20.)

B.II.2.2.2.1.2. Detailed explanation of the intended meaning
B.II.2.2.2.1.2.1. Short explanation by means of a brief survey

> Essence, cause, fruit, function, endowment, manifestation,
> phases, all-pervasiveness of suchness, unchangingness,
> and inseparability of the qualities should be understood
> as intended to describe the meaning of the absolute expanse.

It should be understood that the intention behind the following ten points is to determine the meaning of the dharmadhatu, which is by nature utterly pure, being equivalent to the true state of everything or the absolute truth. They represent a systematic order that classifies this meaning fully and properly:

The points "essence" and "cause" describe the features of purity and purification. The points "fruit" and "function" describe the feature of accomplishment. The topic "endowment" describes the multitude of qualities. The topic "manifestation" describes the fact that there is [a difference in] manifestation due to different kinds of individuals. The topic "phases" describes the fact that there is only a classification in terms of names. The topic "all-pervasiveness" describes the fact that suchness is all-pervasive like space. The topic "unchangingness" describes the fact that the dharmadhatu is at all times free from change, and the topic "inseparability of the qualities" describes the fact that the qualities are completely inseparable [from it].

B.II.2.2.2.1.2.2. Detailed classification of the meaning of the brief survey
B.II.2.2.2.1.2.2.1. Essence and cause
B.II.2.2.2.1.2.2.1.1. Joint explanation of what is to be purified and the means
of purification

> **Just as a jewel, the sky, and water are pure**
> **it is by nature always free from the poisons.**
> **From devotion to the Dharma, from highest wisdom,**
> **and from samadhi and compassion [its realization**
> **arises].**

Just as a precious jewel, the sky, and water are by nature pure, likewise the tathagatagarbha or dharmadhatu is by nature always free from the defilement of the mental poisons and thus utterly pure. Whereas this is the meaning of the essence, the cause that completely purifies the adventitious defilements consists of devotion towards the Mahayana Dharma, of highest discriminative or analytical wisdom realizing the non-existence of a self, of limitless samadhi endowed with bliss, and of great compassion focusing on sentient beings as its point of reference. The realization arising from these [purifying causes] is to be known as enlightenment. (See also Part Three, annotation 21.)

B.II.2.2.2.1.2.2.1.2. Separate explanation of the essence of each
B.II.2.2.2.1.2.2.1.2.1. The essence being what is to be purified

[Wielding] power, not changing into something else,
and being a nature that has a moistening [quality]:
these [three] have properties corresponding
to those of a precious gem, the sky, and water.

When considered from the viewpoint of the specific characteristic
of each, the three aspects of nature explained above are to be known
[to have properties corresponding to the specific characteristics of a
precious jewel, the sky, and water, respectively]. Since the dharmakaya wields the power to accomplish all wishes and intentions just as
they are, and so on, it has a property corresponding to that of a precious [wish-fulfilling] gem. Since throughout all phases suchness does
not change into another nature, it has a property corresponding to
that of the sky. Since the disposition is a nature having a moistening
quality, as it is endowed with compassion that pervades all beings, it
has a property corresponding to the quality of water.

When considered from the viewpoint of the general characteristic
native to all three [there is also a common property]. Since they are
permanently free from defilement and by nature utterly pure, they
have a property corresponding to the quality of a wish-fulfilling gem,
the sky, and water, which are [also] by nature pure.

B.II.2.2.2.1.2.2.1.2.2. The cause being the means of purification
B.II.2.2.2.1.2.2.1.2.2.1. The way the four veils to be abandoned are given up

Enmity towards the Dharma, a view [asserting
an existing] self, fear of samsara's suffering,
and neglect of the welfare of fellow beings
are the four veils of those with great desire,
of tirthikas, shravakas, and pratyekabuddhas.
The cause that purifies [all these veils]
consists of the four qualities [of the path],
which are outstanding devotion and so on.

Generally speaking there are three types of sentient beings, namely
those who desire existence, those who desire freedom from existence,
and those who desire neither of these two. These individuals are the
basis for four types of veils that arise in their streams of being and are
to be abandoned. These four veils are hostility towards the Mahayana
Dharma, a view asserting the person and so on to be an existing self,
desire for personal happiness and peace that results from fear of the
suffering of samsara, and unconcern about the accomplishment of the

welfare of fellow beings. In the given sequence [these correspond to the following individuals]: Firstly there is a correspondence to those who desire existence. These are beings who have the disconnected disposition and beings of great desire who have definitely fallen into the cycle of existence. Secondly there is a correspondence to those who desire freedom from existence. These are the tirthikas [and so on] who desire freedom from existence but apply inappropriate means, and the shravakas and pratyekabuddhas who desire freedom from existence and apply appropriate means. Due to [the presence of these individuals] there are four types of veils preventing the immediate manifestation of the tathagatagarbha. The first obscures the aspect of the purity of the dharmakaya. The second obscures the aspect of its being true self. The third obscures the aspect of its being true happiness, and the fourth obscures the aspect that the dharmakaya is of true permanence. The cause that purifies these veils consists of the four qualities of the path, which are outstanding devotion towards the sacred Dharma and so on, that is, the perfection of discriminative wisdom, immeasurable samadhi, and great compassion. (See also Part Three, annotation 22, and Part Four, note 2.)

B.II.2.2.2.1.2.2.1.2.2.2. The way to become an heir of the Victorious One by means of the antidote

> Those whose seed is devotion towards the supreme vehicle,
> whose mother is analytical wisdom generating the buddha
> qualities,
> whose abode is the blissful womb of meditative stability,
> and whose nurse is compassion, are heirs born to succeed
> the Muni.

There are four reasons due to which the son of a Chakravartin has the power to become the legitimate successor to the king. These are the seed of the king, his pure queen, the unimpaired abode of her womb, and the exceptional nurse who nourishes the child as he grows. Using this example it can be said that devotion towards the supreme vehicle is the seed of the Buddha. Discriminative wisdom that realizes the true nature of everything is like the mother, generating all buddha qualities. Since the happiness of meditative stability, such as "the treasury of space" and so on, augments these qualities, it is similar to the abode of the womb. Since great compassion nourishes whatever has been generated, it is like a nurse. Whoever arises from these four qualities is called a bodhisattva or an heir or child of the Victorious One, since he is born to succeed the Muni and has the power to be his successor. (See also Part Three, annotation 23.)

B.II.2.2.2.1.2.2.2. Fruit and function
B.II.2.2.2.1.2.2.2.1. Joint explanation of what is to be attained and what causes attainment

> **The fruit is the perfection of the qualities**
> **of purity, self, happiness, and permanence.**
> **Weariness of suffering, longing to attain peace,**
> **and devotion towards this aim are the function.**

The absolute expanse has two particular features, which are its fruit and its function. The particularity of the fruit consists of the perfection of four qualities, being true purity, true self, true happiness, and true permanence. Since it acts to induce weariness of the suffering of samsara, longing to attain the peace of nirvana, and devotion towards this aim, it has a particular function. (See also Part Three, annotation 24.)

B.II.2.2.2.1.2.2.2.2. Separate explanation of the essence of each
B.II.2.2.2.1.2.2.2.2.1. The fruit being what is to be attained
B.II.2.2.2.1.2.2.2.2.1.1. The way to eliminate whatever is incorrect and thus needs to be abandoned

> **In brief, the fruit of these [purifying causes]**
> **fully divides into the remedies [for the antidotes],**
> **which [in their turn] counteract the four aspects**
> **of wrong beliefs with regard to the dharmakaya.**

The causes purifying the dharmadhatu are devotion, discriminative wisdom, meditative stability, and compassion. Put briefly, the fruit of these four [purifying] causes consists of four aspects: With regard to the dharmakaya, the children entertain a strong attachment in terms of the belief in purity, in the existence of a self, in happiness, and in permanence. Shravakas and pratyekabuddhas reverse these four aspects of an exaggerated view [of a view wrongly asserting reality where it is not present]. In doing so they get attached to [their vision of] impurity, non-existence of self, suffering, and impermanence. The four aspects of the [true] purity of dharmakaya and so on act as the remedies for this attachment. [The four purifying causes] are the means to bring about their perfection. Thus the full division [of the fruit] is achieved. (See also Part Three, annotation 25.)

B.II.2.2.2.1.2.2.2.2.1.2. The way a fourfold fruit is attained by abandonment

> The [dharmakaya] is purity, since its nature is pure
> and [even] the remaining imprints are fully removed.
> It is true self, since all conceptual elaboration
> in terms of self and non-self is totally stilled.
> It is true happiness, since [even] the aggregates
> of mental nature and their causes are reversed.
> It is permanence, since the cycle of existence
> and the state beyond pain are realized as one.

Buddha-dharmakaya, which is the fruit, has the general characteristic of having been by nature utterly pure since beginningless time, and it has the specific characteristic of the adventitious stains along with their remaining imprints being eliminated without any exception. Thus it constitutes the perfection of purity.

The conceptual elaboration consisting of the belief in the existence of a self as it is imputed by the tirthikas and so on, and the conceptual elaboration consisting of the belief in the non-existence of a self as it is imputed by the shravakas and so on, have been totally stilled and pacified without any remainder. Thus it is the perfection of true self.

All suffering has been ceased without any exception. This is because karma and the mental poisons have been totally eliminated, up to the point that [even] the skandhas, which are of mental nature, and their causes have been exhausted. These causes are on one hand the subtle mental poisons present on the level of the remaining imprints of ignorance, and on the other hand the undefiled karma. Since even these causes have been entirely reversed and exhausted, the dharmakaya is the perfection of happiness.

Samsara and nirvana, the cycle of existence and the state beyond torment and pain, have been realized as being equal in that they are not two different things that should be rejected and adopted, respectively. Thus the two benefits are uninterrupted and the dharmakaya constitutes the perfection of permanence.

In this context the great omniscient Dolpopa has stated:

> Furthermore, since the absolute expanse is by nature completely pure, there is not even the slightest need to remove a fault in terms of the impermanence of samsara. Therefore it does not fall into the extreme of nihilism. Since it has been spontaneously present since beginningless time, there is not even the slightest need to add a quality in terms of the permanence of nirvana. Therefore it does not fall into the extreme of eternalism. Not falling into either of these, it is established as the nirvana free from the two extremes.

(See also Part Three, annotation 26.)

B.II.2.2.2.1.2.2.2.2.1.3. The way this attainment liberates one from the two extremes

> Their analytical wisdom has cut all self-cherishing without
> exception.
> Yet, cherishing beings, those possessed of compassion do not
> adhere to peace.
> Relying on understanding and compassionate love, the means
> to enlightenment,
> noble ones will neither [abide] in samsara nor in a [limited]
> nirvana.

By means of discriminative wisdom realizing the non-existence of a self, bodhisattvas have cut, without any exception, all the cherishing and attachment of viewing the skandhas as a self, along with the dormant tendencies of this attachment. Since this [craving] is eliminated, they do not fall into the extreme of existence as do those who are dominated by great desire. Yet, due to their great compassion they cherish all sentient beings. They feel linked and close to them all and therefore bring about their benefit. For this reason bodhisattvas possessing compassionate love do not fall into another extreme either. They do not attain that state of peace that merely consists of the pacification of suffering, as do shravakas and pratyekabuddhas. Thus they rely on two particular means to attain unsurpassable enlightenment. These are the understanding or discriminative wisdom realizing the non-existence of a self, and the great love and compassion focused on sentient beings as their point of reference. Relying on these particular means, the noble heirs of the Victorious One who cultivate their practice on this basis will not dwell in any extreme. Neither abiding in the extreme of samsara in terms of existence, nor abiding in the extreme of nirvana in terms of [mere] peace, they have achieved the direct manifestation of non-abiding nirvana. (See also Part Three, annotation 27.)

B.II.2.2.2.1.2.2.2.2.2. The function being what causes attainment
B.II.2.2.2.1.2.2.2.2.2.1. Explanation of the disposition's function by means of the contrary

> If the buddha element were not present,
> there would be no remorse over suffering.
> There would be no longing for nirvana,
> nor striving and devotion towards this aim.

[Here the presence of the disposition to buddhahood is proven by using the contrary, i.e. its supposed non-presence, as a means of proof.]

Supposing that the buddha element was definitely not present, not a single person would grow to feel sorrow and remorse over the suffering of samsara. No one would long to attain nirvana. No one would strive for this aim, exerting himself to apply the means to attain it, nor would anyone have devotion in terms of the wish: "If only I attained it!" Contrary to this, the generation of sorrow, remorse, and so on is present. Since these are the function of the disposition, the disposition to buddhahood is established as being present.

B.II.2.2.2.1.2.2.2.2.2.2. Explanation of the particular feature being the power of the disposition by means of deduction

> That with regard to existence and nirvana their respective fault
>   and quality are seen,
> that suffering is seen as the fault of existence and happiness as
>   the quality of nirvana,
> stems from the presence of the disposition to buddhahood.
> "Why so?"
> In those who are devoid of disposition, such seeing does not
>   occur.

There are individuals who possess the so-called four wheels. These consist of the fact that one relies on a saintly being, lives in a favorable place, has formerly practiced virtue, and makes genuine and pure wishing prayers. With regard to samsara and nirvana, or to existence and peace, such an individual sees them for what they are. He perceives their respective fault and quality and sees that suffering is the fault of samsara and that happiness is the quality of nirvana. Upon seeing this, such a person feels weariness with the fault, which is the suffering of samsara, and joy over the quality, which is the happiness of nirvana. This weariness and joy arise from the presence of the disposition to buddhahood. One might wonder for what reason this can be said. The reason is that this understanding of what is to be adopted and what is to be rejected will not be present in someone who is subject to craving for what is wrong and does not have the awakened disposition. Such a person does not see the respective fault and quality of existence and peace until he has developed devotion towards the teaching of one of the three vehicles, depending upon which of these is suitable for this particular person. In this context [the root text speaks of there being no disposition]. Since it is impossible that the naturally present disposition is not there, this explanation is rather [to be understood] by means of the different kinds of disposition, and it seems that by the term "non-present disposition" the unawakened disposition is taught. (See also Part Three, annotation 28 and Part Four, note 1.)

B.II.2.2.2.1.2.2.3. Endowment
B.II.2.2.2.1.2.2.3.1. Joint explanation of the qualities of cause and fruit

> Like the great sea, it holds qualities
> immeasurable, precious, and inexhaustible.
> Its essence holds indivisible properties.
> Thus [the element] is similar to a lamp.

This element has two types of qualities: those in terms of the cause and those in terms of the fruit.

The qualities in terms of the cause: As, for example, the great ocean contains in its vast vessel an immeasurable amount of jewels and water, likewise the element of the Tathagata is the abode that [unifies] the vessel of devotion, the immeasurable jewel-qualities of analytical wisdom and samadhi, and the inexhaustible waters of compassion.

The qualities in terms of the fruit: Its essence has qualities that are inseparable from it, these being the first five kinds of clairvoyance, unpolluted primordial wisdom, and abandonment. Taking an example, it is therefore similar to a lamp in that the three properties of a lamp, which are light, warmth, and color, are inseparable from the lamp itself. (See also Part Three, annotation 29.)

B.II.2.2.2.1.2.2.3.2. Particular explanation of the individual essence of each
B.II.2.2.2.1.2.2.3.2.1. Endowment in terms of the cause

> Unifying the elements of dharmakaya,
> a victor's wisdom, and great compassion,
> it is shown as being similar to the sea
> by the vessel, the gems, and the water.

The dharmadhatu contains devotion, which is the cause of the completely pure dharmakaya, discriminative wisdom and samadhi, which are the causes for the attainment of the primordial wisdom of a Victorious One, and compassion, which is the element or the cause for the manifestation of the great compassion of a buddha. Since it hosts these without any exception, it has three properties corresponding to the examples of the vessel, the jewels, and the water. Due to this correspondence the dharmadhatu is shown as being similar to the great ocean.

B.II.2.2.2.1.2.2.3.2.2. Endowment in terms of the fruit

> Clairvoyance, primordial wisdom, and absence of pollution
> are totally indivisible and native to the unstained abode.
> Thus it has properties corresponding
> to the light, heat, and color of a lamp.

The sugatagarbha or the element, the abode which is by nature free from defilement, possesses [seven] particular properties corresponding, if one takes an example, to the particular properties of a lamp. These are the first five kinds of clairvoyance, unpolluted primordial wisdom, and abandonment, which is freedom from defilement. The first five kinds of clairvoyance overcome the darkness of their opposites. Unpolluted primordial wisdom [overcomes] the veils, and through abandonment, in terms of freedom from defilement, [the aspects of] purity and clear light [are present]. The sugatagarbha has [furthermore] a general property that also corresponds to that of a lamp. Just as the three particular properties of a lamp are inseparable from it, likewise the element possesses these seven properties of no-more-learning in such a way that they are completely inseparable from it. For these reasons it possesses properties corresponding to the light, heat, and color of a lamp, and to the fact that these are indivisible from the lamp itself.

The seven properties of no-more-learning exist as the fruit aspect of the element and are therefore the endowment in terms of the fruit. (See also Part Three, annotation 30.)

B.II.2.2.2.1.2.2.4. Manifestation
B.II.2.2.2.1.2.2.4.1. Short explanation of the reason

> Based upon the manifestation of suchness dividing
> into that of an ordinary being, that of a noble one,
> and that of a perfect buddha, He who Sees Thatness
> has explained the nature of the Victor to beings.

The manifestation of suchness fully divides into three aspects: the suchness of an ordinary being, the suchness of a noble one, and the suchness of a perfect buddha. Taking these different manifestations as a basis, the Omniscient One who Directly Sees Thatness has explained the nature of the victorious Tathagata, or in other words, the completely pure dharmadhatu, in a very clear way to those fortunate beings who have become [suitable] disciples. (See also Part Three, annotation 31, and Part Four, note 3.)

B.II.2.2.2.1.2.2.4.2. Detailed explanation of the reason

> [It manifests as] perverted [views in] ordinary beings,
> [as] the reversal [of these in] those who see the truth,
> and [it manifests] as it is, in an unperverted way,
> and as freedom from elaboration [in] a tathagata.

There are three particular ways in which [suchness] manifests in terms of an understanding. Since ordinary beings who are children [in comparison to noble ones] believe in permanence, it manifests as a perverted or wrong sense-perception, as a wrong way of thinking, and as wrong views. Noble ones who follow [the path of] practice and thus see the Four [Noble] Truths have reversed this distortion. In them it manifests in the manner that the firm belief in permanence is abandoned. A tathagata has abandoned the two veils. Therefore it manifests as it is, in accordance with reality, in an unperverted way, and as freedom from any conceptual elaboration. In this way the individuals who constitute the basis divide into three different kinds. Accordingly, suchness or the dharmadhatu, which is supported by this basis, also gains three different aspects. It should be noted that the topic "manifestation" will be explained below in yet another manner by means of four aspects. (See also Part Three, annotation 32.)

B.II.2.2.2.1.2.2.5. Phases
B.II.2.2.2.1.2.2.5.1. The way a name is attached to three phases

> **The unpurified, the both unpurified and purified,**
> **and the utterly purified [phases]**
> **are expressed in their given order**
> **[by the names] "being," "bodhisattva," and "tathagata."**

There are three different phases. The unpurified phase is the one in which the absolute expanse or the tathagatagarbha has not been purified from the adventitious defilements even to a minute degree. The both unpurified and purified phase is the one in which the tathagatagarbha is not completely purified from all [defilements] to be abandoned through seeing and meditation, but is purified [from these] to a certain degree. The utterly purified phase is the one in which the tathagatagarbha is completely purified from the two veils. These three phases are expressed and explained by means of three different names, which are "being," "bodhisattva," and "tathagata." Considering the fact that there are three different ways of manifestation, one might wonder whether there are different kinds of suchness. This section has been elucidated in order to dispel such doubts. (See also Part Three, annotation 33.)

B.II.2.2.2.1.2.2.5.2. The way these three names contain six topics

> **The element as contained**
> **in the six topics of "essence" and so on**
> **is explained in the light of three phases**
> **by means of three names.**

In the foregoing sections the element that is by nature completely pure has been elucidated extensively by means of six topics: the topic "essence" and so forth, that is, the [further] topics "cause," "fruit," "function," "endowment," and "manifestation." This element is only explained as being of different kinds inasmuch as there are three phases: the unpurified phase, the partly unpurified and partly purified phase, and the utterly purified phase. These are identified by means of the three names "being," "bodhisattva," and "tathagata." With regard to the essence of the subject, however, there is not the slightest difference. (See also Part Three, annotation 34.)

B.II.2.2.2.1.2.2.6. All-pervasiveness
B.II.2.2.2.1.2.2.6.1. Explanation of the essence

> **Just as space, which is by nature free from thought,**
> **pervades everything,**
> **the undefiled expanse, which is the nature of mind,**
> **is all-pervading.**

Space, for example, which is by nature free from thought and unobscured, pervades and embraces everything visible in an undifferentiated way. Likewise, the dharmadhatu, which has been free from defilement since beginningless time, or in other words, clear light, the nature of mind, also pervades all the phases of the individual in an undifferentiated and all-embracing way.

B.II.2.2.2.1.2.2.6.2. Explanation of the different types

> **As the general feature [of everything], it embraces [those with]**
> **faults,**
> **[those with] qualities, and [those in whom the qualities are]**
> **ultimate**
> **just as space [pervades everything] visible,**
> **be it of inferior, average, or supreme appearance.**

The dharmadhatu, which is by nature completely pure, is the general feature (Tib. *spyi'i mtshan nyid*) or true state (Tib. *chos nyid*) of all phenomena. Therefore this dharmadhatu pervades all phases. It equally permeates the phase of an ordinary being who is beset with faults, the phase of a bodhisattva who has qualities, and the phase of a tathagata in whom the qualities are ultimate. Taking an example, this is similar to the way in which space pervades everything visible, permeating a visible object of inferior appearance, such as a vessel made of clay, in the same way as one of average appearance, such as a vessel made of copper, and one of supreme appearance, such as a vessel made of gold.

B.II.2.2.2.1.2.2.7. Unchangingness
B.II.2.2.2.1.2.2.7.1. Concise explanation of the essence

> Having faults that are adventitious
> and qualities that are its nature,
> it is afterwards the same as before.
> This is dharmata ever unchanging.

Although with regard to the dharmadhatu three phases are present, it does not have the fault of not being changeless. In the unpurified phase faults are present. These faults, however, do not truly exist. They are merely adventitious and able to be removed. In the purified phase, qualities have emerged. The nature of these qualities, however, is not something that has newly arisen. They are spontaneously present. For these reasons the dharmadhatu is afterwards, in the completely purified phase, the same as it was before in the unpurified phase. It does not undergo the slightest change. This changelessness is the nature or true state of the dharmadhatu.

B.II.2.2.2.1.2.2.7.2. Detailed explanation of unchangingness throughout the three phases
B.II.2.2.2.1.2.2.7.2.1. Unchangingness in the unpurified phase
B.II.2.2.2.1.2.2.7.2.1.1. The way the essence is not polluted by the defilements

> [Though] space permeates everything,
> it is never polluted, due to its subtlety.
> Likewise the [dharmadhatu] in all beings
> does not suffer the slightest pollution.

Uncompounded space, for example, permeates all compounded visible objects in an all-pervasive way. Yet space is subtle. It is not coarse as is a visible object. Due to this subtlety it is not in the slightest polluted by the faults of the visible, such as being impermanent and so forth. Likewise the tathagatagarbha, the dharmadhatu which is clear light, abides all-pervasively within all beings as the nature of their minds. Yet this dharmadhatu is by nature completely pure. For this reason it never suffers the slightest pollution from the faults of beings, such as their mental poisons and so on.

B.II.2.2.2.1.2.2.7.2.1.2. The way there is appearance of arising and disintegration as far as the subject is concerned

> Just as at all times worlds arise
> and disintegrate in space,
> the senses arise and disintegrate
> in the uncreated expanse.

At all times and throughout all phases the worlds of the outer vessel rely on the opportunity provided by space. They appear on this basis as something that first comes into existence and finally disintegrates. In the same way the sense faculties, here standing for the skandhas, elements, and entrances of beings, rely on the quality of the dharmadhatu: the fact that the dharmadhatu is not created by causes and conditions. Though they appear on this basis as something that first comes into existence and in the end disintegrates, with regard to the tathagatagarbha, or true state, arising and disintegration do not exist. (See also Part Three, annotation 35, and Part Four, note 4.)

B.II.2.2.2.1.2.2.7.2.1.3. The way the true state is not harmed by destruction

Space is never burnt by fires.
Likewise this [dharmadhatu]
is not burnt by the fires
of death, sickness, and aging.

All compounded things are burnt by three types of fire, being the fire at the end of time, the fire of hell, and natural or ordinary fire. Until now, however, space, being uncompounded, has never been burnt by any of these three types of fire. As shown by this example, all sentient beings are burnt by the three fires of death and so on. This dharmadhatu or buddha nature, however, is never even singed by any of these three fires. It is not burnt by the fire of death, corresponding to the fire at the end of time, of sickness, corresponding to the fire of hell, or of aging, corresponding to natural fire. (See also Part Three, annotation 36.)

B.II.2.2.2.1.2.2.7.2.1.4. Detailed explanation of interdependent origination
B.II.2.2.2.1.2.2.7.2.1.4.1. Explanation of the way generation takes place, by
  combining an example and its meaning
B.II.2.2.2.1.2.2.7.2.1.4.1.1. Example

Earth rests upon water and water upon wind.
Wind fully rests on space.
Space does not rest upon any of the elements
of wind, water, or earth.

At the time when the element of the world comes into existence and while it abides, the great circle of the earth is based upon the circle of water. Water is based upon the circle of wind. Wind fully rests upon space. Although they rely on it, space in its turn does not rest upon any of the elements of wind, water, or earth. This is because space does not depend upon causes and conditions.

B.II.2.2.2.1.2.2.7.2.1.4.1.2. Meaning

Likewise skandhas, elements, and senses
are based upon karma and mental poisons.
Karma and poisons are always based
upon improper conceptual activity.
The improper conceptual activity
fully abides on the purity of mind.
Yet, the nature of the mind itself
has no basis in all these phenomena.

Corresponding to the example given above, the five skandhas, the eighteen elements, and the six sense-faculties, all of which are bound up with pollution, along with the six sense-objects are based upon karma and the mental poisons. Karma and the mental poisons are always based upon improper conceptual activity, such as perceiving as a self [what does not exist as a self] and so on. The improper conceptual activity is fully based upon the purity of the mind, which is by nature clear light. Yet, this luminous nature of mind is not based upon any of these adventitious phenomena. This is because this clear light, which is the nature of mind, is uncreated. (See also Part Three, annotation 37.)

B.II.2.2.2.1.2.2.7.2.1.4.1.3. *Joint explanation of the example and its meaning*

The skandhas, entrances, and elements
are to be known as resembling earth.
Karma and the mental poisons of beings
should be envisaged as the water element.
Improper conceptual activity is viewed
as being similar to the element of wind.
[Mind's] nature, as the element of space,
has no ground and no place of abiding.

The five skandhas, which attract suffering, the twelve entrances, and the eighteen elements form on the support of karma and the mental poisons. This is to be understood as being similar to the way in which the circle of earth comes into existence on the basis of water. The element of water acts as the condition bringing about the formation of the circle of earth. Similar to this, the polluted karma and the mental poisons of beings should be known to constitute the condition for the formation of the skandhas, entrances, and elements. The element of wind acts as the basis for the circle of water. The improper conceptual activity should be viewed and understood as being similar to this, since it stirs up mental poisons and karma and fully activates them. The element of space acts as the basis for everything and yet is not based upon anything. In the same way the nature of mind, the tathagatagarbha, acts as the support for everything adventitious, yet its very own essence has no basis in any ground and does not abide anywhere. (See also Part Three, annotation 38.)

B.II.2.2.2.1.2.2.7.2.1.4.1.4. The way generation takes place

> The improper conceptual activity
> rests upon the nature of the mind.
> Improper conceptual activity brings about
> all the classes of karma and mental poisons.
> From the water of karma and mental poisons
> the skandhas, entrances, and elements arise.
> As this [world] arises and disintegrates,
> they will arise and disintegrate as well.

In the same way as the circle of wind rests upon space, the thoughts constituting an improper conceptual activity rest upon the luminous nature of the mind in such a way that they obscure it. As wind supports water, the improper conceptual activity creates all the different kinds of opportunity for the development of mental poisons and karma. In the same way as the ground of the earth emerges from the circle of water being churned, likewise the polluted skandhas, entrances, and elements, all the existences consisting of suffering, emerge from the water-like karma and mental poisons. Therefore the skandhas, entrances, and elements bound up with pollution will arise and disintegrate, just as this vessel of the world arises and disintegrates.

B.II.2.2.2.1.2.2.7.2.1.4.2. Explanation that the essence is undefiled and free from extremes
B.II.2.2.2.1.2.2.7.2.1.4.2.1. The way the essence is free from arising and cessation

> The nature of mind as the element of space
> does not [depend upon] causes or conditions,
> nor does it [depend on] a gathering of these.
> It has neither arising, cessation, nor abiding.

Like the uncreated element of space, the nature of mind, which is luminous dharmadhatu, does not depend upon productive causes and it does not depend upon simultaneously active conditions. It therefore does not depend upon a gathering of these causes and conditions either. For this reason it does not have an initial arising nor a final disintegration, nor does it abide in the meantime. Therefore it does not suffer the slightest change through the three properties native to everything created. (See also Part Three, annotation 39.)

B.II.2.2.2.1.2.2.7.2.1.4.2.2. The way its purity is not touched by defilements

This clear and luminous nature of mind
is as changeless as space. It is not afflicted
by desire and so on, the adventitious stains,
which are sprung from incorrect thoughts.

The nature of space is not changed through clouds, smoke, and so on. In the same way, the tathagatagarbha, the clear and luminous nature of the minds of all beings, is changeless. It is not in the slightest altered by the fact that the veils are purified or unpurified, and so on. There are adventitious defilements consisting of the affliction of birth, the affliction of karma, and the affliction of the mental poisons such as desire, hatred, mental blindness, and so on, all of which are sprung from improper conceptual activity, from incorrect thoughts that conceive in a way not corresponding to reality. The true state is changeless since it is by nature utterly pure and will constantly remain unafflicted by these adventitious defilements, which are able to be removed.

B.II.2.2.2.1.2.2.7.2.1.4.3. Summary of the example and meaning of arising and disintegration
B.II.2.2.2.1.2.2.7.2.1.4.3.1. Summary of the way the nature of mind is free from arising and disintegration

It is not brought into existence
by the water of karma, of the poisons, and so on.
Hence it is also not consumed by the cruel fires
of dying, falling sick, and aging.

This nature of mind, or luminous dharmadhatu, is not generated and brought into existence by the wind of improper conceptual activity, by the waters of karma and the mental poisons, and so on. Hence it is also not consumed and destroyed by the cruel fires of dying, falling sick, and aging, which [correspond respectively to] the fire at the end of time, the fire of hell, and ordinary fire. This is because it is of an uncompounded nature and thus does not change into something else.

B.II.2.2.2.1.2.2.7.2.1.4.3.2. Summary of the way disintegration takes place

The three fires of death, sickness, and aging
are to be understood in their given sequence
as resembling the fire at the end of time,
the fire of hell, and an ordinary fire.

In their given sequence the three fires of death, sickness, and aging are to be understood as being similar to three fires, which are the fire at the end of time, the fire of hell, and ordinary fire. This is due to the following reasons: Just as the vessel of this world is destroyed by the fire at the end of time, the skandhas of this life are destroyed by the fire of death. Just as the fire of hell generates suffering, so also does the fire of sickness. Just as ordinary fire causes the final ripening of anything compounded, the fire of aging causes the final ripening of the skandhas.

B.II.2.2.2.1.2.2.7.2.2. Unchangingness in the partly unpurified and partly purified phase

B.II.2.2.2.1.2.2.7.2.2.1. Explanation of the fact that there is no change through birth and so forth

B.II.2.2.2.1.2.2.7.2.2.1.1. The way bodhisattvas appear as being subject to change although they are not

> Having realized thatness, the nature of the [dharmadhatu], just as it is,
> those of understanding are released from birth, sickness, aging, and death.
> Though free from the destitution of birth and so on, they demonstrate these,
> since by their [insight] they have given rise to compassion for beings.

Noble bodhisattvas have directly realized thatness. They have realized the nature or the way of existence of the tathagatagarbha, of the dharmadhatu, just as it is. Since they abide with this realization, they are liberated from birth, which brings new skandhas into existence, from death, which ends the stream of being, from sickness, which generates suffering, and from aging, which transforms the stream of being. With their insight they are free from the suffering and destitution of birth and so on, which come about due to the predominating influence of karma and mental poisons. They are completely pure and not subject to change. Yet, due to their realization of the dharmadhatu just as it is, bodhisattvas who possess understanding have given rise to great compassion for all those beings who have not gained such insight. Their compassion leads them to wish that all sentient beings may be freed from their suffering to its last traces. Since they abide with this great compassion, they adhere to and stay within samsara. By the power of their wishing prayers for the benefit of others, and so on, they are born into any existence corresponding to their intention. In order to reverse the belief in permanence, they die, fall ill, age, and so on. Thus they show themselves to the vision of others (Tib. *gzhan snang*) as someone who is impure as well, and subject to change. (See also Part Three, annotation 40.)

B.II.2.2.2.1.2.2.7.2.2.1.2. Detailed explanation of the foregoing section's meaning
B.II.2.2.2.1.2.2.7.2.2.1.2.1. The way bodhisattvas are not subject to the change caused by suffering

> **The noble have eradicated the suffering**
> **of dying, falling ill, and aging at its root,**
> **which is being born due to karma and poisons.**
> **There being no such [cause], there is no such [fruit].**

The members of the Assembly of noble bodhisattvas have eradicated the sufferings of helplessly and powerlessly dying, falling ill, and aging at their root. The causes of these sufferings are improper mental activity, mental poisons, and karma, and the fact that one is born within samsara due to their predominating influence. Since bodhisattvas are free from these causes, they are also free from the change caused by suffering, which is their fruit.

B.II.2.2.2.1.2.2.7.2.2.1.2.2. The way they appear as being subject to change out of their compassion

> **Since they have seen reality as it is,**
> **they are beyond being born and so on.**
> **Yet, as the embodiment of compassion itself**
> **they display birth, illness, old age, and death.**

The noble heirs of the Victorious One see reality as it is. They directly perceive the dharmadhatu, which is unborn and changeless. For this reason they are beyond the sufferings of being helplessly delivered to a birth in samsara and so on. Although they are completely liberated from these sufferings, they show themselves in manifold appearances totally subject to change. For those beings who have not gained a realization such as theirs they have become the embodiment of great compassion. Out of this compassion they display the appearance of birth and are born in an existence corresponding to their intention. They demonstrate the appearance of death, sickness, and aging, and thus lead the disciples to complete maturation in correspondence with their respective karmic fortunes.

B.II.2.2.2.2.1.2.2.7.2.2.2. Identification of the qualities of the heirs of the Victorious One who dwell on the ten bodhisattva levels

B.II.2.2.2.2.1.2.2.7.2.2.2.1. The qualities of a bodhisattva who has first given rise to bodhichitta

> After the heirs of the Victorious One
> have realized this changeless state,
> those who are blinded by ignorance
> see them as being born and so forth.
> That such seeing should occur is truly wonderful and amazing.
> When they have attained the field of experience of the noble
> they show themselves as the field of experience of the children.
> Hence means and compassion of the friends of beings are
> supreme.

The heirs of the Victorious One who dwell on the first bodhisattva level have directly realized the changeless true state, the nature of mind which is luminous clarity. Having gained this realization they are liberated from the process of birth and death, which is engendered by karma and the mental poisons. In spite of this, the disciples whose eyes of discriminative wisdom are blinded by ignorance see them as being born, dying, and so on. That the bodhisattvas should be seen in this way and upon this basis bring about the benefit of these disciples is an activity which is truly wonderful and amazing. They have attained the path on which the mind itself is seen directly. This is the object of experience of the noble ones, which is far away from sin, from any unvirtuous phenomenon. Having attained this path they are liberated from birth and death, which are caused by karma and mental poisons. Although they are liberated from these, they demonstrate manifold illusory appearances as the field of experience of the children, or of ordinary beings. They show themselves as being born and so on, and thus lead the disciples to complete maturation. For this reason the bodhisattvas have become the best possible friends and relatives of all sentient beings without exception. Therefore their skill in method by which they accomplish the benefit of others through the means of attraction, and their great compassion which is fully alerted towards this aim, are supreme. (See also Part Three, annotation 41.)

B.II.2.2.2.2.1.2.2.7.2.2.2.2. The qualities of a bodhisattva who has gained access to supreme conduct

> Though they are beyond all worldly matters,
> these [bodhisattvas] do not leave the world.
> They act for the sake of all worldly beings

within the world, unblemished by its defects.
As a lotus will grow in the midst of water,
not being polluted by the water's [faults],
these [noble ones] are born in the world
unpolluted by any worldly phenomena.

Due to the power of their discriminative wisdom, bodhisattvas who
dwell on one of the bodhisattva levels reaching from the second up to
the seventh inclusively are completely beyond all worldly conduct.
Yet, under the influence of their compassion they do not leave the world.
Instead they enact amid the world the vast and powerful bodhisattva
conduct. For the sake of the worldly beings, in order to lead the disciples to full maturation, they adopt the course of action of being born
within the world and so on. Yet, in doing so they are not in the slightest polluted by any defilement, by the defects of the world. Though
lotus flowers, for instance, grow in the midst of water, they are not
polluted by the water's faults or defilements and so on. Likewise these
noble heirs of all Victorious Ones are born within the world for the
sake of the other beings, and yet not in the slightest polluted by the
worldly phenomena or faults, such as the mental poisons and so forth.

*B.II.2.2.2.1.2.2.7.2.2.2.3. The qualities of a bodhisattva who has attained the
level of non-returning*

Viewing the accomplishment of their task,
their understanding always blazes like fire.
And they always rest evenly balanced
in meditative stability, which is peace.

With regard to the accomplishment of their task, the accomplishment of benefit for all other beings, bodhisattvas who dwell on the
eighth bodhisattva level always manifest their own understanding
without deliberate effort in a blazing manner. This is similar to the
way in which a mighty fire, for instance, will burn by its own force on
dry and desiccated wood. Yet, what is more, simultaneously they are
always and uninterruptedly absorbed in evenness. They evenly abide
in the balanced state of the samadhi of meditative stability in which
the conceptual elaboration in terms of characteristics is completely
pacified. This is because they have gained mastery of non-conceptual
primordial wisdom (Tib. *mi rtog pa'i ye shes*). (See also Part Three, annotation 42.)

B.II.2.2.2.1.2.2.7.2.2.2.4. The qualities of a bodhisattva who has reached the last birth

> By the power of their former [prayers]
> and since they are free from all ideation,
> they do not exert any deliberate effort
> to lead all sentient beings to maturation.
> These [heirs of the Victorious One] know precisely
> how and by what [method] each should be trained—
> through whatever teachings, form kayas, conduct,
> and ways of behavior are individually appropriate.
> Always [acting] spontaneously and without hindrance
> for sentient beings whose number is limitless as space,
> such [bodhisattvas] who possess understanding
> truly engage in the task of benefitting beings.

Due to the powerful influence of the wishing prayers they formerly uttered and the further deeds they performed while traveling the ninth bodhisattva level and the levels below, bodhisattvas who dwell on the tenth bodhisattva level act spontaneously. They are free from all thoughts and ideation, having eliminated these in the process of a complete transformation of state (Tib. *gnas yongs su gyur pa'i tshul gyis spangs*). For these reasons, these bodhisattvas who have reached the last existence (Tib. *srid pa tha ma pa*) do not need to exert any deliberate effort in order to lead all beings who are their disciples to complete maturation. They also know the aspects of training. They know the ways and methods to train any disciple. They do so through the activity of speech, teaching the Dharma in accordance with the respective wishes and mental dispositions [of the disciples], through the activity of the body, showing many illusory appearances of form kayas in accordance with the karmic fortune of the disciples, through the vast and powerful conduct that brings about the benefit of others, and through various ways of behavior such as sitting, standing up, and so on, using whichever of these is appropriate. In this way these heirs of the Victorious One have full, unmistaken, and precise knowledge of the activity as it is individually appropriate.

They manifest without deliberate effort and in various ways. This is to be understood as follows: The actors are the bodhisattvas who possess understanding. Their objects of action are beings whose number is as limitless as space. Towards this endless number of sentient beings they always act spontaneously, without deliberate effort, by means of actions that are unhindered and meaningful in every respect. The purpose of these actions is the complete maturation of all those beings who are their disciples. Towards this purpose they engage in the activity which by its very nature accomplishes the benefit of these disciples, and they do so in a true and unmistaken way. (See also Part Three, annotation 43, and Part Four, note 5.)

B.II.2.2.2.1.2.2.7.2.2.2.5. Explanation of the difference as far as the accomplishment of the two benefits is concerned

> The way the bodhisattvas [unfold activity]
> in the post-meditative phase
> equals the tathagatas' [action] in the world
> for beings' true liberation.
> Though this is true, indeed, whatever difference lies
> between the earth and an atom or else between
> [the water in] the sea and in an ox's hoofprint,
> is the difference between a buddha and a bodhisattva.

The way in which a bodhisattva who dwells on the tenth bodhisattva level engages in activity equals that of all tathagatas who embody ultimate abandonment and realization. With respect to leading others to complete maturation in the post-meditative phase they are equal. Such a bodhisattva has attained the particular qualities of the six types of clairvoyance, of the ten kinds of mastery (Tib. *dbang bcu*), and so forth. Therefore he also acts in the world spontaneously and without deliberate effort in order to truly liberate all sentient beings who have become disciples from samsara's ocean of suffering. Though it is true indeed that such a bodhisattva is like a buddha as far as the [fulfillment of] others' benefit is concerned, there is an extremely great difference with respect to personal benefit, which consists of the qualities of abandonment and realization. Consider, for example, the difference between the great globe of the earth and an atom, or between the amount of water contained in the large ocean and in the hoofprint of an ox. In this measure, the difference between the ultimate qualities of a perfect buddha and the qualities of the path of a bodhisattva who dwells on the tenth bodhisattva level is extremely great.

The way reference is made here to the bodhisattva levels corresponds to the way in which the omniscient Dolpopa has clearly elucidated the intended meaning of Asanga's great commentary. On the other hand the omniscient Rangjung Dorjé [the third Karmapa] makes a slight difference. He holds that the two stanzas "By the power of their former [prayers]..." and so on, explain the way in which a bodhisattva who dwells on the ninth bodhisattva level is free from deliberate effort and has attained true discriminative awareness. In Rangjung Dorjé's opinion, the stanza "Always [acting] spontaneously and without hindrance..." and so on then explains the quality of the immeasurable benefit of others, as is native to a bodhisattva who dwells on the tenth bodhisattva level. (See also Part Three, annotation 44, and Part Four, note 6.)

B.II.2.2.2.1.2.2.7.2.3. Unchangingness in the utterly purified phase
B.II.2.2.2.1.2.2.7.2.3.1. Concise explanation of the reason for its unchangingness

> [The dharmakaya] does not change into something else, since
>   it has inexhaustible properties.
> It is the refuge of beings, since [it protects them] without any
>   limit of time, until the final end.
> It is always free from duality, since it is foreign to all ideation.
> It is also an indestructible state, since its nature is uncreated.

The dharmadhatu in the utterly purified phase is the dharmakaya. This dharmakaya has the attribute of permanence (Tib. *rtag*), being unchangingness itself. It does not change into something else in the sense of one physical form being abandoned to be replaced by another. This is because, even in the expanse of the nirvana free from any remainder of skandhas, it possesses immeasurable properties, these being the inexhaustible absolute qualities. Likewise it has the attribute of steadfastness (Tib. *brtan*). It is the supreme refuge of all sentient beings, unfailing and undeceptive. This is because it possesses qualities protecting them without any limit of time, until the final end, as long as samsara may last. This undefiled dharmadhatu has the attribute of peace (Tib. *zhi*). It is always free from the duality of samsara and nirvana. This is because it is without any ideation as to the punishment and comfort represented by these. It also has the attribute of immutability (Tib. *g.yung drung*). It is a lastingly indestructible state, since it possesses the quality of being a nature not created by karma and mental poisons. (See also Part Three, annotation 45.)

B.II.2.2.2.1.2.2.7.2.3.2. Detailed explanation of its meaning
B.II.2.2.2.1.2.2.7.2.3.2.1. Presentation of freedom from birth and so forth in
  terms of statement and proof
B.II.2.2.2.1.2.2.7.2.3.2.1.1. Concise explanation of each individually

> It is not born and it does not die.
> It suffers no harm and does not age
> since it is permanent and steadfast,
> the state of peace and immutability.

This completely pure and luminous dharmakaya is not initially born and does not finally die. It does not suffer the harm of sickness and does not undergo a process of change and aging in the meantime. This is because in the given sequence it is permanent, steadfast, peaceful, and immutable.

B.II.2.2.2.1.2.2.7.2.3.2.1.2. Detailed explanation combining them

> It is not [even] born in a body of mental nature,
> since it is permanent. Steadfast it does not die,
> not [even] through the death and transmigration
> that constitute an inconceivable transformation.
> Since it is peace, it does not [even] suffer harm
> from illnesses caused by subtle karmic imprints.
> Since it is immutable, there is not [even] aging
> induced by compositional factors free from stain.

There is hardly any need to mention that this buddha nature in terms of the dharmakaya does not undergo the slightest change due to an ordinary birth and so on. It is free from any initial birth, not even being born in a body of mental nature. This is because it is unchanging and permanent. Likewise this dharmakaya is free from a final death. It does not even die due to the complete transformation caused by death and transmigration taking place in an inconceivable way. This is because it is unfailing and steadfast. In the meantime it is not harmed by sickness. It is not even harmed by the sicknesses caused by the subtle veil consisting of the remaining imprints of ignorance. This is because it is peace, being free from dualistic perception and so forth. It is free from the property of aging. It does not even age due to the compositional factors constituting the undefiled karma. This is because it is of indestructible nature and thus immutable. (See also Part Three, annotation 46.)

B.II.2.2.2.1.2.2.7.2.3.2.2. Summary of its meaning

> [Combining] sentences from the foregoing
> two by two, the uncreated expanse should be known
> [as possessing] in the same sequence
> the attributes of being permanent and so forth.

Of the foregoing verses the two sentences "[The dharmakaya] does not change into something else . . ." and "It is not [even] born . . ." refer to the attribute of permanence. Likewise the two sentences "It is the refuge of beings . . ." and "Steadfast it does not die . . ." refer to the attribute of steadfastness. The two sentences "It is always free from duality..." and "Since it is peace..." refer to the attribute of peace, and the two sentences "It is also an indestructible state..." and "Since it is immutable..." refer to the attribute of immutability. In the same sequence in which these four attributes are given in the foregoing sections, the true state, the expanse not created by causes and conditions, is to be known from the sutras [teaching the meaning of buddha nature] as being permanent and so on, that is, permanent, steadfast, peaceful, and immutable.

B.II.2.2.2.2.1.2.2.7.2.3.2.3. Explanation of the reason for its establishment as being permanent and so forth

> **Since it is endowed with inexhaustible qualities, [the dharmakaya]**
> **is unchangingness itself and thus [has] the attribute of permanence.**
> **Equaling the uttermost end it is refuge itself**
> **and thus [holds] the attribute of steadfastness.**
> **Since absence of thought is its nature, it is dharmata**
> **free from duality and thus [has] the attribute of peace.**
> **Hosting uncreated qualities, it is immutability itself**
> **and thus [possesses] the attribute of indestructibility.**

Even in the expanse of the nirvana without remainder, this dharmakaya by nature completely pure is endowed with an endless number of inexhaustible qualities. Therefore, not undergoing the slightest transformation into something else, it is unchangingness itself and thus possesses the attribute of permanence. It is protective and uninterrupted in a way that equals the uttermost end of samsara. Therefore it is refuge itself forever unfailing and thus possesses the attribute of steadfastness. Its nature is absence of thought. There is no ideation in terms of the two extremes. Therefore it is the dharmata, the true state free from the duality of existence and [mere] peace, and thus possesses the attribute of [true] peace. It has qualities that are not created, that are not an artifice brought about by causes and conditions. Therefore it is lastingly indestructible and thus possesses the attribute of immutability.

B.II.2.2.2.2.1.2.2.8. Inseparability of the qualities
B.II.2.2.2.2.1.2.2.8.1. Short explanation by means of names

> **Why is it the dharmakaya, the tathagata,**
> **the noble truth, and the absolute nirvana?**
> **Its qualities are inseparable, like the sun and its rays.**
> **Thus other than buddhahood there is no nirvana.**

Why is this tathagatagarbha in the utterly purified phase the dharmakaya of all buddhas? Why is it also the tathagata, the noble truth and the absolute nirvana? This is because these are just synonymous terms. Just as, for instance, the orb of the sun and its rays cannot be separated, these four qualities are inseparable from the svabhavikakaya (Tib. *ngo bo nyid sku*, "the essence body of buddhahood"). The svabhavikakaya is therefore stated as being equivalent to nirvana. And again, the absolute qualities such as the ten powers and so forth are completely inseparable. For these reasons, other than perfect buddhahood, there is nothing else that is the actual or true nirvana. (See also Part Three, annotation 47.)

B.II.2.2.2.1.2.2.8.2. Detailed explanation of their essence
B.II.2.2.2.1.2.2.8.2.1. Detailed explanation of the synonymous names
B.II.2.2.2.1.2.2.8.2.1.1. The fact that the names have been given due to the meaning [of the dharmadhatu]

> **Since the unpolluted expanse has, put briefly,**
> **four different types of meaning,**
> **it should be known in terms of four synonyms:**
> **the dharmakaya and so forth.**

Put briefly, the tathagatagarbha in terms of the unpolluted dharmadhatu has four different types or aspects of meaning, which will be explained below. In correspondence to these it should therefore be known in terms of the four synonymous names mentioned above, which are the dharmakaya and so on.

B.II.2.2.2.1.2.2.8.2.1.2. Combination of the names and the meaning

> **Buddha qualities are indivisible.**
> **The disposition is attained as it is.**
> **The true state is [always] free from any fickleness and deceit.**
> **Since beginningless time the nature has been peace itself.**

The absolute qualities, the powers and so on, which are the properties of a buddha, are completely indivisible from the dharmadhatu free from defilements. In the light of this meaning, this undefiled expanse is called the dharmakaya (Tib. *chos sku*, " the body of qualities"). The disposition to [becoming] this buddha, which is the true state present since beginningless time, is directly attained as it is. In the light of this meaning, the undefiled expanse is called the Tathagata (Tib. *de bzhin gshegs pa*, "the One Gone to Suchness"). Its nature is the true state, which does not change into something else, is free from any

The Unassailable Lion's Roar 145

deceit, and at all times free from fickleness or unreliability. This true state has become the field of experience of the primordial wisdom of the noble ones. In the light of this meaning, the undefiled expanse is called the Noble Truth. This dharmadhatu has been by nature utterly pure since beginningless time and the adventitious defilements have been totally pacified up to their very end. In the light of this meaning the undefiled expanse is expressed by the term "nirvana" (Tib. *mnya ngan las 'das pa*, "the state beyond any torment and pain").

B.II.2.2.2.1.2.2.8.2.2. Detailed explanation of their essential meaning
B.II.2.2.2.1.2.2.8.2.2.1. Detailed explanation of the fact [that a buddha and nirvana] are no different

> Direct perfect enlightenment [with regard to] all aspects,
> and abandonment of the stains along with their imprints
> [are called] buddha and nirvana respectively.
> In truth, these are not two different things.

All aspects of the knowable—all absolute and relative phenomena—are directly known. Through this knowledge one is immediately and perfectly enlightened. This is the aspect of realization. All the adventitious defilements—the two veils along with their remaining imprints—are abandoned without any exception. This is the aspect of abandonment. These two qualities have been led to ultimate perfection. They are therefore named "perfect buddha" ["perfectly awakened and expanded"] from the viewpoint of the former aspect, and "nirvana" ["gone beyond any torment and pain"] from the viewpoint of the latter aspect. These two aspects are contained in one and the same meaning, the meaning of the tathagatagarbha, whereas a difference only lies in the convention of the different terms. In the sense of the absolute field of experience of the noble ones' primordial wisdom the qualities of realization and abandonment are therefore completely inseparable and do not exist as two different things.

B.II.2.2.2.1.2.2.8.2.2.2. Detailed explanation of the meaning of liberation

> Liberation is distinguished by indivisibility
> from qualities present in all their aspects:
> innumerable, inconceivable, and unpolluted.
> Such liberation is [also called] "tathagata."

Since the qualities are not incomplete, all aspects are fully present. Since the types of qualities are beyond any end, they are innumerable. Since one cannot fathom their number and inherent power, they are inconceivable. Since the two veils along with the remaining imprints are eliminated, they are unpolluted. The dharmakaya has the characteristic of being inseparable from these four qualifications. The fact that this dharmakaya has become directly manifest is called ultimate nirvana, or in other words, liberation. In the light of the fact that suchness (Skt. *tathatā*) is directly realized, such true qualified liberation (Tib. *thar pa mtshan nyid pa*) is also called "tathagata."

B.II.2.2.2.1.2.2.8.2.3. Detailed explanation of these by means of examples
B.II.2.2.2.1.2.2.8.2.3.1. The fictitious example of the painters
B.II.2.2.2.1.2.2.8.2.3.1.1. Example

> Suppose some painters mastered their craft,
> each with respect to a different [part of the body],
> so that whichever part one would know how to do,
> he would not succeed with any other part.
> Then the king, the ruler of the country,
> hands them a canvas and gives the order:
> "You all together paint my image on this!"
> Having heard this [order] from the [king]
> they carefully take up their painting work.
> While they are well immersed in their task,
> one among them leaves for another country.
> Since they are incomplete
> due to his travel abroad,
> their painting in all its parts
> does not get fully perfected.
> Thus the example is given.

The cause through which one accomplishes the four qualities mentioned above is primordial wisdom realizing emptiness endowed with all supreme aspects (Tib. *rnam kun mchog ldan gyi stong pa nyid*). Therefore this primordial wisdom is taught by means of the example of the painters as given in the *Ratnacudasutra* (Tib. *rin chen gyis zhus pa'i mdo*). The example is as follows:

Suppose there is a gathering of many painters, each of whom is highly specialized and has mastered his craft with respect to a different part of the body, such as the head and so forth. Whichever part of the body one of them knows how to do, he will not succeed with any other part. Then, when they are assembled, the king, the ruler of the country, hands them a canvas and gives the following order: "You all together paint my royal image on this canvas!" Having heard this command from the king, each of them carefully takes up his painting work, whatever he is able to execute. While these painters are immersed in their task, the one among them who knows how to paint the head leaves for another country. This painter having traveled abroad, they are incomplete. Hence the painting of the king does not get fully perfected in all its parts. (See also Part Three, annotation 48.)

B.II.2.2.2.1.2.2.8.2.3.1.2. Meaning

> Who are the painters of these [parts of the image]?
> They are generosity, morality, patience, and so on.
> Emptiness endowed with all supreme aspects
> is described as being the form [of the king].

One may wonder what is illustrated by the artists who execute the different parts of this painting. They stand for generosity free from any attachment, moral discipline free from the pollution of the defects [of body, speech, and mind], patience never disturbed by anger in any respect, and so on, that is, for diligence delighting in virtue, meditative stability being one-pointed with regard to its focus, and discriminative wisdom completely and thoroughly discriminating phenomena. Emptiness endowed with all supreme aspects of means is equivalent to the direct manifestation of the dharmakaya. This is said to be similar to the well-painted form of the king being fully perfected. (See also Part Three, annotation 49.)

B.II.2.2.2.1.2.2.8.2.3.2. Explanation by means of the non-fictitious example of the sun
B.II.2.2.2.1.2.2.8.2.3.2.1. Presentation of the corresponding qualities

> Illuminating, radiating, and purifying,
> and inseparable from each other, analytical wisdom,
> primordial wisdom, and total liberation
> correspond to the light, rays, and orb of the sun.

Discriminative or analytical wisdom, primordial wisdom, and complete liberation (Tib. *rnam grol*) are inseparable from the four qualities [dharmakaya, tathagata, noble truth, and nirvana]. In their given sequence they illuminate, radiate, and purify, and these three [aspects] are not separate from each other. For these reasons they have properties corresponding to those of the sun: to the clarity of its light, the radiation of its rays, the purity of its orb, and to the fact that these three are not separate from each other. (See also Part Three, annotation 50.)

B.II.2.2.2.1.2.2.8.2.3.2.2. Explanation of buddhahood as being nirvana

**One will therefore not attain nirvana
without attaining the state of buddhahood.
Just as one could not see the sun
if one were to eliminate its light and its rays.**

Therefore, as has been explained in detail in the foregoing sections, one will not attain the ultimate nirvana completely liberated from all the veils without attaining perfect buddhahood endowed with the vision of the primordial wisdom that is free from attachment with regard to everything knowable. This is similar to the example that one could not see the completely pure orb of the sun if one were to eliminate its clear light and its beaming rays.

B.II.2.2.2.1.2.3. Summary of the meaning of the explanation

**In this way the nature of the Victorious One
is expressed [by] the "Tenfold Presentation."**

Such as it has been explained in detail in the foregoing sections, the nature of the victorious Tathagata, or in other words, the dharmadhatu, the true state, has been well expressed and clearly elucidated in a systematic order by means of "the Tenfold Presentation" starting with the topic "essence" and ending with the topic "inseparability of the qualities."

B.II.2.2.2.1.3. Explanation of the way the defilements are to be purified though the essence is unchanging, by means of examples
B.II.2.2.2.1.3.1. Concise summary

**This [tathagatagarbha] abides within the shroud of the afflictions,
as should be understood through [the following nine] examples:**

This tathagatagarbha, the true state by nature pure, abides within the many-millionfold shroud of the afflictions. These are defilements that are by nature adventitious. Although they [have been] close to buddha nature since beginningless time, they are not connected with it. This is clearly and fully illustrated by means of nine examples, which should be understood as being given in accordance with the *Tathagatagarbhasutra* (Tib. *de bzhin gshegs pa'i snying po'i mdo*).

B.II.2.2.2.1.3.2. Explanation of the nature of the Victorious One and the defilements by means of nine examples
B.II.2.2.2.1.3.2.1. Concise explanation
B.II.2.2.2.1.3.2.1.1. What is obscured and what causes obscuration alternately expressed through an example followed by its meaning

> Just like a buddha in a decaying lotus, honey amidst bees,
> a grain in its husk, gold in filth, a treasure underground,
> a shoot and so on sprouting from a little fruit,
> a statue of the Victorious One in a tattered rag,
> a ruler of mankind in a destitute woman's womb,
> and a precious image under [a layer of] clay,
> this [buddha] element abides within all sentient beings,
> obscured by the defilement of the adventitious poisons.

Just as a good buddha statue is present within the shroud of a decaying lotus (1), just as pure honey is present amid a big swarm of bees (2), just as the grain is contained in its husk (3), just like gold in the midst of filth (4), just like a precious treasure in the ground under a poor man's house (5), just like the shoot of a mighty tree grows and increases from a tiny fruit (6), just like a statue of the Victorious One inside a tattered rag (7), just like a universal ruler of mankind in the womb of a woman of miserable appearance (8), and just as at the time when the mold is removed a precious image is present under a layer of clay (9), this undefiled expanse, the buddha element, definitely abides within all sentient beings, obscured by the defilement of the adventitious mental poisons.

B.II.2.2.2.1.3.2.1.2. Both example and meaning expressed separately

> The defilements correspond to the lotus,
> the insects, the husk, the filth, the earth,
> the fruit, the tattered rag, the pregnant woman
> direly vexed with burning suffering, and the clay.
> The buddha, the honey, the grain, the gold,
> the treasure, the nyagrodha tree, the precious statue,
> the continents' supreme ruler, and the precious image
> are similar to the supreme undefiled element.

The mental poisons, the adventitious defilements obscuring the inherently pure element, correspond to the lotus flower, the bees, the husk, the filthy material, the heap of earth, the skin of the fruit, the tattered rag, the woman who is direly tormented by the burning suffering of being destitute and without protection, and to the element of black clay.

The buddha statue, the honey, the grain, the pure gold, the precious treasure, a mighty tree such as a nyagrodha, the statue made from precious material, the supreme universal monarch who rules the four continents, and the precious golden image correspond to the tathagatagarbha, the supreme element, which is completely pure and free from any defilement.

B.II.2.2.2.1.3.2.2. Detailed explanation

All of the following nine examples are presented in three parts, which are the example itself, its meaning, and their function. First the example is given, then its meaning is explained, and finally both example and meaning are combined and their function is elucidated.

B.II.2.2.2.1.3.2.2.1. Example and meaning of the buddha and the lotus
B.II.2.2.2.1.3.2.2.1.1. Example

> Seeing that in the calyx of an ugly-colored lotus
> a tathagata dwells ablaze with a thousand marks,
> a man endowed with the immaculate divine vision
> takes it from the shroud of the water-born's petals.

Inside the closed calyx of a lotus that has an ugly color and a repugnant smell dwells a statue of the Tathagata, ablaze with a thousand pure and beautiful marks. A man who is endowed with the clairvoyance of immaculate divine vision sees this, and upon being aware of it, removes the buddha statue from the shroud of the petals of the water-born [flower].

B.II.2.2.2.1.3.2.2.1.2. Meaning

> Likewise the Sugata with his buddha eye perceives his own
>   true state even in those
> who must abide in the hell of direst pain.
> Endowed with compassion itself, which is unobscured and
>   endures to the final end,
> he relieves them from their obscurations.

Likewise, with their eye of primordial buddha wisdom, the Sugatas perceive that the tathagatagarbha, the true state illuminating their own being, is even present within those who have to abide in the hell of direst pain (Skt. *Avīci*, Tib. *mnar med*). Being endowed with discriminative wisdom, compassion, and activity, which are free from the veils and enduring up to the last, until the far end of samsara, they relieve the disciples from their adventitious obscurations.

B.II.2.2.2.1.3.2.2.1.3. Both combined

> Once his divine eye sees the Sugata abiding within the closed
> ugly lotus,
> the man cuts the petals. Seeing the perfect buddha nature
> within beings,
> obscured by the shroud of desire, hatred, and the other mental
> poisons,
> the Muni does likewise and through his compassion defeats
> all their veils.

Once someone who possesses divine vision sees this statue of the Sugata abiding within the bud of the closed ugly lotus, he will cut off the petals in order to remove the statue. Likewise the Munis see that the nature of perfect buddhahood is present within all sentient beings, obscured by the shroud of the defilements, by desire, hatred, and the other mental poisons. Through the might of their limitless compassion for all those beings who do not realize this [presence], the awakened Munis also unfold their activity, thus overcoming these adventitious veils, just as the petals obscuring the statue are removed.

B.II.2.2.2.1.3.2.2.2. Example and meaning of the honey and the bees
B.II.2.2.2.1.3.2.2.2.1. Example

> Honey is surrounded by a swarm of insects.
> A skillful man in search of [honey]
> [employs], upon seeing this, suitable means
> to fully separate it from the host of bees.

Honey is present in the midst of a surrounding swarm of bees. Upon seeing that there is honey among the bees, a capable and skillful man whose aim is to get this honey makes use of suitable means. Letting smoke rise and so on, he completely separates the honey from the host of bees and procures the honey.

B.II.2.2.2.1.3.2.2.2.2. Meaning

> Likewise, when his eye of omniscience
> sees the honey-like element of awareness,
> the Great Sage causes its bee-like veils
> to be fully and radically abandoned.

Likewise the Buddha, the Great Sage, sees with his eye knowing all phenomena that the element of [self-sprung] awareness is present within all beings, contained in the shroud of the mental poisons like honey surrounded by bees. Upon seeing this, he teaches the path by means of which the bee-like veils covering this element are fully and radically abandoned and the element is realized. Thus he causes the direct manifestation of the dharmakaya.

B.II.2.2.2.1.3.2.2.2.3. Both combined

**Aiming to get honey that is obscured by millions and millions
    of honeybees,
the man disperses all these bees and procures the honey, just
    as he wishes.
The unpolluted knowledge present in all sentient beings is
    similar to the honey,
and the Victor skilled in vanquishing the bee-like poisons
    resembles the man.**

When honey is obscured by millions and millions of honeybees, a man who is skillful and in search of honey disperses these bees by means of suitable methods and procures the honey, just as he wishes. The unpolluted knowledge, the sugatagarbha, is present within all beings, contained in the shroud of their defilements. Thus it is similar to the honey surrounded by bees. The Victorious One (Skt. *jina*, Tib. *rgyal ba*) is skilled in the methods to overcome the bee-like mental poisons obscuring the element. Thus he is similar to the skillful man whose aim is to get the honey.

B.II.2.2.2.1.3.2.2.3. Example and meaning of the grain and the husk
B.II.2.2.2.1.3.2.2.3.1. Example

**A grain when still in its husk
is not fit to be eaten by man.
Those seeking food and sustenance
remove this [grain] from its husk.**

Since a grain that still has its husk is not edible for man, those human beings who seek palatable food and nourishment must remove this grain from the inside of its husk.

B.II.2.2.2.1.3.2.2.3.2. Meaning

**[The nature of] the Victorious One, which is present within
    beings**

[but] mixed with the defilement of the poisons, is similar to this.
While it is not freed from being mingled with the pollution of
these afflictions,
the deeds of the Victor will not be [displayed] in the three
realms of existence.

The nature of the Victorious One, which is present within all sentient beings but mixed with the defilement of the mental poisons, is
similar to this example. As long as it is not freed from being mingled
with the defilement of the mental poisons, the deeds of the Victorious
One will not be displayed in the three realms of existence. Buddha
activity unfolds in order to separate this nature from its veils.

B.II.2.2.2.1.3.2.2.3.3. Both combined

Unthreshed grains of rice, buckwheat, or barley, which not
having emerged from their husks
still have husk and beard, cannot be turned into delicious food
that is palatable for man.
Likewise the Lord of Qualities is present within all beings, but
his body is not liberated from the shroud of the poisons.
Thus his body cannot bestow the joyous taste of Dharma upon
sentient beings stricken by the famine of their afflictions.

When ripe grains of rice, buckwheat, or barley have not been well
threshed until the husk and spelt are cleared away, when they have
therefore not emerged from their husks and still have husk and beard,
they cannot be turned into delicious food that is palatable for human
beings. Likewise the sugatagarbha, the Lord of Qualities, is present
within all beings. Yet, while his body is not liberated from the shroud
of the mental poisons, it cannot bestow the taste of the joy of sacred
Dharma upon those sentient beings who are stricken by the famine of
their afflictions.

B.II.2.2.2.1.3.2.2.4. Example and meaning of the gold and the filth
B.II.2.2.2.1.3.2.2.4.1. Example

While a man was traveling, gold he owned
fell into a place filled with rotting refuse.
This [gold], being of indestructible nature,
remained for many centuries just as it was.
Then a god with completely pure divine vision saw it there
and addressed a man: "Purify this supremely precious gold
lying here in this [filth], and [then convert it into something]
that is worth being made from such a precious substance!"

When a man who was traveling had reached a crossroads, out of negligence and lack of attentiveness he dropped a great lump of gold he owned into a place filled with rotting refuse. The nature of gold is such that it will not diminish or be destroyed even after many years. Thus this gold stayed in the midst of this filth just as it was, unblemished for many centuries. Then a god who possessed completely pure vision saw that there was a large lump of gold in the midst of this filth. Upon seeing this he turned to a man who was in search of gold and said: "Purify this supremely precious lump of gold that is lying in this heap of refuse from its defilement and convert it into a piece of jewelry or something similar that is worth being made from such a precious substance!"

B.II.2.2.2.1.3.2.2.4.2. Meaning

> Likewise the Muni sees the quality [of] beings,
> which is sunken in the filth-like mental poisons,
> and pours his rain of sacred Dharma upon them
> to purify the muddiness of their afflictions.

Likewise the great Muni, the Perfect Buddha, sees that the sugatagarbha, the quality of beings, which is sunken in the mud of the filth-like mental poisons, is present within all sentient beings. Upon seeing this he pours the mighty rain of his sacred Dharma upon all those beings in order to purify this mud of their afflictions.

B.II.2.2.2.1.3.2.2.4.3. Both combined

> Once the god has seen the gold that has fallen into the place
> full of rotting refuse,
> insistently he directs the man's attention to this supremely
> beautiful thing so he may completely cleanse it.
> Seeing within all beings the precious perfect buddha that has
> fallen into the great filth of the mental poisons,
> the Victorious One does likewise and teaches the Dharma to
> persuade them to purify it.

As soon as the god has seen the gold that has fallen into the place full of rotting refuse, with insistence he shows the man this supremely beautiful gold so that he may completely cleanse it, and he incites him to purify it. Similarly the omniscient Victorious One sees that the nature of a perfect buddha, resembling the precious [gold], is present within all sentient beings, but has fallen into the great filth of the mental poisons.

Upon seeing this he teaches the Dharma to all those beings in the measure of their karmic fortune, so that they may purify their [buddha] nature.

B.II.2.2.2.1.3.2.2.5. Example and meaning of the treasure and the earth
B.II.2.2.2.1.3.2.2.5.1. Example

> If an inexhaustible treasure were buried
> in the ground beneath a poor man's house,
> the man would not know of it, and the treasure
> would not speak and tell him "I am here!"

If a great inexhaustible treasure were buried in the ground beneath a poor man's house, the man would not know that this treasure was there, and the treasure would also not be able to speak to the man and tell him "I am here!" Therefore the man would have to experience the suffering of poverty.

B.II.2.2.2.1.3.2.2.5.2. Meaning

> Likewise a precious treasure is contained in each being's mind.
>   This is its true state,
> which is free from defilement. Nothing is to be added and
>   nothing to be removed.
> Nevertheless, since they do not realize this, sentient beings
> continuously undergo the manifold sufferings of deprivation.

Likewise the precious treasure of the sugatagarbha is contained within the minds of all sentient beings. This is the true state [of the mind], which is by nature free from defilement. To this true state no quality that was previously not present is to be added. No defilement is to be removed from it, [since the defilements] to be abandoned are not truly existent. Nevertheless, sentient beings do not realize that this true state is present within themselves. Therefore, although the direct manifestation of the qualities is at hand, they must continuously experience the deprivation of the manifold aspects of the suffering of samsara.

B.II.2.2.2.1.3.2.2.5.3. Both combined

> When a precious treasure is contained within [the ground
>   beneath] a poor man's house,
> the treasure cannot tell him "I am here!" [and] the man does
>   not know of its presence.

> Like the poor man, beings are [unaware] that Dharma's
> treasure lies in the house of their minds
> and the great Sage truly takes birth within the world to cause
> them to attain [this treasure].

When a precious treasure is contained in the ground underneath a poor man's house, this precious treasure cannot tell the man "I am here!" and the poor man will not know that this treasure is there. Through his being ignorant of this he is not liberated from his suffering of poverty and deprivation. All beings are equally [unknowing] and thus resemble the poor man. Although the treasure of dharmakaya abides within their own mind's house, they are unaware of it. In order to cause those beings to actually attain the treasure of dharmakaya, which is present within themselves, the great Sage, the Buddha Bhagavat, truly takes birth in the endless realms of the world and teaches the sacred Dharma.

B.II.2.2.2.1.3.2.2.6. Example and meaning of the shoot and the fruit-skin
B.II.2.2.2.1.3.2.2.6.1. Example

> The seed contained in the fruit of a mango or similar trees
> [is possessed of] the indestructible property of sprouting.
> Once it gets plowed earth, water, and the other [conditions],
> the substance of a majestic tree will gradually come about.

Although it is contained inside the skin of a fruit of a mango, a nyagrodha, or similar trees, a tree seed has the capacity to generate a mighty tree. It has an indestructible property in that there is no hindrance that could obstruct the sprouting of the shoot. Once it has all the necessary conditions collected together, such as well-plowed earth, water, manure, warmth, and so on, it will gradually develop in substance until a genuine king of trees has come about.

B.II.2.2.2.1.3.2.2.6.2. Meaning

> The fruit consisting of the ignorance and the other defects of
> beings
> contains in the shroud of its peel the virtuous element of the
> dharma[kaya].
> Likewise, through relying on virtue, this [element] also
> will gradually turn into the substance of a King of Munis.

The fruit, which consists of the mental poisons, of ignorance and the other defects of beings, contains within the shroud of its skin the element of the dharmakaya, the expanse of all virtue. Similar to the way in which a mighty tree comes about when all the favorable conditions [for its growth] are present, this element will also turn into the substance of a buddha, a King of Munis, when one relies on the necessary condition, which is the virtue of the two accumulations, and thus gradually travels the paths and levels.

B.II.2.2.2.1.3.2.2.6.3. Both combined

> By means of water, sunlight, wind, earth, time, and space, the
>   necessary conditions,
> the tree grows from within the narrow shroud of the fruit of a
>   banana or mango.
> Similarly the fertile seed of the Perfect Buddha, contained
>   within the fruit-skin of the mental poisons of beings,
> also grows from virtue as its necessary condition, until the [shoot
>   of] Dharma is seen and augmented [towards perfection].

What has come forth is moistened by water, ripened by sunlight, increased by wind, supported by earth, strengthened by the passing of time, provided with the opportunity to unfold by space, and so on. Due to these necessary conditions a mighty tree is gradually growing from its abode within the narrow shroud of the fruit-skin of a banana or mango. Similarly the seed of the Perfect Buddha, which is contained within the fruit-skin of the mental poisons of beings, resembles the shoot. Just as a tree grows from the meeting of the necessary conditions, the virtue of the two accumulations acts as the necessary condition, on the basis of which the shoot of the Dharma is seen on the path of seeing, augmented on the path of meditation and led to ultimate perfection on the path of no more learning.

B.II.2.2.2.1.3.2.2.7. Example and meaning of the statue and the tattered rag
B.II.2.2.2.1.3.2.2.7.1. Example

> An image of the Victorious One made from precious material
> lies by the road, wrapped in an evil-smelling tattered rag.
> Upon seeing this a god will alert the [passersby]
> to its presence by the road to cause its retrieval.

Suppose a statue of the Victorious One made from invaluably precious material is lying at a crossroads, wrapped in an evil-smelling tattered rag, and people heedlessly pass it by, unaware of its presence. When a god sees what is lying there, he will alert the passersby to the fact that a statue is lying by the road and show it to them, so that they retrieve this statue from its evil-smelling covering.

B.II.2.2.2.1.3.2.2.7.2. Meaning

Likewise, being possessed of unhindered vision
[the Buddha] sees the substance of the Sugata
wrapped in the multitude of the mental poisons,
even in animals, and teaches the means to free it.

Since beginningless time the sugatagarbha has been wrapped in the evil-smelling rags of the afflictions, in the various aspects of the three poisons and the other defilements [up to] the remaining imprints. The eye of a buddha sees that this substance of the sugatagarbha is even present within animals. Upon seeing this he opens an endless number of gates of the sacred Dharma. He teaches the means to practice the path, so that this dharmadhatu may be released from its adventitious veils, just as the [rag] enveloping the statue is removed.

B.II.2.2.2.1.3.2.2.7.3. Both combined

When his eye perceives the statue of the Tathagata, which is of
    precious nature
but wrapped in a stinking rag and lying by the road, the god
    points it out to passersby, so that they retrieve it.
Likewise the Victor sees that the element, wrapped in the
    tattered garments of the poisons and lying on samsara's road,
is present even within animals, and teaches the Dharma so that
    it may be released.

When the god's eye perceives that a statue of the Tathagata, which is made from a material of precious nature but wrapped in a stinking rag, is lying by a crossroads unnoticed by the men passing by, he will show it to those men and tell them: "There is a statue here!" so that it may be retrieved from the tattered rags. Similarly the Victorious One sees the buddha element which, wrapped in the tattered garments of the mental poisons, is lying on samsara's road. He sees that it even abides within animals and teaches the Dharma so that it may be released from these rags of the mental poisons.

B.II.2.2.2.1.3.2.2.8. Example and meaning of the universal monarch and the woman
B.II.2.2.2.1.3.2.2.8.1. Example

A woman of miserable appearance
who is without protection and abides in a poorhouse
holds in her womb a glorious king,
not knowing that a lord of man dwells in her own body.

A woman of miserable appearance and complexion, having neither protection nor refuge, abides in poorhouses, cheap hostels, and at cross-roads. She bears in her womb an infant who is endowed with the signs and will become a glorious universal monarch. And yet, since this child is obscured by the shroud of her womb, she does not know that this being dwelling in her own body is a ruler of mankind. Being ignorant of this she suffers and is stricken with the fear of being slandered, treated with contempt, and abused by others.

B.II.2.2.2.1.3.2.2.8.2. Meaning

> Birth in an existence is similar to the poorhouse.
> Impure beings are like the woman bearing [a king] in her womb.
> Since he is present within her, she has protection.
> The undefiled element is like [the king] who dwells in her womb.

Since births in the various places of samsaric existence are accompanied by suffering, they are similar to living in a poorhouse, in the abodes of those who have neither protection nor refuge. Since all beings who are not purified from the adventitious afflictions have protection and refuge and yet are ignorant of this, they are similar to the woman who has a king in her womb. Since a king is present within this woman, it will become apparent that she has protection. Since within those beings the true state, the tathagatagarbha, is present, they are accompanied by the best possible protection. Once this element, which is by nature completely pure and free from any defilement, has directly revealed itself, they will be sheltered from all their fear. Therefore the element is similar to the king who dwells in this woman's womb.

B.II.2.2.2.1.3.2.2.8.3. Both combined

> A ruler of the earth dwells in the womb of a woman who has an unpleasant appearance and whose body is dressed in dirty clothes.
> Nevertheless she has [to abide] in a poorhouse and undergo the experience of direst suffering.
> Likewise, beings deem themselves unsheltered though a protector resides within their own [minds].
> Thus they have to abide in the ground of suffering, their minds being unpeaceful under the predominating drive of the mental poisons.

A universal monarch, a ruler of the earth, dwells within the womb of a woman who has an unpleasant appearance and whose body is dressed in dirty clothes. Although this ruler resides in her own womb, being ignorant of this, she has to abide in a poorhouse and undergo the experience of direst suffering, of being destitute, subject to contempt, abused, and neglected. Similarly all sentient beings have a protector and refuge, this being the sugatagarbha which resides within their own minds. Yet, since they do not know this, they deem themselves without any protection and refuge. Thus those beings whose minds are unpeaceful due to the predominating influence of the mental poisons have to abide within the cycle of existence, the ground of suffering.

B.II.2.2.2.1.3.2.2.9. Example and meaning of the golden image and the clay
B.II.2.2.2.1.3.2.2.9.1. Example

> An artistically well designed image of peaceful appearance,
> which has been cast in gold and is [still] inside [its mold],
> externally has the nature of clay. Experts, upon seeing this,
> will clear away the outer layer and cleanse the gold therein.

When an image, which is artistically well designed in all its parts, pure, and beautiful in its peaceful appearance, has been cast in gold and is still inside its black mold, it is covered by clay and thus externally has the nature of earth. Upon seeing this, experts who know that a golden image is contained in the covering mold will clear away the outer layer in order to remove the traces of clay remaining on the golden image enclosed therein.

B.II.2.2.2.1.3.2.2.9.2. Meaning

> Likewise those of supreme enlightenment
> fully see that there are defilements [on] the luminous nature,
> but that these stains are just adventitious,
> and purify beings, who are like jewel mines, from all their veils.

Similarly the Victorious Ones fully see that there are defilements on the luminous nature of the minds of beings, but that these are just adventitious, being able to be removed. Upon seeing this they clear away these veils, which are similar to the mold. Once they are awakened and expanded in supreme enlightenment, they teach the sacred Dharma and purify beings, who are like jewel mines, from all their obscurations.

B.II.2.2.2.1.3.2.2.9.3. Both combined

Recognizing the nature of an image of peaceful appearance,
flawless and made from shimmering gold,
while it is [still] contained in its mold, an expert removes the
   layers of clay.
Likewise the omniscient know the peaceful mind, which is
   similar to pure gold,
and remove the obscurations by teaching the Dharma, [just as
the mold] is struck and chipped away.

Suppose there is an image of peaceful and beautiful appearance that is flawless and completely pure, made from unalloyed, shimmering gold, but which at the time of its casting is contained within a mold of black clay. An expert skilled in the making of statues would recognize its nature and remove the external layers of clay. Similarly the Buddhas who know the entirety of the knowable recognize the sugatagarbha, the true state of the mind, which is by nature peaceful, and thus similar to completely pure gold. They remove the veils that hinder the direct realization of the element by teaching the Dharma as the means to their removal, acting just as one who strikes the clay, chipping it away to remove the mold.

B.II.2.2.2.1.3.2.3. Summary of the meaning

The lotus, the bees, the husk, the filth,
the earth, the skin of the fruit, the tattered rag,
the woman's womb, and the shroud of clay
[exemplify the defilements], while [the pure nature]
is like the buddha, the honey, the kernel, the gold,
the treasure, the great tree, the precious statue,
the universal monarch, and the golden image.
It is said that the shroud of the mental poisons,
[which causes the veils] of the element of beings,
has had no connection with it since beginningless time,
while the nature of mind, which is devoid of stains,
[has been present within them] since beginningless time.

By "the ugly lotus," "the bees," "the husk of the grain," "the filthy mud," "the ground," "the skin of the fruit," "the evil-smelling tattered rag," "the woman's womb," and "the shroud of black clay," the nine examples for the defilements causing the obscuration are summarized, whereas through the statements "like a buddha adorned with the signs and marks," "like honey endowed with the essence of taste," "like a ripe grain," "like a lump of gold that does not change into something else," "like a great inexhaustible treasure," "like a great fruit-bearing tree," "like a beautiful precious statue," "like a universal monarch," and "like an image of unalloyed gold," the nine examples for the buddha nature that is obscured are explained concisely.

The meaning illustrated through these examples is as follows: It is said that the shrouds of the mental poisons causing the obscuration of suchness, of the element of beings, are naturally present, and yet have no connection with it. For this reason they are adventitious. Nevertheless they are also simultaneously present with the dharmadhatu and have remained close to it since beginningless time. Wherever these shrouds of the mental poisons are, there is the tathagatagarbha as well. The nature of the minds of beings is contained within them. This tathagatagarbha, which has ever been free from any defilement and is coemergent primordial wisdom, has remained close to them since beginningless time.

B.II.2.2.2.1.3.3. The way the defilements are purified
B.II.2.2.2.1.3.3.1. Explanation of the nine defilements

> The nine aspects of defilement: desire, aversion,
> and mental blindness, their fierce active state,
> the remaining imprints [of unknowing], the defilements
> to be abandoned on the paths of seeing and meditation,
> and the defilements based upon the impure levels
> and the pure levels respectively, are fully taught
> by the shroud of the lotus and the other examples.
> [When] classified, the shroud of the secondary poisons
> is beyond any end. But when it is comprised concisely,
> the nine defilements of desire and the other afflictions
> are well explained in the given order by the nine similes
> of the shroud of the lotus and the subsequent examples.

If the adventitious defilements veiling the dharmadhatu, which is by nature completely pure, are comprised concisely by means of the families they belong to, there are nine aspects:

The first three aspects provide the condition of the karma of immovability (Tib. *mi g.yo ba'i las*). These are the remaining imprints of desire, aversion, and ignorance, which is mental blindness with respect to thatness.

The fourth aspect provides the condition of virtuous and unvirtuous karma. It consists of the fiercely active state of these three poisons, the state in which they immediately manifest. These three are presented as one aspect.

The fifth aspect provides the condition producing a body of mental nature. This is the ground of the remaining imprints of ignorance (Tib. *ma rig bag chags kyi sa*).

The sixth aspect consists of the defilements exclusively abandoned on the path of seeing.

The seventh aspect consists of the defilements exclusively abandoned on the path of meditation.

The eighth aspect comprises the defilements based upon the stream of being of an individual who dwells on one of the seven impure [bodhisattva] levels. Only their elimination generates the pure [bodhisattva] levels.

The ninth aspect comprises the defilements based upon the stream of being of an individual dwelling on one of the pure [bodhisattva] levels. Their elimination generates the end of the continuum.

In their given sequence these nine aspects are fully and thoroughly explained by the nine examples of the shroud of the lotus, the bees, and the following [seven].

When the shroud of the secondary mental poisons that obscure the element is fully classified in terms of subject matter, there are eighty-four thousand different major types, which in their turn split up into ever further kinds. This process is beyond any end and corresponds to the different kinds of primordial wisdom of a tathagata, which are similarly endless in number.

The lines starting with "But when it is comprised concisely..." and ending with "... and the subsequent examples," have been elucidated in the foregoing sections and are easily comprehended from the words of [Asanga's] commentary.

B.II.2.2.2.1.3.3.2. Explanation of the question: In which individual's stream of being are they present?

> **These defilements cause in their given sequence**
> **the four impurities of children, the impurity of arhats,**
> **the two impurities of followers of the path of training,**
> **and the two impurities of those with understanding.**

With regard to the statement of the Bhagavan: "All beings possess the tathagatagarbha," there are different classes of beings who are veiled by these nine aspects of obscuring adventitious defilements. These are the impurities of the children or of ordinary beings, of shravaka and pratyekabuddha arhats, of those who generally follow the path of training, and of bodhisattvas who particularly possess understanding. Furthermore, in their given sequence the first four veils are the dormant tendencies of the three poisons, which constitute the impurity of the children dwelling in the higher realms, and the fiercely active state of these three poisons, which constitutes the impurity of the children bound to the desire realm. The following veil is the ground of the remaining imprints of ignorance, which constitutes the impurity of arhats. The following two veils are those to be abandoned through seeing and meditation, respectively. These constitute the impurities of ordinary beings on the path of training and of noble ones on the path of training. The last two veils are the defilements based upon the seven impure bodhisattva levels and those based upon the three pure bodhisattva levels. These constitute the impurities of bodhisattvas who have not reached final [accomplishment] and of those who have reached final [accomplishment]. These impurities are the pollutions respectively prevailing in these individuals and foremost to be abandoned, since they constitute their [immediate] hindrance that prevents the ultimate dharmadhatu from revealing itself directly.

B.II.2.2.2.1.3.3.3. Detailed explanation of the way the defilements are purified
B.II.2.2.2.1.3.3.3.1. The three dormant tendencies

> **When a lotus [just] born from the mud**
> **appears to [a beholder], it delights his mind.**
> **Yet later it changes and becomes undelightful.**
> **The joy born from desire is similar to this.**
>
> **Bees, when extremely agitated,**
> **will fiercely use their stings.**
> **Similarly, hatred, once arisen,**
> **brings suffering to the heart.**
>
> **The kernel of rice and so on**
> **is obscured by its outer husk.**
> **Likewise the vision of the [true] meaning**
> **is obscured by the eggshell of ignorance.**

When a lotus flower freshly born from the mud appears to a beholder soon after its arising, it will greatly delight his mind. Yet later, without a long time passing, it changes and becomes faded and undelightful. The dormant tendencies of the mental poison of desire are similar to this. When greed born from improper mental activity directly manifests, joy and delight are present. When later it ceases, there is no longer any delight. This greed is therefore said to be similar to the delight upon seeing the lotus, while the dormant tendencies of desire are similar to the lotus [itself].

Bees are attached to their honey. When someone else takes the honey away, their minds are extremely agitated by anger. They fiercely attack and sting this person, causing a burning pain. Similarly, when the dormant tendencies of anger and hatred increase until anger has actually arisen, this also generates a burning suffering in the hearts of oneself and the others [involved]. Thus the dormant tendencies of hatred are said to be similar to bees.

The kernels of rice and other grains cannot be seen since they are concealed by their husks, by the beards and different layers of skin. Likewise the vision of the meaning of the tathagatagarbha, of the dharmadhatu, which is by nature clear light, is also obscured by the dormant tendencies of mental blindness, of ignorance, and so on, which are similar to an eggshell. Thus they cause it not to be seen. In this way the dormant tendencies of mental blindness are said to be similar to the husk.

B.II.2.2.2.1.3.3.3.2. The defect of their fiercely active state

Filth is repugnant.
Being the cause for those bound up with greed
to indulge in sense pleasures,
the active state [of the poisons] resembles it.

Filthy and rotten things belong to the repugnant part. They involve danger, and are to be feared. The state in which the three poisons rise up and become directly manifest is the cause for beings in the desire realm who are bound up with greed to get immersed in many forms of evil conduct, to indulge in sense pleasures and pursue various other inferior aims. The fiercely active state of the mental poisons is therefore similar to a great heap of filth. It is the abode of affliction, of anxiety and mental disturbance. Thus the direct manifestation of the three poisons is said to resemble filth.

B.II.2.2.2.1.3.3.3.3. The fault of the ground of the remaining imprints of ignorance

When wealth is hidden, one is ignorant of it
and therefore does not obtain the treasure.
Likewise self-sprung [wisdom] is veiled in arhats
by the ground of remaining imprints of ignorance.

When a great treasure representing inexhaustible wealth is hidden and obscured by a vast amount of earth, the poor do not know that there are riches [at hand] and thus will not obtain this treasure. Similarly the vision of self-sprung primordial wisdom endowed with inexhaustible qualities is veiled within arhats by the ground of remaining imprints of ignorance. For this reason the arhats, resembling the poor, are prevented from seeing it. Thus the complex of the remaining imprints of ignorance is explained as being similar to earth.

B.II.2.2.2.1.3.3.3.4. The defilements to be abandoned on the paths of seeing and meditation of the common vehicle

> As by gradual growth from bud to shoot
> the skins of the seed are cut,
> the vision of thatness averts
> [the stains] to be abandoned by seeing.
>
> Through their junction with the noble path
> they have overcome the essential part of the transitory
>   collection.
> What their wisdom must abandon [on] the path of meditation
> is explained as being similar to tattered rags.

By the gradual growth of a tree bud into a sprout, a shoot, and finally a tiny trunk with small branches and leaves, the skins of the seed are progressively cut. Similarly the gradual vision of thatness or of the absolute dharmadhatu progressively averts the mental poisons that are to be abandoned through seeing. Through the section containing this statement, the defilements to be abandoned through seeing are explained as being similar to the skin of a fruit.

Arhats have joined with [or attained] the direct vision of the actual state of the Four Truths that constitute the Noble Path. Through this vision they have overcome the essential or main part of the defilements belonging to the so-called transitory collection and the views related to it. The views of the transitory collection consist of the belief that the five skandhas constitute a self, something that belongs to a self, and similar notions. Once the true state has been seen directly, defilements are [still] present within the stream of being of an arhat. These defilements are to be abandoned through primordial wisdom on the path of meditation. They are the remainders that are present after the coarse aspect has been exhausted. These remainders are explained as being similar to dirty shreds of a garment. Through the section containing this statement, the defilements to be abandoned through meditation are said to resemble tattered rags.

B.II.2.2.2.1.3.3.3.5. The defilements of the seven impure levels in particular

The stains based on the seven [impure] levels
resemble the defilements of the shrouding womb.
Concept-free primordial wisdom [is released]
like the mature [prince] from the womb's confine.

Since they veil what needs to be seen and involve deliberate effort, the stains based on the seven impure [bodhisattva] levels resemble the defilements of the shrouding womb. Once it is completely freed from these stains, like being released from the confines of the womb, completely concept-free primordial wisdom directly reveals itself on the eighth bodhisattva level and the levels above, doing so spontaneously and without any deliberate effort. This direct revelation of concept-free primordial wisdom is similar to the full development and birth of the Chakravartin king. Through the statement contained in this section the defilements based on the seven [impure levels] are said to be similar to the shroud of the womb.

B.II.2.2.2.1.3.3.3.6. The defilements to be overcome by vajra-like samadhi

The defilements connected with the three [pure] levels
should be known as being similar to the layer of clay.
They must be overcome by the vajra-like samadhi
of [those] who are the embodiment of greatness.

Since the subtle defilements connected with the three pure [bodhisattva] levels can be abandoned without exerting deliberate effort, they should be known as being similar to the fine layer of clay, which only just covers the golden image a tiny bit. They are to be overcome by the vajra-like samadhi of those great [bodhisattvas] who are themselves the embodiment of the remedy. By the statement in this section, the defilements based on the three pure [bodhisattva] levels are said to be similar to [traces of] clay.

B.II.2.2.2.1.3.3.3.7. Summary of the meaning

Thus desire and the further of the nine defilements
correspond to the lotus and the following examples.

In the foregoing sections, corresponding properties have been extensively related to each other. In the way shown there and in their given sequence, desire, hatred, and the further of the nine adventitious

defilements that obscure the dharmadhatu have properties corresponding to those of the lotus, the bees, and the following examples. Since
each of these defilements and examples have an individual corresponding property, one example and one meaning are respectively combined.
This does not mean, though, that whatever has been explained as the
obscuration of a particular [individual] is exclusive, in that it does not
veil the previously mentioned of the nine [individuals] as well.

B.II.2.2.2.1.3.4. The gradual stages of realization
B.II.2.2.2.1.3.4.1. Short explanation of what is illustrated by the nine examples

> **Its nature unifying three aspects, the element has properties**
> **that correspond to those of the Buddha and the other similes.**

The nature of the element unifies three aspects, as will be explained
in the following sections. With these three aspects the tathagatagarbha
has properties that correspond to those of the buddha statue, the honey,
and the further of the nine similes illustrating buddha nature.

B.II.2.2.2.1.3.4.2. Individual classification of their meaning

> **Its nature is dharmakaya, suchness,**
> **and also the disposition. These are to be**
> **known by the [first] three examples,**
> **the [fourth] one, and the [following] five.**

One may wonder: What are the three aspects of the nature of the
sugatagarbha or dharmadhatu?

The three aspects are its nature in terms of the dharmakaya, which
is luminous clarity, its nature in terms of suchness, which is unchanging, and its nature in terms of the disposition, which accomplishes the
state of buddhahood. These three aspects must be understood by
means of what is illustrated by the nine examples. By means of the
first three examples of the buddha statue and so on, the element is to
be understood as having the nature of the dharmakaya, by means of
the example of gold as having the nature of suchness, and by means
of the last five examples of the treasure and so forth as having the
nature of the disposition.

B.II.2.2.2.1.3.4.3. Detailed explanation of the essence of the different kinds
B.II.2.2.2.1.3.4.3.1. Example and meaning of the dharmakaya
B.II.2.2.2.1.3.4.3.1.1. Explanation of the different aspects of the dharmakaya

The dharmakaya is to be known [in] two aspects.
These are the utterly unstained dharmadhatu
and the cause conducive to its [realization],
which is teaching in the deep and manifold way.

When classified in terms of what is actual or real and what is imputed, the nature in the sense of the dharmakaya is also to be known
in two aspects: The real or actual aspect (Tib. *mtshan nyid pa*) is the
dharmakaya in the sense of realization. This is the tathagatagarbha,
the dharmadhatu, which is utterly free from defilement and by nature
clear light. It exists as the field of experience of the self-aware primordial wisdom of all buddhas. The imputed aspect is the dharmakaya in
the sense of teaching. This is the cause conducive to the attainment or
realization of this actual or real dharmakaya. It consists of the teachings of the words of the Buddha, from which true awareness will
emerge in accordance with the respective karmic fortunes of the disciples. These two aspects are classified in terms of the object to be
expressed and the means of expression, or in other words, in terms of
fruit and cause.

When the dharmakaya in the sense of teaching is categorized into
an internal classification, there are also two aspects: The first is teaching in the way of the deep Dharma. This is teaching from the viewpoint
of thatness or the absolute truth. It stems from the bodhisattva pitaka.
The second aspect is teaching in the vast and manifold way. This is
teaching from the viewpoint of the relative truth in accordance with
the varied mental dispositions of beings. It stems from the twelve
branches of the supreme speech of the Buddha (Tib. *gsung rab yan lag
bcu gnyis*), from the sutras, and so on. (See also Part Four, note 7.)

B.II.2.2.2.1.3.4.3.1.2. Combination of these with their examples

[The dharmakaya] being beyond the worldly,
no example for it can be found in the world.
Therefore the element and the Tathagata
are explained as being [slightly] similar.
Teaching in the deep and subtle way
is like the one single taste of honey,
while teaching through various aspects
resembles grain in its variety of husks.

The dharmakaya in the sense of the completely pure nature, being
what is to be realized, is truly beyond all worldly phenomena. Therefore no example whatsoever to illustrate it can be found in the world.

For this reason the statue of the self-sprung Tathagata abiding within the lotus, and the element that is by nature completely pure, are explained as having an only slight similarity. The cause conducive to the realization of this element is teaching in the mode of the absolute. This is subtle and deep, since it is difficult to fathom and holds benefit. It shows all phenomena as being of one single taste in the light of their suchness. Therefore this teaching is like the different kinds of honey, which are of one taste in that they are equally sweet and delicious. Teaching in the way of the various aspects of means consists of the twelve branches of the supreme speech of the Buddha and so forth. To facilitate realization of the actual meaning, the vast aspect of teaching gradually provides a connection with various meanings requiring interpretation (Skt. *neyārtha*, Tib. *drang don*). It should therefore be known to resemble grain, which is fit to be turned into edible food, abiding in the enclosures of its various husks.

B.II.2.2.2.1.3.4.3.2. Example and meaning of suchness

> Since the nature is unchanging,
> full of virtue, and utterly pure,
> suchness is said to correspond
> to the shape and color of gold.

Although the nature of mind is connected with the endless suffering incurred by the mental poisons, it is unchanging, luminous clarity, and utterly pure. Therefore it is called "suchness." Just as pure gold is unchanging, this suchness does not change into another nature throughout all phases. Just as gold is beautiful and can be turned into an ornament, it is by nature full of virtue and supreme. Just as the essence of gold has no stain, it has been utterly pure and free from defilement since beginningless time. For these reasons, this suchness, the dharmadhatu, is said to have properties corresponding to the shape and color of pieces of pure gold.

B.II.2.2.2.1.3.4.3.3. Example and meaning of the disposition
B.II.2.2.2.1.3.4.3.3.1. Presentation of the two types of disposition by means of their examples

> Similar to the treasure and the fruit of a tree,
> the disposition is to be known in two aspects,
> as it has existed [as] the nature since beginningless time
> and has become supreme [through] right cultivation.

The aspect of nature called "the disposition to buddhahood" is also to be known in two aspects. The first is the disposition that has existed since beginningless time (Tib. *thog ma med pa nas gnas pa'i rigs*) as the nature of mind. This is similar to an underground treasure, since it is not accomplished through deliberate effort. The second aspect is the disposition that is expanded (Tib. *rgyas 'gyur gyi rigs*) or unfolded. Just as the fruit of a tree increases into something new by means of the necessary conditions, this is equivalent to supreme ability unfolding through right cultivation by means of the necessary conditions of learning and reflection.

B.II.2.2.2.1.3.4.3.3.2. Explanation of the way the three kayas are attained from these

> The attainment of the three kayas of a buddha
> is seen to stem from the twofold disposition.
> By the first aspect there is the first [kaya],
> through the second there are the latter two.

The attainment of the three kayas of a perfect buddha is seen as the fruit stemming from the twofold disposition. These are the disposition in terms of the nature and the expanded disposition acting as the cause of the three kayas.

(1) Once the numerous accumulations of primordial wisdom have been led to final perfection, the disposition that exists as the nature will have become free from all the adventitious stains without any remainder. Through this the first kaya is attained. This is the svabhavikakaya, the true state possessing the two types of purity.

(2) Through final perfection of the accumulation of merit, the disposition that is expanded has room to unfold. Due to this, the latter two kayas are attained. These are the sambhogakaya and nirmanakaya, which appear to the near and distant disciples, respectively.

In this context the venerable Karma Thrinläpa states the following:

> Nowadays most of those who interpret the five Dharmas of Maitreya hold that the expanded disposition is compounded, in that it has come about through causes and conditions. As a proof they quote the above statement [which is also contained in the *Mahayanasutralamkara* (Tib. *mdo sde rgyan*)]: "it has become supreme [through] right cultivation" (B.II.2.2.2.1.3.4.3.3.1). On this basis they say: "The disposition that is expanded is the proper cultivation of the roots of virtue." This can only be considered as an assertion comparable to the noise of the rabbit.

The glorious Third Karmapa Rangjung Dorjé said in *The Profound Inner Meaning* (Tib. *zab mo nang don*): "Moreover, when some think that the expanded disposition is newly arisen, this is not the case…" This quote, as well as further statements he made, corresponds in content to this present text. It is therefore not held here that the expanded disposition consists of the proper cultivation of the roots of virtue. On the contrary, it has been present since beginningless time. Yet, in the phase of an ordinary being it is obscured by the veils so that complete maturation and activity cannot unfold. Therefore it lacks the ability to accomplish the benefit of sentient beings to a large extent. The [inherent] ability of this disposition unfolds, though, when the roots of virtue that form the accumulation of merit are properly cultivated on the path of training. For this reason, once the veils are purified, the activity of the form kayas, which are adorned with the thirty-two qualities of complete maturation, unfolds in the phase of a buddha. This is expressed in the passage: "it has become supreme [through] right cultivation." This passage corresponds in content to the passage: "Similar to…the fruit of a tree" (B.II.2.2.2.1.3.4.3.3.1) and to the passage further above: "The seed contained in the fruit of a mango or similar trees" (B.II.2.2.2.1.3.2.2.6.1). If with regard to this fact one sees the necessity to claim that this disposition [as it is explained in the context of the nine examples and their respective meanings by means of the example of the fruit-skin and the shoot] is the proper cultivation of the roots of virtue, this is, I think, an exaggerated interpretation.

(See also Part Four, note 8.)

B.II.2.2.2.1.3.4.3.3.3. Combination of these with their examples

The beautiful svabhavikakaya
is like the statue of precious material,
since [it exists] naturally, is not created,
and is a treasure of gem-like qualities.
Wielding the sublime majesty of the Great Dharma,
the sambhoga[kaya] resembles the Chakravartin.
Being of the nature of a [mere] representation,
the nirmana[kaya] is similar to the golden image.

The svabhavikakaya, which is the absolute kaya, is by nature clear light and is supremely beautiful due to the glory of its qualities. It should be known as being similar to the statue of the Buddha made from precious material, since it has naturally existed since beginningless time. It is not newly created by means of deliberate effort and it has qualities, the powers and so on, similar to an inexhaustible treasure of gems.

The sambhogakaya [the kaya of perfect enjoyment], which appears to beings of pure vision, wields the sublime glory of the majesty of the Mahayana Dharma in its deep and vast aspects. It therefore resembles the precious Chakravartin who enjoys the wealth of his seven possessions, which are the four continents and so on. (See also Part Four, note 9.)

The nirmanakaya, which appears to all sentient beings in common, is like the golden image. Because of the power resulting from the realization of the absolute kaya, it has the effect or nature of appearing to the minds of the disciples as a mere representation of whatever form is suitable to train any of them.

B.II.2.2.2.1.3.4.3.4. The way these are to be realized through faith

This truth of the Self-Sprung Ones
is to be realized through faith.
The orb of the sun blazes with light,
[but] is not seen by the blind.

This true nature of all self-sprung buddhas, who have not come about through conditions but have been spontaneously present from the very beginning, is within all sentient beings. Nevertheless ordinary beings, shravakas, pratyekabuddhas, and those bodhisattvas who have newly entered [the path] do not realize it directly, as it is. Relying on the trustworthy words of the Buddha they [first] have to realize it in a general way by means of faith, devotion, and finally firm conviction. This is similar to the example of the orb of the sun, which blazing with light is still not seen by the blind.

B.II.2.2.2.1.3.5. Explanation of the very nature itself
B.II.2.2.2.1.3.5.1. Essence

Nothing whatsoever is to be removed.
Not the slightest thing is to be added.
Truly looking at truth, truth is seen.
When seen, this is complete liberation.

This sugatagarbha, or this element by nature completely pure, does not have any afflicting fault whatsoever. There are no stains existing in the nature of the element that are formerly present and have to be removed. Its nature is such that it has been free from all the adventitious stains without any exception since beginningless time.

Similarly, not in the slightest way is there any completely purified quality that is formerly not present and has to be added. Its nature is such that the absolute qualities, the powers and so on, have been spontaneously present since beginningless time and are equivalent to the true state, which is completely indivisible.

Thus the object to be perceived is suchness, the true dharmadhatu, which is free from the two extremes. The perceiving subject is the authentic discriminative wisdom, which knows the absolute. Through looking directly at this true dharmadhatu by means of this discriminative wisdom, and through resting within it in meditative equipoise, one will become supremely familiar with it, and primordial wisdom, which directly sees the authentic meaning of the actual true state, will gradually arise. Through this [seeing] one attains complete liberation from the adventitious stains that are to be abandoned. [First] one will be completely freed from the stains to be abandoned through seeing on the path of seeing. [Subsequently] one will be completely freed from the stains to be abandoned through meditation on the path of meditation. [Finally] one will be completely freed from the two veils along with their remaining imprints without any exception on the path of final perfection (Tib. *mthar phyin pa'i lam*).

B.II.2.2.2.1.3.5.2. The way it is empty and not empty

The element is empty of the adventitious [stains],
which are featured by their total separateness.
But it is not empty of the matchless properties,
which are featured by their total inseparability.

The true nature of mind is free from there being anything to be removed or added, and thus is devoid of extremes.

This element is empty of the adventitious stains, which have the feature of being totally separate from it, along with the fact that they are able to be removed. For this reason the element is free from the extreme of assertion or overstatement (Tib. *sgro 'dogs*) in the sense of [falsely] stating existence.

Yet, this element is not empty of the powers and so on, the unsurpassable properties or qualities, which have the feature of being totally inseparable from it and thus are not able to be removed. For this reason the element is free from the extreme of denial or understatement (Tib. *skur 'debs*) in the sense of [falsely] stating non-existence.

Since the simultaneous presence [of existence and non-existence] is a contradiction, it is also freed from the extreme of there being both existence and non-existence.

Since this is so, it is also freed from the extreme of there being neither of these two that have been refuted, of there being neither existence nor non-existence.

For this reason it is completely freed from the two extremes, or in
other words, from the four extreme views. This complete freedom from
the four extreme views is the way unperverted emptiness is. This is
thatness [the simple state of everything].

B.II.2.2.2.1.4. The necessity to explain the element
B.II.2.2.2.1.4.1. Short explanation of question and answer
B.II.2.2.2.1.4.1.1. Question

> [The sutras of the second turning of the wheel of Dharma]
>   state in numerous places
> that all knowable [phenomena] are in all ways empty like a
>   cloud, a dream, or an illusion.
> Why is it then, that in [the sutras of the third turning of the
>   wheel of Dharma]
> the Buddha, having said this, declared that buddha nature is
>   present within beings?

In the transition to the following verses it is said in [Asanga's] commentary:

> The element being so difficult to see that it is not [even] the object
> of experience of the supreme noble ones who dwell on the level
> where freedom from attachment is finally perfected, one may
> wonder why its presence was taught to the children.

This question is implicitly contained in the section commented here.
The literal question is as follows: It is said in numerous places in the
great, the middling, and the other prajnaparamitasutras, in which on
the occasion of the second turning of the wheel of Dharma the teaching on the absence of characteristics was expounded:

> ...Appearance, but not true and devoid of entity like a cloud, a
> dream, or an illusion; thus all knowable phenomena starting from
> form up to omniscience appear, but are empty in all ways and
> devoid of entity, without the slightest exception.

Why is it then, that after having extensively taught this, the Buddha
taught on the occasion of the third turning of the wheel of Dharma in
numerous lectures, the tathagatagarbhasutras, and so on, which finally
identify the absolute: "Buddha nature, the dharmadhatu, which is by
nature completely pure and luminous clarity, has been spontaneously

present within all sentient beings since beginningless time"? Does it not follow that there is a contradiction between the second and the third turnings of the wheel of Dharma?

B.II.2.2.2.1.4.1.2. Answer

**With regard to faintheartedness, contempt for inferior beings,
perceiving the untrue, disparaging the true nature,
and exceeding self-cherishing, he said this to persuade those
who have any of these five to abandon their defects.**

This and the following sections explain why there is no contradiction between the teachings of the second and the third turnings of the wheel of Dharma. They explain the necessity for which the presence of buddha nature is taught in the tathagatagarbhasutras and so on.

The teaching that buddha nature is present within every sentient being is necessary, since the Buddha has given it in order to persuade those who have any of the following five faults to abandon these: The first of these faults is faintheartedness, which hinders one from exerting effort and striving for enlightenment. The second is contempt for "inferior beings," which hinders one from [developing] love and compassion for others. The third is distorted perception, which comes about through not perceiving an object in its true way of existence. The fourth is disparaging the true nature [by] denying the existence of the sugatagarbha, and the fifth is exceeding self-cherishing and attachment to oneself.

B.II.2.2.2.1.4.2. Detailed explanation of their meaning
*B.II.2.2.2.1.4.2.1. The intention of the teaching of the second turning of the
 wheel of Dharma*
B.II.2.2.2.1.4.2.1.1. Short explanation

**The final truth is in every respect
devoid of anything compounded.
The poisons, karma, and their product
are said to be like a cloud and so on.**

What was meant when the Buddha said, on the occasion of the second turning of the wheel of Dharma, that all phenomena are devoid of entity?

The meaning is that the final true nature is in every respect devoid of the adventitious stains, which are compounded. The afflictions of birth and so on, which appear due to the affliction of the mental poisons, the affliction of karma, and due to the skandhas and so on, which are the product of the full ripening of the mental poisons and karma, do not truly exist. With the words "like a cloud and so on" they are said to be like a cloud, a dream appearance, an illusion, or a deceptive apparition.

B.II.2.2.2.1.4.2.1.2. Detailed explanation

The mental poisons are like a cloud.
Karma resembles a dream experience.
The skandhas produced by the poisons and karma
are similar to an illusion or a deceptive apparition.

The omnipresent afflictions of desire and the other mental poisons are like a cloud, since they pervade the sky-like nature of mind and since they are adventitious. The omnipresent affliction of karma, unvirtuous action, and so on, which is fully activated by attachment and so forth, is similar to a dream experience. This is because it is generated by a distorted understanding and [thus] is a deluded imagination. The omnipresent affliction of birth is due to the skandhas and so on, which are the fruit of the full ripening of karma and mental poisons. This is similar to an illusion or a deceptive apparition, since it depends upon conditions and is not real.

B.II.2.2.2.1.4.2.2. The reason for the teaching of the third turning of the wheel of Dharma

For the time being it was thus expounded.
Additionally in this unsurpassable continuity
it was then taught: "The element is present,"
so that the five evils would be abandoned.

[The teachings of the three turnings of the wheel of Dharma were given] in order to guide the disciples gradually. With respect to the first turning of the wheel of Dharma, which consists of the teachings on the Four Noble Truths, some might think that form and so on are truly existent. In order to cause the abandonment of this attachment to the immediate semblance, the Buddha said for the time being, on the occasion of the second turning of the wheel of Dharma, which expresses the absence of characteristics: "All phenomena are emptiness, appearance but devoid of entity, like a cloud, a dream, or an illusion." Thus he gave an explanation that mainly and almost exclusively teaches the absence of an existing essence. Without abandoning his explanation that solely elucidates this [essencelessness], he then additionally gave the cycle of teachings pertaining to the highest or the last of the three turnings of the wheel of Dharma, which finally defines the absolute. He did so in order to demonstrate the deepest aspect. His aim was to cause the abandonment of the five evils of faint-heartedness and so on and the subsequent attainment of qualities such as delight in the Dharma and so forth. With this intention he said here in the context of the explanation of the ultimate, which is comparable to a continuity, since the uninterrupted dharmadhatu is taught: "This element that is by nature completely pure, the tathagatagarbha, is all-pervasively present within all [sentient beings]." And he explained this extremely clearly by means of a vast number of examples, reasons, and so forth.

B.II.2.2.2.1.4.2.3. Detailed explanation of this reason
B.II.2.2.2.1.4.2.3.1. The way the five evils come about

> As long as they have not heard this,
> bodhichitta will not be born in those
> whose minds are feeble and fainthearted,
> stirred by the evil of self-contempt.
> Having engendered [a little] bodhichitta,
> some proudly imagine: "I am supreme!"
> Towards those who have not developed it
> they are imbued with notions of inferiority.
> In those who entertain such thoughts,
> true understanding will not arise.
> They hold the untrue [to be true]
> and thus will not realize the truth.
> Being artificially produced and adventitious,
> these faults of beings are not truly [existent].
> In truth these evils do not exist as self,
> but exist as the qualities by nature pure.
> While they hold the evils, which are untrue, [to be true]
> and disparage the true qualities, [denying their presence,]
> even those of understanding will not attain the love
> that perceives the similarity of oneself and others.

If the Buddha had not taught: "This buddha nature is all-pervasively present within all beings" and one could therefore not hear this teaching, there would be the following consequences. As long as sentient beings have not heard this, five faults will arise within them:

Some individuals' minds are feeble and fainthearted because of the evil of self-contempt and lack of drive, so that they think: "How could someone like me attain unsurpassable enlightenment?" Special bodhichitta expresses itself in the wish: "May the true Buddha, which is my own nature, reveal itself!" In those beings this special bodhichitta will not be born.

Bodhichitta consists of the wish: "May I accomplish buddhahood for the sake of the others!" Some, through having developed this only a little bit, get arrogant and conceited so that they imagine: "I follow the Great Vehicle! Therefore I am extraordinary and supreme!" Towards other beings who have not engendered bodhichitta they are imbued with the notion: "These are inferior!" This is due to their ignorance of the fact that suchness is present in these other beings as well.

In those individuals who entertain such thoughts, who believe that buddha nature does not exist, true understanding free from assertion and denial will not arise. Therefore they fall into the evil of overstatement and hold what is not true—the relative, adventitious stains—to be truly existent.

On the other hand they also fall into the evil of understatement. They will not realize that the dharmadhatu, which contains the absolute qualities, is spontaneously present. In this way they do not realize the truth. Thoroughly analyzing, one finds that these faults of beings are artificially produced by causes and conditions and are adventitious, being able to be removed. These adventitious stains are therefore not truly existent. In truth these adventitious evils, since they do not exist in terms of a self of the person or a self of phenomena, exist as the powers and so on, as the absolute qualities that are by nature completely pure.

When one falls to assertion or denial, believing that the adventitious evils, which are not the truth, exist as the nature, or believing that the dharmadhatu, which contains the true qualities, has not been spontaneously present since beginningless time, the evil of exceeding self-cherishing and attachment to oneself will arise. Thus not even bodhisattvas possessing understanding will attain the great love that sees oneself and all sentient beings as having the same nature, as being equally the absolute buddha.

Therefore the dharmadhatu has been clearly elucidated in order to cause the abandonment of these evils.

In this context the venerable Mikyö Dorjé [the eighth Karmapa] has said:

> Here some Tibetan scholars consider the words in the *Mahayana Uttara Tantra Shastra:* "The tatagathagarbha is present within all beings" as a statement requiring interpretation, inasmuch as to

their opinion this was only said in order to eliminate the five faults. If this was so, it would follow that there would be no need to eliminate the five faults. It would also not be a fault to have contempt for inferior beings. The tathagatagarbha would not be present within sentient beings. There would be no need to take the teachings on the tathagatagarbha as being a valid truth. This would be a statement requiring interpretation. To deny the existence of the sugatagarbha as dharmakaya would also not be a fault, but a correct statement expressing the actual way of existence, since with regard to something that never existed one cannot fall into the extreme of understatement. Also faintheartedness would be justified, since no sugatagarbha would be present in one's own stream of being and a teaching aimed against faintheartedness would therefore be a statement that does not correspond to reality. Further, it follows from this opinion that the noble Asanga, for instance, was not a person of authority, since in his system he would not present the holy teachings of the Buddha, of Maitreya, and so on, which "have been given for a specific purpose and when taken literally lead to contradiction," as a statement that is "not to be understood in the literal sense." Since we find ourselves unable to follow those who are capable of walking over the Protector Asanga, we will follow the Noble One himself.

B.II.2.2.2.1.4.2.3.2. The way qualities are attained once the five evils are abandoned

> Once one has heard this, joy will be born.
> Respect as towards the Buddha, analytical wisdom,
> primordial wisdom, and great love will arise.
> Through the arising of these five qualities,
> one is rid of the faults and sees similarity.
> [By realizing] the absence of defects and the presence of
>   qualities,
> and through love, [seeing] the equality of oneself and [all]
>   beings,
> buddhahood will be quickly attained.

Through the fact that in the context of the Buddha's words containing the definitive meaning (Tib. *nges don*, Skt. *nitārtha*), it is said that "the dharmadhatu of the Tathagata is all-pervasively present within all beings," and through the disciples having thoroughly heard this, [five qualities will arise]:

Through the notion, "direct revelation of my own nature is great enlightenment," joy and willingness towards the hardships and burdens of the path will be born.

Through knowing that the nature of others is also buddha, the respect one has for one's teacher will equally arise towards anyone else.

With regard to the relative, adventitious stains, which do not exist in terms of the two aspects of self, the discriminative wisdom knowing them to be non-existent arises.

With regard to the absolute dharmadhatu, which exists in terms of the nature, the primordial wisdom knowing it to be existent arises.

Through seeing one's own nature and that of others equally as buddha, great love, which wishes to do others good, is born.

Since in this way five qualities arise, this results in the benefit that one is free from the defects of faintheartedness and so on and sees buddha nature to be equally present within all.

Through the realization that the faults, the adventitious stains, do not exist, whereas the naturally pure qualities exist and everyone has them, and through the great love seeing the equality of oneself and all beings in that all have the tatagathagarbha, one will gradually accomplish the path. Through this one will without any doubt quickly attain the fruit, unsurpassable buddhahood, which is the final perfection of the two benefits.

♦ This was the section "Tathagatagarbha," the first [chapter] of *The Commentary on the Highest Continuity of the Mahayana Dharma which Analyzes the Disposition of the Rare and Sublime Ones.*

With this the complete explanation of the first chapter, teaching the nature of the Tathagata, the ground to be realized, is achieved.

CHAPTER TWO

The Fifth Vajra Point: Enlightenment

B.II.2.2.2.2. Enlightenment is the realization
B.II.2.2.2.2.1. Short explanation of the essence of the subject to be explained

With its purity, attainment, freedom,
benefit for oneself and others, [their] basis,
depth, vastness, and greatness of nature,
duration, and suchness [it has eight qualities].

Enlightenment is the essence of realization. It is the fruit of the final perfection of the path and possesses the following eight particular qualities: It is purified from the veils. It is attained through the power of meditation, which constitutes the path. It is free from anything to be abandoned. It is the accomplishment of benefit for oneself and others. It possesses the powers and so forth, the basis of these benefits. It contains the division of [the three kayas]: the dharmakaya which is deep, the sambhogakaya which is vast, and the nirmanakaya which is the embodiment of greatness. It is durable in that it exists as long as samsara lasts. Its nature is suchness, the true state [of everything].

B.II.2.2.2.2.2. Concise summary of the way of explanation

By [the topics] essence, cause, fruit,
function, endowment, manifestation,
permanence, and inconceivability,
the level of a buddha is presented.

By means of the following eight topics the ultimate fruit is therefore presented as being the level of buddhahood:

The topic "essence" describes the fact that it possesses the two types of purity: in addition to the sphere being by nature completely pure it is free from the adventitious stains, from anything to be abandoned.

The topic "cause" describes the means to attain this [enlightenment] as being the practice of the path of the meditative and post-meditative phases.

The topic "fruit" describes the fact that due to the practice of the path it is free from the pollution of the two veils.

The topic "function" describes the fact that due to the veils being abandoned it accomplishes two benefits: benefit for oneself and others.

The topic "endowment" describes the fact that it possesses inconceivable qualities providing the basis for these two benefits.

The topic "manifestation" describes the fact that these qualities manifest through the division of the three kayas: the svabhavikakaya, sambhogakaya, and nirmanakaya.

The topic "permanence" describes the fact that [of] these kayas [the first] will last as long as there is space and [the latter two] as long as there are sentient beings.

The topic "inconceivability" describes the way the final ultimate [fruit] actually is as being inconceivable to ordinary beings. (See also Part Three, annotation 51.)

B.II.2.2.2.2.3. Detailed explanation by combining these
B.II.2.2.2.2.3.1. Detailed explanation of essence and cause
B.II.2.2.2.2.3.1.1. Concise explanation of the way purity is attained

> [Enlightenment, of which the Buddha] said: "It is by nature clear light," is similar to the sun and space.
> It is free from the stains of the adventitious poisons and hindrances to knowledge, the veils of which obscured it [like] a dense sea of clouds.
> Buddhahood is permanent, steadfast, and immutable, possessing all the unpolluted buddha qualities.
> It is attained on the basis of [two] primordial wisdoms: [one is] free from ideation with regard to phenomena, [the other is] discriminative.

The state of a buddha, which possesses the two types of purity, is enlightenment, of which the words of the Buddha conveying the definitive meaning state: "It is by nature clear light." This enlightenment has four particularities:

(1) It is similar to the sun in that primordial wisdom has expanded, and it is similar to space in that there is [the aspect] of abandonment, which constitutes purity. This is the particularity in terms of the essence.

(2) It is free from the pollution of the veils of the adventitious mental poisons and hindrances to knowledge, which obscured it like a dense sea of clouds. This is the particularity of abandonment, or of the fact that all obscurations have been eliminated.

(3) When buddhahood has directly revealed itself, it possesses the entirety of the unpolluted buddha qualities, such as the powers and so forth. With regard to this, buddhahood represents the essence of permanence, steadfastness, and immutability. This is the particularity in terms of the way in which it is endowed with qualities.

(4) This enlightenment is attained on the basis of the practice of the path by means of the [two] primordial wisdoms present during meditation and in the post-meditative phase, respectively. The first is primordial wisdom that is completely free from ideation with regard to all phenomena, and the second is primordial wisdom that fully and thoroughly discriminates all objects of knowledge. This is the particularity in terms of the cause. (See also Part Three, annotation 52, and Part Four, note 11.)

B.II.2.2.2.2.3.1.2. Detailed explanation of its meaning
B.II.2.2.2.2.3.1.2.1. Essence

Buddhahood is indivisible, yet can be divided
according to its property of [twofold] purity.
[Thus] it has two features, which are abandonment
and primordial wisdom, similar to space and the sun.

The enlightenment of a buddha exists indivisibly from the completely pure nature that is the essence of all [sentient beings]. When additionally, at the end [of the purifying process] it has also become free from the adventitious stains, it possesses two types of purity [purity of nature and purity in terms of purification] and can be divided according to this property of twofold purity. Thus it possesses two characteristics, which are best possible abandonment and realization. Just as space is by nature completely pure, it is totally pure from the two veils. This is the characteristic of abandonment. Just as the sun is by nature clear light, it is luminous clarity, this quality being inseparable from the nature of primordial wisdom. This is the characteristic of realization. (See also Part Three, annotation 53.)

B.II.2.2.2.2.3.1.2.2. The way it possesses qualities

Luminous clear light is not created.
It is indivisibly manifest [in the nature of beings]
and holds all the buddha properties
outnumbering the grains of sand in the river Ganges.

The dharmakaya, which is by nature luminous clear light, is an unpolluted sphere. It is not created by causes and conditions, yet is indivisibly manifest within the nature of all sentient beings. Since beginningless time it has spontaneously possessed all the properties of a buddha, such as the powers and so forth. These qualities are immeasurable and their number is beyond that of the grains of sand in the river Ganges. (See also Part Three, annotation 54.)

B.II.2.2.2.2.3.1.2.3. The meaning of the stains

By nature not existent, pervasive,
and adventitious, the veils of the poisons
and of the hindrances to knowledge
are described as being similar to a cloud.

Since beginningless time the stains by their very nature have never been truly existent. In the unpurified phase they pervade everything, and they are adventitious since they are able to be removed. For these three reasons the veil of the mental poisons, which constitutes the obstacle to liberation, and the veil of the hindrances to knowledge, which constitutes the obstacle to omniscience, are said to be similar to a cloud. Just as a cloud veils the sun and the sky, these two veils obscure the nature of clear light in the phase of ordinary beings. (See also Part Three, annotation 55.)

B.II.2.2.2.2.3.1.2.4. The cause by which one becomes free from these [veils]

Twofold wisdom causes release from the two veils.
Since there is the one that is free from ideation
and the one ensuing from this in post-meditation,
it is held that there are [two] primordial wisdoms.

Through freeing oneself from the two veils of the mental poisons and hindrances to knowledge, the vimuktikaya (Tib. *rnam par grol ba'i sku*, "the kaya of complete liberation") and the dharmakaya (Tib. *chos kyi sku*, "the kaya of qualities") are directly revealed. The cause bringing about this fruit consists of the fact that twofold primordial wisdom is jointly cultivated. The two primordial wisdoms are the ones realizing correctly and completely. In the phase of meditative equipoise, bodhisattvas cultivate primordial wisdom that is completely free from ideation. This acts as the remedy for the three realms of existence. This cultivation mainly purifies the veil of the mental poisons. In the postmeditative phase ensuing from [meditative equipoise], they cultivate the primordial wisdom that fully and thoroughly discriminates all objects of knowledge, as many as there are, in their deep and vast aspects, and so on. This cultivation mainly purifies the veil of the hindrances to knowledge. For this reason these are considered as being two primordial wisdoms. (See also Part Three, annotation 56.)

It should be understood that in the context dealt with above, the first three stanzas explain the topic "essence." This points out that [enlightenment] possesses twofold purity. The last stanza explains the topic "cause." This points out that it is primordial wisdom that brings about the attainment [of this twofold purity].

B.II.2.2.2.2.3.2. Detailed explanation of the fruit
B.II.2.2.2.2.3.2.1. Concise explanation of freedom from stains by means of examples
B.II.2.2.2.2.3.2.1.1. The fruit of liberation from the veil of the mental poisons

> Like a lake filled with unpolluted water gradually overspread
>   by lotus flowers,
> like the full moon released from Rahu's mouth and the sun
>   liberated from a sea of clouds,
> it is free from affliction. Being free from pollution and
>   possessing qualities,
> [buddhahood] is endowed with the brilliant light rays [of
>   correct and complete vision].

[The state of a buddha] is completely liberated from the affliction of desire. Thus it is similar to the example of a beautiful lake, free from any pollution of mud or dirt and filled with an abundant amount of water, which is covered by a wealth of gradually spreading lotus flowers.

It is liberated from the affliction of aversion and hatred. Inasmuch as that, it is like the full moon, which is released from the inside of the demon Rahu's mouth.

It is completely liberated from the evil affliction of ignorance, which is similar to a dense sea of clouds. For this reason it is like the orb of the sun with its clear radiant light.

Since it is free from the adventitious stains and since it possesses the final ultimate qualities of best possible abandonment and realization, it is perfect buddhahood, endowed with the brilliant light rays of correct and complete vision. (See also Part Four, note 12.)

B.II.2.2.2.2.3.2.1.2. The fruit of liberation from the veil of the hindrances to knowledge

> Being similar to the [statue of the] Muni, the leader of beings,
> and to the honey, the grain, the precious gold, the treasure, the
>   mighty tree,
> the Sugata's statue [made from] immaculate precious material,
> the ruler of the earth, and the golden image, [a buddha] has
>   gained victory.

Perfect buddhahood has gained victory over the veil of the hindrances to knowledge, eliminating them without any exception. Thus it is similar to the statue of the Muni, the leader of beings, which is liberated from the shroud of the lotus. It resembles the honey separated from the bees, the grain removed from its husk, the precious gold freed from the rotting rubbish, the treasure brought to light from underground, and the mighty tree grown from the seed. It is like the statue of the Sugata made from immaculate precious material that is removed from the tattered rags, like the Chakravartin, the ruler of the earth, born from the womb, and like the golden image cleansed from the traces of clay.

B.II.2.2.2.2.3.2.2. Detailed explanation of the reason for this
B.II.2.2.2.2.3.2.2.1. The fruit attained through meditative equipoise and the post-meditative phase

> Purity from the adventitious afflictions
> of desire and the other mental poisons
> is like the water of the lake and so forth.
> When put concisely it can be fully shown
> as the fruit of wisdom free from ideation.
> The actual attainment of the buddhakaya,
> which has all supreme aspects, is explained as the fruit
> of primordial wisdom ensuing from this after meditation.

The lake filled with unpolluted water and the other examples have three particular properties. Purity from the adventitious afflictions of desire and the other mental poisons is similar [to these examples].

Briefly, the means to achieve this purity and to then attain the three antidotes, which are meditative stability and so forth, can be fully described as being the fruit of freedom. This is primordial wisdom free from ideation, which is present during meditative equipoise. Through eliminating the veil of the hindrances to knowledge one attains the buddhakaya, which has all supreme aspects of qualities. The means for the authentic attainment of this buddhakaya is explained as being the fruit of cultivation. This consists of learning and so forth by means of the worldly primordial wisdom ensuing from this meditative equipoise in the post-meditative phase.

B.II.2.2.2.2.2.3.2.2.2. The fruit of purification from the three poisons

> Having eliminated the silt of desire,
> he lets the waters of meditative stability
> flow onto the lotus[-like] disciples,
> and thus resembles the lake of pure water.
> Having freed himself from the Rahu of hatred,
> he pervades beings with the light rays
> of his great love and compassionate concern,
> and thus is similar to the immaculate full moon.
> Totally freed from the clouds of unknowing
> and dispelling [its] darkness within beings
> through the light rays of primordial wisdom,
> buddhahood is similar to the unpolluted sun.

Within his own stream of being, a buddha has eliminated all desire, which is comparable to silt polluting the mind. He has eradicated all attachments of the three realms of existence without any exception. To the multitude of other beings, who are comparable to the lotus flowers, he teaches the Dharma. By means of his teaching he lets the waters of the samadhi of meditative stability flow onto the disciples' streams of being and moistens them with calm abiding (Skt. *śamatha*, Tib. *zhi gnas*) and special insight (Skt. *vipaśyanā*, Tib. *lhag mthong*). For these reasons a buddha who has led the two benefits to final perfection resembles a delightful lake filled with an abundance of pure water and overspread by lotus flowers.

He has completely liberated his own stream of being from the veil of hatred, which totally haunts the mind with tormenting thoughts when facing anything unpleasant and is thus comparable to the vicious Rahu. He takes care of all sentient beings, not neglecting a single one, and pervades the disciples with his great love and compassion. [A buddha's love and compassion] are comparable to light rays, his love expressing itself in the wish that all other beings may meet with goodness, and his compassion taking form in the wish that their streams of being may be free from suffering. For these reasons a buddha who has finally perfected the two benefits resembles the immaculate full moon released from the [demon's] mouth.

He has completely liberated his own stream of being from the veil of not knowing, which is similar to a dense sea of clouds. He has freed himself from all the ignorance and bewilderment of the three realms of existence. To the great multitude of beings who are his disciples he teaches the Dharma in accordance with their streams of being. Through his teaching he dispels all the darkness of their ignorance by means of the light rays of primordial wisdom. For these reasons buddhahood in which the two benefits are finally perfected resembles the unpolluted and luminous sun, which is freed from clouds. (See also Part Three, annotation 57.)

B.II.2.2.2.2.3.2.2.3. Combination of the meaning with the nine examples

> Since [enlightenment has] peerless properties,
> since it bestows the taste of sacred Dharma,
> and since it is free from the peel [of the veils],
> it is like the Sugata, the honey, and the grain.
> Since it is purified, since [beings'] poverty
> is dispelled by the wealth of its qualities,
> and since it grants the fruit of total liberation,
> it is like the gold, the treasure, and the tree.
> Representing the jewel of the dharmakaya,
> and [the attainment of] the supreme lord of humans,
> and [manifesting in] the likeness of a precious image,
> they are like the bejeweled, the king, and the golden.

Final ultimate enlightenment, which has the two types of purity, possesses peerless properties in that only a buddha has its qualities. It bestows the taste of the sacred Dharma upon the disciples, granting them the most excellent essence of its deep aspect. It is free from the peel of the two veils along with their remaining imprints. For these reasons and in the same sequence, it resembles the Sugata having come to light from the lotus, the honey separated from the bees, and the grain having emerged from the husk.

It is by nature free from stains and in addition to that is completely purified from the adventitious faults. By means of the inexhaustible wealth of its qualities it dispels all the poverty and destitution of the disciples, not leaving a single trace. It grants the disciples the fruit of great bliss, which completely liberates them from all their suffering. For these reasons it is like the pure gold cleansed from the filth, like the great treasure having come to light from the shroud of the earth, and like the mighty fruit-bearing tree.

The dharmakaya has directly revealed itself. Possessing immeasurable qualities, it is similar to a jewel that is the source [of the fulfillment] of all wishes and needs. The sambhogakaya is attained, being the supreme leader and lord of all disciples, especially of all human beings. The nirmanakaya is demonstrated. It is similar to the form of an image made from precious gold, in that it manifests in various illusory appearances. For these reasons buddhahood is like the bejeweled statue freed from the tattered rags, like the Chakravartin released from the shroud of the womb, and like the golden image freed from the traces of clay.

Through the first stanza of the foregoing section, buddhahood is explained as being the final ultimate fruit, through the second as being liberated from the veils, and through the third as representing the complete perfection of the three kayas.

B.II.2.2.2.2.3.3. Detailed explanation of its function
B.II.2.2.2.2.3.3.1. Concise explanation of the way the two benefits are accomplished
B.II.2.2.2.2.3.3.1.1. The function of the essence

> Rid of pollution [and] all-pervasive, [true buddhahood] has an
>   indestructible nature
> since it is steadfast, at peace, permanent, and unchanging. As
>   the abode [of qualities]
> a tathagata is similar to space. For the six sense-faculties of a
>   saintly being
> it forms the cause to experience their respective [pure] objects
>   [of perception].

The true absolute state of a buddha is equivalent to final ultimate abandonment in that it is free from even the slightest trace of pollution along with its remaining imprints. It is equivalent to final ultimate realization in that it pervades the whole range of the knowable in terms of "as it is" and "as much as there is," in its absolute and relative aspects or in its ways of being and of appearance. This true buddhahood, which has best possible abandonment and realization, is of an uncompounded and lastingly indestructible nature. This is because it is free from death, birth, sickness, and aging and is therefore steadfast, permanent, at peace, and unchanging. Buddhahood being such, its attainment means that one's own benefit is finally perfected. Since it is the abode of all unstained [lit. "white"] properties, it also finally perfects the benefit of others. A buddha who has gone into the very essence of suchness, into the true state itself, is similar to uncreated space. The own essence of space is not such that it fulfils a function, and yet it unfolds activity, providing the prerequisite for visible objects to be seen and so forth. Similar to that, a buddha acts as a cause with respect to the six sense-faculties of a saintly being who has karmic fortune. Once the six sense-faculties of such a person have become supreme, buddhahood represents the cause for the pure object of perception corresponding to each sense faculty to be experienced and realized. (See also Part Three, annotation 58.)

B.II.2.2.2.2.3.3.1.2. The function in terms of there being purity throughout all phenomena

> It is the cause for visible objects, which are non-arising,
>   to be seen,
> for good and pure speech to be heard,
> for the pure scent of the moral conduct of the Sugata to be
>   smelled,
> for the flavor of sacred Dharma [of] the great noble ones
>   to be tasted,
> for the blissful touch of samadhi to be felt,
> and for the mode [of the Dharma], which is by essence deep,
>   to be realized.
> When reflected upon in a very fine way, a sugata bestowing
>   true bliss
> is like space, devoid of any reasons.

The Sugata constitutes the cause for manifold sensory objects, such as the form kayas and so forth, to be perceived [and yet known] as being merely relative. This perception occurs through the power of having previously gathered the accumulations. The objects perceived are non-arisings in that they are not made from the elements. One beholds [pure] physical form, hears the good and pure speech of the Mahayana Dharma, smells the pure scent of the moral conduct of the Sugata, and tastes the flavor of the nectar of the sacred Dharma that is the object of experience of the great noble ones. Through samadhi one attains suppleness or malleability (Tib. *shin sbyangs*). The Sugata is the cause for [a noble one] to feel the blissful touch arising from this suppleness and to realize the mode of the Dharma, which is deep according to its own essence.

Therefore, when reflected upon in a very fine way by means of the intelligence analyzing the absolute, a sugata bestowing true bliss is similar to space. Like space he is devoid of any reasons that generate a fruit, and yet he generates all goodness for the disciples.

Here Rongtönpa explains in his own commentary:

> Since the Sanskrit term "buddhi" has two meanings, which are "non-arising" [i.e. karma, mental poisons, and self-attachment will never arise again] and "wielding power" (Tib. *dbang 'byor*), it is [literally] translated [in the root text] as "non-arising" (Tib. *'byung med*). Yet, as for the meaning it is better to translate it as "wielding power," having in view the point of its taking form, which is equivalent to wielding or being possessed of power.

(See also Part Three, annotation 59.)

B.II.2.2.2.2.3.3.2. Detailed explanation of the meaning
B.II.2.2.2.2.3.3.2.1. Explanation of the way the two benefits are accomplished, combined with their respective classification

In brief, [two kayas] are to be understood
as functions of the two primordial wisdoms:
the vimuktikaya [representing] perfection,
and the dharmakaya [representing] refinement.
Vimuktikaya and dharmakaya are to be known
in terms of two aspects and [a common] one,
as they are free from pollution and all-pervasive,
uncreated and thus embody the ground [of virtue].

Briefly speaking, the functioning of the two kayas is to be understood as the function of the two primordial wisdoms, which are present on the path of training during meditative equipoise and during the post-meditative phase, respectively.

During meditative equipoise one contemplates [the true nature] as it is [and thus gains correct knowledge]. Through this contemplation one perfectly attains final ultimate abandonment. This is equivalent to the vimuktikaya, the kaya in terms of being completely liberated from anything to be abandoned. During the post-meditative phase one trains oneself in an unperverted way with regard to the manner in which [anything relative], as much as there is, exists [and thus gains complete knowledge]. Through this training one fully refines final ultimate realization. This is equivalent to the dharmakaya.

In this context the kaya in terms of complete liberation from the veils and the dharmakaya, which is the support of primordial wisdom, are each to be known as having an individual aspect, namely the two aspects of freedom from pollution and all-pervasiveness, respectively. They are further to be known as having one [common] aspect in that they are both uncreated. This is because the vimuktikaya is free from even the slightest pollution and thus has [the aspect of abandonment], and the dharmakaya pervades all objects of knowledge without any remainder and thus has [the aspect of] realization. Their common aspect is due to the fact that they are both of a nature that is not created by causes and conditions. It is taught that these constitute the best possible benefit for oneself. Since they are the abode [of all virtue], of all unstained [lit. "white"] properties, they also provide the best possible benefit for others.

B.II.2.2.2.2.3.3.2.2. Particular explanation of the best possible benefit for oneself

> Since the mental poisons along with their remaining imprints
>   are ended,
> [the vimuktikaya] is free from any pollution.
> Since there is no attachment and obstruction,
> [the dharmakaya] is considered as pervasive primordial
>   wisdom.
> Being of a nature forever indestructible
> [neither kaya] is something that is created.
> While "indestructibility" is the [concise] explanation [of
>   uncreatedness],
> it is taught in more detail through [the topic] "steadfast" and
>   so forth.
> "Destructibility" is to be understood [in terms of] four aspects,
> since it constitutes the contrary of "steadfastness" and so on.
> These are decay, drastic change, being cut-off, and
>   transmigration,
> which is inconceivable [and] a transformation [in various] ways.
> Since [the vimuktikaya and dharmakaya] are free from these
>   [features],
> they are to be known as steadfast, peaceful, permanent, and
>   unchanging.

Since all the adventitious mental poisons along with their remaining imprints are ended, having been eliminated without exception at their very root, the vimuktikaya has the aspect of being free from any pollution. Likewise the dharmakaya is considered as having the aspect of pervading the full range of the knowable, as much as there is, by means of the realization of primordial wisdom. This is equivalent to correct and complete knowledge. Correct knowledge results from the fact that perverted perception has been exhausted; hence there is no attachment and fixation to objects. Since all aspects [of the relative world] have become apparent, there is no hindrance with regard to objects [of perception]. Thus there is complete knowledge. Furthermore, both kayas have the aspect of not being created by causes and conditions in their own right. For this reason they are of a nature that is forever indestructible, or in other words, unchanging. In this context their indestructibility is briefly explained by means of the reason of their uncreatedness. "Indestructibility" is then taught in detail through the four topics of steadfastness and so forth, the latter [three] being peace, permanence, and unchangingness.

Then, if these are analyzed from the viewpoint of their opposite sides, all created or composite things are found to be subject to four ways of destruction for the following reasons: Contrary to being steadfast they are not stable; contrary to being at peace they are unpeaceful; contrary to being permanent they are impermanent; and contrary to being unchanging they are subject to manifold changes.

One may wonder in what way they are mutable. Mutability has four aspects: Reaching the point when they are fully ripened, all compounded things become rotten and old; this is the process of aging, which is equivalent to putrefaction and decay. The elements undergo a total change; this is the aspect of sickness, which consists of suffering. The course of the previous existence is cut and the following one is achieved; this is the aspect of being born. Then there is the process of dying; this implies a change that is inconceivable and takes place in manifold ways.

Since with respect to the vimuktikaya and dharmakaya these four aspects of destruction are not present, in the same sequence they are to be considered as being the embodiment of steadfastness, peace, permanence, and immutability. (See also Part Three, annotation 60.)

B.II.2.2.2.2.3.3.2.3. Particular explanation of the best possible benefit for others

As absence of pollution and [primordial] wisdom are the
   support for the unstained properties
[to come forth in the disciples], they are [also] the abode [of the
   best possible benefit for others].
Space is not a cause, and yet the cause
for all visible things to be seen,
for sound, odor, flavor, touch,
and phenomena to be heard and so on.
Just so, they cause the unstained qualities

to arise as objects sensed by those
[whose vision is] stable by junction
with the unveiled [seeing of] the two kayas.

Thus these aspects of abandonment and realization, which are freedom from any pollution and primordial wisdom having revealed itself directly, are the support or ground for the outstanding qualities, for the unstained properties of virtue, to come forth within the disciples' streams of being in accordance with their respective karmic fortunes. For this reason they are also the abode of the best possible benefit of others.

This can be shown by means of an example: Space does not constitute a cause that brings about any generation, and is devoid of the characteristics of the visible and so forth. Yet it is still established as being a cause in that it provides the prerequisite and opportunity for visible things to be seen by the sense faculty of the eye, for sounds to be heard by the ear, and so on—which is to say, for odors to be smelled by the nose, for flavors to be tasted by the tongue, for touches to be felt by the body, and for phenomena to be thought by the mind. In the same way, [the aspects of abandonment and realization] act as a cause: Cultivating the path of junction, one becomes free from the veils that prevent one from seeing the two buddhakayas. Through the cultivation of this path one's understanding is profound and stable. The six sense-faculties of heirs of the Victorious One who are endowed with karmic fortune have become supreme by means of [this cultivation]. Thus their object of perception or field of experience is the dharmakaya and the visible kayas. By the power of seeing the visible kayas, and so forth, the unpolluted qualities—such as the marks, signs, and so on—arise on the relative level. From seeing the dharmakaya, and so forth, the numberless unstained qualities—such as the powers, fearlessnesses, and so on—will reveal themselves directly on the absolute level. The cause for the arising [of these qualities] is [joint] abandonment and realization.

B.II.2.2.2.2.3.4. Detailed explanation of endowment
B.II.2.2.2.2.3.4.1. Concise explanation through listing the names [of the qualities]

Buddhahood is inconceivable, permanent, steadfast, at peace,
and immutable.
It is utterly peaceful, pervasive, without thought, and unattached like space.

It is free from hindrance and coarse objects of contact are
eliminated.
It cannot be seen or grasped. It is virtuous and free from
pollution.

Buddhahood, which is equivalent to the attainment of great enlightenment, is endowed with fifteen ultimate qualities, listed [below]:

(1) It cannot be conceived by means of study and so on.
(2) Being free from birth it is permanent.
(3) Being free from aging it is steadfast.
(4) Being free from sickness it is at peace.
(5) Being free from death it is immutable.
(6) Being free from suffering it is utterly peaceful.
(7) Due to complete understanding it pervades the knowable.
(8) Due to correct understanding it is free from thought.
(9) The veil of the mental poisons having been abandoned, it is
without any attachment, like space.
(10) The veil of the obstructions to knowledge having been abandoned, it is at all times free from any hindrance with regard
to all objects [of perception].
(11) The veil of the obstructions to meditative equipoise having
been abandoned, coarse objects of contact are eliminated. (See
also Part Three, annotation 61.)
(12) Being free from the features of the visible it cannot be seen.
(13) Being free from characteristics it cannot be grasped.
(14) Being by nature pure it is virtuous.
(15) Being purified from the adventitious stains it is free from
pollution.

B.II.2.2.2.2.3.4.2. Detailed explanation of the meaning [of the qualities]
B.II.2.2.2.2.3.4.2.1. Concise explanation of who is endowed with qualities

As was explained, the vimuktikaya and the dharmakaya
[accomplish] benefit for oneself and benefit for others.
These [kayas], being the support of this twofold benefit,
possess the qualities of being inconceivable and so forth.

As has been explained already, the vimuktikaya and the dharmakaya, which embody abandonment and realization, accomplish the
best possible benefits for oneself and others. This is because complete
liberation from all the fetters of anything to be abandoned is the
achievement of personal benefit, and the activity [unfolding] on the
support of the qualities of the dharmakaya, which is equivalent to

realization, accomplishes the benefit of others. These two kayas thus forming the support of this twofold benefit for oneself and others are to be known as possessing the fifteen qualities or properties of being inconceivable and so forth.

B.II.2.2.2.2.3.4.2.2. Definition of the qualities that constitute endowment
B.II.2.2.2.2.3.4.2.2.1. Detailed explanation of the reason why they are deep
B.II.2.2.2.2.3.4.2.2.1.1. General explanation of the way they are inconceivable

> **Being the object of the omniscient primordial wisdom,**
> **buddhahood is not an object for the three types of insight.**
> **So even those with a wisdom body must realize**
> **that [buddha enlightenment] is inconceivable.**

The enlightenment of a buddha is exclusively the object of perception of the omniscient primordial wisdom. As such it is not an object or field of experience for the three types of discriminative wisdom, which result from study and so forth. For this reason it is said:

> Those beings who are different from a buddha must realize that the ultimate kaya of primordial wisdom possesses the quality of being inconceivable, in that it cannot be conceived just as it is by saying: It is this!

Or else:

> All the noble ones below those who have a wisdom body must realize that it is inconceivable.

(See also Part Three, annotation 62.)

B.II.2.2.2.2.3.4.2.2.1.2. Detailed explanation of the specifics

> **Being subtle it is not an object for study.**
> **Being absolute it cannot be reflected upon.**
> **Dharmata is deep. Hence it is not an object**
> **for any worldly meditation and so on.**

Since the absolute Buddha is extremely subtle and difficult to realize, it is not an object of experience [for] the discriminative wisdom resulting from study. Likewise it is not an object of the discriminative wisdom resulting from reflection, since the ultimate truth must be realized through self-aware primordial wisdom. Since suchness or the dharmata is deep and hard to explore, it is not an object of experience of any type of consciousness that consists of a discriminative wisdom resulting from worldly meditation, and so forth [i.e., this is the first quality]. (See also Part Three, annotation 63.)

B.II.2.2.2.2.3.4.2.2.1.3. Combination of the reasons with an example

Why [is it hard to realize]? Like the blind with regard
to the visible, the children have never seen it before.
Even noble ones [see it] as babies [would glimpse]
the sun from within the house where they are born.

One may wonder for what reason it is so difficult to realize. This is because the children, all ordinary beings, are like people blind from birth who have not seen the various aspects of the visible at all, ever before [in their lives]. Similar to the example, all children without exception have never before seen unpolluted suchness directly, not even to the slightest extent. And even those noble heirs of the Victorious One who dwell on the tenth bodhisattva level are like newborn children who faintly glimpse the light rays of the orb of the sun from within the house where they were born, but are not able to view it fully and perfectly. They see the dharmakaya directly to a small extent but are not able to apprehend it immediately in its full perfection.

B.II.2.2.2.2.3.4.2.2.2. Explanation of the reason for the next [fourteen qualities]
B.II.2.2.2.2.3.4.2.2.2.1. The qualities of being unchanging

Since it is free from being born, it is permanent.
Since it is without cessation, it is steadfast.
Since these two are not present, it is peaceful.
It is immutable, for the dharmata [ever] remains.

Because this unpolluted buddha has been free from being born [or coming into existence] due to causes and conditions since beginningless time, it has the quality of being permanent (2). Because something that has not come into existence [will not end and thus] is without cessation, it has the quality of being steadfast (3). Because it is not disturbed and made restless through the two aspects of birth and cessation, this buddha has the quality of being peaceful (4). As such it has the quality of being immutable (5). The reason is that the dharmata, the true state of everything, which is by nature nirvana, beyond any torment, is unchangingness itself and has remained since beginningless time.

B.II.2.2.2.2.3.4.2.2.2.2. The qualities of abandonment and realization

It is utter peace, since the truth of cessation [is revealed].
Since everything is realized, it pervades [all the knowable].
Since it does not dwell upon anything, it is without ideation.

> Since the mental poisons are eliminated, it has no attachment.
> Since the veil of the hindrances to knowledge is cleansed,
> it is in all ways unobstructed [with regard to complete insight].
> Being free from its two [obstacles], it is suited for [samadhi]
> and thus relieved from the touch of coarse objects of contact.

The enlightenment of a buddha has the quality of great bliss, all suffering being utterly pacified (6). This is because the final ultimate truth of cessation is revealed directly, as everything to be abandoned has been ended without any exception. Likewise all aspects of the knowable are immediately realized. For this reason it has the quality of pervading the full range of whatever is to be known. This is equivalent to complete insight (7). Since it does not dwell upon any focus or characteristic whatsoever, it has the quality of being without ideation. This is equivalent to correct insight (8). These two aspects are the particularities in terms of realization and bliss.

Since the veil of the mental poisons, which constitutes the obstruction to liberating other beings, is eliminated along with its remaining imprints, it possesses the quality of having no attachment to the field of correct insight (9). Since all the veils of the hindrances to knowledge, which constitute the obstruction to omniscience, are totally purified without any exception, it has the quality of being unobstructed in all ways with regard to the field of complete insight (10). Being free from the veil of meditative equipoise, which consists of the two [obstacles] of agitation (Tib. *rgod*) and dullness (Tib. *bying*), and so on, body and mind are smooth [and malleable] and thus suited for samadhi. For this reason it has the quality of being relieved of meeting any sensation of coarse objects of contact (11).

B.II.2.2.2.2.3.4.2.2.2.3. The qualities of purity and purification

> Since it is not something visible, it cannot be seen.
> Since it is free from features, it cannot be grasped.
> It is virtuous, [the dharmadhatu] being by nature pure,
> and it is free from stains, since pollution is abandoned.

Since enlightenment is not something visible that consists of a gathering of subtle particles, and since it is totally beyond all conditioned phenomena, it cannot be seen by means of the ordinary sense-faculty (12). Since it is free from features in terms of the conceptual elaboration of signs, definitions, and so forth, and since it is totally beyond all phenomena of consciousness, it cannot be grasped by the ordinary intellect (13). It has the quality of ultimate virtue, since it embraces the dharmadhatu, which is by nature utterly pure (14). It has the quality of being extremely stainless, since all the adventitious pollutions along with their remaining imprints have been abandoned without any exception and it is in consequence totally purified (15).

B.II.2.2.2.2.3.5. Detailed explanation of its manifestation
B.II.2.2.2.2.3.5.1. Concise explanation through listing the characteristics
B.II.2.2.2.2.3.5.1.1. Explanation of who realizes the essence

What is the nature of dharmadhatu? It is without beginning, middle, and end.
It is totally indivisible and far away from the two [extremes], rid of the three [veils], unpolluted, and not an object of thought.
Its realization is the vision of a Yogi who Dwells in Meditative Equipoise.

What is the nature of the dharmadhatu? It possesses five characteristics: It is without coming into existence in a beginning, without abiding during an intermediate phase, and without ceasing at an end. Thus there is the characteristic of being uncreated (1). Spaciousness and awareness cannot be split into different things at all. Thus there is the characteristic of being indivisible (2). It does not dwell in the two extremes of assertion and denial. Thus there is the characteristic of being unperverted (3). It is free from the three veils. Thus there is the characteristic of being totally purified (4). It is by nature free from any pollution and does not constitute an object for the thoughts of a reasoner. Thus there is the characteristic of clear light (5). The direct realization of the dharmadhatu possessing these five characteristics is the realization of the dharmakaya. This is seen as it is by a tathagata. It is the vision of a Yogi who Dwells in Meditative Equipoise in such a way that he never rises from the dharmata, the true state of everything. (See also Part Three, annotation 64.)

B.II.2.2.2.2.3.5.1.2. Concise explanation of the particularity of the dharmakaya

The unpolluted sphere of a tathagata possesses the [four] qualities [of realization].
It cannot be fathomed and [in number] is beyond the grains of sand in the river Ganges.
It is inconceivable and peerless and there is furthermore elimination of all faults along with their remaining traces.

This unpolluted sphere of a tathagata, which is the dharmakaya, has the four qualities of best possible realization: It cannot be fathomed in terms of any measure (1). [Its virtues are] countless, their number being beyond that of the grains of sand in the river Ganges, as many as there may be (2). Due to its depth it is inconceivable (3), and it is peerless, unequaled by anything else (4). Furthermore there is the quality of best possible abandonment (5), since the faults of the two veils along with their remaining imprints have been eliminated without exception. The dharmakaya is therefore to be understood in terms of possessing five qualities.

B.II.2.2.2.2.3.5.1.3. Concise explanation of the particularity of the sambhogakaya

> Through various aspects of the sacred Dharma, through bodies shot with light rays,
> and through its readiness to accomplish the task of the total liberation of beings,
> its deeds resemble the activity of a king of wish-fulfilling jewels.
> [It appears as] a variety of things, yet is not of the nature of these.

The sambhogakaya has five qualities or particular properties: It has mastery over teaching the various aspects of the sacred Dharma, demonstrating its deep and its vast aspects. Thus the flow of pure speech is uninterrupted (1). It shows itself in various appearances through bodies endowed with the light rays of the signs and marks. Thus the flow of displaying pure physical form is uninterrupted (2). There is [constant] readiness to accomplish the task of totally liberating the disciples' streams of being. Thus the flow of pure mental activity is uninterrupted (3). Acting without any deliberate effort, spontaneously and without thought, its deeds resemble the activity of a king of wish-fulfilling jewels (4). It appears to the disciples as a variety of things, and yet demonstrates at the same time that it is not of the nature or essence of these (5).

B.II.2.2.2.2.3.5.1.4. Concise explanation of the particularity of the nirmanakaya

> [The nirmanakaya persuades] the worldly beings to enter the path towards peace.
> He fully matures them and, granting prophecy, [becomes] the cause [of their release].

> These form [kayas] remain forever in this [world]
> like the realm of form within the realm of space.

First the nirmanakaya persuades the worldly beings to enter the path towards the nirvana which is peace (1). Thereupon during an intermediate period he leads them to reach full maturation on the path of the Great Vehicle (2). Finally he becomes the cause of their liberation and release through granting them prophecy with regard to their enlightenment (3). The visible kayas endowed with these three particular properties are the nirmanakayas, which appear in various ways. They remain forever in this world as long as samsara lasts. This is because they dwell uninterruptedly within the dharmadhatu just as, for example, the inanimate and animate constituents (Tib. *snod bcud,* lit. "vessel and content") of the realms of desire and form dwell within the realm of space. (See also Part Three, annotation 65.)

B.II.2.2.2.2.3.5.2. Detailed explanation of their meaning
B.II.2.2.2.2.3.5.2.1. Common classification

> The Omniscience of All the Self-Sprung Ones is given
> the name of "Buddhahood." Its meaning is [also termed]:
> "Most Supremely Beyond Torment," "The Inconceivable,"
> "Foe-Vanquisher," and "Quintessence of Self-Awareness."
> When these are categorized, they can be fully divided
> into [three] properties, which are the qualities of depth,
> vastness, and greatness, or the nature [kaya] and so on.
> [The benefits] are fulfilled through these three kayas.

Great enlightenment is self-sprung (Tib. *rang byung*) (1) in that it does not depend upon extraneous conditions. The Self-Sprung Ones [who have reached great enlightenment] are omniscient (2); they know all aspects of the knowable (Tib. *shes bya thams cad mkhyen pa*) and thus possess primordial wisdom. With respect to their having primordial wisdom, there are the aspects of best possible abandonment and realization. From the viewpoint of there being these aspects, the Omniscience of the Self-Sprung Ones is called Buddhahood (Tib. *sangs rgyas nyid*) [*sangs rgyas* means "awakened and expanded" and is explained as "awakened from the sleep of ignorance and expanded with regard to the knowable," this being equivalent to the aspects of abandonment and realization, or correct and complete insight] (3). What this expresses is also called Supremely Beyond Torment, or Highest Nirvana (Tib. *mchog tu mnya ngan las 'das*) (4), since great enlightenment does not abide within the two extremes of existence and peace. It is called The Inconceivable (Tib. *bsam du med pa*) (5), since it is beyond any object of experience of reasoning and argumentation. It is the Foe-Vanquisher or arhat (Tib. *dgra bcom pa*) (6), since it has gained victory over the objects of samsara [having vanquished all enemies, which are karma and the mental poisons]. It has become the Quintessence of Self-Awareness (Tib. *so so rang gis rig pa'i bdag nyid*) (7).

When great enlightenment expressed by means of these seven synonymous names is categorized, it can be fully divided into three properties, which are the qualities of depth, vastness, and greatness. It is deep since it is difficult to realize. It is vast since it wields power, and it is the embodiment of greatness since it corresponds to any karmic fortune. In the same sequence there are therefore three kayas: the svabhavikakaya, the kaya of the nature or essence that is deep, and so forth. "And so forth" refers to the sambhogakaya, which is vast, and to the nirmanakaya, which is the embodiment of greatness. Through these three kayas benefit for oneself and others is achieved spontaneously and without interruption. (See also Part Three, annotation 66.)

B.II.2.2.2.2.3.5.2.2. Presentation of each individually
B.II.2.2.2.2.3.5.2.2.1. Presentation of the dharmakaya or svabhavikakaya
B.II.2.2.2.2.3.5.2.2.1.1. Concise explanation of the qualities and characteristics

Of these, the svabhavikakaya
of the buddhas is to be known
as having five characteristics
and, if condensed, five qualities:

In this way ultimate enlightenment is classified in terms of three kayas. Of these the svabhavikakaya, or essence kaya of all buddhas, which constitutes best possible benefit for oneself, has five particularities or characteristics. These are the characteristics of being uncreated and so forth. The number of its qualities is extremely great. Yet, when these are summarized and put briefly, it is to be known as having five types of qualities that are indivisibly native to it. These are the qualities of being unfathomable and so forth.

B.II.2.2.2.2.3.5.2.2.1.2. Detailed explanation of their essence
B.II.2.2.2.2.3.5.2.2.1.2.1. Explanation of the five characteristics

It is uncreated and totally indivisible.
The two extremes are completely abandoned.
It is definitively freed from the three veils—
the mental poisons and the obstructions

> to knowledge and meditative equipoise.
> It is unpolluted and not an [object of] thought.
> Being the field of the yogis and the dharmadhatu,
> being by essence pure, it is luminous clarity.

The svabhavikakaya, which constitutes the ultimate [kaya], has the following five particular characteristics:

(1) It is uncreated and totally indivisible. It is uncreated since it is far away from the aspects of arising, abiding, and disintegration, which are the properties of anything compounded, that is, created [by causes and conditions]. And it is totally indivisible since the unpolluted dharmadhatu and final ultimate primordial wisdom are entirely mixed into one.

(2) The two extremes of eternalism and nihilism are completely abandoned, eternalism being equivalent to an exaggerative [view in that existence is asserted where it is not present] and nihilism being equivalent to a depreciating [view in that existence is denied where it is present].

(3) It is definitively freed from the three veils, which are the veil of the mental poisons, the veil of the obstructions to knowledge, and the veil of the obstructions to meditative equipoise. The first-mentioned veil consists of avarice and so forth. The second-mentioned veil does not contain any mental poisons but constitutes the obstacle that hinders one from understanding the knowable. The third-mentioned veil is a particular aspect of the veil of the obstructions to knowledge. It consists of not knowing how to rest evenly in meditative equipoise just as one wishes. Freedom from these [three] constitutes the characteristics of being free from the veils or obscurations.

(4) It is free from the pollution of the mental poisons and is not an object or field of experience for any thought or conceptualization.

(5) It is the field of experience of the self-aware primordial wisdom of those ultimate yogis who always rest evenly in the meditative equipoise in which means and discriminative wisdom are in union. The deep dharmadhatu has been by essence utterly pure since beginningless time. For these reasons it has the characteristic of being by nature luminous clarity. (See also Part Three, annotation 67.)

B.II.2.2.2.2.3.5.2.2.1.2.2. Explanation of the five qualities

> The svabhavikakaya truly has
> the final and ultimate qualities
> of being unfathomable, countless,
> inconceivable, unequaled, and pure.

> Since it is vast, not to be numbered,
> not an object of reasoning, and unique,
> and since the remaining traces are eliminated,
> it is in the same order unfathomable and so on.

The svabhavikakaya possesses the following five final and ultimate qualities: It cannot be fathomed or evaluated by means of signs and marks (1). It cannot be expressed by means of numbers (2). It cannot be conceived by means of the intellect (3). It is not equaled by anything else (4). It is utterly pure (5).

When [viewed] in true perspective the svabhavikakaya and its five qualities are indivisible. There are five reasons: Its essence is vast like space (1). One cannot pinpoint it in any way saying: "This is its number!" (2). It is in no way and no respect an object or field for reasoning, argumentation, or dialectics (3). It is a unique quality in that only a buddha embraces it (4). The two veils along with their remaining imprints are eliminated without exception (5).

Therefore the qualities of being unfathomable and so forth are to be understood in the same sequence in combination with the five reasons of being vast and so on.

B.II.2.2.2.2.2.3.5.2.2.2. Presentation of the sambhogakaya
B.II.2.2.2.2.2.3.5.2.2.2.1. Detailed explanation of the presentation

> It perfectly enjoys the various aspects of Dharma
> and appears [in the form] of natural qualities.
> Corresponding to the pure cause of its compassion,
> the benefit of sentient beings is uninterrupted.
> Totally without any thought and spontaneously
> it wholly grants all wishes exactly as they are
> by miraculous powers, like a wish-fulfilling gem.
> It therefore fully abides in Perfect Enjoyment.

The sambhogakaya (Tib. *longs spyod rdzogs pa'i sku*, "the kaya of perfect enjoyment") has the following five [particular qualities]:

(1) It perfectly enjoys the wealth of the various aspects of the Mahayana Dharma in its features of depth and vastness, [of teaching the ultimate and the relative truth].

(2) To the pure among the disciples it always appears in the form of natural qualities adorned with signs and marks that are not just illusory.

(3) Uninterruptedly it brings about the benefit of all sentient beings. [This activity] constitutes the fruit that corresponds to its pure and immaculate cause, which is great compassion.

(4) Its activity manifests spontaneously, totally without thought and deliberate effort. By means of this activity it grants all wishes of the disciples just as they are and thus wholly fulfils any of their expectations and hopes.

(5) Due to the surface underneath it, a wish-fulfilling gem appears in various colors, but does not exist as the essence of these. Likewise, due to [different wishes and needs of] the disciples, the sambhoga-kaya manifests in perfect play by means of various miraculous powers, but does not exist as the essence of these [manifestations].

Thus it possesses five particularities. Through the manner in which it is endowed with these it fully abides as the Kaya of Perfect Enjoyment of the Mahayana Dharma.

B.II.2.2.2.2.3.5.2.2.2.2. The five properties taught in summarized form

Since the stream of verbal expression, display [of form],
and action [of mind] is uninterrupted and not a product,
and since it shows that it is not of the essence of these,
it is taught here in five aspects, as "various" and so on.

The clear verbal expression of instruction, which is the action of speech, the display of physical appearance, which is the action of the body, and mental activity, which is the action of mind, are an uninterrupted stream (1-3). These three types of action are spontaneous and are not the products of deliberate effort (4). Due to the power of [the disciples'] karmic fortunes it appears in various ways, but at the same time shows that it is not of the essence of these (5). With respect to these five properties it is taught here in this chapter, which explains the sambhogakaya, in terms of five particularities. These are [enjoyment of the] variety [of Dharma], and so on.

B.II.2.2.2.2.3.5.2.2.2.3. The way it appears due to conditions

Due to the various colors [of its background] a gem appears [in manifold colors],
[but] is not a thing fulfilling their function.
Likewise the All-Pervasive [Ones] appear due to the manifold conditions [set by beings]
without being a thing fulfilling their function.

Due to the condition provided by the various hues of the colorful cotton forming its background, a precious wish-fulfilling gem lying upon it appears, because of its brilliant transparence, in manifold [colors], though it is not a thing fulfilling their function. Likewise, as shown by this example, perfect buddhas who are the embodiment of great compassion, pervading all sentient beings (Tib. *skye dgu*) by means of it, appear in a totally illusory manifestation of color, size, and so forth. They do so due to the condition set by the beings who are to be trained, reflecting their [different] temperaments, wishes, aspirations, and so forth, though they are not a thing fulfilling the function of these [conditions].

B.II.2.2.2.2.3.5.2.2.3. Presentation of the nirmanakaya
B.II.2.2.2.2.3.5.2.2.3.1. The way the twelve deeds of the supreme nirmanakaya
are demonstrated

> [The Supreme Nirmanakaya] knows the world and having
>   gazed upon
> all worldly [beings demonstrates] out of his great compassion
> [twelve wondrous deeds]. Without moving away from the
>   dharmakaya
> he manifests through various [aspects] of an illusory nature.
> Having [first] been born spontaneously in a [divine] existence
> he then leaves the realm of Tushita and passes [into this
>   world].
> He enters [his mother's] womb, takes birth, and gains perfect
>   skill,
> mastering all the various fields of handicraft, science, and art.
> He mirthfully enjoys amusement among his spouse and her
>   retinue.
> Feeling weariness and renunciation he practices as an ascetic.
> Then he goes to Awakening's Heart and defeats the hosts of
>   Mara.
> [He finds] perfect enlightenment and turns the wheel of
>   Dharma.
> He passes into nirvana [the state beyond any torment and
>   pain].
> Within all the [endless] fields totally infested with impurity
> he shows these deeds as long as [beings] abide in existence.

When the phrase "[he] shows or demonstrates" is to be put down to a basis of explanation, [one might wonder]:

(a) For what reason does [the Supreme Nirmanakaya] demonstrate activity? The reason is that out of his inconceivable great compassion towards all sentient beings beyond end in number, he wishes to take them in his protection and care.

(b) In what way does he demonstrate it? By means of his primordial wisdom, which knows all the realms of the world, as many as there are, he thoroughly gazes upon and beholds all worldly beings who are to become his disciples, without exception. Resting evenly within the unchanging sphere of the dharmakaya, within the primordial wisdom that knows correctly, he thereupon [demonstrates activity] without in any way moving away from his resting in this meditative equipoise. (See also Part Three, annotation 68.)

(c) What does he demonstrate? By means of various aspects that are of an illusory nature he truly and perfectly demonstrates twelve sublimely wondrous deeds. This can be illustrated by the way in which the King of the Shakyas [Buddha Shakyamuni] acted. The basis of his activity was such that this great being was first born spontaneously in a divine existence as "Dampa Tog Karpo" in the realm of Tushita. Having led the extremely vast assembly of gods to maturity and liberation he left the realm of Tushita and passed into the world of Zambuling, this being the first of his twelve deeds. He entered the womb of his pure mother (2) and took birth from her womb (3). He gained perfect skill, mastering all the various fields of handicraft, science, and art (4). He mirthfully enjoyed amusement in the surrounding of his spouse and her retinue (5). Experiencing weariness and renunciation he left the palace where he dwelt with his queen (6) and trained himself severely as an ascetic (7). He went to Bodhgaya, "the Heart of Enlightenment," and entered the Vajra Seat (8). Through the might of his love he overcame all the classes of Maras along with their host [of evil forces] (9), and found great enlightenment, awakening directly and perfectly (10). He turned the Wheel of Dharma in three stages (11) and went into nirvana, the state beyond any torment and pain (12).

(d) Where does he demonstrate [these deeds]? Within all the endless fields totally infested with impurity, the realms of the world and so forth [stricken by unbearable suffering].

(e) How long does he demonstrate them? As long as a [single] disciple still abides in samsaric existence he demonstrates them, spontaneously and without interruption.

B.II.2.2.2.2.3.5.2.2.3.2. The way the disciples are gradually guided, this being the function of the [twelve deeds]
B.II.2.2.2.2.3.5.2.2.3.2.1. The way the ordinary beings are guided to enter the lesser vehicles

> **With the words "impermanent," "suffering," "selfless," and**
>   **"peace"**
> **[the Buddhas] who know all means persuade sentient beings**
> **to generate weariness with the three realms of existence**
> **and to fully enter into the state beyond torment and pain.**

"Everything compounded is impermanent. Everything bound up with pollution is suffering. All phenomena are devoid of self-entity. Nirvana is supremely in peace and comfort." With these words and so forth, which expound the Great Bonds (Tib. *sdom chen po*) or guiding principles of Dharma summarizing all the teachings, the buddhas who know the methods to tame the disciples address sentient beings who are to be tamed.

To those who are attached to and hold on to samsara they describe extensively and in manifold ways what a great punishment and ordeal the three realms of existence actually are. [By means of these teachings] they incite them to generate weariness with and renouncement of cyclic existence. They persuade them to find access to and fully follow either of the paths of the shravakas or the pratyekabuddhas. Thus they cause [those beings clinging to existence] to first enter, for a little while, the state beyond torment and pain (Skt. *nirvāṇa*), which is [mere] peace in that only the faults of samsara are most closely pacified.

B.II.2.2.2.2.3.5.2.2.3.2.2. The way those following the lesser vehicles are ripened by means of the Mahayana

> Those who have perfectly followed the path of peace
> believe that they have attained the state of nirvana.
> By the *White Lotus of Dharma Sutra* and similar aspects
> of his sacred teaching he explains the nature of phenomena.
> Thus he causes them to refrain from their former belief,
> to fully adopt skillful means and discriminative wisdom,
> and gain maturity on the [path of the] supreme vehicle.

The shravaka and pratyekabuddha paths constitute the means through which one gains peace for oneself, totally pacifying the suffering of samsara. Those who have perfectly followed these paths have attained arhathood or self-enlightenment, respectively. When this is achieved, they hold the belief that they have attained nirvana, though they have not yet reached the final ultimate state. To those arhats [the Buddha] teaches the *White Lotus of Dharma Sutra* (Skt. *Saddharmapuṇḍarīkasūtra*), the *Mahaparinirvanasutra*, and similar aspects of the sacred Dharma, where it is said:

> There is only one vehicle that illustrates the actual nature of all phenomena, this being the union of emptiness and compassion. Hence there is also only one nirvana, and this results from having traveled this path.

Through these teachings he causes the shravakas and pratyeka-buddhas to turn away from the notion that they have attained ultimate enlightenment, though this is not yet the case. He persuades them to rely on the [appropriate] means and on the discriminative wisdom through which one realizes all phenomena as being emptiness. The appropriate means is great compassion, which consists of the wish to lead all sentient beings to liberation. Thus he causes them to fully adopt and gather the two accumulations of merit and primordial wisdom, and leads them to gain maturity in the course of the Mahayana, which is supreme, being the highest of the three vehicles. In this way he guides them onto the truly authentic path. (See also Part Three, annotation 69.)

B.II.2.2.2.2.3.5.2.2.3.2.3. The way those following the Great Vehicle are joined with complete liberation

Then he grants them prophecy of their supreme enlightenment.

Thus having led [the shravakas and pratyekabuddhas] to gradually gain maturity on the path of the Great Vehicle, they attain the eighth bodhisattva level and the levels above. [Then] he grants them prophecy regarding their futures as unsurpassable Kings of Dharma whose enlightenment, constituting total release, is supreme among the three types of enlightenment. [He foretells the details] as it is stated in the *Mahayanasutralamkara* (Tib. *mdo sde rgyan*):

> Furthermore the buddhafield and the name, the time [to appear] and the name of the eon, the retinue as well as the sacred teachings. Abiding in this nature he is asserted as such...,

and so forth.

B.II.2.2.2.2.3.5.2.3. Summary of their meaning
B.II.2.2.2.2.3.5.2.3.1. Summary into three [kayas] with reference to reasons

Since [these kayas] constitute depth, best possible power,
and supreme guidance in tune with the aims of the children,
they should be known in accordance with this number
as being deep, vast, and the embodiment of greatness.

Since it is subtle and difficult to realize, it constitutes depth. It possesses the best possible power to accomplish the benefit of others. Since he teaches the children or ordinary beings in a way that is in tune with their wishes and aims, he constitutes supreme guidance in the cycle of existence. For these reasons these three kayas should be known, when referred to in accordance with the number [of reasons], as the deep svabhavikakaya, the vast sambhogakaya, and the nirmanakaya embodying greatness.

B.II.2.2.2.2.3.5.2.3.2. Summary into two [kayas] with reference to the way they are

> Here the first is the dharmakaya,
> and the latter are the form kayas.
> As the visible abides in space,
> the latter abide in the first.

Here in this chapter explaining the buddhakayas, the first kaya, the kaya constituting depth, is to be understood as being the dharmakaya [the kaya in terms of nature], since it is equivalent to the nature of all phenomena and since it is not a field of experience for an other-aware cognition (Tib. *gzhan rig*). The latter two kayas, these being the sambhogakaya and the nirmanakaya, are the form kayas or visible kayas (Skt. *rūpa kāya*, Tib. *gzugs sku*), since they appear to the disciples in tune with their respective karmic fortunes.

Taking an example, [the relationship between] these [kayas should] also [be understood as follows]: All the various compounded visible things abide within the uncompounded sphere of space. In the same way, the latter-mentioned form kayas, which appear in various ways, abide in the unchanging sphere of the first-mentioned dharmakaya.

B.II.2.2.2.2.3.6. Detailed explanation of its permanence
B.II.2.2.2.2.3.6.1. Concise explanation of the reason

> There is permanence [since] the causes are endless and
> sentient beings inexhaustible [in number].
> They have compassionate love, miraculous power, knowledge,
> and utter [bliss].
> They are masters of [all] qualities. The demon of death has
> been vanquished.
> Being not of the essence [of the compounded] it is the [true]
> protector of all worldly [beings].

In brief these three kayas of a tathagata are permanent for ten reasons:
There are seven reasons why with regard to the visible kayas the accomplishment of the benefit of others is always permanent:

(1) The causes, which consist of the two accumulations and so forth, are endless.
(2) There is no end to exhausting the number of sentient beings to be trained.
(3) There is uninterruptedness through great compassionate love.
(4) Mastery is gained on the support of miraculous powers.
(5) There is knowledge [seeing] the oneness of samsara and nirvana.

(6) They possess utter bliss, free from any pollution.

(7) They are the masters of all qualities or properties.

There are three reasons why the dharmakaya is permanent, since it is unchanging:

(1) The demon of the Lord of Death has been vanquished.

(2) It is not of the essence of whatever is compounded.

(3) It proves to be the protector and refuge of all worldly beings.

B.II.2.2.2.2.3.6.2. Detailed explanation of its meaning
B.II.2.2.2.2.3.6.2.1. The seven reasons why the visible kayas are permanent

> Having offered bodies, lives, and goods
> they [purely] uphold the sacred Dharma.
> In order to benefit all sentient beings
> they fulfill their vow as initially taken.
> Buddhahood supremely expresses itself
> as compassion both cleansed and purified.
> Appearing on the feet of miraculous powers
> they [can] act forever by means of these.
> By knowledge they are freed from the belief
> fixed on the duality of samsara and nirvana.
> They always possess the best possible bliss
> of samadhi, beyond ideation [and end].
> While acting in the world [for other's good]
> they are unsullied by all worldly phenomena.

There are four reasons why the visible kayas of a buddha stay in samsara for the benefit of the other beings:

(1) Having offered their bodies, lives, and goods throughout three countless kalpas they uphold the sacred Dharma as comprised by the two accumulations.

Then one may wonder: "So all causes beyond end are complete. But is there also a necessity [to stay]?" (2) There is the necessity to always stay for the benefit of others due to the following reason: When they initially generated bodhichitta in order to benefit all sentient beings, they vowed to free all disciples without any exception from the cycle of existence. There is the necessity to fulfill this vow to its full extent. [Thus they will stay permanently] since the number of disciples is inexhaustible.

Then one may wonder: "So there is necessity, but is there also such a noble wish?" (3) There is the wish to accomplish the benefit of all others, since buddhahood supremely expresses itself as great compassion, cleansed of karma and mental poisons and purified from the veil of the hindrances to knowledge.

Then one may wonder: "So there is the wish to accomplish the benefit of others, but is it not satiated and exhausted by rendering benefit in the course of one lifetime?" (4) There is the ability to always stay for the sake of others. The reason is that they possess ability provided by the support [lit. "feet"] of miraculous powers, on the basis of which the appearance of the visible kayas is displayed. Through these miraculous powers they have the ability to act forever, as long as samsara may last.

There are three reasons why they do not forsake the world:

"So there is permanent abiding for the sake of others. But will there not be an urge to leave samsara, there being the view of samsara and nirvana being different in that samsara is considered as something to be abandoned, whereas nirvana should be adopted?"

(1) They do not have any notion of abandoning and adopting with respect to samsara and nirvana. This is because they know the nature of all objects of knowledge just as it is, they know the way they are. By this knowledge they are freed from the belief that is fixed on the duality of samsara and nirvana, wherein samsara is viewed as being something to be abandoned, while nirvana is viewed as being something to be adopted.

"When they abide in samsara, are they not harmed by the suffering experienced in the cycle of existence?"

(2) They are not harmed, since they always possess the best possible bliss of samadhi, which is inconceivable and beyond any end.

"So they are not harmed by suffering, but are they not affected by its faults?"

(3) It is impossible for them to be harmed by the faults of samsara for the following reason: When they act within the world for the sake of others, they are not sullied by worldly phenomena such as karma, mental poisons, suffering, and so forth.

B.II.2.2.2.2.3.6.2.2. Explanation of the three reasons why the dharmakaya is permanent

Free from dying, it is the attainment of peace.
In this sphere the demon of death cannot roam.
The state of the Muni being of uncreated nature
has been fully pacified since beginningless time.
For all those who are bereft of permanent shelter
it provides the most delightful refuge, and so on.

There are three reasons why buddha dharmakaya is permanent and unchanging:

(1) Since it is free from transmigration and change in that it does not die, the attainment of the dharmakaya is the abode of peace. Within this sphere the demon of the Lord of Death cannot roam.

(2) The dharmakaya of the Muni has a nature not created by causes and conditions. As such it is fully pacified, not having undergone birth, death, and so on, since beginningless time.

(3) For all those shelterless sentient beings endless in number it is the final and ultimate refuge, the most delightful protector, guardian-friend, and so on.

B.II.2.2.2.2.3.6.3. Summary of its general meaning

The first seven reasons clarify
the permanence of the form kayas,
while the latter three illustrate
why the dharmakaya lasts forever.

Through the first seven reasons, that is, "the causes are endless" and so forth, the visible kayas are clarified and taught as being permanent, in that there is uninterruptedness in always [bringing about] the benefit of others. Through the latter three reasons, that is, "The demon of death has been vanquished" and so on, buddha dharmakaya is illustrated and taught as permanence in the sense of being unchanging.

Thus these are also explained in the *Mahayanasutralamkara* (Tib. *mdo sde rgyan*): "Their permanence is that of nature, of uninterruptedness, and of continuity." This is to say that the dharmakaya is permanent in terms of its nature, the sambhogakaya is permanent in terms of its being uninterrupted, and the nirmanakaya is permanent in terms of its being continuous. (See also Part Three, annotation 70.)

B.II.2.2.2.2.3.7. Detailed explanation of inconceivability
B.II.2.2.2.2.3.7.1. Concise illustration of the way it is inconceivable

It is not an object of speech and is embraced by the absolute.
It is not a field for ideation and is beyond any example,
unexcelled and not embraced by existence and peace.
Even the noble cannot conceive the sphere of the Victor.

This great enlightenment, which is equivalent to suchness free from any pollution, is not an object to be expressed by speech. It is embraced by or consists of the absolute. It is not a field accessible to ideation. It is beyond any example and unexcelled. It does not consist of existence or peace. Thus it is the sphere or the object of perception of the primordial wisdom of a perfect buddha, of a victor alone. For the above reasons even the noble ones who dwell on the tenth bodhisattva level cannot conceive of it [as it actually is]. (See also Part Three, annotation 71.)

B.II.2.2.2.2.3.7.2. Detailed explanation of the reason for this
B.II.2.2.2.2.3.7.2.1. Gradual explanation through eight logical reasonings

> It is inconceivable since it cannot be verbally expressed.
> It is inexpressible since it consists of the absolute [truth].
> It is absolute since it cannot be [intellectually] scrutinized.
> It is inscrutable since it cannot be inferentially deduced.
> It is not deducible since it is peerless, the highest of all.
> It is the highest of all since it is not comprised by anything.
> It is uncomprised since it does not dwell [on any extreme].
> This is because there is no dualistic idea of quality and fault.

(1) This enlightenment, which takes form as the complete perfection of the three kayas, is even inconceivable for [a bodhisattva] who dwells on the tenth bhumi, since it cannot be expressed by means of speech.

(2) It is inexpressible since it consists of the absolute [truth], whereas any object of speech is invariably part of the relative.

(3) It is absolute since it cannot be intellectually scrutinized or investigated by means of thought, whereas any aspect of the relative is invariably an object of thought.

(4) It is intellectually inscrutable since it cannot be deduced by means of signs and examples, whereas any object of thought is invariably able to be deduced from examples.

(5) It is not deducible since it is unequaled and peerless, the highest of all, whereas anything that can be deduced from examples has qualities corresponding to those of the example. Enlightenment is not similar to any of that.

(6) It is the highest of all since it is not comprised by existence and peace, whereas anything that has an equal is comprised by either existence or peace [i.e. by either samsara or the provisional nirvana reached by shravaka and pratyekabuddha arhats].

(7) It is not comprised by existence and peace since it does not abide in either of the extremes of existence and peace.

(8) This is because there is no [dualistic] idea in terms of ideating peace as being a quality and existence as being a fault.

B.II.2.2.2.2.3.7.2.2. Summary into six causes

For the [first] five reasons the dharmakaya is subtle
and thus beyond the reach of thought. For the sixth
the form kayas are inconceivable. [They show appearance]
but are not something that fulfils the function of this.

For the [first] five reasons, that is, "it is not an object of speech " and
so on, the dharmakaya is taught to be not conceivable for ordinary
beings in terms of being able to say: "It is this!" This is because it is
extremely subtle and profound and thus difficult to explore. For the
sixth reason, that is, "not embraced by existence and peace," the illusory manifestations of the visible kayas, the number of which is beyond any end, are taught to be inconceivable. This is because they
appear as the phenomena of existence and peace—they appear to be
born, to cease, and so forth, but are themselves not something that
fulfils the function of these [appearances].

B.II.2.2.2.2.3.7.2.3. Explanation of the way it is difficult to realize

Since through peerless primordial wisdom, great compassion,
    and further attributes
all qualities are finally perfected, the Victor is inconceivable.
Thus the last mode of the Self-Sprung Ones is not even seen
by those Great Sages who have received "the Empowerment
    [of Splendorous Light Rays]."

Through peerless primordial wisdom, great compassion, and its
further attributes it constitutes the final ultimate perfection of [all]
qualities. For this reason, the state of all victors, embracing the dharmakaya and the visible kayas, does not abide in either extreme of samsara
or nirvana and is therefore inconceivable. Thus "the last mode of the
Self-Sprung Ones" is not even seen as it is by the Great Sages who
have received the Empowerment of Splendorous Light Rays and
thereby dwell on the tenth bodhisattva level.

[The formulation in the root text: "the last mode of the Self-Sprung
Ones" can be explained in two ways]:

There are eight qualities of the Self-Sprung Victorious Ones. The
last, being the mode in which they are inconceivable, is not even seen
as it is [by a tenth level bodhisattva].

Or else: Bringing to mind how bodhichitta was developed for the
first time, the final mode in which one directly and perfectly awakens
and expands [in buddhahood] is not even seen as it is [by a tenth
level bodhisattva].

In this context the Lion of Speech Rongtön remarks:

> Since this mentions the term *dbang* [which is here explained as being short for *dbang bskur*, "empowerment"], it is commented: "It is not even known by those who have attained the eighth [bhumi] by attaining the ten powers (Tib. *dbang bcu*)." Drawing that connection does not correspond to the meaning of the chapter.

♦ This was the section "Enlightenment," the second chapter of *The Commentary on the Highest Continuity of the Mahayana Dharma which Analyzes the Disposition of the Rare and Sublime Ones.*

With this the complete explanation of the second chapter, teaching enlightenment or the means of realization, is achieved.

CHAPTER THREE

The Sixth Vajra Point: Qualities

B.II.2.2.2.3. The qualities are the attributes [of realization]
B.II.2.2.2.3.1. Concise explanation of their number combining them with the two kayas
B.II.2.2.2.3.1.1. Explanation classifying them in terms of kaya and primordial wisdom

**Benefit for oneself and benefit for others are equivalent
to the ultimate kaya and the relative kayas based upon it.
Being the fruits of freedom and complete maturation
these are [endowed with] sixty-four types of qualities.**

What is called "buddha" is fully classified by best possible benefit for oneself and best possible benefit for others, both being finally perfected. These are equivalent to the ultimate dharmakaya, constituting the basis, and to the relative visible kayas based upon it. The dharmakaya represents benefit for oneself and the visible kayas represent benefit for others. Thus "buddha" is also that which has the nature of the two kayas. If these are classified with respect to their endowment, or in other words, with respect to the qualities supported by them, both together have sixty-four types of qualities: the dharmakaya possesses thirty-two qualities, which are the fruit of freedom, and the visible kayas [also] have thirty-two qualities, which are the fruit of complete maturation. (See also Part Three, annotation 72.)

B.II.2.2.2.3.1.2. The qualities combined with these individually

**The abode adhering to [benefit] for oneself
is the kaya being [wisdom's] sacred object.
The symbolic kaya of sages is the ground
of best possible [benefit] for other beings.**

The first kaya has the qualities of freedom,
which are the qualities of power and so on.
The second has those of full maturation,
which are the marks of a great being.

The abode or ground adhering to and spontaneously fulfilling every best possible benefit for oneself is the dharmakaya having immediately revealed itself as the object or field of experience of the sacred and authentic wisdom of the noble. The visible kayas of the Great Sages, of perfect buddhas, teaching by mere symbols and terms, are the abode or ground giving rise to and spontaneously fulfilling every best possible benefit for all other beings who are their disciples. Of these, the dharmakaya, which is the first to reveal itself, possesses the ten powers, the four kinds of fearlessness, and so forth, in such a way that they are completely inseparable from it. These qualities fully unfold their different types exclusively due to freedom from the veils, which has come about through gathering the accumulation of primordial wisdom. The second kaya, which is the [division of the] visible kayas, possesses the thirty-two signs of a great being and so forth. These are the qualities that emerge due to the accumulation of merit through which the power of the essence was gradually matured to its full extent.

B.II.2.2.2.3.2. Detailed explanation of the different classes of qualities
B.II.2.2.2.3.2.1. Concise explanation combining the meaning with an example

Power is like a vajra against the veil of unknowing.
Fearlessness acts like a lion amidst [any] assembly.
Like space are the unmixed features of the Tathagata,
like a water-moon the two facets of the Muni's teaching.

The ten powers of a victor relinquish the veils of unknowing and so on at their very root, while nothing else is able to overcome these veils. For this reason they are like a vajra [when compared to] a material thing. The four fearlessnesses are like a lion, the king of all animals, since there is no intimidation when amidst any assembly. Since the eighteen unmixed features of a tathagata have nothing in common with anything else, they are like space, which has nothing in common with the four elements. The two aspects of teaching [manifesting] as the visible kayas of the Muni are like [the reflection of] the moon in water. This is because they appear in various [forms] by the power of devotion, but do not exist as the essence of these.

B.II.2.2.2.3.2.2. Detailed explanation presenting each individually
B.II.2.2.2.3.2.2.1. Illustration of the fruit of freedom
B.II.2.2.2.3.2.2.1.1. The ten powers
B.II.2.2.2.3.2.2.1.1.1. Depiction of the essence of the point to be demonstrated

> **Knowing what is worthwhile and worthless,**
> **knowing the ripening product of all action,**
> **knowing faculties, temperaments, and wishes,**
> **knowing the path reaching the entire range,**
> **knowing meditative stability and so on—**
> **when it is afflicted or without pollution—**
> **memory of past states, divine sight, and peace**
> **are the ten aspects of the power of knowledge.**

(1) From having previously given rise to bodhichitta and having relied on the sacred commitment represented by the [bodhisattva] vow, there is knowledge as to how an agreeable product of ripening is gained through [the practice of] virtue and how a disagreeable product of ripening is harvested. Thus there is knowledge of what is worthwhile and advisable, of what is worthless and inadvisable (Tib. *gnas dang gnas min*), and so forth.

(2) Through the teaching on action and its fruit (Skt. *karma*, Tib. *las 'bras*) there is knowledge of the product, of all actions' complete ripening.

(3) Since the Dharma has been taught in correspondence to the faculties [of beings], there is knowledge [and recognition] of supreme and lesser faculties, respectively.

(4) Since there was manifestation in correspondence to the temperaments [of beings], there is knowledge of the various temperaments.

(5) Since there was manifestation in correspondence to the wishes [of beings], there is knowledge of the various wishes and aspirations.

(6) From having cultivated all vehicles there is knowledge of the path reaching the entire range of samsara and nirvana. [This is to say that a buddha fully knows all the paths leading into cyclic existence as well as those leading to complete liberation].

(7) From wholehearted dedication to samadhi there is knowledge of meditative stability and so on, knowing when it is afflicted or without pollution.

(8) Resulting from inexhaustible virtue there is memory of previous states [of existence].

(9) From supreme noble-mindedness towards sentient beings and so on there is knowledge of birth and the transmigration of death, [which are seen] through divine vision.

(10) Through teaching the Dharma in order to exhaust pollution there is attainment of the power of knowing that all affliction is appeased and pollution is exhausted.

These ten aspects of power vanquish everything that is to be abandoned, each in correspondence to its respective cause. Having directly revealed themselves, they overcome the Four Maras, or in other words, anything belonging to the part that is non-conducive to oneself and [all] others.

B.II.2.2.2.3.2.2.1.1.2. Clarification through examples as the means of demonstration

> [Knowing] the worthwhile and worthless, complete ripening,
>   the various temperaments, paths, and aspirations of beings,
> their manifold faculties, the defiled and the utterly pure,
>   remembrance of previous states [of existence], divine sight,
> and [knowing] the way in which [all] pollution is exhausted
>   piercingly destroys the armor of ignorance, fells its trees
> and smashes its unshakable walls, laying them in utter ruin.
>   Such power, therefore, resembles an [indestructible] vajra.

(1) Knowing which cause and result are worthwhile and worthless, respectively;

(2) knowing that action and its complete ripening are done and must be harvested by oneself (Tib. *bdag gir bya ba*);

(3) knowing the various temperaments or dispositions of the disciples;

(4) knowing the various different paths of beings;

(5) knowing the various aspirations or ways of mindedness of sentient beings;

(6) knowing which of the manifold faculties of the disciples such as faith and so on are excellent or not excellent [as yet];

(7) knowing the difference and particularity of meditation, of resting evenly in meditative equipoise and so on, in terms of knowing whether it is bound up with defilement or utterly purified, respectively;

(8) clairvoyance in terms of remembering previous states of existence;

(9) knowing birth and the transmigration of death by means of divine vision;

(10) knowing the way in which [all] pollution of oneself and other sentient beings is exhausted.

These powers of knowledge [overcome] their respective counterparts, which are non-conducive. These consist of the veils of not knowing and so on, which are comparable to an impenetrable armor, to firm and unshakable walls, and to a dense forest of trees. In the respective order they piercingly destroy [this armor], they smash [these walls] laying them in utter ruin, and they fell [these trees of ignorance]. Therefore, the powers of the Victor resemble an [indestructible] vajra [when compared to] a material thing.

B.II.2.2.2.3.2.2.1.2. The four fearlessnesses
B.II.2.2.2.3.2.2.1.2.1. Concise explanation of the essence

> Perfectly enlightened [in] all phenomena,
> setting an end to [all] hindrances,
> teaching the path, and showing cessation
> are the four aspects of fearlessness.

On the path of training, buddhas have taught the Dharma without greed and avarice, being guided by a calm and impartial mind. In the meantime [while following the path] they have not relied on adverse phenomena. They have kept to the path of all virtuous [lit. "white"] phenomena and taught the Dharma without any pride. For these reasons, no opponent can defeat their sacred words when they state: "I am directly and perfectly enlightened within the sphere of all phenomena!" proclaiming this to be the best possible realization and benefit for oneself (1). No one whosoever can contest them when they state: "Set an end to attachment and so forth, the hindrances to liberation!" teaching these to be the impediments to the benefit of others (2). No other follower of Dharma can oppose them when they teach the path that definitively brings forth the benefit of others, showing the thirty-seven dharmas conducive to enlightenment as being the path of liberation (3). And no one whosoever can defeat them when they demonstrate having attained cessation itself, where everything that is to be abandoned has been ceased, declaring this to be the best possible abandonment and benefit for oneself (4).

For these reasons buddhas have attained physical well-being, freedom from intimidation, and mental dauntlessness. There are therefore the qualities in terms of the four aspects of the fearlessness native to all buddhas. (See also Part Four, note 10.)

B.II.2.2.2.3.2.2.1.2.2. Detailed explanation of the function

> Knowing and causing [others] to know all the different aspects
> of things that are to be known of oneself and others,
> having abandoned and causing abandonment of all things that
> are to be abandoned, having relied on what is to be relied upon,

having attained and causing attainment of the Peerless and
Stainless to be attained,
they relate their own truth to others. Thus the Great Sages are
unhindered anywhere.

The function of these [four fearlessnesses] is as follows: Perfect buddhas themselves know the truth of suffering in every respect. They know all the things that are to be known in relation to oneself and others, and they cause the other beings to gain this knowledge (1). They themselves have abandoned everything contained in the truth of origination. They have abandoned all things to be abandoned in relation to oneself and others, and they lead the other beings to abandon them as well (2). They themselves have relied on the truth of the path. They have relied on everything that needs to be relied upon in relation to oneself and others, and cause the other beings to gain access to this reliance (3). They themselves have attained the truth of cessation. They have attained the peerless and stainless state that is to be attained by oneself and others, and they manifest for all other sentient beings so that they attain it as well (4). Having themselves made the meaning of the Four Noble Truths immediately apparent, they truthfully relate this meaning to all other beings. For these reasons the perfect buddhas are the great sages who manifest in an unhindered way with respect to teaching the sacred Dharma in any assembly, be it a gathering of monks, of Brahmins, and so on.

B.II.2.2.2.3.2.2.1.2.3. Clarification by means of examples

The lord of animals is ever fearless to the far ends of
the jungle,
undauntedly roaming amongst the [other] animals.
In [any] assembly the Lord of Munis is a lion as well,
remaining at ease, independent, stable, and endowed
with skill.

The lion, the lord of animals, is ever fearless to the far ends of the jungle and undauntedly roams among the other animals. Likewise, in the midst of any gathering or assembly, the Lord of Munis is a lion amongst humans as well. He fearlessly remains at ease. Seeing that other beings are not his equal he is independent from and unimpressed by others. His samadhi is stable, and since he has [even] traversed [and left behind] the ground of the remaining imprints of ignorance, he is constantly endowed with skill and energy.

B.II.2.2.2.3.2.2.1.3. The eighteen unmixed features
B.II.2.2.2.3.2.2.1.3.1. Concise explanation of the essence

> There is no delusion and no idle talk.
> The Teacher's mindfulness is unimpaired.
> Never is his mind not resting evenly.
> There is no harboring of various ideas.
> There is no equanimity without analysis.
> His aspiration, diligence, mindfulness,
> and discriminative wisdom are unimpaired,
> as are total release and its eye of wisdom.
> All action is preceded by primordial wisdom
> and this is unobscured with regard to time.
> Thus these eighteen features and others
> are the unmixed qualities of the Teacher.

The [unmixed features] have four sections:

(a) Six pertain to conduct: As far as his physical behavior is concerned there is no delusion (1). As far as his verbal behavior is concerned there is no idle talk (2). Likewise the Teacher's mindfulness does not suffer any impairment (3). His mind is never such that it does not rest evenly in meditative equipoise (4). There is also no harboring of various ideas (5). There is no equanimity without individually analyzing each and every thing (6).

(b) The six unmixed features of realization: His aspiration does not suffer any impairment (7). His diligence (8), mindfulness (9), discriminative wisdom (10), and total release from the veils (11) do not get impaired and do not deteriorate in any way. His vision of the primordial wisdom of total release does not get diminished (12).

Here the reason why the different kinds of samadhi are enumerated is the intention [of showing them] to collectively stand for the fact that a buddha never has a mind that does not dwell in meditative equipoise.

(c) The three unmixed features of activity: The activities of body (13), speech (14), and mind (15) are preceded by primordial wisdom and are achieved manifesting in its likeness.

(d) The three unmixed features of primordial wisdom: Since his intellect has been purified with respect to all knowable phenomena of the three times (16-18), he has attained the unobscured vision of primordial wisdom that is free from obstruction and without attachment with regard to the three aspects of time [these being past, present, and future].

Such are the eighteen features; in addition to these there are further ones: His physical body is beyond measure and [the height of] his ushnisha cannot be perceived. At first sight and merely through being seen he pacifies the faults of sentient beings. In the sutras it is said that his robes do not touch his body, keeping a space as broad as four fingers. These and others are also the unmixed qualities of the Teacher. They equally result from the fact that a buddha previously, while following the path of training, showed the unmistaken path to all beings who had gone astray or lost the way, and so on. For this reason these qualities are especially wonderful and have nothing in common with those of shravakas, pratyekabuddhas, and so forth.

B.II.2.2.2.3.2.2.1.3.2. Detailed explanation of the function

> Delusion, idle talk, forgetfulness, mental agitation, ideation of
>   duality, and indifferent equanimity:
> the Sage does not have any of these. His aspiration, diligence,
>   and mindfulness,
> his utterly pure and unstained discriminative wisdom, his
>   constant total release,
> and his primordial wisdom of liberation seeing all fields of the
>   knowable do not suffer any impairment.
> His three activities are preceded [by primordial wisdom] and
>   display themselves in its likeness.
> He manifests his vast definitive knowing, always unhindered
>   in its vision of the three times.
> By such insight he is fearless and supremely turns the Great
>   Wheel of Pure Dharma for beings.
> Endowment with great compassion and quintessence of
>   victory are what all buddhas will find.

Delusion with respect to the body, idle talk with respect to speech, forgetfulness with respect to the mind, mental agitation in terms of not resting evenly in meditative equipoise, ideation of duality in terms of samsara and nirvana being viewed differently, indifferent equanimity in terms of not being alert and analyzing: the Sage is without any of these.

His aspiration, diligence, mindfulness, and his utterly pure and unstained discriminative wisdom, his being always totally released, and his primordial wisdom of liberation seeing all fields of the knowable, do not suffer any impairment.

Whichever of the three activities of body, speech, and mind a buddha displays, they are all preceded by primordial wisdom, which constitutes the cause for his behavior. And while his respective behavior lasts it manifests in the likeness of primordial wisdom.

He manifests his vast definitive knowing always unhindered in its view of the three aspects of time, which are past, future, and the moment arising right now.

Having attained such realization and insight as it is represented by the eighteen [unmixed features], he is without any fear and thus supremely turns the Great Wheel of Sacred Dharma for beings.

Endowment with great compassion constitutes the benefit of others, and quintessence of victory over the foes, which are equivalent to everything that is to be abandoned, constitutes one's own benefit. Having previously cultivated the path that corresponds to and takes care of each individually, and having rid themselves of the adventitious pollutions, this is what all buddhas will find or discover directly.

B.II.2.2.2.3.2.2.1.3.3. Clarification by means of examples

> The nature of any of the properties native to earth and so on is
> not the nature of space.
> Any of the features of space, such as being non-obstructive
> and so on, is not a feature of the visible.
> Earth, water, fire, air, and space, being equally [elements], have
> something in common in the world.
> The unmixed qualities and worldly beings have nothing in
> common, not even as much as a single atom.

The individual nature of anything compounded is not the nature of space; any of the properties of the four elements of earth and so on, such as being solid, moist, and so forth, are not native to space. Any of the individual features of space, such as not obstructing other phenomena, offering an opportunity [for their arising], and so on, are not native to anything visible. Thus, space pervades anything visible and yet has nothing in common with it; similarly the great compassion of a buddha pervades all beings, and yet his unmixed qualities have nothing in common with sentient beings.

When viewed in true perspective, though, the unmixed qualities cannot be illustrated by means of [the example of] space either: the constituents of earth, water, fire, air, and space have something in common in the world, in that they are just elements and so on, whereas the eighteen unmixed qualities of a buddha have nothing in common with the worldly beings, not even as much as a single atom. For this reason they constitute a particularity that is even beyond any example.

B.II.2.2.2.2.3.2.2.2. Explanation of the fruit of maturation
B.II.2.2.2.2.3.2.2.2.1. The different kinds of signs intended to be illustrated

His perfectly even [soles] are marked with wheels.
His feet are broad and his ankles are not visible.
His fingers and toes are long and the digits
of his hands and feet are entwined by a web.
His skin is soft and his flesh remains youthful.
His body has seven elevated and rounded parts.
His calves are like those of an antelope and
his secret parts are hidden as are an elephant's.
His [mighty] torso is similar to that of a lion.
[The hollow] between his clavicles is well filled.
The curve of his shoulders is perfect and beautiful.
His hands and arms are rounded, soft, and even.
His arms are long and his utterly immaculate body
is enfolded in the mandala of an aureole of light.
His neck, unblemished [in hue], resembles a conch.
His cheeks are like those of the king of all animals.
His forty teeth are equal [in number in both his jaws].
His teeth are supremely pure and most beautifully set.
They are totally immaculate and aligned in even rows.
The eye-teeth are of supreme and excellent whiteness.
His tongue is long, his speech unlimited and inconceivable.
His sense of taste is supreme, and the Self-Sprung's voice
is like the kalavinka's call and the melody of Brahma.
His pure eyes are like blue lotuses, his eyelashes [dense]
as those of an ox. He has the stainless white urna hair
embellishing his face and the ushnisha crowning his head.
His skin is pure and delicate and of the color of gold.
Extremely fine and soft, each of the hairs on his body
curls from one pore to the right and upwards to his crown.
His immaculate hair resembles [in color] a deep-blue gem.
Well-proportioned in stature like a perfect nyagrodha tree,
the Great Sage who is all-good and without any example
has an unbreakable body possessed of Narayana's strength.
These thirty-two marks, which one cannot conceive or grasp
and which are resplendent [in their brightness and beauty],
the Teacher has described as the signs of a lord of humans.

A self-sprung buddha possesses thirty-two pure and beautiful marks which are as follows:

(1) Previously, while following the path of training he has taken and kept his vows in the most sincere and perfect manner and he has sought his guru and kept to his company. Due to that, the soles of his

feet are perfectly even like the belly of a tortoise and marked with the image of a thousand-spoked wheel. In the prajnaparamitasutras (Tib. *sher phyin*) it is said that the palms of his hands are also marked with wheels. This [sign] is attained from having practiced generosity purely and genuinely. As for their shape, the wheels on the palms have spokes, the tips of which are sharp and pointed like a sword, while those of the wheels on the soles are slightly rounded in shape.

(2) Since he has genuinely adopted the virtuous dharmas, and since he has not killed, even for the sake of another sentient being, his heels are as broad as his entire feet and the ankles do not protrude [and are thus not visible].

(3) From having protected sentient beings who were meant to be killed and from having relieved their fear, [a buddha] possesses the sign that his fingers and toes are as long as his palms and soles.

(4) He has kindly looked after his own following by means of the four essentials of partnership, and he has not divided the following of others by creating disharmony through calumny and slander. For this reason the digits of his hands and feet are connected by a [delicate] web. (See also Part Four, note 13.)

(5) From having freely given all kinds of food and clothing, his skin is soft and the flesh [of his body] remains perfectly firm and youthful. In this context it is also said: "The skin of his hands and feet [is soft] . . ." When this connection is made, though, the statement below: "His hands and arms are smoothly rounded, soft, and even" becomes a repetition.

(6) From having given a great number of things, such as delicious food and drink, seven parts of his body—his palms, soles, shoulders, and neck—are elevated.

(7) He has cultivated and preserved the teachings on the five sciences given by the Buddha. For this reason his calves resemble those of an antelope: beautiful in their delicate magnificence, and yet well-rounded and firm. (See also Part Four, note 14.)

(8) Since he has guarded the secret words [from evil forces] and since he has abandoned sexual conduct, his secret parts are concealed in a recess as are those of an elephant or a bull.

(9) Since he has not killed, [even] for the sake of others, and since he has gradually practiced and developed his own vast virtue, his torso is mighty as that of a lion.

(10) From his having genuinely practiced virtue and having given medicine and so forth the hollow between his clavicles is well filled [and thus not visible].

(11) He has taken all fear from his fellow beings and has made them fearless through addressing them in ways that are friendly, skillful, and so on. For this reason the curve of his shoulders is perfectly round and beautiful.

(12) Since he was [always] ready and made any effort to act as a friend towards all other sentient beings, his hands and arms are beautiful, being soft to the touch, smoothly rounded and evenly shaped.

(13) Since he has extended his giving hand to all beggars, not neglecting a single one, his arms are long, reaching to his knees when unbent.

(14) Since he has practiced the ten virtues without ever contenting himself, his immaculate body, completely purified from any flaw, is enfolded in the mandala of an aureole of light.

(15) From having given medicine and so on to the sick, and from having praised the Buddha, his neck is unblemished in hue and beautiful in shape like a conch.

(16) From having himself abandoned senseless words, and from having caused the other beings to connect with [the practice of] virtue, his cheeks are like those of a lion, the king of all animals.

(17) Through viewing all sentient beings as being equal to himself [and worthy of respect] he has given up all slanderous and abusive talk. For this reason his forty teeth are of equal number in both his jaws, there being twenty in each.

(18) Since he has averted any discordancy and since he has always uttered truthful words, his teeth are supremely pure and most beautifully set, not showing any gap.

(19) From having given pleasant riches to others, and from having himself kept to a livelihood that was utterly pure, his teeth are immaculate, free from any flaw, and of similar length, aligned in even rows.

(20) He himself has guarded his three gates of action [of body, speech, and mind], and has shown honor and respect to all his fellow beings. For this reason his eye-teeth are very sharp and of supreme and excellent whiteness.

(21) From having spoken only truthful words in a gentle manner his tongue is long, his speech is unlimited, and its meaning is inconceivable.

(22) Since he has tended the sick and has given them tasty medicine and so on, his sense of taste is supreme.

(23) Through uttering pure and gentle words he helped all beings to understand the sacred Dharma. For this reason his speech is amiable, like the call of the kalavinka bird or the melody of Brahma.

(24) Since he has looked upon all beings with loving eyes, as if each were his only child, his pure eyes are like blue utpala lotuses.

(25) Since his gaze was unmoved and free from anger and scorn, his eyelashes are dense and shining as those of an ox.

(26) From having praised all supreme beings he possesses the stainless white urna hair, which embellishes his face.

(27) Since he has granted gifts to temples, monasteries, and so on, and since he has respectfully carried the guru on the crown of his head, he has the ushnisha, which being very straight, invisibly crowns the center of his head.

Authentic scriptures state: "... has [the ushnisha] on the center [of his head]" (Tib. *dbus ldan*), whereas in most places it is said: "...has the ushnisha on his head" (Tib. *dbu ldan*). This is not just the mark of having the ushnisha, though, [as this can also be the case with certain beings bound to samsara]. It is illustrated as being special and different from the mark of an ordinary being. The mark of the Muni is especially excellent through its being perfect, clear, and situated in its place.

(28) Since his mind was suited to seek the Dharma, and since he has given housing and so on to others, his skin is pure and delicate.

(29) Since a buddha who is supreme among all sentient beings has offered clothing and seats pleasant to the senses, his skin is of the color of gold.

(30) He has forsaken the worldly hustle and bustle and increased any virtue he had genuinely adopted, such as having a mind suited to seek the Dharma and so on. For this reason the hairs on his body are extremely fine and soft; each grows from one pore and curls to the right upwards towards the crown of his body.

(31) Because of his compassionate love towards all, and because he has abandoned any impulse to strike or use weapons, his hair is immaculate and resembles in color a deep-blue gem.

(32) He has donated monasteries, groves, and so on, and he has connected others with [the practice of] samadhi. For this reason his physical stature is well-proportioned, like the mandala of a perfect nyagrodha tree. And the all-good Buddha, the Great Sage who is without any example, has a firm and unbreakable body possessing the strength of Narayana.

These thirty-two [marks], which one cannot conceive of or grasp and which are resplendent in their brightness and beauty, the Teacher has described in the *Ratnadarikasutra* (Tib. *bu mo rin chen gyis zhus pa'i do*) as being the signs of a buddha, a lord of humans.

This passage differs from the way in which the pure marks [of a buddha] are defined in the *Abhisamayalamkara* (Tib. *mngon rtogs rgyan*), where each is only mentioned, but the meaning is the same. When here the number of thirty-two is established, this mainly refers to the body being taught as the basis of thirty-two qualities. Differing from other [scriptures], the fact that [his soles] are perfectly even and marked with wheels is taken as one [mark]. The fact that [his feet are] broad and his ankles not visible is [also] considered as one. So is the fact that the hairs on his body are extremely fine and grow from one pore, curling to the right upwards to his crown. This is the intended meaning of the *Ratnadarikasutra*. Then, one may wonder what other ways there are besides summarizing [the marks of a perfect buddha] into thirty-two. Apart from [their classification] into thirty-six as was just explained, elsewhere examples are also given of eighty pure [marks] being the qualities of complete maturation. Other than that, all buddha qualities, as many as there are, are [described as] those of complete maturation, being equivalent to the fruit of the complete ripening of the accumulation that has been gathered on the path of training. What is mainly viewed [in the description given] here is the question of which family or category the [different qualities] belong to. Viewing the fruit of meditative equipoise, which is the accumulation of primordial wisdom, there are thirty-two qualities of freedom. Viewing the fruit of the phase ensuing from meditative equipoise, which is the accumulation of merit, there are thirty-two qualities of complete maturation. The establishment of the number of sixty-four qualities is [therefore] only made in terms of a general and rough classification.

B.II.2.2.2.3.2.2.2.2. Summary through examples, being the means of illustration

> Just as in autumn the form of the moon is seen
> in a cloudless sky and in the deep blue water of a lake,
> the form of the All-Embracing is seen by the Victor's heirs
> in the perfect buddha mandala [and in the world].

At the time of autumn when there are no clouds, the form of the full moon is seen in the round of the sky and in the deep blue water of a clear and unpolluted lake. Similar to this example, the two visible kayas of an all-pervasive buddha, which are the sambhogakaya and the nirmanakaya, will be seen in the same sequence by those heirs of the Victor who dwell on the tenth bhumi and by ordinary disciples, within the perfect buddha mandala and within the mandala of the world, respectively.

B.II.2.2.2.3.2.3. The way these are to be realized from the words of the Teacher

These sixty-four qualities
each combined with its cause
should be known in their order
to follow the *Ratnadarikasutra*.

These sixty-four qualities of freedom and complete maturation, which is to say the ten powers, the four fearlessnesses, the eighteen unmixed features, and the thirty-two pure marks, each combined with its individual essence and cause, have the following source of explanation: In the order as given above they should be known to be explained following the words of the sutra called *The Oral Instructions of the Great Vehicle Requested by the Maiden Rinchen* (Skt. *Ratnadārikāsūtra*, Tib. *bu mo rin chen gyis zhus pa'i theg pa chen po'i man ngag*).

B.II.2.2.2.3.2.4. Explanation by once more summarizing meaning and example
B.II.2.2.2.3.2.4.1. General teaching of the reason for the similarity of meaning and example

Being unchangeable and never weakened,
dissimilar and unmoving, they are taught
by the examples of the vajra, the lion,
space, and the moon in sky and water.

The ten powers of a tathagata are not changed or influenced by their respective non-corresponding or opposite sides. The four kinds of fearlessness are never weakened in their courage and thus are similar to a lion. The eighteen unmixed features have nothing in common with and are not similar to those of the shravakas and so forth. The two visible kayas endowed with the pure marks and signs appear to those to be trained in such a way that they do not move away or separate from the dharmakaya, which is similar to space. The four sections of qualities are therefore taught in their given sequence by means of four examples. These are the material substance of a vajra, the lion being the lord of all animals, uncreated space, and the moon, which is of lustrous brightness, being not polluted in any way [seen in the sky and in water].

B.II.2.2.2.3.2.4.2. Explanation of each individually by combining [meaning and example]
B.II.2.2.2.3.2.4.2.1. Explanation of the fruit of freedom

B.II.2.2.2.3.2.4.2.1.1. Illustration of the powers by means of examples
B.II.2.2.2.3.2.4.2.1.1.1. Illustration of the individual kinds

Of the powers, six powers, three, and one,
in this sequence, have totally dispelled
[the veils of] knowledge and meditation,
along with that of the remaining imprints.
Resembling armor, a wall, and a tree,
they were pierced, shattered, and felled.

Of the ten powers, the first six powers, the middling three, and the last power, in this sequence, have totally dispelled the veils of the hindrances to knowledge and of the hindrances to meditative equipoise, along with the veil of the remaining karmic imprints. For this reason they are like a vajra, because these three veils, resembling armor, a wall, and a tree, were in this order pierced, shattered, and felled by the powers.

B.II.2.2.2.3.2.4.2.1.1.2. Illustration of their common feature

Being firm, essential, steadfast, and unchangeable
the powers of the Great Sage are similar to a vajra.
Why are they firm? Because they are essential.
Why essential? Because they are steadfast.
Why steadfast? Because they are unchangeable.
Being unchangeable, they are like a vajra.

The ten powers are the quintessence of firmness, essentiality, steadfastness, and unchangeability. Since they possess these four qualities or properties, all ten powers of the Great Sages, of all perfect buddhas, are similar to a vajra. Then one may wonder: "For what reason are they firm?" "Because they are the essential core of all phenomena of samsara and nirvana." "Why are they essential?" "Because they are steadfast, being uncreated and spontaneously present." "Why are they steadfast?" "Because they cannot be changed or influenced by concepts, characteristics, and so on, by anything that belongs to the nonconducive side." Furthermore, since in this way they have overcome everything to be abandoned and will never again be changed by anything to be abandoned, the ten powers resemble a vajra [when compared to] a material thing.

B.II.2.2.2.3.2.4.2.1.2. Illustration of the fearlessnesses by means of examples
B.II.2.2.2.3.2.4.2.1.2.1. Concise teaching

> Since he is not intimidated, is independent,
> stable, and [possessed of] best possible skill,
> the Muni is like a lion. The Lion [of Mankind]
> does not have fear in any assembly whatever.

A buddha is not intimidated by anyone, whoever he may be, and he is unimpressed by and independent with regard to others. His intellectual power is supremely stable and he possesses the best possible skill and energy in overcoming the non-conducive side. Thus being endowed with four types of qualities, the Lord of Munis resembles a lion who due to having four qualities is free from fear amidst the animals. Similar to that, the Lion of Mankind abides in the midst of any assembly, endless in number, without having any [feelings of] fright or fear.

B.II.2.2.2.3.2.4.2.1.2.2. Detailed explanation

> Knowing everything directly, he always remains
> totally fearless of anyone, no matter of whom.
> Seeing that even pure beings are not his equal,
> he is unimpressed and not daunted [by others].
> His mind being one-pointed as to all phenomena,
> [his samadhi] is the quintessence of stability.
> He possesses skill, having crossed the earth
> of the latencies of unknowing, ever so [subtle].

Thus possessing [these] four qualities, a buddha directly knows all the aspects of the knowable without any exception, and is therefore able to answer all questions to whoever deems himself knowledgable. For this reason he remains totally fearless of any hostile opponent, counterpart, and so on, no matter what kind of person he may be. He sees that all beings who are purified from the veils to a certain respective extent—that is, shravaka and pratyekabuddha arhats, and even bodhisattvas who dwell on the tenth bodhisattva level—are not his equal and that he is more highly evolved than [all of] them. For this reason he is unimpressed and not daunted by anyone whosoever. His mind abides one-pointedly and without ideation with regard to all phenomena [in terms of their ultimate and relative aspects, seeing them] correctly as they are and completely, as many as there are. For this reason his samadhi is always stable. He has even crossed and fully left behind the veil of the earth of the latencies or remaining imprints of unknowing, which being ever so subtle are the hardest to abandon. For this reason he possesses best possible skill and energy in overcoming anything that belongs to the non-conducive side. [With these] he has the four qualities [of fearlessness].

B.II.2.2.2.3.2.4.2.1.3. Illustration of the unmixed features by means of examples

> The understanding of worldly beings, of listeners,
> of biased practitioners, of those who have insight,
> and of self-sprung buddhas getting ever subtler
> and progressively refined, there are five similes:
> Sustaining the life of all worldly beings, [buddhas]
> are likened to earth and water and to fire and air.
> Away from the features of the worldly and of those
> being beyond the world, they are similar to space.

Earlier the unmixed features were described by the example of space, and in addition to that earth, water, fire, air, and so on were mentioned to supplement it. One may wonder for what purpose these examples are given. The understanding of ordinary worldly beings, of listeners (Skt. *shravakas*), of pratyekabuddhas practicing their own benefit in a biased, one-sided way, of bodhisattvas who have insight, and of buddhas who are self-sprung, is progressively more subtle and profound [and] finally supreme. The characteristics of earth, water, fire, and wind, which are taken as examples, are progressively subtler from the former to the next. Since, therefore, understanding is facilitated when combining the meaning with these examples, the five examples of earth and so on are given. Furthermore, these five examples are applied since buddhahood constitutes the ground providing sustenance of life for all the worlds. Earth forming the basis, water bringing about cohesion, fire bringing about ripening, air preventing putrefaction, and space offering the opportunity for all of these, they proffer the possibility of life. Similar to the last-mentioned [example of space], the unmixed features of a buddha are far away from the characteristics or qualities of ordinary worldly beings, as well as of those of noble shravakas, pratyekabuddhas, and bodhisattvas who are beyond the worldly. They have nothing in common with these characteristics. For this reason they are similar to space, which is beyond the characteristics of the four [other] elements.

B.II.2.2.2.3.2.4.2.1.4. Summary of the way they are indivisible

> So the dharmakaya fully divides
> into these thirty-two qualities,
> indivisible like a precious gem
> in its light, radiance, and shape.

Thus these thirty-two qualities of freedom are fully divided by the ultimate dharmakaya and they are indivisibly inherent and native to it. As, for example, the light shining forth from a precious jewel, its clear radiance, and its beautiful shape are inseparable from the gem itself, the thirty-two qualities are inseparable from the dharmakaya.

B.II.2.2.2.3.2.4.2.2. Explanation of the fruit of maturation
B.II.2.2.2.3.2.4.2.2.1. The way the marks are based upon the two kayas

> Granting satisfaction whenever they are seen,
> the qualities called "the thirty-two [marks]"
> adhere to two kayas, being the illusory kaya
> and the kaya perfectly rejoicing in Dharma.

The qualities of complete maturation, called "the thirty-two marks [of a Great Being]," satisfy and content the mind whenever they are seen. They adhere to the nirmanakaya and the sambhogakaya, which is to say, the illusory kaya and the kaya that perfectly rejoices in Dharma. These are the two visible kayas, since they embody the buddha qualities appearing to the disciples.

B.II.2.2.2.3.2.4.2.2.2. The way the two kayas are illustrated by the example of the moon

> Those far from and close to purity [see them]
> as the mandalas of the world the Victor,
> like the form of the moon in water and sky.
> Thus these [kayas] are beheld in two ways.

There are disciples who are far away from being utterly purified from the veils that constitute the hindrance to seeing the visible kayas, and there are others who are very close to it. The former are ordinary beings, shravakas and so on, and the latter are bodhisattvas who dwell on the ten bhumis. In the given sequence, the nirmanakaya appears to ordinary beings in the mandala of the world and its circumstances, and the sambhogakaya appears to the bodhisattvas in the mandala of the Victorious One and his retinue. This is, for example, like seeing the form of the moon in pure water and like seeing it in the sky. Thus there are two kinds of disciples who see these two kayas which are embellished by the pure marks. For this reason, though one longs for the direct revelation of the visible kayas, one needs karmic fortune, consisting of [appropriate] purification. (See also Part Three, annotation 73.)

♦ This was the section "Qualities," the third chapter of *The Commentary on the Highest Continuity of the Mahayana Dharma which Analyzes the Disposition of the Rare and Sublime Ones.*

With this the complete explanation of the third chapter, teaching the sixty-four qualities or branches [of enlightenment], is achieved.

CHAPTER FOUR

The Seventh Vajra Point: Activity

B.II.2.2.2.4. Activity is the action [of realization]
B.II.2.2.2.4.1. Concise teaching
B.II.2.2.2.4.1.1. Concise teaching [of activity] being spontaneous

> An All-Embracing One always has spontaneous access
> to the disciples' temperaments, the means of training,
> the [various] trainings that suit their temperaments,
> and to seeking them wherever they are, at the right time.

When buddhas bring about the benefit of beings, they know the temperaments and constitutions of the endless number of sentient beings who are to be trained. They know their dispositions, their latent tendencies, their wishes, thoughts, and so on. In accordance with these they teach the means of training, whichever is appropriate for any [individual]. They take care that the trainings as they suit the various temperaments of the disciples establish them in the higher states of existence and in the state representing the definitive good. They go to any place within the endless realms of the world and seek every disciple no matter where each may live, doing so whenever the right time to train them has come. While engaging in all of these, the All-Embracing Ones, the perfect buddhas, are always totally free from concepts and so on. They do not have to exert any deliberate effort and spontaneously have access [to all these activities].

B.II.2.2.2.4.1.2. Concise teaching [of activity] being uninterrupted

> Having multitudes of supremely precious qualities and the
> waters of the ocean of primordial wisdom, possessing the
> sunlight of merit and wisdom,

it is the definitive accomplishment of all vehicles without exception. [Enlightenment] is vast, without middle or end, and thus all-pervasive like space.

Fully seeing that buddhahood, the treasure of the unpolluted qualities, is [present] within all sentient beings without the slightest distinction,

the wind of the Buddhas' sublime compassion totally dispels the clouds of afflictions and hindrances to knowledge, which have spun their net about it.

It is stated in the scriptures:

The activity of the Victor is uninterrupted and unceasing for the following reasons: [Buddhas] have an immeasurable multitude of supremely precious qualities, which are dharani, samadhi, and so on, and there is the great ocean of the ten bodhisattva levels, completely filled with the waters of unpolluted primordial wisdom. These latter constitute the cause that definitively reveals release (Tib. *nges par 'byin pa'i rgyu*). They are endowed with the accumulations of merit and wisdom, which are similar to the light rays of the sun, causing the ripening of all sentient beings. These constitute the supportive cause (Tib. *nye bar ston pa'i rgyu*). Through these, all vehicles or paths of beings are definitively accomplished without any exception. Sprung from this accomplishment they possess the best possible causes and they have attained the best possible fruit that can result from these. This is great enlightenment, which is pervasive as space, being vast and without middle or end. For these reasons buddha activity is uninterrupted or ever-present. Furthermore, once they have attained enlightenment, they perfectly see that true and ultimate buddhahood has been present in all sentient beings without any differentiation since beginningless time. Similar to a treasure, it is within all beings, possessing qualities that are by nature free from any pollution, such as the powers and so on. Since the buddhas help all these sentient beings to fully get hold of this treasure, their activity does not cease. The nature of the Victorious One, which itself is similar to space, is obscured by the adventitious pollutions of the veils of the afflictions and hindrances to knowledge. These obscurations, being similar to a net of clouds that has spun about it, need to be removed; the condition that will clear them away is the force of the great compassion of the Victors. This is similar to a fierce and mighty wind, constituting the ability to utterly dispel all the clouds of pollution. For these reasons as well, buddha activity is uninterrupted.

When put concisely, [this can be explained as follows]: Temporarily a buddha joins all sentient beings with the two accumulations and the ten bodhisattva levels and finally with ultimate enlightenment. Furthermore, through his great compassion a buddha overcomes all the obscurations of beings. Buddha activity is therefore taught as being uninterrupted or ever-present.

B.II.2.2.2.4.2. Detailed explanation
B.II.2.2.2.4.2.1. Teaching of the summarized meaning of spontaneity
B.II.2.2.2.4.2.1.1. Manifesting free from ideation

> **For whom? How? By which training?**
> **Where? and When? Since ideation**
> **as to such [questions] does not occur,**
> **the Muni always [acts] spontaneously.**

"For the sake of which disciple should I manifest?" "Through which method should I train them?" "Which activity of training should be applied?" "To which place of living of a disciple should I go?" "And when should I do so? What is the appropriate time?" Any ideation in terms of such questions does not occur and there is no movement initiated by deliberate effort. For this reason, the activity of a Muni, a perfect buddha, always manifests spontaneously.

B.II.2.2.2.4.2.1.2. Manifesting unmistakenly as to place and time

> **The temperaments of the disciples,**
> **which of the many means for each,**
> **which training at what place and time:**
> **[He is not mistaken as to any of] these.**

A buddha is spontaneously familiar with the temperaments of the disciples, who have manifold wishes and aspirations. The same is true of the many methods of training: he intuitively knows through which of the three vehicles and so on each disciple will be trained most beneficially in accordance with his individual aspiration. He also has spontaneous access to the different activities of training, knowing which will establish [the disciples] temporarily in the higher states of existence and finally in the state that is definitively good (Tib. *nges par legs pa*). He intuitively knows where and when, [the right] time and place. He will go to the place where any disciple lives, no matter who, and will do so when the right time to train this particular disciple has come. In this as well a buddha is unmistaken and [his activity] manifests spontaneously, without any deliberate effort.

B.II.2.2.2.4.2.2. Explanation of the classified meaning of uninterruptedness
B.II.2.2.2.4.2.2.1. Concise teaching enumerating names

Since, with regard to the definitive revelation of release,
its support, its fruit, those being fully sustained,
their obscurations, and the condition cutting these veils,
there is no ideation, [buddha activity is uninterrupted].

The activity through which buddhas bring about the benefit of beings is uninterrupted. This is because it manifests owing to the following six [points], doing so effortlessly and without any ideation:

(1) The [primary] cause of activity is the path that will definitively reveal release (Tib. *nges 'byin gyi lam*). A buddha has formerly relied [on it] in the most authentic manner.

(2) There are the two accumulations, which are the cause supportive to this total release.

(3) There is enlightenment, which is the fruit of this cause and condition.

(4) There is a cause for enlightenment, [as] there are sentient beings [who need to be] fully sustained and [thus] are the object for the manifestation of activity.

(5) In their streams of being obscurations are present that need to be cleared away.

(6) There is great compassion constituting the necessary condition for the activity that cuts these [obscurations]. (See also Part Three, annotation 74.)

B.II.2.2.2.4.2.2.2. Detailed explanation of the different kinds of meaning

The ten levels definitively reveal release.
The two accumulations provide their cause.
Supreme enlightenment is the fruit of these.
Enlightenment in beings is fully sustained.
These are obscured by the endless afflictions,
the secondary afflictions, and the latencies.
A buddha's great compassion is the condition
that, at all times, vanquishes these [veils].

From the very beginning, when starting from samsara until at last enlightenment is reached, [one follows] the path that definitively leads up to and reveals release within the final or ultimate state. This path is the condition or cause of [buddha] activity and is equivalent to the ten bodhisattva levels. While one gradually travels through these ten levels, the qualities they represent will ever increase. The supportive cause of [buddha] activity is the two accumulations of primordial wisdom and merit, or in other words, of wisdom and [skillful] means. The ultimate fruit of these causes and conditions is the attainment of great enlightenment, which is authentically perfected, unsurpassable, and supreme. Once enlightenment is attained, it is seen that there is an object for the manifestation of [buddha] activity, as all sentient beings also possess buddha nature. When this is seen, sentient beings are fully sustained. This buddha nature [within beings] is obscured by the endless afflictions, the secondary afflictions, and the accompanying latencies or karmic imprints. These adventitious defilements must be overcome; the condition that at all times vanquishes these veils is great compassion, out of which the path is taught. For the first-mentioned reasons and the latter-mentioned as well, buddha activity is uninterrupted.

In this context Rongtönpa the Great has said, explaining this section very well:

> Therefore, what is the cause for activity to be uninterrupted? It stems from having formerly traveled the paths and gone through the accumulations. Through the attainment of what fruit is it uninterrupted? Through the attainment of enlightenment. What object is there for it to be uninterrupted? Since the nature of enlightenment is present in all sentient beings and is identical [with enlightenment itself] (Tib. *tshul du*), the veils obscuring it are cleared away by great compassion.

B.II.2.2.2.4.2.2.3. Illustration of these by means of examples

These six points, being similar
to an ocean, the sun, space,
a treasure, clouds, and wind
are to be grasped accordingly.

Six points or meanings serve as the reasons why the activity of a tathagata is uninterrupted or ever-present. These are to be understood through combining one meaning with an example, respectively. In their given sequence they are to be grasped as being similar to a vast ocean, to the unpolluted sun, to the element of space, to a great treasure, to a multitude of clouds that are to be dispelled, and to the force of a mighty wind dispelling [these clouds].

B.II.2.2.2.4.2.2.4. Detailed explanation combining example and meaning

Holding wisdom's waters and qualities
like gems, the levels are like an ocean.
Closely sustaining all sentient beings,
the two accumulations are like the sun.
Being vast and without any middle or end,
enlightenment is like the element of space.
Genuine perfect awakening is dharmata,
hence beings' nature is like a treasure.
Adventitious, pervasive, and not existent,
its afflictions are like a host of clouds.
Always ready to dispel these [afflictions],
compassion is similar to a merciless wind.

They contain the waters of unpolluted primordial wisdom and hold gems of qualities such as clairvoyance and so forth. For this reason the ten bodhisattva levels, being the cause that definitively reveals release, are like an ocean. Since they benefit all sentient beings, sustaining them with happiness and well-being, the two accumulations of merit and primordial wisdom, which constitute the supportive cause, are like the sun. Pervading everything it is vast, and being without middle or end it is deep and profound. For this reason great enlightenment, which is the fruit of these [causes], is like the element of space. Dharmata, the actual state of a truly perfect buddha, has been spontaneously present since beginningless time [and] contains an inexhaustible wealth of qualities. For this reason sentient beings must be fully sustained and the tathagatagarbha, their element that is by nature pure, is similar to a great treasure. They are adventitious, being able to be removed; they pervade the nature and ultimately do not truly exist. For this reason the afflictions obscuring the element that is by nature utterly pure are similar to a dense host of clouds. It is always present and ready to teach the path that dispels these cloud-like afflictions. For this reason great compassion, which provides the condition to eliminate all veils, is similar to the force of an extremely fierce and merciless wind.

B.II.2.2.2.4.2.2.5. Summary of the way it is uninterrupted

Their release [is accomplished] for the sake of others.
They see the equality of themselves and sentient beings
and their activity is not completed to its full extent.
Thus their deeds will never cease while samsara exists.

Previously, while following the path of training, they have vowed to liberate all sentient beings without any exception and they have accomplished their release [from the cycle of existence] through the practice of the path, which is solely for the sake of the benefit of others. After having attained enlightenment for the benefit of others they have seen that they themselves and all sentient beings are equal as far as buddha nature is concerned. Thus they know that it is meaningful to unfold activity. There is no end to the number of the species "sentient beings." Therefore their activity of establishing all those sentient beings on the level of buddhahood is not completed to its full extent. For these reasons the deeds of the buddhas are uninterrupted and will never cease as long as samsara has not been emptied.

B.II.2.2.2.4.3. Very detailed explanation in combination with examples
B.II.2.2.2.4.3.1. Concise teaching of the different kinds of examples

A tathagata is similar to Indra,
to the drum [of the gods], clouds,
to Brahma, the sun, a precious gem,
to an echo, to space, and the earth.

There are nine examples to illustrate how the activity of all buddhas manifests in accordance with the karmic fortune of the disciples, doing so in such a way that it is free from ideation, spontaneous, and uninterrupted:

(1) The example illustrating the body is the appearance of the reflection of Indra in a lapis lazuli ground.

(2) The example for the speech exhorting [beings to practice] the sacred Dharma is the drum of the gods.

(3) Clouds are the example for the way in which knowledge and compassionate love pervade everything.

(4) The example illustrating the various illusory manifestations of the body is Brahma, who without moving away from his own abode brings about the benefit of the gods of the realm of desire by means of an illusory appearance.

(5) The way in which light rays issue from the sun is the example for the spreading radiance of primordial wisdom.

(6) The example for the inconceivable secret aspect of mind is a precious [wish-fulfilling] gem that brings forth any necessities that are desired.

(7) The example for the inconceivable secret aspect of a tathagata's speech is an echo resounding from a rock—the way in which an echo is not real and yet demonstrates various articulate sounds.

(8) The example for the inconceivable secret aspect of the body is space, which is in no way existent and yet appears everywhere.

(9) The example for compassion fulfilling the benefit of others is the earth providing the basis for everything else.

In this context the omniscient Dolpopa has said:

> Since they are free from arising and ceasing, buddhas have the characteristics of the uncompounded in their full division. This being so, the question may arise: "How can they manifest uninterrupted and spontaneous activity as long as samsara lasts?" In order to eliminate the delusion of those who have given rise to such doubts and uncertainties, and to then inspire devotion towards the inconceivable object represented by a buddha, [activity] is explained by many clarifying examples.

B.II.2.2.2.4.3.2. Detailed explanation of the examples and their meaning

B.II.2.2.2.4.3.2.1. Combining each example and meaning in terms of its individual essence

B.II.2.2.2.4.3.2.1.1. The body demonstrating illusory appearance

B.II.2.2.2.4.3.2.1.1.1. Presentation of the example

B.II.2.2.2.4.3.2.1.1.1.1. The way it appears

> **If the surface of the ground here changed**
> **into the nature of immaculate lapis lazuli,**
> **because of its purity one would see in it**
> **the [appearance of] the Lord of All Gods**
> **with his following of many young goddesses.**
> **One would see his sublimely beautiful palace**
> **"the All-Victorious" and other divine abodes,**
> **the gods' various palaces and manifold wealth.**

There is a tradition according to which the appearance of the Lord of Gods will become visible to an inhabitant of Zambuling who possesses merit. This tradition is as follows:

Through the power of former virtue the surface of the ground here in Zambuling will become utterly pure and will have the immaculate nature of precious lapis lazuli. Since the ground is extremely pure and brilliant, one will see the Lord of All Gods in it, together with his retinue of hosts of young goddesses. One will see the sublimely beautiful palace of the king, called "the All-Victorious," and other divine abodes besides, such as "the Garden of Joy" and so forth. The various splendid residences of the gods will appear filled with manifold wealth and riches for the gods to delight in. All this will appear on the ground of this earth and be seen by the worldly human beings.

B.II.2.2.2.4.3.2.1.1.1.2. The function

> Once the assembly of men and women
> who inhabit the surface of the earth
> saw this appearance, each would say:
> "Before a long time passes, may I too
> become like this Lord of the Gods!"
> Prayers like these they would utter
> and to achieve this feat would adopt
> genuine virtue and remain within it.

In this way the assembly of men, women, and so on of Zambuling, all those who live on the surface of this earth, will see the appearance of the Lord of Gods with his retinue and inconceivable treasures. Once they have beheld this, this seeing will act as the condition for them to wish: "Before a long time passes, may we too become like this Lord of the Gods!" Prayers such as these they will utter and, in order to attain this state of the Lord of Gods, they will genuinely adopt the practices of virtue such as generosity and so forth, and will remain in and keep to these practices. This illustrates that the appearance of the Lord of the Gods has a special function.

B.II.2.2.2.4.3.2.1.1.1.3. The way it becomes meaningful

> "This is just an appearance!" There would not be
> any such understanding. Still their virtuous deeds
> would lead them to be reborn in a divine existence
> after they departed from the surface of the earth.
> These appearances are totally free from ideation
> and do not involve the slightest movement at all.
> There is nothing of this kind, and yet nevertheless
> they are accompanied by great benefit on the earth.

"When we see Indra and so on, this is the mere appearance of a reflection, whereas the real substance of the god and so forth has not come here!" These men and women who have engaged very well in the practice of unstained virtuous deeds, such as guarding their moral conduct and so on, will not have any such correct understanding. Nevertheless, the power of having practiced virtue after they took the reflection for the real thing will lead them to be reborn as gods, whoever they wish to be, once they die and depart from the human bodies they have on the surface of the earth.

The shining forth of these appearances is completely free from ideation in terms of any particular motivation. There is not even the thought: "I will incite the inhabitants of Zambuling to enter [the practice of] virtue!" These appearances do not involve the slightest movement at all, and thus are free from deliberate effort. There is nothing of this kind, and yet in reality this appearance connects those who abide in the places of humans on the surface of this earth with virtue. It makes them adhere to it and leads them to the state they formerly wished for. This being so, it is accompanied by and entails great benefit.

B.II.2.2.2.4.3.2.1.1.2. Explanation of the meaning
B.II.2.2.2.4.3.2.1.1.2.1. The way of appearance

> **Those endowed with unpolluted faith and so forth,**
> **having cultivated the qualities of faith and so on,**
> **will see in their own minds the Buddha's appearance,**
> **which is perfect and has special signs and marks.**
> **They will see the Buddha while he is walking,**
> **while he is standing, sitting, or resting in sleep.**
> **They will see him in manifold forms of conduct:**
> **when explaining the teaching leading to peace,**
> **when silently resting in meditative equipoise,**
> **or when displaying various forms of miracles.**
> **Possessed of great splendor and magnificence,**
> **[the Buddha] will be seen by all sentient beings.**

As is shown by the example, [first] one has to rid [one's mind] of the pollution of distrust and so on, of everything that belongs to the opposite side of faith, diligence, and so forth. Once this pollution is eliminated, one has to gradually cultivate all the qualities, such as faith, diligence, mindfulness, and so on. Through the power of this cultivation one's own mind will become clear and the visible kaya of the Perfect Buddha, endowed with the thirty-two pure signs and the eighty special marks, will appear in it. He will be seen in manifold forms of conduct, at times walking or standing, sitting on a seat or resting in sleep, going somewhere, and so forth. He will be seen while explaining the teaching of the peace of nirvana to the disciples, and at other times while not teaching the Dharma but resting in meditative equipoise, immersed in the truth within. Beings will see him displaying various forms of miracles, such as magical illusions and so on. Thus all sentient beings of karmic fortune will see the Buddha in an endless number of illusory appearances, such as an appearance surrounded by a mandala of light and thereby endowed with great splendor and magnificence, and so forth.

B.II.2.2.2.4.3.2.1.1.2.2. Striving [to achieve it]

Once having seen this, they too will wish
to fully join what is named "buddhahood,"
and adopting its causes in a genuine way
they will attain the state they longed for.

Having seen the visible kaya appearing in one's pure mind, one
will have the longing to attain the state of a buddha as well. Out of
this wish and in order to quickly attain buddhahood, one will fully
unite with the practices of virtue, such as studying [the Dharma] and
so forth. In a genuine manner one will adopt the causes that accomplish this [aim]. These causes are bodhichitta in terms of motivation
and bodhichitta in terms of application, which consists of the practice
of the ten perfections, and so on. Through gradually cultivating these
causes one will eventually attain the state of a perfect buddha, the
ultimate fruit one was longing for.

B.II.2.2.2.4.3.2.1.1.2.3. Free from ideation and yet bringing about benefit

These appearances are totally free from ideation
and do not involve the slightest movement at all.
There is nothing of this kind, and yet nevertheless
they are accompanied by great benefit in the world.
"This is the appearance of my own mind."
Worldly beings do not have such insight.
Yet, their seeing of this visible kaya
will become meaningful for these beings.
Relying on gradually beholding this form,
all those who follow the [Great] Vehicle
will see their genuine inner dharmakaya
by means of the eye of primordial wisdom.

A buddha who appears in the pure mind is totally free from ideation in terms of any particular intention, such as thinking: "I must
bring about the benefit of sentient beings in such and such a way!"
His appearance does not involve any movement, and thus is free from
deliberate effort. This being so, nevertheless the seeing of a buddha's
visible appearance is accompanied by and entails great benefit in the
world. This is because it immediately links the disciples with vast
amounts of the roots of virtue and eventually links them with the state
of omniscience.

"This is just the reflection of the true buddha that appears in my
own pure mind, but it is not the ultimate buddha itself." Children, or

in other words, worldly beings, do not have any such insight. They do not understand the endless number of illusory appearances of the visible kayas as they truly are. Nevertheless, beholding the buddhakaya will become very meaningful for the onlooking disciples. [They will want] to attain buddhahood. Relying on the gradual vision of the visible kayas they will follow the Mahayana in order to achieve this aim, and will practice the path in accordance with the profound mode of this vehicle. In doing so, those of karmic fortune [will discover] clear light, the true nature of mind that needs to be realized through self-awareness. The true nature of mind is no other than emptiness endowed with all supreme aspects. This is the dharmakaya [the body of qualities] and it will be seen directly and in clear precision by means of the eye of concept-free primordial wisdom present during meditative equipoise.

B.II.2.2.2.4.3.2.1.1.3. Detailed explanation of the example

> If the whole earth became rid of fearful places
> and turned into an even surface of lapis lazuli
> that was flawless, radiant, and beautiful,
> having a gem's qualities and unstained luster,
> various divine abodes and the form of their Lord
> would shine forth within it because of its purity.
> Then, as the earth gradually lost these properties,
> they would be invisible again and appear no more.
> Yet, for their real attainment the men and women
> would side with the vows of individual release,
> with penitence, authentic giving, and so forth,
> scattering flowers and so on with longing minds.

Suppose through the power of virtue, the great earth, the whole of Zambuling, became rid of rocky ravines and other fearful places and turned into an even surface, smooth as the palm of a hand and made from flawless lapis lazuli. Radiant and beautiful, it would possess a luster free from any stain such as containing flaws of less precious materials (Tib. *rngul*) and so on, and all the qualities of a precious gem would be complete. Thus it would be arranged in the likeness of an ornament. Since this ground would be extremely pure, the various divine abodes such as the Lord of the Gods' sublime palace called "the All-Victorious," and so on, would shine forth within it. And the reflections of the King of the Gods and his retinue would clearly appear. Later these properties of [the earth] would gradually be lost. Due to that, these reflections would become invisible again and appear no more: they would have arisen and ceased. Yet, through the power of having seen these reflections all the men and women would side with [the practice of virtue]. To attain the state of Indra in its real substance they would [adopt] the vows of individual release, speaking the truth and so forth, and would practice penitence (Tib. *brtul zhugs*). They would genuinely train in generosity, giving material goods and so on, and then proceed to moral discipline, to meditation, and so on. With longing minds they would scatter flowers and so forth, and joining the palms of their hands would utter prayers to be reborn as gods. In this way they would train on the path in order to attain the visible kaya [they had formerly seen].

B.II.2.2.2.4.3.2.1.1.4. Precise depiction of the meaning

> Likewise, to attain the state of a Lord of Munis shining forth in
>   their minds, which are similar to pure lapis lazuli,
> the heirs of the Victor, their vision filled with sheer delight,
>   give rise to bodhichitta in the most perfect manner.

Those human beings who have seen the reflection of Indra are filled with aspiration towards him. Likewise, the bodhisattvas, the heirs of the Victor, whose minds are filled with sheer delight in the Buddha, give rise to bodhichitta, to the mind aspiring to unsurpassable enlightenment, in the most perfect manner. They do so since they [feel the] need to attain the state of the Lord of Munis, whose appearance shines forth in their own pure minds, which are similar to pure lapis lazuli.

B.II.2.2.2.4.3.2.1.1.5. Summary of the way in which there is freedom from arising and cessation

> Just as mirrored by the purified lapis lazuli ground
> the physical appearance of the Lord of Gods is seen,
> likewise the kaya of the Lord of Munis is reflected
> in the purified ground of sentient beings' minds.
> Whether these reflections will rise or set in beings
> owes to their own minds being sullied or unstained.
> Like the form [of Lord Indra] appearing in the worlds,
> they are not to be viewed as "existent" or "extinct."

When in the world of human beings the ground consists of lapis lazuli, having become purified and free from any pollution of dust and so on, the reflection of the Lord of Gods will appear in it together with all his wealth. In the same sense the reflection of the kaya of the Lord of Munis possessed of the pure marks will shine forth in the ground of the minds of beings. This will happen once the disciples' minds have become purified and are free from the stains of distrust and so forth. Also, just as described in the example, the reflection of the buddhakaya will seem to appear and disappear in sentient beings to be trained. This is due to the way their own minds manifest. When their minds have become pure and are not stained by lack of faith and so on, then through the power of this mental condition the visible kaya will seem to rise [in them]. Whereas, when their minds are utterly impure and sullied by distrust and so on, then through the power of this frame of mind the visible kaya will seem to have set. In the example the reflection of the Lord of the Gods seems to appear and disappear, depending upon the ground in the worlds of human beings, which is either pure or impure. Yet, the Lord of the Gods himself does not move away from his own abode. In the same sense, the visible kaya seems to arise and cease depending upon the disciples being pure or impure. Yet the ultimate dharmakaya is not to be viewed in any way in terms of "arising and ceasing" or in terms of "existent and extinct." This is because it is both uncreated and uninterruptedness itself. (See also Part Three, annotation 75.)

B.II.2.2.2.4.3.2.1.2. The speech expressing the oral instructions
B.II.2.2.2.4.3.2.1.2.1. Presentation of the example

> By the power of the gods' former virtue
> the Dharma drum [arose] among them.
> Involving no effort, origin, or thought,
> no vibration and no intention at all,
> the drum resounds again and again
> with "impermanence" and "suffering,"
> "non-existence of self" and "peace,"
> admonishing all the careless gods.

In the sky above the roof of the beautiful palace "the All-Victorious" there is the great drum of Dharma called "Donator of Teaching's Sound," which arose among the gods by the power of their former unstained virtuous deeds. From this drum articulate sound arises without involving any effort in terms of someone beating it and so on. There is no origin that produces the sound such as a tongue, throat, and so on, no intention in terms of a thinking mind, and no visible basis in terms of vibration. It is free from any ideation such as thinking: "I will produce a sound." Without there being any of these, the sounds of: "All compounded things are impermanent!" "Everything bound up with pollution is suffering!" "All phenomena are devoid of self!" and "Nirvana is peace!" arise from it again and again. Thus it admonishes all the gods who have become careless, seeking distraction in the pleasures of the senses, to turn [their minds] to Dharma.

B.II.2.2.2.4.3.2.1.2.2. Teaching the meaning

> Likewise, though free from effort and so on,
> the buddha speech of the All-Pervading Ones
> permeates sentient beings without exception,
> teaching Dharma to those of karmic fortune.

Similar to the foregoing example, the perfect buddhas who pervade existence and peace are without the five [aspects mentioned above]. Though they are free from the deliberate effort of articulating the Dharma and so on, they permeate all sentient beings without any exception by means of their buddha speech. To those of karmic fortune they teach the Dharma in correspondence to their respective capacities and gifts.

B.II.2.2.2.4.3.2.1.2.3. The function of the meaning and the example
B.II.2.2.2.4.3.2.1.2.3.1. Detailed explanation

> Just as the sound of the drum arises
> among the gods from their own deeds,
> the Dharma spoken by the Muni arises
> in the world from beings' own deeds.
> Just as the sound [of the drum] accomplishes peace
> without effort, origin, visible form, or intention,
> likewise the Dharma causes accomplishment of peace
> without deliberate effort or any other such feature.

The sound of the great drum arises among the gods due to the power of their own virtuous deeds. Similar to that, the appearance of the Munis who utter Buddha Dharma in the world of the disciples arises from the virtuous deeds done by all sentient beings themselves. The sound of the drum [comes about] without the effort of someone [beating it], without any place of origin, without basis in terms of a visible form, and without thinking in terms of intention. And yet, the sound of the drum, though it has none [of these features] at all, admonishes the gods to [turn their minds towards] Dharma and thus accomplishes peace. Likewise a buddha is free from any deliberate effort of teaching the Dharma and so on. And yet this Dharma, though it has none [of these features] at all, causes the disciples to pacify their suffering and to accomplish nirvana, the state beyond any torment and pain.

B.II.2.2.2.4.3.2.1.2.3.2. Summary of the meaning

> The sound of the drum in the city of the gods acts as the cause,
>   yielding the gift of undauntedness and granting them
>   victory
> over the host of the asuras, when these, driven by their
>   poisons, make war upon them, and it dispels the gods'
>   reveling in play.
> Likewise, arising in the worlds from the cause of meditative
>   stability, formless dimension, and so on, it expresses the
>   mode
> of the unsurpassable path, which will fully overcome all
>   affliction and suffering and thus lead all sentient beings to
>   peace.

The sound of the great drum that is present in the city of the gods, suspended in the sky above the sublime palace "the All-Victorious," acts as the cause yielding the gift of fearlessness to the gods. At the time when the gods have gone into the dense forests, and the asuras, generating the mental poison of hatred, make war upon them, this fearlessness grants them victory over the host of the demigods. The sound of the drum dispels the gods' reveling in various plays, their distraction and indulgence in sense pleasures, and thus gradually leads them to enlightenment. Similarly the speech of the Buddha arises in the worlds of the disciples from their reliance on virtues such as the practice of the samadhis of meditative stability and of the formless dimensions (Tib. *gsugs med*), and so on. Due to this cause, buddha speech fully overcomes the afflictions of all sentient beings, which constitute the cause, and their suffering, which constitutes [its] fruit. It perfectly expresses the Great Vehicle, the mode of the unsurpassable path [leading to] peace, to the pacification of all suffering without exception.

B.II.2.2.2.4.3.2.1.2.4. Expressing its specialty

> Universal, of benefit, bestowing bliss,
> and endowed with threefold miracle,
> the Muni's melody is by far superior
> to the cymbals treasured by the gods.

Being there for all the endless number of disciples, [manifesting] in tune with the very own wishes and motivations of each, it is universal, the quintessence of freedom from any smallness and limitation (Tib. *nyi tshe ba ma yin pa nyid*). Since ultimately it joins them with the state representing the definitive good, it is the quintessence of benefit. Since meanwhile it joins them with the joy of the higher states of existence, it is the quintessence of bliss. It is endowed with three types of miraculous display. These are displaying miraculous powers (Tib. *rdzu 'phrul gyi cho 'phrul*), displaying all-pervasive expression (Tib. *kun tu brjod pa'i cho 'phrul*), and displaying the miraculous effects of teaching the Dharma (Tib. *rjes su bstan pa'i cho 'phrul*). Through these it is the quintessence of definitive release from all suffering. Since it possesses these four qualities or properties, the melody of the Muni articulating the teaching of all perfect buddhas is superior to and by far more excellent than the cymbals that are in the possession of the gods. These cymbals are limited and of small reach. They neither constitute benefit nor happiness or definitive release. (See also Part Three, annotation 76.)

B.II.2.2.2.4.3.2.1.2.5. Explanation in combination with the three miraculous displays

> The mighty sound of the drum in the divine realms
> does not reach the ears of those dwelling on earth,
> whereas the drumming sound of Buddha's [speech]
> even reaches the subterranean worlds of samsara.
> Millions of divine cymbals resound among the gods
> to set the fire of lust ablaze and to fan its flames.
> The single melody of Those of Compassionate Being
> manifests to fully quench all the fires of suffering.
> The beautiful and bewitching sound of the cymbals
> causes among the gods increase of their distraction,
> whereas the speech of the compassionate Tathagata
> exhorts [us] to reflect and commits the mind to samadhi.
> Any cause of happiness for earthly beings and gods
> in whichever sphere of the world without exception,
> briefly spoken, fully depends upon this melody
> that pervades all the worlds, not forsaking one.

Though the mighty sound of a heavenly drum pervasively reaches all the endless abodes of the gods, it is still limited and does not reach the ears of those sentient beings who dwell on the surface of the earth. Whereas, when a buddha utters Dharma at the right time, the sound of this drum reaches everywhere, pervading even those disciples who dwell in the subterranean worlds of samsara. For this reason [the speech of a buddha] is totally unlimited and is therefore of special excellence.

In this context the noble Karma Thrinläpa has said:

> The drum mentioned here is to be taken as belonging to the [class of] ordinary heavenly cymbals and drums, which are different from the great drum [of Dharma]. This passage is an expanded explanation of the foregoing section starting with: "Universal, of benefit, bestowing bliss...," whereas the great drum has been explained in an earlier section by means of one stanza in terms of a particular property that is distinct from the ordinary [heavenly] cymbals. To think that the line: "...does not reach the ears of those dwelling on earth" includes the statement that the great drum is not heard by human beings and so on who dwell on the earth is therefore erroneous. This opinion contradicts the statement that the Four Guiding Principles of Dharma and so forth, which arise from the sound of the great heavenly drum, admonish the gods and turn them away from their careless pursuit [of sensual pleasures]. So if we nowadays heard this from someone and thereupon spoke accordingly, we would insult our own [intelligence]. That we should not do!

(See also Part Three, annotation 77.)

There are many millions of different kinds of divine cymbals among the gods. Yet, these only resound in order to set ablaze the fire of craving for the happiness derived from sense pleasures, and to increase it, fanning its flames. Thus they are of no benefit. The melodious speech of perfect buddhas, who are the embodiment of great compassion, is just of one kind. Yet, with its single melody it leads all disciples of karmic fortune to fully quench the fires of their manifold suffering along with its causes, and to attain the state beyond torment and pain. Since [the speech of the Buddha] manifests for this purpose, it is beneficial and thus again especially excellent.

In the divine realms, the sound of the cymbals, which are beautifully shaped and bewitching the very moment one hears them, is varied and manifold. Yet, it acts as the cause that makes the mind yearn for objects and increases its being totally distracted and scattered. Therefore, this sound does not constitute [any true] happiness. Contrary to that, the speech of tathagatas who are endowed with great compassion itself acts as the cause that exhorts the disciples to reflect and to commit their minds to meditative stability and samadhi. For this reason it constitutes happiness and thus is also especially excellent.

In brief, the cymbals treasured by the gods do not constitute what will definitively reveal release. As opposed to that, there is a cause relinquishing all suffering and the sources of suffering experienced by gods, by humans dwelling on the earth, and so forth, in whichever sphere of the world without exception. All suffering being ended, it will increase unpolluted great bliss. Such a cause is said to fully depend upon the melody of buddha speech, which wielding three types of miraculous display pervades all world spheres, not forsaking one. For this reason it constitutes definitive release from suffering and is therefore also especially excellent.

Here, through these four stanzas [each consisting of four lines], what is limited or unlimited, what is beneficial or non-beneficial, what [yields] happiness or non-happiness, and what definitively reveals release or does not, is taught extensively.

B.II.2.2.2.4.3.2.1.2.6. Where the power of speech does not enter and where it is unhindered

Without [an intact sense of] hearing
one cannot experience subtle sound,
and all [its manifold variations]
do not even reach the ears of a god.
Likewise, as the field of experience
of the very finest primordial wisdom,
the subtle Dharma only reaches the ear
of someone whose mind is rid of poison.

Just as, for example, without an intact sense of hearing one does not experience subtle sound and cannot hear it, similarly those who do not have the [respective] karmic fortune do not hear the melody of buddha speech. All the different variations and particularities of sound do not even reach the ears of someone who has attained divine hearing, and are only heard by some. Likewise, the extremely subtle and profound teaching of a buddha does not reach the ears of all the disciples. This Dharma is exclusively the field of experience of the very finest primordial wisdom. As such it only reaches the ears of someone who has great karmic fortune, having become a supreme disciple whose mind is rid of the mental poisons. (See also Part Three, annotation 78.)

B.II.2.2.2.4.3.2.1.3. The way the mind is pervasive through knowledge and compassionate love
B.II.2.2.2.4.3.2.1.3.1. Short presentation of the example of clouds

The monsoon clouds in summertime
continuously and without any effort
pour down their vast masses of water,

causing on earth the best possible crops.
Just so, from the cloud of compassion
the rain of the Victor's pure teaching
pours down its waters without ideation,
causing a harvest of virtue for beings.

In summertime, during the rainy season, the clouds [of the monsoon] continuously and without any effort pour down vast masses of water onto the earth, thus causing the best possible crops. Similarly, the rain of the sacred Dharma pours down without any ideation from the cloud of the Victor's compassion and acts as the cause for the best possible harvest of virtue in the mindstreams of sentient beings.

B.II.2.2.2.4.3.2.1.3.2. Detailed explanation of the example
B.II.2.2.2.4.3.2.1.3.2.1. Presentation of the meaning and the example

Just as the wind-born clouds cause rain to fall
when the worldly beings follow the path of virtue,
from the buddha cloud called by compassion's wind,
pure Dharma rains to nurture the virtue of beings.

When the worldly beings follow the path of the ten virtuous deeds, the clouds born from the call of the wind release their waters and cause rain to fall. Similarly, in order to increase and actualize the harvest of virtue in beings, the mighty rain of the sacred Dharma falls from the buddha cloud, called by the wind of loving kindness and compassion.

B.II.2.2.2.4.3.2.1.3.2.2. Explanation of the meaning through corresponding properties

Through great knowledge and compassionate love with regard
to existence
it abides in the midst of space unsullied by change and non-
change.
Holding the essence of the unpolluted waters of dharani and
samadhi,
the cloud of the Lord of Munis is the cause of the harvest of
virtue.

Through great knowledge and compassionate love with regard to the existence of the disciples, it abides in the midst of the space of dharmadhatu, which is not sullied by change and non-change nor by samsara and nirvana. It pours down the rain of Dharma, which holds the essence of the unpolluted waters of dharani and samadhi. For these reasons the cloud of the compassion of the Lord of Munis constitutes the cause that increases the harvest of virtue in [all] sentient beings.

B.II.2.2.2.4.3.2.1.3.3. The way there is change in terms of the vessel

Water that is cool, delicious, soft,
and light when it falls from the clouds
acquires on earth very many tastes
by touching salty and other grounds.
When the waters of the noble eightfold [path]
rain from the heart of the vast cloud of love,
they will also acquire many kinds of tastes
by the different grounds of beings' make-up.

When water having the eight properties—being cool, delicious, soft, light, and so forth—falls from the clouds, it is just of one kind. Yet, on the surface of the earth, through its contact with salty and other grounds, with good and poor soils that are present there, it acquires very many tastes, such as a sweet or a bitter flavor and so on. In the same sense, when raining from the heart of the extremely high and vast cloud of compassionate love, the waters of the teachings of the noble eightfold path are one and the same. Yet, due to the ground, which is the mindstream and make-up of beings to be trained, due to their different aspirations, it acquires many kinds of tastes, such as the flavor of the shravaka vehicle and so on. In this way it seems to be of various kinds.

In his commentary to Vasubandhu's *Treasury of Knowledge* (Skt. *Abhidharmakośaṭīkā*, Tib. *chos mngon pa'i mdzod kyi 'grel bshad*), Yashomitra describes the eight properties of water as follows:

It is cool, delicious, light, and soft,
of clear transparency and unpolluted.
Drinking it does not cause any harm
to the stomach or to the throat.

In this context the Venerable Seventh [Karmapa] has said:

The Victorious One has spoken all his sublime words solely in the light of the definitive meaning (Tib. *nges don*). Due to the various ways of understanding of the disciples, they are grasped as being provisional, as being a meaning requiring interpretation (Tib. *drang don*), and so forth. The presentation in terms of "definitive" and "provisional" is therefore made from the viewpoint of the disciples. Yet, from the viewpoint of the own essence of the teachings itself they are all exclusively a definitive meaning.

This seems to finally conclude the intended meaning of this present text, the *Uttara Tantra*. Similar to that it is stated in Chandragomin's *Letter to a Disciple* (Skt. *Śiṣya-lekha*, Tib. *slob ma la springs pa'i spring yig*):

The nectar of Dharma, the cause of supreme nirvana, is of single
taste.
Like a stream of rain it falls down and dispels the scorching heat.
Depending on the vessel this will turn into different kinds of flavor.

Lobpön Pawo [Ashvaghosha] has also said:

There being many aspirations
and meeting with many targets,
from the command of one speech
seemingly there will be many.

B.II.2.2.2.4.3.2.1.3.4. Effortless manifestation
B.II.2.2.2.4.3.2.1.3.4.1. Concise presentation

Those of devotion towards the supreme vehicle,
those who are neutral, and those with animosity
are three groups [of beings] who are similar
to humans, peacocks, and craving spirits.

According to the dispositions of sentient beings there are three different groups or skandhas. The first group is certain in that there is
faith and devotion towards the rainfall of the sacred Dharma of the
supreme vehicle. The second is uncertain in that beings of that group
are neutral, dwelling between faith and non-faith towards this vehicle.
The third group is certain in a perverted way in that there is animosity
towards the supreme vehicle. In the given sequence these three groups
are similar to humans who rejoice over the rainfall in the hot season,
to peacocks who dwell in between, who neither like nor dislike this
rain, and to craving spirits who have aversion towards it.

B.II.2.2.2.4.3.2.1.3.4.2. Detailed explanation
B.II.2.2.2.4.3.2.1.3.4.2.1. Combination of example and meaning in terms of
corresponding properties

At the end of spring, when there are no clouds, human beings
and the birds that rarely fly
[are unhappy or neutral, respectively]. When rain is falling in
summertime, the craving spirits suffer.
Similar to this example, the arising and non-arising of the
Dharma-rain from the host of clouds of compassion
also [leads to opposite reactions] in worldly beings who long
for Dharma or are hostile to it, respectively.

In the hot season at the end of spring, when there are no clouds,
human beings are unhappy, the peacocks who [rarely fly and thus] do

not continuously move in the sky react with indifference, and the craving spirits are happy. When in summertime the rain falls onto the earth, human beings are happy, peacocks are again indifferent, and it causes suffering to the craving spirits, since to them it transforms into a rain of hailstones. Similarly, when the rain of the sacred Dharma brought forth by the host of the clouds of compassion arises in the worlds, it leads those who long for Dharma to be happy, leaves those who are neutral indifferent, and makes those who are hostile to Dharma unhappy. Its non-arising again makes the hostile ones happy, leaves the neutral ones indifferent, and makes those longing for Dharma unhappy. For this reason the three species of beings [who react differently] at the time of rainfall and the three types of skandhas [or dispositions to Dharma] of beings in the world have similar properties and are thus combined in terms of example and meaning.

B.II.2.2.2.4.3.2.1.3.4.2.2. *The way it is not discriminatory*

> When releasing a deluge of heavy drops or hurling down
>   hailstones and thunderbolts,
> a cloud does not heed any tiny beings or those who have
>   sought shelter in the hills.
> Likewise the cloud of knowledge and love does not heed
>   whether its vast and subtle drops
> will purify the afflictions or [increase] dormant tendencies
>   towards holding the view of a self.

When it releases a deluge of heavy drops of water or hurls down hailstones and thunderbolts in a screaming gale, a cloud is heedless [of the consequences] and does not think: "I will cause benefit or harm." It does not attend to the fact that these, once they have fallen on the fields, will harm all those many tiny beings who live on the ground, whereas they will not do any harm to the beings who took shelter in the hills and will even be of benefit to them. Likewise the cloud of knowledge and compassionate love releases the drops of emptiness and skillful means such as generosity and so on, of [teaching] in the subtle and the vast way. In doing so, it does not attend to the fact at all that these will purify the afflictions of those who have devotion towards the Great Vehicle, whereas they may increase the dormant tendencies towards holding the view of an [existing] self in those who are hostile to it. It causes the rain of Dharma to fall without any such notion.

B.II.2.2.2.4.3.2.1.3.5. Connection with the property conducive to eliminating suffering
B.II.2.2.2.4.3.2.1.3.5.1. Depiction of suffering and its elimination

> In this cycle of beginningless birth and death five paths are
> open for sentient beings to tread.
> Just as no sweet scent is found in excrement, no happiness will
> be found among the five types of beings.
> Their suffering resembles the continuous pain arising from
> fire and weapons, or [from a wound] being touched by salt,
> and so on.
> The great rain of sacred Dharma pours down in cascades from
> the cloud of compassion, fully soothing and appeasing this
> [pain].

The twelve branches of interdependent origination, which are compounded by and consist of the active state of the three mental poisons repeatedly evolve in an ongoing cycle. Due to this cycle there is the suffering of being born, of dying, and so on. [To beings caught in this cycle, the suffering it involves] is without beginning and end. They do not have the certainty that it has only arisen from these [poisons]. And those who do not practice the path of release do not have any certainty either that [suffering] will be ended when [the practice of] this [path] is finalized. In this place of beginningless and endless suffering there are five paths open for sentient beings to tread. These are the three kinds of evil wanderings (Tib. *ngan song:* of hell beings, craving spirits, and animals) and the two paths of gods and men. Just as in excrement and similar unclean things no sweet scent is to be found at all, there is also not the slightest opportunity for happiness in the cycles of existence of the five kinds of beings. This is because [the cycle of existence] is the abode of suffering itself, being direly and utterly steeped in the three kinds of suffering, the eight kinds of suffering, and so on. The specific suffering ingrained in this cycle of existence is comparable to the feeling of pain arising from being forever burnt by an enormous fire, from being continuously cut by sharp weapons, or from a raw wound coming in touch with salt, and so on. For anyone who abides in this [state] extremely hard to endure, a buddha [manifests] the cloud of great compassion, consisting of the wish to liberate all these [beings] from their suffering. From the cloud of his compassion he releases the mighty rain of the sacred Dharma in its vast and deep aspects. When the meaning of this Dharma is practiced, it fully soothes and appeases all the cruel fires of suffering. A buddha makes its rain fall uninterruptedly and in accordance with the specific karmic fortune of each [sentient being].

B.II.2.2.2.4.3.2.1.3.5.2. Realizing in terms of change

> "[Even] gods have the suffering of death and transmigration,
> and man suffers from desperate strife!" Realizing this,
> those endowed with discriminative wisdom have no desire for
> even the highest [state] of a lord of humans or gods.
> There is wisdom [from the past] and they faithfully follow the
> sublime words of the Tathagata,
> so insight makes them see: "This is suffering! This is its cause!
> And this is cessation of misery!"

"Even gods are subject to the suffering of death and transmigration, which will lead them to fall [into a lower state of existence]. And human beings suffer as well—they have the suffering of holding on to and protecting whatever is there and of desperately striving for whatever is not there for them. Beside that, they are subject to other sufferings, such as hunger and thirst, weariness and fatigue, and many others." Those skillful ones who possess the discriminative wisdom that understands the nature of samsara and nirvana realize this. For this reason they have no desire, not even for the highest state of a god or a human being. They neither long for the state of Indra, the lord of the gods, and so on, nor do they long for the state of a Chakravartin, the lord of mankind, and so on. Throughout their former existences they have attained discriminative wisdom and [generated] utter faith in the sublime words of the Tathagata, which are free from any pollution. By the power of this faith they continue to follow these words in this life as well, and carry out the aspects of study and reflection in the right fashion. Resulting from this [practice] there is completely pure discriminative wisdom that realizes the non-existence of a self and thus constitutes the path. Through this wisdom they truly and unmistakenly see: "The aspect of the fruit, anything that is bound up with pollution, constitutes in its entirety nothing but suffering. The entirety of the mental poisons and karma, anything that is of this kind, constitutes its cause, the origination of all suffering. The point where the cycle of existence and action in terms of cause and fruit have ceased without any exception is the state of nirvana, which constitutes cessation [of all suffering and pain]."

B.II.2.2.2.4.3.2.1.3.5.3. Seeing the way of the four truths

In the case of disease, one needs to diagnose it, remove its cause,
attain the happy state [of health], and rely on suitable medicine;
similarly one needs to recognize suffering, remove its cause,
come in touch with its cessation, and rely on the suitable path.

Intelligent people who wish to get rid of the suffering caused by a
disease and to attain the happiness of health must first find out what
the disease is—they must diagnose its nature. Thereupon they have
to abandon the cause that has generated this disease, such as unhealthy
food and so on. They have to attain the happy state of freedom from
sickness and to do so rely on good medicine, the means to achieve this
aim. Similar to this example, those who have the intelligence of wishing to get rid of the suffering of samsara and to attain the happiness of
nirvana must first understand what suffering is. They must recognize
that the whole of samsara, which consists of the fruit of anything bound
up with pollution, is in its entirety nothing but suffering. Upon this
recognition they have to remove its cause, the origination of all suffering, to its full extent. This consists of karma and the mental poisons.
They must come into direct contact with the cessation [of suffering],
which is free from these stains, and attain the happiness of nirvana.
As the means towards this aim they must rely on the five paths, which
are free from pollution, and gradually incorporate them into their
streams of being.

B.II.2.2.2.4.3.2.1.4. Emitting illusory manifestations
B.II.2.2.2.4.3.2.1.4.1. Short presentation of the example and its meaning

Just like the way in which Brahma,
without departing from his abode,
effortlessly shows his appearance
in all the residences of the gods,
without moving from dharmakaya
the Muni effortlessly demonstrates
illusory appearances in every realm
to beings who have karmic fortune.

Without moving from his abode "the Brahma Heaven," Brahma the
Great effortlessly shows an illusory appearance, manifesting in his
likeness in all the residences of the gods of the desire realm. Similar to
that, without moving from the dharmakaya of all buddhas, a Muni
effortlessly demonstrates physical appearances of an illusory nature

(Skt. *nirmāṇakāya*, Tib. *sprul sku*) in all the realms of the world to those disciples who have karmic fortune.

B.II.2.2.2.4.3.2.1.4.2. Detailed explanation

When Brahma, never departing from his palace, has manifested
in the desire realm, he is seen by the gods.
This vision incites them to emulate him and to abandon their
delight in [sensuous] objects.
Similarly, without moving from dharmakaya, the Sugata is
seen in all spheres of this world
by beings of karmic fortune. This vision incites them to
emulate him and to dispel all their pollution.

When Brahma, never departing from his own palace, has manifested
an illusory appearance in his own likeness among the gods of the desire realm, this is seen by the gods addicted to desire. Then these gods
who envisage this appearance as Brahma are incited to emulate him
and to abandon their delight in sensuous objects. Similar to this example, the Sugatas do not move from the dharmakaya. Without there
being any such agitation, their visible kayas are seen in all spheres of
the world by those beings who have karmic fortune. The vision of
these kayas also incites the disciples [to emulate the Sugatas] and [thus]
always dispels all their pollution.

B.II.2.2.2.4.3.2.1.4.3. Presentation of the cause of seeing

By his own former wishing prayers
and the power of the virtue of the gods
Brahma appears without deliberate effort.
So does the self-sprung illusory kaya.

In former times Brahma himself uttered wishing prayers [to become
able] to fulfill the benefit of the gods. The gods, who whenever they
desire something act accordingly, accumulated merit conducive to seeing Brahma in the future. By the power of these supplications and this
virtue, something that appears to be Brahma is shown without effort
in the realm of desire. Similar to that, the illusory kaya of self-sprung
perfect buddhas [comes about] as well. By the power of prayers prior
to buddhahood and by the power of virtue enacted by sentient beings
who are to be trained, manifold appearances, which are totally illusory, are demonstrated. They issue from dharmakaya in such a way
that they do not involve any deliberate effort.

B.II.2.2.2.4.3.2.1.4.4. Explanation of the twelve deeds of the nirmanakaya

> He moves from [Tushita] and enters the womb, gets born, and
> goes to his father's palace.
> He enjoys amusement and then seeks solitude, undergoes
> austerity, and defeats all evils.
> [In Bodhgaya] he finds great enlightenment and shows the
> path to the citadel of peace.
> The Muni, having shown [these deeds], becomes invisible to
> those of no karmic fortune.

When the right time for the disciples has come, buddhas demonstrate twelve deeds. [The Buddha Shakyamuni] moved away from Tushita and entered his mother's womb. He was born and went to his father's palace where he gained skill in all sciences, arts, and crafts. He enjoyed amusement with his spouse and her retinue. Seeking solitude, he renounced the householder's life and the worldly bustle and became a monk. For six years he practiced austere asceticism. Then he went to Bodhgaya, "the Heart of Awakening," defeated all the Maras and evil forces and found great enlightenment. He turned the wheel of Dharma showing the path that leads to nirvana, the citadel of peace. Having shown these eleven [deeds] he passed into nirvana and became invisible to the eyes of those who do not have the karmic fortune of being able to see a buddha.

B.II.2.2.2.4.3.2.1.5. The way primordial wisdom manifests
*B.II.2.2.2.4.3.2.1.5.1. Presentation of the manifestation and non-manifestation
of primordial wisdom*

> When the sun blazes down, lotuses and so on open
> while simultaneously kumuta flowers totally close.
> On the benefit and fault of the water-born flowers' opening
> and closing
> the sun does not shed any thought. The sun of the Noble acts
> likewise.

When the rays of the sun blaze down with scorching heat, all the lotus flowers will fully open, while simultaneously the kumuta flowers will totally close. Yet, the orb of the sun does not give any thought to the benefit and fault represented by the opening and closing of the water-born flowers. It manifests without any ideation in terms of thinking: "I must make the lotuses open and I must make the kumuta flowers close." Here as well, the sun of the Great Noble One, of the Perfect

Buddha, does likewise. When he blazes with his light rays of sacred Dharma, the lotus of understanding of those who are able to be trained will fully blossom. Simultaneously the kumuta flower of the minds of those who are not able to be trained will totally close. The Buddha also perfectly manifests without any ideation as to the benefit and harm represented by these [effects].

B.II.2.2.2.4.3.2.1.5.2. Explanation of its manifestation's activity

> As the sun shining its own light
> simultaneously and without thought
> makes lotus flowers open their petals
> and brings ripening to other [crops],
> so the sun of the Tathagata manifests,
> shedding its rays of the sacred Dharma
> on the lotus-like beings to be trained
> without harboring any thought or idea.

The orb of the sun, without any thought or intention, simultaneously shines its innumerable light rays. Through these it causes all lotus flowers to open their buds and to fully blossom. And it makes other especially excellent crops ripen into a perfect harvest. Similarly the orb of the sun of the Tathagata, of the Perfect Buddha, also radiates its innumerable light rays of the sacred Dharma simultaneously. Thus it causes the lotus-like beings to be trained to fully open the petals of their qualities and makes the crops of their virtue mature. Yet, in doing so, a buddha also manifests spontaneously and without harboring a thought or idea as to any of these [effects].

B.II.2.2.2.4.3.2.1.5.3. They way primordial wisdom radiates

> By the dharmakaya and the visible kayas
> the sun of omniscience rises in the sky,
> which is the very heart of enlightenment,
> to shed light beams of wisdom on beings.

When, for example, the orb of the sun rises in the expanse of the sky, its light rays dispel the darkness of the world. Similarly the sun of the omniscient King of Dharma rises in the sky, which is the direct revelation of the very heart of enlightenment, free from all extremes of conceptual elaboration. It does so with the completely perfect mandalas of the two kayas, which are the ultimate dharmakaya representing benefit for oneself and the relative (Tib. *tha snyad*) visible kayas representing the benefit of others. By means of his primordial wisdom of [correct and complete] knowledge, the Buddha sheds manifold light beams of the sacred Dharma onto beings to be trained without any exception. Thus he also dispels the darkness of their unknowing.

B.II.2.2.2.4.3.2.1.5.4. The way there is manifold manifestation

In all disciples, as in water vessels,
simultaneously the sun of the Sugata
is mirrored in countless reflections
owing to the purity [of these beings].

The reflection of the sun will appear simultaneously in many vessels filled with clear water. Similar to this example, like the reflection of the sun countless visible kayas of the Sugata are simultaneously mirrored in the endless number of the disciples, thus bringing about the best possible benefit for others. This happens to all disciples whose mindstreams are completely purified from the stains of the mental poisons and so on and who are therefore like vessels filled with clear water.

B.II.2.2.2.4.3.2.1.5.5. The gradual manifestation of primordial wisdom
B.II.2.2.2.4.3.2.1.5.5.1. Concise presentation

[From] within the space of dharmadhatu,
which continuously pervades everything,
the buddha sun shines on the disciples
[like] on mountains, as merited by each.

The utterly pure dharmadhatu, which continuously pervades anyone whose state is relative (Tib. *chos can*) in a totally indivisible way, is similar to the sphere of space. Perfect buddhas resemble the great sun. Having arisen in the space of dharmadhatu they gradually shine on the mountain-like disciples as is merited by each, and corresponding to their respective karmic fortunes.

B.II.2.2.2.4.3.2.1.5.5.2. Detailed explanation

Just as the rising sun with thousands of far-reaching beams
illuminates all the worlds and then gradually sheds its light
on the highest mountains, then the medium-sized, and the small,
the buddha sun gradually shines on the assembly of beings.

When rising in the expanse of space, the sun, which is endowed with many thousands of far-reaching light rays, illuminates all the worlds of the four continents with its beams. Then it gradually sheds its light first on the highest mountains, then on those of medium size, and finally on the small. The sun of an omniscient buddha who is endowed with the far-reaching light rays of primordial wisdom is similar to that. Rising within dharmadhatu's space it also shines gradually on the assembly of sentient beings. First it illuminates disciples of supreme karmic fortune, then those whose karmic fortune is of medium quality, and finally those whose karmic fortune is poor. In this way a buddha leads all disciples step-by-step to complete maturation.

B.II.2.2.2.4.3.2.1.5.6. The special excellence of its function
B.II.2.2.2.4.3.2.1.5.6.1. Presentation in terms of being beyond the example

> **The sun does not radiate to the depth of space in every field,
> nor can it show
> the meaning of the knowable [to those] confined to the
> darkness of unknowing.
> Appearing in clarity through a multitude of light emitting
> various colors,
> Those of Compassionate Nature show the meaning of the
> knowable to beings.**

The sun does not have the ability to send out light rays pervading the depth of space of every field in the ten directions. It also does not show the meaning of the knowable to beings whose eyes of understanding are shut through the darkness of unknowing. Perfect buddhas, whose nature is great compassion, are clearly apparent in the ten directions, their light emitting the various colors of the three vehicles' sacred Dharma teaching. In doing so they show the meaning of the knowable to all sentient beings. For this reason, although the sun and the light rays of compassion [radiating from] the Victor's sun are linked in terms of example and meaning, the latter are totally beyond this example.

B.II.2.2.2.4.3.2.1.5.6.2. Depiction of its specific function

> **When a buddha goes to the city [of the disciples], people
> without eyes become sighted.
> Being freed from all meaningless things they see the meaningful and experience [happiness].
> When blinded by delusion they fall into existence's sea and are
> wrapped in the darkness of views,
> the light of the buddha sun illumines their vision and they see
> the very point they never saw before.**

When a buddha goes to the city of the disciples, the impairments causing harm (Tib. *nyer 'tshe*) to the higher states of existence are cleared away: blind people [who have no eyes] become sighted and see the visible, the deaf hear sound, and so on. They free themselves from the multitude of sufferings of the evil wanderings, which are meaningless in that they are without any happiness. They see what is meaningful [and will lead to] happiness. Once established in the delightful wanderings (Tib. *bde 'gro*) they experience happiness and well-being. Then there are those who possess the quality of the higher states of existence, of the delightful wanderings, but who are blinded by ignorance and have fallen into the ocean of existence. In consequence they are wrapped in the darkness of inferior views. In those beings the sunlight of the Buddha's compassion illuminates insight and understanding. They expel the ocean of existence and clear away the darkness of delusion whereupon they see thatness, the true nature they never saw before. For this reason [the sun of the Buddha's compassion] is especially excellent in terms of its function as well.

B.II.2.2.2.4.3.2.1.6. The secret aspect of mind
B.II.2.2.2.4.3.2.1.6.1. The way manifold wishes are accomplished without ideation

> A wish-fulfilling gem, though free from thought,
> grants all those who dwell in its field of activity
> each of their desires simultaneously,
> doing so in the most perfect manner.
> Likewise beings of different ways of thinking,
> when they rely on the wish-fulfilling Buddha,
> will hear various kinds of teachings,
> though he generates no ideas of these.

A precious wish-fulfilling gem is totally free from any intention in terms of thinking: "I will give something to this [person]!" And yet when beings with different thoughts in mind dwell in the vicinity of its field of activity and pray to it, it grants all their wishes simultaneously and without exception. It fulfils each and every one of their desires, whatever they may be, such as nourishment, clothing, grain, medicine, a place of living, and so on, not getting mixed up and doing so in the most perfect manner. Likewise, the immeasurable number of disciples who, being endowed with the three kinds of disposition and so on, have different thoughts and aspirations, will also hear various teachings when they rely on the precious wish-fulfilling gem that is a perfect buddha. They will hear the teachings of the three vehicles and so on, corresponding to their individual karmic fortunes. Though he fulfils the benefits of all these disciples completely and in the most perfect manner, a buddha is totally free from ideation while giving these teachings. There is not the slightest intention in terms of thinking: "I will give this particular instruction to this [disciple]!"

B.II.2.2.2.4.3.2.1.6.2. The way there is continuous manifestation without deliberate effort

As a precious gem, which is free from thought, fully bestows
the desired riches on others, doing so without any effort,
the Muni always stays for others' sake, as merited by each
and as long as existences last, doing so without any effort.

A precious wish-fulfilling gem is free from any thought or intention. And [yet] it bestows on other beings who pray to it all riches and goods, no matter what they may desire, doing so without any effort or labor. Likewise buddhas, the Lords of Munis, stay in endless samsara, always and ever-presently, as long as existences may last. To accomplish the final benefit of the other beings who are to be trained, they teach the Dharma as it is suited to and merited by each, doing so without any effort or labor in terms of ideation and so on.

B.II.2.2.2.4.3.2.1.6.3. Presentation of similarity in terms of being difficult to find

The good jewel lying underground or in the ocean
is very hard to find for beings wanting it.
Likewise, one should understand that beings held in the grip
of the poisons,
and whose karmic gifts are poor, will hardly see the Sugata in
their minds.

A precious wish-fulfilling gem granting all desires and necessities is contained in the depth of the great ocean or lies hidden underground in the great earth. Because of this, beings of poor merit who desire the pure gem and look for it have extreme difficulty in finding it. Likewise, one should understand that it is extremely difficult for the endless number of beings abiding in samsara to see the appearance of the two kayas of the Sugata in their own minds, which are bound up with pollution. This is because the karmic gifts of these beings are extremely poor and they are in the [iron] grip of various mental poisons and secondary afflictions.

B.II.2.2.2.4.3.2.1.7. The secret aspect of speech

Just as the sound of an echo arises
due to the perception of others,
without thought or purposeful labor
and neither abiding without or within,
so the speech of the Tathagata arises
due to the perception of others,
without thought or purposeful labor
and neither abiding without or within.

An echo resounding from a rock and so on comes into appearance as various sounds. Yet, in terms of its necessary condition it only appears and arises due to the perception or faculty of cognition of others—of those who hear it—and it does so in accordance with their very own way of expressing themselves. The rock and so forth in its turn is without any intentional thought or purposeful labor and effort. It does not think: "I will utter this particular thing to this particular person!" The own essence of the sound, furthermore, neither abides outside the rock and so on, nor does it abide within it. Likewise, when the Tathagatas expound the sacred Dharma, the sound of their speech comes into appearance as various tones. Yet, this also, in terms of the disciples, only appears and arises due to the perception of others—of those who listen to it—and it does so in accordance with their very own individual ways of thinking and frames of mind. A buddha in his turn is without the slightest thought or intention, and he is free from any deliberate effort or labor. A buddha does not think: "I will teach this particular subject to this particular person!" Furthermore, the own essence of the sound [of his speech] neither abides on the surface of nor within his body.

B.II.2.2.2.4.3.2.1.8. The secret aspect of body

Space is nothing at all and does not appear.
It is neither an object [of the senses] nor a support.
It is totally beyond being a path for the eye.
It has no form and is not to be demonstrated.
Nevertheless it is seen as being high and low,
but it is not at all like that.
Likewise all [his appearances] are seen as Buddha,
but he is not at all like that.

Space does not exist as a thing at all and it does not appear to the sense faculties and consciousnesses. It does not exist as their object and is also not a supportive ground for them. In particular, it is totally beyond being a path for the sense faculty of the eye. It does not exist as form obstructing [other things from being seen] and it cannot be demonstrated as another object in terms of being able to say: "It is this!" Uncreated space, which has these features, is seen in various ways. Some people perceive appearances arising in its middle as being high, and appearances arising at its fringe as being low. It is also seen in terms of shape and color. In actual fact, though, space appears as various things, but does not truly exist like that. Likewise all the illusory appearances, infinite in number, demonstrating the twelve deeds and so on, which are due to the aspirations and ways of thinking of the disciples, are seen to exist as Buddha. In actual fact, though, the true and ultimate Buddha, which appears in various ways, as something that arises, ceases, and so on, does not really exist like that, because the true Buddha is unchanging.

B.II.2.2.2.4.3.2.1.9. The way compassion manifests

Everything that grows from the earth
will increase and become firm and vast
on the support of its thought-free soil.
Likewise, relying on the Perfect Buddha,
who [like] the earth is free from thought,
every root of virtue of sentient beings
without exception will flourish and grow.

All the fruit trees, groves, flowers, and so on that grow from the great earth rely on the support of its ground, which is free from any deliberate effort or intention. The earth does not think: "I must generate all these [plants]!" Relying on its thought-free soil, [vegetation] that has not been there before will grow and increase into something new, what was there before will develop firm and stable roots, and everything will flourish, becoming ever more vast and expanded. For this reason the earth provides sustenance and the basis of living for sentient beings. A perfect buddha is similar to the great earth. Just like the earth, he is free from any deliberate effort or intention. A buddha does not think: "I must accomplish the benefit of these [beings]!" When beings to be trained rely on this effortless and thought-free Victor, all the immeasurable crops of their roots of virtue, represented by the two accumulations, will increase, become stable and firm, vast and expanded. For this reason a buddha provides sustenance and the basis of living for all sentient beings, endless [in number].

B.II.2.2.2.4.3.2.2. Summary of the meaning of this chapter by expressing its purpose
B.II.2.2.2.4.3.2.2.1. The different kinds of the examples' purpose and meaning
B.II.2.2.2.4.3.2.2.1.1. The way the immediate purpose and the intrinsic purpose is achieved

> **It is not obvious that one could act**
> **without exerting deliberate effort.**
> **Therefore nine examples are taught**
> **to cut the doubts of the disciples.**
> **The place where these nine examples**
> **were explained in very great detail**
> **is the sutra which through its very name**
> **teaches their necessity and purpose.**
> **Adorned with the far-reaching light**
> **of knowledge arisen from hearing it,**
> **those of insight will quickly enter**
> **the field of experience of a buddha.**

For ordinary beings it is not at all obvious that someone could act in spontaneous ways and that his actions could come about without the slightest need of deliberate effort and labor. Ordinary beings cannot see that, as such activity does not form an object of their understanding. For this reason, doubts will arise when the disciples reflect: "If the activity of a buddha is free from deliberate effort, and [yet] acts in such a way that it spontaneously fulfils the benefit of sentient beings, there is a contradiction!" In order to eliminate and cut such doubts, [arisen from] mental poisons, the nine examples of the reflection of Indra and so on are used to explain very clearly in what way action is carried out without involving deliberate effort. Furthermore, the place in the supreme words of the Buddha where the nine examples illustrating buddha activity along with their detailed reasons are fully and clearly explained, is the sutra named *Adornment with the Light of Primordial Wisdom Entering the Domain of the Buddha* (Skt. *Sarvabuddhaviṣayāvatārajñānālokālaṃkāra-sūtra;* Tib. *sangs rgyas kyi yul la 'jug pa ye shes snang ba rgyan*). In this sutra, the fact that there is a need to speak in examples and the way their intrinsic purposes are achieved are explained very well. It says there:

> Bodhisatttvas who have gained insight will understand these supreme words of the Buddha and the commentaries on their intended meaning. From hearing these, discriminative wisdom will arise, totally adorning these bodhisattvas by its utterly pure light, so that they quickly find access to the domain of the activity of a

buddha. First they gain access to all the ways of accomplishing activity spontaneously and without deliberate effort by means of thought, [by means of the discriminative wisdoms arising from learning and reflection]. Then later, in the end, they will manifest [this feat] in terms of actually accomplishing it, [through the discriminative wisdom arising from meditation].

Thus there is the immediate purpose of cutting all doubts as to the actual way activity is, whereas in the long term there is also the purpose of actually entering the domain or the field of experience of a buddha.

2.2.2.4.3.2.2.1.2. Presentation of a summary of the example and the meaning

This point is made clear in the nine examples
of Indra's reflection in lapis lazuli and so on.
Their concise meaning, when grasped precisely,
is to [illustrate] display [of physical form],
speech, and the all-pervasiveness [of mind],
illusory emanation, radiation of wisdom,
the secret aspects of body, speech, and mind,
and the fact that compassion itself is attained.

The nine examples of the reflection of Indra appearing in the pure lapis lazuli ground and so on are expressed in great detail in the foregoing sections in order to illustrate what is meant by activity unfolding without deliberate effort. When grasped precisely, the concise meaning of what is shown by the examples can be explained as follows:

(1) Through the example of Indra the display of the illusory manifestation of the body is explained.

(2) The drum illustrates speech expressing the sacred Dharma.

(3) The clouds clarify [the way in which] mind is all-pervasive by means of knowledge and compassionate love.

(4) Brahma stands for the illusory emanation of body and speech.

(5) The sun illustrates the mind radiating the light rays of primordial wisdom.

(6-8) Through the jewel, the echo, and space the three secret aspects are explained: the jewel represents the secret of mind, the echo that of speech, and space that of the body.

(9) The example of the earth explains that the embodiment of great compassion is attained, fully constituting the basis and ground of all qualities. This attainment provides sustenance and the basis of living for all sentient beings, limitless in number.

B.II.2.2.2.4.3.2.2.1.3. Applying the examples in three ways

All streams of effort being fully appeased
and the mind being free from all ideation
is similar to Indra's reflection appearing
within stainless lapis lazuli and so forth.
Appeasement of effort is the proposition;
mind free from ideation its justification.
In order to establish the meaning of this nature
the similes of Indra's form and so on are given.

When perfect buddhas accomplish the benefit of others, they manifest in such a way that all streams or channels of deliberate effort involving a focus [of perception] are totally appeased without any exception. This is because final and ultimate compassion, which is by nature clear light, has revealed itself directly. This compassion is such that all thoughts are totally eliminated, and it is without any ideation. This is similar to the example of the reflection of Indra, the lord of the gods, appearing in the world of humans once the ground has turned into flawless lapis lazuli. Here, as in the other examples, action takes place though there is no exertion of deliberate effort. [Buddha activity is to be understood] accordingly. In this context, with the statement: "All streams of deliberate effort involving a focus [of perception] are totally appeased" the proposition or thesis (Tib. *dam bca'*) is evolved. And the statement: "since the final and ultimate mind free from all ideation has revealed itself directly" constitutes the justification or proof of this thesis (Tib. *gtan tshigs*). In order to establish the meaning of a nature that represents spontaneous accomplishment of the benefit of others, and yet is free from any deliberate effort whatsoever, as an object of understanding of the disciples, there are the examples of the reflection of Indra, the sound of the great drum, and so on, as given in the foregoing sections. Through these this nature is illustrated.

B.II.2.2.2.4.3.2.2.1.4. The meaning of the chapter is freedom from deliberate effort

Here the meaning of the chapter is as follows:
The nine aspects of physical display and so on
[show] that the Teacher has no birth and death,
and yet perfectly manifests without any effort.

Here, in this chapter treating buddha activity, its meaning illustrated by means of examples is as follows: Through the nine points explained before (i.e. the aspects of display of illusory physical appearance, verbalizing instruction, and so on), the Teachers, the perfect buddhas, are shown to perfectly manifest, though they are free from being born, dying, and so on—they are rid of all compounded phenomena. Nevertheless they manifest in such a way that they accomplish activity for the disciples, doing so without there being any ideation, deliberate effort, or labor in terms of having to think: "I should do this or that!"

B.II.2.2.2.4.3.2.2.2. Specifically explaining the way it has been shown by examples
B.II.2.2.2.4.3.2.2.2.1. The different kinds of examples

Something that, similar to Indra, the drum, clouds, Brahma, the sun, the precious king of wish-granting gems, an echo, space, and the earth, effortlessly and as long as existence may last fulfils others' benefit is only conceived of by [supreme] yogis.

Buddha activity is something spontaneous and uninterrupted. It is explained in nine examples that illustrate it quite closely. In these it is shown as being similar to the reflection of Indra, to the sound of the great drum, to the way in which clouds pervade the sky, to the illusory emanation of Brahma, to the light rays of the sun, to a mighty king of supremely precious wish-fulfilling gems, to an echo resounding from a rock, and so on: that is, to the great element of space, and to the ground of the earth, which provides the support for everything else. The way in which activity unfolds, accomplishing the benefit of others in such a way that it is spontaneous and free from deliberate effort, and at the same time uninterrupted, [not ceasing] as long as the existences of endless samsara may last, is [only] conceived of by those yogis who are utterly supreme [i.e. a buddha himself]. For ordinary beings, though, it is inconceivable.

B.II.2.2.2.4.3.2.2.2.2. Explanation in combination with their meaning

[Kayas] are displayed like the Lord of Gods appearing [in] the gem.
Explanation being well bestowed resembles the drum of the gods.
With cloud-hosts of insight and deep concern, the All-Embracing pervades the limitless number of beings up to existence's peak.
Like Brahma, not moving from his sphere devoid of pollution, he perfectly displays a manifold number of illusory appearances.

Like a sun, primordial wisdom perfectly radiates its brilliance.
Buddha mind resembles a pure and precious wish-fulfilling
jewel.
Buddha speech has no letters, like an echo resounding from rock.
Similar to space, his body is pervasive, formless, and permanent.
Like the earth, a buddha is the ground holding without
exception
and in any way all medicinal herbs of beings' unstained
qualities.

Perfect buddhas fulfill the benefit of others in the following way:

(1) The reflection of Indra, the lord of the gods, appears in the human world when the ground there has changed into a surface of precious lapis lazuli. Similar to this example there is the appearance of physical form. A buddha, without moving from the dharmakaya, displays an endless number of illusory form kayas to disciples who have karmic fortune.

(2) Likewise, in order to incite those not practicing meditation to do so, and to fully liberate those who practice meditation, there is the advice of speech. The way in which the teaching resulting from this advice is well explained is similar to the great drum of the gods expounding the Four Great Guiding Principles of Dharma.

(3) Buddhas embody pervasiveness in that their minds embrace all the knowable. Thus there is primordial wisdom that knows correctly and completely. They have great compassionate concern, consisting of the wish to free [all sentient beings] from the suffering of samsara. Filled with this wish they are like hosts of clouds reaching everywhere. Their manifestations pervade all sentient beings, all their disciples beyond any count, wherever they dwell, up to the peak of existence.

(4) Just as Brahma shows appearance in the desire realm without moving away from the realm of form, a buddha perfectly displays a manifold number of different physical and verbal appearances in accordance with his own aspiration, and yet does not move away at all from the unpolluted abode of the dharmadhatu.

(5) As the sun disperses the brilliance of its light rays, a buddha based upon primordial wisdom perfectly radiates brilliant light rays of the sacred Dharma, beyond any end in number.

(6) A buddha has the inconceivable secret aspect of mind which, though totally free from ideation, grants all wishes and needs. In this respect there is similarity to a supremely precious wish-fulfilling jewel, which is utterly pure and free from stain.

(7) Just like an echo resounding from a rock and so on, the secret aspect of the speech of all perfect buddhas is heard in various ways, and yet does not exist as the essence of letters [the basis of words and names].

(8) The secret aspect of the body is similar to space in that it pervades everything, is permanent, and appears in various shapes and so on, and yet does not exist as form.

(9) As the earth provides the basis for the arising and growth of crops and so on, a buddha is the basis for all medicinal plants without exception, these being the unstained virtuous qualities of all sentient beings, immeasurable in number. Buddhas provide the ground that makes all these crops flourish in the streams of being of the disciples, making them firm, stable, wide, and expanded in every respect. Such is the attainment of the level of all buddhas who are endowed with great compassion; it represents a total transformation of state in every respect and without exception. (See also Part Three, annotation 79.)

B.II.2.2.2.4.3.2.3. Specific explanation through a very condensed summary
B.II.2.2.2.4.3.2.3.1. The way there is appearance and yet freedom from birth and death
B.II.2.2.2.4.3.2.3.1.1. The example of [dependence on] faculties

> The cause for the Buddha to be seen in the mind
> similar to pure lapis lazuli
> is the purity of this ground,
> [achieved] by a firm faculty of irreversible faith.
> Since virtue arises and ceases,
> the form of a buddha arises and ceases.
> Like Indra, the Muni who is dharmakaya
> is free from arising and ceasing.

If buddhas are always free from arising and ceasing, one may wonder for what reason they are seen as if they were arising and ceasing. Based upon the gathering of the roots of virtue, the surface of the earth transforms into pure lapis lazuli. The kaya of all perfect buddhas will be clearly seen in one's own mind once the mind has become lucid and free from pollution, being thus [comparable to] the pure lapis lazuli. The cause of this seeing, or in other words, the means that purify the mind, are the faculties of faith and so on (i.e. of diligence, mindfulness, samadhi, and discriminative wisdom) having become extremely firm and stable through no longer being reversed by anything belonging to the unconducive side, such as lack of confidence and so on. In the context [of the example], the reflection will appear and disappear due to the surface of the earth being pure or impure, respectively. Similarly the roots of virtue of the disciples, their faith and other qualities, arise and cease. Due to this arising and ceasing, respectively, the relative form kayas of all buddhas appear as if they were arising and ceasing. Nevertheless, the own essence of Indra does not move away from the thirty-three [divine] abodes. Likewise the omniscient Muni is the ultimate dharmakaya, which does not suffer any change. For this reason the own essence of a buddha is free from arising and ceasing.

B.II.2.2.2.2.4.3.2.3.1.2. The way it is free from birth and death, since it is uninterrupted

> Effortlessly, like [Indra] he manifests his deeds,
> displaying [physical appearance] and so forth,
> from birthless and deathless dharmakaya
> for as long as samsaric existence may last.

Further, one may wonder for what reason activity emerges effortlessly and uninterruptedly. Though Indra and the other examples are free from deliberate effort, they bring about the benefit of others through their reflection shining forth and so on. Likewise, all buddhas are also free from any kind of deliberate effort in terms of ideation, intention, and so on. They do not depart from birthless and deathless dharmakaya, which has immediately revealed itself. In this effortless and unmoving way they manifest their spontaneous deeds uninterruptedly and ever-presently, as long as samsara is not emptied and the endless existences of the disciples may last. They display illusory appearances through [the aspect of] body, express instruction through [the aspect of] speech, pervade everything with their knowledge and compassionate love through [the aspect of] mind, and so on.

B.II.2.2.2.2.4.3.2.3.2. The way there is special excellence superior to the corresponding property
B.II.2.2.2.2.4.3.2.3.2.1. Concise presentation

> The condensed meaning of the examples is [contained] herein.
> Their order is also [not arbitrary], as they are abandoned such
> that properties not in tune are eliminated
> [progressing] from the former to the latter.

The briefly condensed meaning of the nine examples illustrating buddha activity and their detailed explanation has been elucidated by the [foregoing] sections. In addition to that it is also explained here that there is a definitive cause for presenting them in this order, for the latter being elucidated after the former. In this context the respective preceding examples are not able to illustrate buddha activity to its full extent. Whatever aspect is a non-corresponding property is gradually eliminated by the following examples. Thus it is expressed by teaching in terms of corresponding qualities.

B.II.2.2.2.4.3.2.3.2.2. Detailed explanation

> A buddha is like the reflection, and yet dissimilar,
> since the reflection is not endowed with his melody.
> He is like the drum of the gods, and yet dissimilar,
> since the drum does not bring benefit everywhere.
> He is similar to a vast cloud, and yet dissimilar,
> since a cloud does not eliminate worthless seeds.
> He is like the mighty Brahma, and yet dissimilar,
> since Brahma does not continuously cause maturity.
> He is like the orb of the sun, and yet dissimilar,
> since the sun does not always overcome darkness.
> He is like a wish-granting gem, and yet dissimilar,
> since the gem's appearance is not so rarely found.
> He is similar to an echo, and yet dissimilar,
> since an echo arises from cause and condition.
> He is similar to space, and yet dissimilar,
> since space is not a ground of pure virtue.
> Being the lasting basis for every goodness,
> the best possible for all without exception,
> for worldly beings and those beyond the world,
> [activity] is similar to the mandala of earth.
> Because based upon all buddhas' enlightenment,
> the path beyond the world will arise, as will
> the path of virtuous deeds, mental stability, and
> the immeasurable and formless contemplations.

(1) The unfolding of the activity of all perfect buddhas is similar to the reflection of Indra appearing in the lapis lazuli surface of the earth, inasmuch as an endless number of illusory physical manifestations is displayed. Nevertheless, the form [of Indra] does not wield a melody, whereas a buddha possesses the melody of his speech expounding the Dharma. For this reason there is a dissimilarity and [a buddha] is more excellent than that.

(2) [Buddha activity] is similar to the great drum of the gods teaching the Four Guiding Principles of Dharma, inasmuch as through the melody of his speech expounding the Dharma various instructions are given. Nevertheless, the great drum is not such that it brings benefit

in whichever direction wished for, whereas a buddha accomplishes benefit pervading all the worlds of the disciples. For this reason there is again a dissimilarity and [a buddha] is more excellent than that.

(3) Viewing the aspect that it pervades all world spheres, buddha activity, which matures all disciples by means of knowledge and compassionate love, has properties similar to those of a vast cloud, which all-pervasively causes the ripening of crops. Nevertheless, a cloud does not eliminate worthless seeds, whereas a buddha causes the elimination of everything that is worthless, of all afflictions such as desire and so on. For this reason there is a further dissimilarity and [a buddha] is more excellent than that.

(4) Viewing the aspect of eliminating worthless seeds, the display of an endless number of illusory appearances is similar to the illusory manifestation of Mahabrahma eliminating the attachment to sense gratifications. Nevertheless, Brahma only brings benefit one time and thus does not continuously cause maturity, whereas a buddha always and uninterruptedly leads the disciples' streams of being to full maturation. For this reason there is again a dissimilarity and [a buddha] is more excellent than that.

(5) Viewing the aspect that all crops, which are the disciples, are continuously lead to maturation, the radiation of an infinite number of light rays of primordial wisdom is similar to the orb of the sun continuously ripening all crops by means of its light beams. Nevertheless, the sun only shines alternately. It does not always overcome darkness, doing so day and night, whereas a buddha always and uninterruptedly overcomes the darkness of unknowing. For this reason, again there is a dissimilarity and [a buddha] is more excellent than that.

(6) Viewing the aspect of darkness being overcome continuously, the secret aspect of mind, radiating the light of totally thought-free primordial wisdom, is similar to a wish-fulfilling gem that through its brilliance continuously overcomes darkness, doing so day and night. Nevertheless, the jewel being present among Nagas and so on, and even among animals, its occurrence is not so hard to find, whereas a buddha does not appear to sentient beings who lack karmic fortune and is thus very hard to find [for those beings]. For this reason there is another dissimilarity and [a buddha] is more excellent than that.

(7) Viewing the aspect of his appearance being difficult to encounter, the secret aspect of speech excellently explaining various teachings is similar to an echo being difficult to encounter, since it does not truly exist either outside or inside [its source]. Nevertheless, an echo

occurs in dependence on adventitious conditions, whereas a buddha, being self-sprung and uncreated, does not appear due to causes and conditions. For this reason there is a further dissimilarity and [a buddha] is more excellent than that.

(8) Viewing the aspect that [buddha activity] is truly uncreated and does not arise from causes and conditions, the secret aspect of body, displaying an infinite number of totally illusory manifestations, is similar to space, which appears as a variety of things and is yet uncreated. Nevertheless, space does not become a basis or ground for virtue, whereas a buddha becomes the basis or ground of all unstained virtuous properties. For this reason there is again a dissimilarity and [a buddha] is more excellent than that.

(9) [Buddha activity] becomes the basis and lasting ground of every goodness without exception, of everything that is best for worldly beings and beings beyond the worldly. For this reason it is similar to the great mandala of the earth, which provides the basis for everything. One may wonder why [a buddha] forms the ground of all [goodness]. This is because the attainment of the great enlightenment of all buddhas constitutes the basis on which the sacred teachings arise. These consist of the three vehicles and so on, constituting the path that leads beyond the worldly. As it is stated in the *Madhyamakavatara* (Tib. *dbu ma la 'jug pa*): "...the shravakas, the mediocre buddhas, and the Lords of Munis [i.e. pratyekabuddhas and perfect buddhas] will arise." Based upon this [great enlightenment], the paths of the ten virtuous actions will arise, constituting the cause of the best possible [feat] of the desire realm. The four stages of meditative stability and the immeasurable contemplations will come about, constituting the cause of the best possible [achievement] of the realm of form. And the formless states of resting evenly in meditative equipoise, constituting the cause of the best possible [feat] of the formless realm, will arise as well. (See also Part Three, annotation 80.)

• This was the section "Unfolding the Activity of the Tathagata," the fourth chapter of *The Commentary on the Highest Continuity of the Mahayana Dharma which Analyzes the Disposition of the Rare and Sublime Ones.*

With this the complete explanation of the fourth chapter, teaching the unfolding of the activity of the Tathagata, is achieved.

CHAPTER FIVE
Benefit

B.II.3. Conclusion of the explanation
B.II.3.1. Benefit
B.II.3.1.1. Presentation of the meaning being inconceivable

Buddha element, buddha awakening,
buddha qualities, and buddha activity
cannot be thought, not even by purified beings.
They are the field of experience of their guides.

The phase in which the naturally pure buddha element is bound up with the adventitious stains is the tathagatagarbha [or heart of buddha]. The phase in which this buddha element is completely and thoroughly purified from all the adventitious stains is the attainment of the great awakening or enlightenment of a buddha. Great enlightenment has all buddha qualities, those special properties which are the powers and so on, possessing them in an indivisible way. Through the force provided by the attainment of these qualities, there is the activity accomplishing the deeds of a buddha spontaneously and without interruption. These four vajra points are in accordance with and accomplish the Three Jewels [of Buddha, Dharma, and Sangha] in their likeness. Their true and actual way of being cannot even be thought by those beings who are to a certain extent completely purified from the adventitious stains and thus dwell on one of the bodhisattva levels. When this is so, what need is there to consider how they might be viewed by ordinary beings, shravakas, and pratyekabuddhas? For them they are inconceivable, as has been explained before. Then one may wonder: Whose field of experience are these four vajra points? They emerge as the field of experience of the primordial wisdom exclusively native to perfect buddhas, the guides of all sentient beings.

B.II.3.1.2. Short teaching of its qualities

> Those of insight who have devotion to this buddha domain
> will become vessels for the multitude of all buddha qualities,
> while those truly delighting in these inconceivable properties
> will exceed in merit [the good actions of] all sentient beings.

Those bodhisattvas of insight who have special devotion to these four points, which are the field of experience of the primordial wisdom exclusively native to perfect buddhas, will become vessels for the immeasurable multitude of buddha qualities, such as the powers and so on. The Mahayana disposition being awakened, they will quickly attain the final ultimate fruit. The benefits of being especially devoted to and truly delighting in these four points, which possess a multitude of unimaginable qualities, are extremely great in number. For this reason ordinary beings will also exceed all those who have no connection with these [four vajra points]. Without exception, they will surpass all their accumulations of merit sprung from generosity and so forth.

B.II.3.1.3. Explanation of its special excellence in comparison with generosity and two further [virtues]
B.II.3.1.3.1. Explanation in comparison with generosity

> Someone striving for enlightenment may turn to the Dharma
> kings, offering golden fields adorned with gems
> of equal [number] to the atoms in the buddhafields, and may
> continue doing so every day.
> Another may just hear a word of this, and upon hearing it
> become filled with devotion.
> He will attain merits far greater and more manifold than the
> virtue sprung from this practice of giving.

Some generous person striving for enlightenment may offer fields made of gold adorned with gems to all buddhas, to all Dharma kings. These [offerings] may be equal in number to the number of atoms in the buddhafields, and he may do so continuously, each single day. As opposed to the merit [arising from] this offering and so on, another person may just hear one single word of the sublime words of the Buddha that teach the four vajra points. Yet, upon hearing it, he may be filled with devotion and thereby gain conviction with regard to them. When this happens, this [person] will attain supreme merit by far greater and much more manifold than the virtue sprung from the generosity of the former.

B.II.3.1.3.2. Explanation in comparison with moral conduct

An intelligent person wishing for enlightenment may by body, speech, and mind
guard a flawless moral conduct and do so effortlessly, even through many eons.
Another may just hear a word of this, and upon hearing it become filled with devotion.
He will attain merits far greater and more manifold than the virtue sprung from this discipline.

An intelligent person who wishes to attain unsurpassable enlightenment may by means of the three aspects of body, speech, and mind guard his own ethical conduct flawlessly, without any stain from breaking moral discipline. He may even do so throughout many kalpas. Another person may just hear one single word of the sublime words of the Buddha that teach the four vajra points. Yet, upon hearing it, he may be filled with devotion, being firmly convinced of them. When this happens, this [person] will attain supreme merit that is by far greater and much more manifold than the virtue sprung from the moral discipline of the former.

B.II.3.1.3.3. Explanation in comparison with meditative stability

Someone here may finally achieve the divine meditative stabilities and Brahma's abode, thus quenching all affliction's fire
within the three realms of existence, and may cultivate these as a means to reach unchanging and perfect enlightenment.
Another may just hear a word of this, and upon hearing it become filled with devotion.
He will attain merits far greater and more manifold than the virtue sprung from this meditation.

An intelligent person here in this world may have finally perfected the four meditative stabilities that are the abode of the gods and the four limitless contemplations that are the abode of Brahma. He may have led them to their peak and may have cultivated them as a means leading to unchanging perfect enlightenment. Another person may just hear one single word of this, yet upon hearing it, may be filled with devotion. When this happens, this [person] will attain benefit and merit by far greater and much more manifold than the virtue sprung from the meditative stability of the former.

B.II.3.1.4. Presentation of the reason for this excellence

> Why [is it so beneficial]? Generosity only yields wealth,
> discipline leads to the higher states of existence, and
>   meditation removes affliction.
> Discriminative wisdom fully abandons all afflictions and
>   [hindrances to] knowledge.
> It is therefore supreme, and its cause is studying these.

One may wonder why it has such great benefit. When not held by discriminative wisdom, extensive generosity will only yield material wealth, extensive discipline will only lead to the higher states of existence, and meditation will only remove the afflictions in terms of suppressing them and keeping them down. As opposed to that, the discriminative wisdom realizing the four vajra points totally abandons all the veils of the afflictions and hindrances to knowledge along with their remaining imprints. For this reason, discriminative wisdom realizing the profound ultimate nature is supremacy itself, and by far more excellent than generosity and so on. Therefore, there are special benefits of a training in the frame of which one studies and reflects upon the sublime words of the Buddha teaching the four vajra points. This is due to the fact that there is only one cause for the realization represented by the discriminative wisdom, which is far more excellent than the virtue resulting from the three [practices] of generosity and so on. This single cause consists of studying the sublime words of the Buddha teaching the four vajra points, of thereupon having faith in them, and training oneself [as to their meaning].

B.II.3.1.5. Very detailed explanation of the benefit
B.II.3.1.5.1. Attainment of enlightenment

> The presence [of the element], its result,
> its qualities, and the achievement of benefit
> are the objects of understanding of a buddha.
> When towards these four, as explained above,
> one of understanding is filled with devotion
> to their presence, ability, and qualities,
> he will be quickly endowed with the fortune
> by which one attains the state of a tathagata.

The element forming the ground to be realized, which has been present since beginningless time, enlightenment, which is the realization transforming the element's state, the qualities, which are the branches of enlightenment, and its action, which is the activity accomplishing the benefit of others, are the objects of understanding of a buddha. Those bodhisattvas possessed of understanding who train themselves in an unperverted way with regard to these four points, as explained above, will quickly harvest the benefit of attaining enlightenment. Devotion towards the fact that the element is present in all sentient beings, that it wields the ability of reaching enlightenment, and that enlightenment has been indivisibly endowed with qualities since beginningless time, will transform into the karmic fortune of quickly attaining the state of a tathagata.

B.II.3.1.5.2. Firm bodhichitta

> Those who realize: "This inconceivable object is present
> and someone like me can attain it;
> its attainment will hold such qualities and endowment"
> will aspire to it, filled with faith.
> Thus becoming vessels of all qualities,
> such as longing, diligence, mindfulness,
> meditative stability, wisdom, and so on,
> bodhichitta will be ever-present in them.

"This element is present within myself and someone like me has the ability to attain enlightenment. Due to the attainment of enlightenment, qualities will emerge such as the powers and so on, and sprung from these there will be endowment with activity fulfilling benefit [for each and every one]." Those who derive such insight from the four profound [vajra] points, which are objects inconceivable to ordinary beings, will aspire to them, filled with the three kinds of faith. Thus they will become vessels for manifold qualities. There will be heartfelt longing in terms of the wish to attain enlightenment, and diligence inspired by delight in enlightenment. There will be mindfulness preventing one from forgetting the means to enlightenment, and meditative stability that is one-pointed as to these means. There will be discriminative wisdom perfectly and thoroughly discerning all phenomena, and so on. In those bodhisattvas who are devoted to and realize these four vajra points, bodhichitta, which consists of the wish to attain perfect enlightenment for the sake of all other fellow beings, will be ever-present and ingrained.

B.II.3.1.5.3. Attainment of complete perfection

[Bodhichitta] being ever-present in them
the heirs of the Victor will not fall back.
The perfection of merit will be refined
until being transformed into total purity.
Once these five perfections of merit
are not ideated in threefold division,
they will become perfect and fully pure,
as their opposite facets are abandoned.

Since bodhichitta, as explained before, is ever-present in them, the heirs of the Victor will not fall back from unsurpassable enlightenment. Wholeheartedly inspired and uplifted by this particular motivation they will fully refine the first five perfections, and transform these into total purity. The first five perfections represent the aspect of application or the accumulation of merit, of generosity, and so on, constituting the means to be of benefit and help to all sentient beings. Then further, not ideating the three circles of actor, action, and the one towards whom the action is directed, these perfections are refined into supremacy. And they will become utterly pure, as the veils of their opposite sides, such as avarice being the contrary of generosity and so forth, are totally and radically abandoned.

B.II.3.1.5.4. Definition of the accumulations

The merit of generosity arises from giving,
that of morality arises from moral conduct.
The two aspects of patience and meditative stability
stem from meditation, and diligence accompanies all.

Formerly, merit was explained as the three aspects of generosity, ethical conduct, and meditation. So one may wonder whether it does not follow that, of the six perfections, three are to be considered as the accumulation of merit and three as the accumulation of primordial wisdom. The first five perfections are considered as being the accumulation of merit. The merit arisen from giving is the perfection of generosity, and the merit arisen from ethical conduct is the perfection of morality. Both aspects of patience and meditative stability are the merit sprung from meditation. Diligence accompanies all three aspects of merit [as mentioned here].

B.II.3.1.5.5. Elimination of the veils
B.II.3.1.5.5.1. Depiction of the veils to be abandoned

**Whatever ideates [in terms of] the three circles
is viewed as the veil of the hindrances to knowledge.
Whatever is the impulse of avarice and so on
is to be regarded as the veil of the mental poisons.**

When it is said: "Discriminative wisdom totally abandons all the afflictions and [hindrances to] knowledge," one may wonder which are the two veils to be abandoned by discriminative wisdom. Any ideation in terms of the three circles—of the giver, the object to whom one is giving, and the action of giving—and so forth is considered to be the veil of the hindrances to knowledge. It constitutes the obstruction to the first five paramitas becoming fully perfected. Any ideation of avarice, desire, anger, sloth, total distraction, and so on is considered to be the veil of the mental poisons. It constitutes the obstruction to the first five perfections becoming totally pure. Thus these [two veils] are to be abandoned.

B.II.3.1.5.5.2. Explanation of wisdom being the supreme remedy

**Since apart from discriminative wisdom
there is no other cause to remove these [veils],
this discriminative wisdom is supreme.
Its ground being study, such study is supreme.**

Since it realizes points such as those [discussed here] in the most excellent way, apart from discriminative wisdom there is no other cause that will eliminate the two veils at their very root. Generosity and so on, when devoid of discriminative wisdom, can only suppress the direct manifestation of the veils but cannot eliminate them to the extent of uprooting their seeds. As opposed to that, the perfection of discriminative wisdom has the ability to eliminate the seeds of the two veils and their remaining imprints up to their very root. For this reason, discriminative wisdom, which forms the accumulation of primordial wisdom, is supreme and more excellent than the five perfections of merit. The ground that will increase such discriminative wisdom is learning the sublime words of the Buddha, which teach subjects such as these four vajra points, along with the commentaries explaining their intended meaning, and doing so in the proper fashion. Although the merit resulting from generosity, ethical conduct, and meditation is extremely manifold, the wisdom of learning a profound teaching such as this is by far more excellent.

B.II.3.2. The way the commentary was composed
B.II.3.2.1. The reason for its composition

**Based on the trustworthy words of the Buddha and on
   scriptures of logic,
I have explained this for the sole purpose
of purifying myself and supporting all those
whose understanding has the best of virtue and devotion.**

The way in which the seven vajra points have been taught in the foregoing sections is not my own artifice or the selfish product of not heeding any instructions. It is based upon many sutras containing the trustworthy words of the Buddha, such as the *Sutra Requested by King Dharanishvara* and so on. Equally it is based on direct recognition in yoga, and on many logical arguments that cut all exaggerative and depreciating [views]. I have composed this *Commentary on the Highest Continuity* in a meaningful way [for two reasons. The first is] to purify the nature of the veils up to the last single seed and remaining imprint. [The second is] to support all those disciples who have the disposition to the Great Vehicle and whose understanding is endowed with the best possible virtue of devotion.

B.II.3.2.2. The basis on which it was composed

**As someone with eyes sees by relying on a lamp,
or on lightning, a jewel, the sun, or the moon,
this has been truly explained by relying on the Muni,
brilliant in meaning, words, phenomena, and power.**

Relying on the outer primary condition, which is the light of a butter-lamp, of lightning, a gem, the sun, or the moon, an individual endowed with a clear consciousness of sight, forming the inner primary condition, will perceive visible things. Seeing them in an unperverted way this individual can also explain them to others. Likewise this *Commentary on the Highest Continuity* has been well explained by relying on the sublime words of the Muni as the outer primary condition. The Muni is endowed with insight into all knowable phenomena by radiating the light of the four kinds of individual and authentic awareness (Tib. *so so yang dag par rig pa bzhi*). [The first of these four is] individual and authentic awareness of the meaning (Tib. *don*), which is equivalent to knowing the intrinsic and general characteristics of all phenomena. [The second is] individual and authentic awareness of the words (Tib. *tshig*), which is equivalent to knowing all denotations without exception. [The third is] individual and authentic awareness of phenomena, which is equivalent to knowing all synonymous names without exception. [The fourth is] individual and authentic awareness of self-reliance and fearless power (Tib. *spobs*), which is equivalent to knowing all knowable objects in an unhindered and unobstructed way. The inner primary condition that was relied upon [when composing this text] is the immediate seeing of the tathagatagarbha by means of the eye of discriminative wisdom. (See also Part Three, annotation 81.)

B.II.3.2.3. Definition of the words of the Buddha

Whatever speech is meaningful and well connected with Dharma,
which removes all afflictions of the three realms
and shows the benefit of the [attainment] of peace,
is the speech of the Sage, while any different speech is other.

Any exalted speech having the four following particular properties is the command of the Victorious One, the sublime speech of the Great Sage, the Buddha: Whatever is expressed holds great meaning and benefit. The words that are the means of expression are well connected with stainless Dharma. Its function is such that it causes elimination of all the afflictions of the three realms of existence. It demonstrates the fruit, showing the benefit of nirvana as being peace, [the state beyond any torment and pain]. Any speech connecting one with [the elimination of all affliction and the attainment of peace] is equivalent to the sacred words of the Buddha. As opposed to that, anything else, since it is different from his command, should not be followed.

B.II.3.2.4. Explanation that everything according with the Buddha's words should be accepted

Whatever someone has explained with undistracted mind,
exclusively in the light of the Victor's teaching,
and conducive to the path of attaining release,
one should place on one's head as the words of the Sage.

Whichever scriptures have been composed by an author with undistracted mind, solely in the light of the Victor's teaching, exclusively expressing its meaning, and thus elucidating all the words of the Buddha and granting excellent explanation conducive to the attainment of the fruit, which is the path leading to liberation, should be placed on the head as the words of the Sage, of the Buddha himself. The reason is that these completely pure scriptures, which comment the intended meaning of the [Buddha's words], are in the likeness of these words themselves.

B.II.3.2.5. One should not teach contradicting the Buddha's words

> There is no one in this world more skilled in Dharma than the
>   Victor.
> No other has such insight, knowing everything without
>   exception [and knowing] supreme thatness the way it is.
> Thus one should not distort the sutras presented by the Sage
>   himself,
> since this would destroy the Muni's manner [of teaching] and
>   furthermore cause harm to the sacred Dharma.

Compared to the Victor, the Perfect Buddha, there is no one in this world as skilled in Dharma. There is no other who has such knowledge consisting of the primordial wisdom that directly knows all aspects, perceiving them the way they are and in an unperverted manner. The Buddha's primordial wisdom knows completely and knows correctly. Thus he knows the whole range of the knowable, as much as there is, without any exception, and he knows everything as it is, in terms of supreme thatness. For this reason whichever sutras the great Sage himself has presented in terms of a definitive and a provisional meaning should not be adulterated and explained in a false way. They should not be distorted through self-styled artifices, such as calling a meaning requiring interpretation a definitive meaning, and a definitive meaning a provisional one. For if one does so, the way in which the Perfect Buddha [has expounded] his pure teaching will be destroyed. One will further cause harm to the sacred Dharma and fall into the great evil of abandoning it.

B.II.3.2.6. Explanation of the fault of contradiction
B.II.3.2.6.1. Defining how the Dharma is abandoned
B.II.3.2.6.1.1. Explanation of how it is abandoned due to the condition of one's stream of being

> Those blinded by poisons [and possessed of] the nature of
>   ignorance
> revile the noble ones and despise the teachings they have
>   spoken.

> Since all this stems from a fixated view, mind should not be
> joined with polluted vision.
> Clean cloth is totally transformed by color, but never is cloth
> [to be treated] with oil.

Those who are blinded by their mental poisons and possessed of the nature of ignorance revile the noble ones who are special objects [of veneration], and despise the teachings these noble ones have spoken. All of this is produced by an inferior view fixated upon one's very own doctrine. Since any holding on to inferior tenets twists what is self-sprung into something bound up with pollution, one should not join one's mind with such fixed and opinionated view. It is suitable, for instance, to transform a clean cloth that is free from stains through color into various hues, but it is not suitable to [treat] such cloth with oil.

B.II.3.2.6.1.2. The ten direct causes for abandoning the Dharma

> Due to a feeble intellect, lack of striving for virtue, reliance
> on false pride,
> a nature obscured by neglect of pure Dharma, taking the
> provisional for the definitive meaning—for thatness,
> craving for profit,
> being under the sway of [inferior] views, relying on those
> disapproving [of Dharma], staying away from those who
> uphold the teachings,
> and due to mean devotion, the teachings of the Foe-
> Vanquishers are abandoned.

It is taught [in the scriptures]: "Thus the definitive meaning, the final and ultimate essence of the teachings of the Great Vehicle, is supremely profound and possesses great benefit." This being so, one might wonder: How could anyone not have devotion and thus totally abandon it? This is not the fault of the Dharma but the fault of such an individual. This relates to the fact that a person will abandon the sacred Dharma for the following [ten] reasons:

(1) Discriminative wisdom thoroughly investigating the profound meaning is faint and a person's understanding and intellectual capacity are extremely feeble.

(2) Since the disposition to be expanded has not been awakened, there is total lack of striving for unstained virtuous properties.

(3) A person relies on false pride, nourishing the conceited idea: "I have qualities!" while what he believes to be a quality is not one at all.

(4) In former lives a person has accumulated the karma through which the sacred Dharma is abandoned, doing so very intensively

and to a great extent. For this reason this person has the nature of being obscured [and blinded] with respect to truth.

(5) The sublime words of the Buddha expressing the provisional meaning are mistakenly held to be a definitive meaning, which is thatness, [the true nature] of all phenomena.

(6) A person is in the grip of very strong craving and greed for the profits of sense gratifications, such as food, clothing, wealth, and so on.

(7) A person is under the sway of being totally fixated upon and indoctrinated by inferior views, such as the views belonging to the transitory collection, and so on.

(8) A person has fallen to the influence of evil friends, having relied on them for a very long time, having totally forsaken the sacred Dharma, and having disapproved of and noisily opposed its deep and vast aspects.

(9) Likewise, for a very long time, a person has stayed away from those who have the characteristics of a saintly being, from spiritual friends who uphold the sacred teachings of the Great Vehicle.

(10) A person has mean devotion and aspiration, in that he delights in what is harmful and wrong, while there is no faith and confidence in the true Dharma and in pure beings.

These are the reasons why the sacred teaching of the tathagatas who have vanquished all foes is abandoned; there is hardly any need to mention that in this way especially the instructions on profound thatness are forsaken. Since this will also damage and cause deterioration of one's own being, those who are skillful will not act like that.

B.II.3.2.6.2. Defining how not to abandon the profound Dharma

> Skillful beings must not be as deeply afraid of fire and cruel poisonous snakes,
> of murderers or lightning, as they should be of the loss of the profound Dharma.
> Fire, snakes, enemies, and thunderbolts [can] only separate us from this life,
> but cannot take us to the utterly fearful states of [the hells] of direst pain.

Pure sentient beings who are skillful in adopting [what is right] and abandoning [what is wrong] should not fear anything frightful in this world as much as the loss of the profound sacred Dharma. They should not be as afraid of being burnt by a raging fire, eaten by a cruel poisonous snake, killed by a murderer, or struck by lightning. These are irrelevant, since the loss of Dharma is to be feared far more than them. When we die from fire, a snake, an enemy, or a thunderbolt, this only has the power to separate us from this very life; it cannot make us go into the evil wanderings, into the utterly fearful states of the hells infested with direst pain (Skt. *Avici*). Whereas, when abandoning the sacred Dharma, one will experience the suffering of the Avici hell.

B.II.3.2.6.3. Explanation that abandoning the Dharma is more grave than the immeasurably negative acts

> Even someone who has relied on evil friends again and again
>   and thus heeded harmful intentions towards a buddha,
> who has committed one of the most heinous acts—killing
>   his father, mother, or an arhat, or splitting the sublime
>   Assembly—
> will be quickly released from these, once genuinely reflecting
>   the dharmata.
> But where would liberation be for someone whose mind is
>   hostile to Dharma?

An individual may have relied again and again on evil and mis-leading friends and thus may have wounded a buddha's body, spilling his blood in the harmful intention of wanting to kill him. He may have committed one of the three most severe acts of killing his father, his mother, or an arhat. Or he may have created a rift in the sublime Assembly, causing division among its members. Even such a person will be quickly released from the karma of the immeasurably negative acts once he closely and genuinely reflects suchness or the dharmata, which is the way in which everything really exists. But where would liberation be for an individual whose mind is hostile to the teaching of the Great Vehicle and who therefore abandons the sacred Dharma? There is no [possibility of] release for such an individual. Since the negativity of abandoning the Dharma is even more severe than having committed the immeasurably negative acts, one should always refrain from this great evil.

B.II.3.3. Dedication and summary of the meaning
B.II.3.3.1. Meaning of the benefits combined with a dedication prayer

> Having properly explained the seven [vajra] points of the
>   jewels, the utterly pure element,
> flawless enlightenment, qualities, and activity, may any virtue
>   I harvest from this

lead all sentient beings to see the Lord of Boundless Life who
is endowed with Infinite Light.
Upon seeing, may their stainless Dharma-eye open and may
they reach highest enlightenment.

Thus I have properly explained the seven points resembling a vajra,
being the Three Rare and Sublime Ones, the element by nature utterly
pure, enlightenment free from pollution, the fact that [enlightenment]
possesses sixty-four qualities, and the manifestation of activity. May
any virtue that I, Maitreya, harvest from this explanation lead all sentient beings, whose number is as infinite as space, temporarily to directly perceive the kaya of Amitayus (Tib. *tshe dpag med*), the great
Sage of Boundless Life who is endowed with Infinite Light. Upon perceiving him, may they also receive his teachings. May their Dharma-
eye be freed from dust and may the realization of the unpolluted path
of seeing be born in them. Finally may they attain unsurpassable supreme enlightenment.

All the virtue of composing this text is dedicated to all sentient beings for their unsurpassable enlightenment. Through this, all followers are advised and encouraged to apply themselves to practice.

B.II.3.3.2. Summary

On what basis, for what reason, and in what way
[this has been given], what it explains
and what cause is conducive [to understanding it]
have been taught by means of four stanzas.
Two stanzas [show] the means to purify oneself
and one [shows] the cause of deterioration.
Thereupon, by means of two further stanzas
the fruit [sprung from deterioration] is explained.
[Being born] in the mandala of a buddha's retinue,
attaining patience and [then] enlightenment:
expressing these qualities, the two aspects of fruit
are explained by the last in a summarized way.

[The following ten points are expressed in the foregoing nine stanzas]:
(1) The basis on which [this text] was explained is taught by means
of the line: "Based on the trustworthy words of the Buddha and on
scriptures of logic..."
(2) The reason or need for explaining it is taught by the lines [con-
tained in the same stanza]: "I have explained this for the sole purpose

of purifying myself and supporting all those whose understanding is endowed with the best possible virtue and devotion."

(3) The way it was explained is taught by the stanza: "As someone with eyes sees by relying on a lamp, or on lightning, a jewel, the sun, or the moon..." and so on.

(4) The essence of the meaning to be explained is taught by the stanza: "Whatever speech is meaningful..." and so on.

(5) What kind of explanation will become a cause conducive to the realization of what is to be understood from this text is taught by the stanza: "Whatever someone has explained with undistracted mind, exclusively in the light of the Victor's teaching..." and so on.

Thus the way the commentary has been undertaken and carried out is extensively taught by the aforementioned four stanzas [the first of these teaching two points].

(6) Through the two stanzas: "There is no one in this world more skilled in Dharma than the Victor..." and so forth it is taught that, as a means of purifying oneself, one should be alert to and avoid the obscuration [resulting from] abandoning the Dharma.

(7) Through the stanza: "Due to a feeble intellect..." and so on one is advised to abandon [the fault of losing the Dharma], since by accumulating the actions of forsaking the Dharma one sets the cause that deteriorates one's nature and being.

(8) Thereupon, through the two stanzas [starting with the words]: "Skillful beings must not be as deeply afraid..." the consequence of abandoning the Dharma is very clearly depicted. It is taught that there will be a twofold fruit: through deteriorating from and losing the profound Dharma one will temporarily take birth in the evil wanderings and will ultimately not attain liberation.

(9) The last stanza is wholehearted dedication [to all sentient beings] expressing [the wish that they may attain] the following qualities: to temporarily be born in the utterly pure mandala of a buddha's retinue and thereupon directly realize the true state of everything; to attain the patience that is not timid regarding the profound meaning and can forbear it; and to finally reach great unsurpassable enlightenment. This dedication is expressed in the stanza: "Having properly explained the seven [vajra] points of the jewels, the utterly pure element..." and so on. Through this last stanza it is well explained in a summarized form that all followers of the sacred Dharma will harvest a twofold fruit, being the best possible temporary and ultimate benefit.

♦ This was the section "Benefit," the fifth chapter of *The Commentary on the Highest Continuity of the Mahayana Dharma which Analyzes the Disposition of the Rare and Sublime Ones.*

With this the complete explanation of the fifth chapter, teaching the benefit, is achieved.

B.II.3.3.3. The way it was perfected

It was translated from Sanskrit into Tibetan by the great Pandita and scholar Sadzana, who was a grandson of the Brahmin Ratnavajra, a great scholar of the Incomparable City of Glory in the land of Kashmir [Shrinagar], and by a Tibetan translator, the Sakya monk Lodän Sherab, in this Incomparable City of Glory.

PART THREE

Explanations by Khenpo Tsultrim Gyamtso Rinpoche

Annotation 1:
(1) The state of a buddha is called "perfect" since the two aspects of abandonment and realization are finally perfected.

(2) The two truths are the absolute and the relative truth.

(3) The Sangha of noble ones consists of those who have directly realized emptiness. They are called "noble" since due to this realization they have reached a higher level of mental development than an ordinary being.

(4) Within the system of the Madhyamaka, "Rangtong Madhyamaka" and "Shäntong Madhyamaka" (Tib. *dbu ma rang stong dang dbu ma gzhan stong*) are distinguished. Literally, Rangtong means "self-empty" and Shäntong "empty of other." In the view of the Rangtong Madhyamaka, "the expanse by nature completely pure" refers to the fact that all phenomena are by nature not truly existent. It is equivalent to emptiness in the sense of complete freedom from conceptual elaboration (Tib. *spros pa*). In the view of the Shäntong Madhyamaka it is the nature of mind, being the inseparable union of spaciousness and awareness (Tib. *dbyings rig dbyer med*).

(5) The defilements from which the element or the tathagatagarbha is purified in the state of enlightenment are the adventitious stains of delusion with regard to appearances, or in other words, the veils of the mental poisons and hindrances to knowledge.

(6) The term "fruit of freedom" is used from the viewpoint of complete freedom from all the defilements consisting of delusion with regard to appearances. With this freedom, the thirty-two qualities of the dharmakaya are attained. The fruit of complete maturation results from the fact that the accumulation of merit has been led to complete maturity. It consists of the thirty-two qualities of the form kayas.

(7) When having reached ultimate direct realization, one has disposal over the means causing all other beings to gain this realization. This is buddha activity, which consists of the power or ability of the qualities, or in other words, of the fact that one wields great qualities, those of freedom and complete maturation.

Annotation 2:
When speaking of the qualities, those of the path and the fruit are to be distinguished. The qualities of the path are those present while the state of buddhahood is not yet reached, which are present on the paths of accumulation, of junction, of seeing, and of meditation. The qualities present on the path of no more learning are the qualities of the fruit.

Nagarjuna's words are to be understood as follows: If the element is present and one practices the sacred Dharma, thus purifying oneself from the defilements, one will attain the fruit on the support of this purification. If the element was not present, not the slightest fruit would be attained, even though one practiced the Dharma and purified oneself from the defilements. This can be illustrated by means of an example: If ore bears gold and is processed, one will obtain gold. If ore is not gold-bearing, no gold will emerge, no matter how long one processes it. The view as it is expressed by Nagarjuna's words corresponds to that of the *Uttara Tantra Shastra*. Nagarjuna has composed two collections of works, which are called "Collection of Reasonings" (Tib. *dbu ma rig pa'i tshogs drug*) and "Collection of Praises" (Tib. *dbu ma stod tshogs*). The *Dharmadhatustava* belongs to the latter. The collection of reasonings contains the view of the second turning of the wheel of Dharma, while the collection of praises contains the approach of the third turning of the wheel of Dharma, which corresponds to the Shäntong view.

When the element, or in other words, the dharmadhatu, the inseparable union of spaciousness and awareness, is described as being by nature completely pure, this means that it is not to be considered as something that is formerly impure and later purified. It is equivalent to the way the mind exists—as the inseparable union of emptiness and clear light. It is always by nature pure, even though the adventitious defilements, which do not affect this purity, have to be removed, just as the dross needs to be removed in order to obtain the pure gold contained therein.

Annotation 3:

"The expanse of the equality of all phenomena" can be explained as follows: The term "phenomena" refers to all outer and inner phenomena, that is, to the phenomena of the basis and to those of the fruit. The phenomena of the fruit consist of the fruits of the three vehicles; the phenomena of the basis comprise all phenomena of samsara without exception. The fact that there is no difference with regard to the essence of phenomena is called "equality." How this is to be understood is often explained through the example of dream. While dreaming, fire and water are equal, as are light and darkness, in that they are equally not truly existent. With regard to their essence there is no difference. The expanse of equality is therefore the expanse of the emptiness of all phenomena.

The term "primary condition" is to be understood by the way in which, for example, the sense faculty of the eye constitutes the primary condition for the eye to perceive visible objects. Without its sense faculty the eye could not perceive anything. Likewise, the presence of the qualities is necessary as they are the primary condition for the manifestation of the inconceivable activity of a buddha's body, speech, and mind. If the qualities were not present, a buddha would not be able to act spontaneously and without deliberate effort for the benefit of all sentient beings.

Annotation 4:

The term "name and form" (Tib. *ming gzugs*) refers to the five skandhas: form (Skt. *rūpa*, Tib. *gzugs*), feelings (Skt. *vedanā*, Tib. *tshor ba*), discrimination (Skt. *saṃjñā*, Tib. *'du shes*), compositional factors (Skt. *saṃskāra*, Tib. *'du byed*), and consciousness (Skt. *vijñāna*, Tib. *rnam shes*). The term is used because, other than form, the remaining four can only be grasped by a name.

When speaking of doubts about the truth and about action and its fruit, this refers to two things: the first are doubts about the meaning or validity of the Four Noble Truths or of the two truths, which are the absolute and the relative truth. The second are doubts about the fact that the practice of virtue acts as the cause giving rise to the fruit of happiness, the fact that suffering will arise on the basis of unvirtuous action, and so on.

The views belonging to the fearful or transitory collection (Skt. *satkāyadṛṣṭi*, Tib. *'jig tshogs la lta ba* [the text translated here reads *'jigs tshogs*) are views such as taking the skandhas as a self or as something that belongs to this self, and so forth. There are twenty of these described, for instance, in the *Madhyamakavatara* (Tib. *dbu ma la 'jug pa*) by Chandrakirti. For further information in English, see Jeffrey Hopkins, *Meditation on Emptiness* (Boston: Wisdom Publications, 1983), pp. 176 f., 258 f.

Annotation 5:

The usage of the terms "subject matter" (Tib. *rdzas*) and "aspect" (Tib. *ldog pa*) can be explained as follows: Taking a flower as an example, the flower itself is the subject matter. From the point of view that it has come into existence due to causes and conditions, the flower is compounded. From the point of view that it undergoes a process of destruction taking place from instant to instant—that it is continuously nearing cessation—the flower is impermanent. This way of distinguishing two different features with regard to the flower is a classification in terms of different aspects. On the basis of the flower itself, however, whatever is compounded is impermanent and whatever is impermanent is compounded. These two aspects have just one essence. With regard to the essence there is no variety. Nevertheless, since the flower is able to appear to thought as having various different features, it gains an according variety in terms of verbal expression. These aspects are a mere difference of terms; on the basis of the subject matter as such, all different aspects are indivisible.

The terms "subject matter" and "aspect" play a very important role in the explanations of valid cognition (Tib. *tshad ma*). Having gained a proper understanding of the meaning of these terms, one will come to understand the way mind manifests. A subject matter is the object of the sense consciousnesses, which are free from thought. An aspect is the object of thought. When the eye-consciousness perceives a flower, it only perceives the subject matter. It does not perceive the flower in terms of "this flower is white, red, compounded, impermanent," and so on. The conceptual mind makes these differences and divides the flower into various aspects, whereas the sense consciousness perceives the subject matter, or the individual characteristic (Tib. *rang mtshan*), of the sense-object just as it comes within the range of perception (Tib. *bzhin shar du*). Therefore the terms "subject matter" and "aspect of the subject matter" refer to the way in which an understanding that is free from thought and one that is bound up with thought manifest. It is very important that these two different ways of manifestation are understood well.

Annotation 6:
Contrary to other worldly beings, arhats have an arising through a body of mental nature and a cessation in terms of an inconceivable type of death.

The omniscient Rongtön was an eminent scholar and the teacher of the Sixth Karmapa Tongwa Dönden. He holds that buddhahood is uncreated in the sense of the fourth criterion of uncreatedness. According to Rongtön, the dharmakaya has the quality of uncreatedness since it does not appear to the disciples as something that arises and ceases, whereas the form kayas are created or compounded since these appear to the disciples as something that arises and ceases.

When it is said that a buddha shows the path in accordance with the respective karmic fortune of the disciples, this means that he adapts his teaching to their respective intelligence and mental capacities. To less gifted disciples he gives a teaching enabling them to reach the state of a shravaka arhat on the basis of the Shravaka Vehicle. He teaches the path of the pratyekabuddhas to disciples of middling gifts, while highly gifted disciples receive the teaching of the path of the Mahayana.

The first three qualities of buddhahood, that is, those of being uncreated, spontaneously present, and not a realization due to extraneous conditions, are the qualities of the dharmakaya, which constitutes the most excellent benefit for oneself. The last three qualities, that is, those of primordial wisdom of knowledge, compassionate love, and ability, are the qualities of the form kayas, which bring about the most excellent benefit of others.

Annotation 7:
(1) The expanse or the open dimension (Tib. *dbyings*), which is complete peace beyond any conceptual elaboration, having neither up nor down, neither middle nor end, is called the dharmadhatu (Tib. *chos kyi dbyings*). It is similar to the depth or sphere of space, which is extremely vast and open and does not obstruct anything. Suchness is equivalent to emptiness. The terms "dharmadhatu," "suchness," and "absolute truth" are synonymous in that both "dharmadhatu" and "suchness" denote emptiness, and the absolute truth is the way everything exists, which is also emptiness. In the context dealt with here, which is to say in the Shäntong view, this emptiness is to be understood mainly in the sense of ultimate emptiness or the ultimate expanse. This is the nature of mind or the way the mind truly exists, being the inseparable union of spaciousness and awareness or of emptiness and clear light. According to the Madhyamaka, however, the nature of mind is to be understood solely from the point of view that all phenomena do not truly exist. In this view it is nothing but empty in the sense of not being accessible to any conceptualization. It is very important to gain a proper understanding of these two different views. What is mainly taught in the system to which the *Uttara Tantra Shastra* belongs is the aspect of awareness (Tib. *rig pa*) or clear light (Tib. *od gsal*), whereas in the system of the Madhyamaka the aspect of emptiness in the sense of freedom from conceptual elaboration is exclusively taught. If one understands well what is meant by the inseparable union of emptiness and clear light, one comes very close to the path of the Vajrayana. In the system of the Vajrayana the nature of mind is then described as the inseparable union of clarity-emptiness (Tib. *gsal stong*), of bliss-

emptiness (Tib. *bde stong*), of appearance-emptiness (Tib. *snang stong*), and of awareness-emptiness (Tib. *rig stong*). These are called the four "joint manifestations" (Tib. *zung 'jug bzhi*). Without knowing the meaning of the inseparable union of spaciousness and awareness one will not be able to understand these. Not having studied the views as presented in the *Uttara Tantra Shastra* and in the Madhyamaka system, one will not come to an understanding of the Vajrayana where the four joint manifestations are introduced. One would find oneself forced to leave the level of the Vajrayana "already reached," in order to study the vehicle of characteristics that forms its basis. It is therefore advisable to study this first. If, for example, someone learns how to fly a plane without being able to drive a car, he might one day have to learn how to drive while he can already fly. Since the first is also much more difficult than the latter, one had better keep the appropriate order. In brief, one should endeavor to study and understand the views of the *Uttara Tantra Shastra* and the Madhyamaka properly, since they equally constitute the cause of one's ability to follow the Vajrayana path.

When it is said that the truth of cessation does not fall into the extreme of nihilism, this means that it does not fall into the extreme view of considering the absolute truth as being just empty in the sense of a bare nothingness or non-presence of anything. To describe this, the commentary partly uses words from the terminology of the Prasangika Madhyamaka. In this terminology the reasoning would be as follows: the truth of cessation does not fall into the extreme of nihilism, since it exists as the object of experience of self-sprung primordial wisdom.

The literal meaning of the Tibetan term "künzob" (*kun rdzob*), which is here translated as "relative," is "false from every angle" or "deceptive." A phenomenon is called "adventitious" when it comes into existence as something fleeting and when it is able to be removed or abandoned. An example for this is water containing mud, which will settle by itself when the water is not stirred, and which does not affect the purity of the water itself. Another example is defilements in the sky such as clouds or smoke, which also do not impair the purity of the sky and are dispelled by a breeze. By means of these examples one should understand that there are defilements in terms of mental poisons and obstructions to knowledge as long as the state of buddhahood is not reached, but that the nature or essence of mind has been pure since beginningless time and is not afflicted in the slightest by the adventitious stains of confusion, by the mental poisons and so on, which are able to be removed. For this reason one can say: "The dharma-dhatu, the absolute truth, does not fall into the extreme of eternalism, since it has been free from arising as a relative, adventitious thing since beginningless time." Generally speaking, the term "eternalism" refers to a view considering a subject that undergoes an arising and a ceasing as something that cannot be destroyed in any way. Here, in this context, the extreme of eternalism consists of a view holding a subject to be truly existent, to be inherently or of itself existent.

The statement that the truth of cessation is completely freed from the conceptual elaboration that consists of the four extreme views, again stems from the terminology of the Prasangika Madhyamaka. According to this terminology the truth of cessation, that is, the dharmadhatu, the absolute truth, is completely freed from the four extreme beliefs in the non-existence of a subject, the existence of a subject, the simultaneous existence and non-existence of a subject, and a presence of a subject that is neither existent nor non-existent. Therefore it is completely freed from the conceptual elaboration that consists of the four extreme views.

In the terminology of the scriptures explaining the dharmadhatu or the absolute truth, the name or the designation of a subject in question is called "symbol" (Tib. *brda*), whereas its properties are called "terms" (Tib. *tha snyad*). When a flower is called a "flower," this is a symbol. When the flower is described as being white, red, or yellow, or as being impermanent, faded, and so on, these are terms. The dharmadhatu, or the ultimate absolute truth, is beyond symbols and it cannot be expressed by means of terms. As such it is completely beyond the field of activity of speech and is therefore inexpressible.

The terms "self-aware" and "other-aware" denote two different types of perception. Whatever is perceived by the different sense consciousnesses—of the eye, the nose, and so on—is an other-aware perception. A self-aware perception does not focus outwards and perceive something else, but perceives its very own essence. At the time when emptiness or Mahamudra is realized, the essence of one's own mind is realized by itself in such a way that there is no duality between an object to be realized and a realizing subject.

The Dharma in terms of the truth of cessation has three qualities, the first being the fact that it is inconceivable. The commentary substantiates this by successive proofs. When these are traced back, the reasoning is as follows:

(1) The true nirvana of the noble ones, constituting the absolute truth, is the object of perception of the self-aware, or self-sprung, primordial wisdom of the noble ones, since it is not an object for an other-aware perception.

(2) The absolute truth is not an object for an other-aware perception since it cannot be explained by means of examples, logical reasonings, and so forth.

(3) It cannot be explained by means of examples, logical reasonings, and so forth since it is inexpressible by means of symbols, terms, and so on and thus beyond the field of activity of speech.

(4) It is beyond symbols, terms, and so on since any ideation is completely pacified.

(5) All ideation is completely pacified since it is beyond the conceptual elaboration consisting of the four extreme views.

An improper conceptual activity (Tib. *tshul bzhin ma yin pa'i rnam par rtog pa*) is a wrong way of thinking, such as taking something that is impure to be pure, something that does not exist as a self to be a self, and so on.

(2) The literal meaning of the Tibetan term "nyönmong" (*nyon mongs*), which is here translated as "mental poisons," is "affliction." The mental poisons are an affliction since they oppress and afflict the mind and above all cause it suffering. The "remaining imprints" (Tib. *bag chags*) are to be understood as the after-effect or the remaining force (Tib. *nus pa*) of the mental poisons. If, for instance, a person has been drinking a considerable amount of alcohol over a long period of time and then stops doing so, he will still feel an urge from time to time, although he has given up his habit completely. The preceding behavior has an after-effect, a remaining force. The traditional example is musk that has been put on a piece of paper. Even after a long time, when the musk itself is completely gone, the smell will still be noticeable.

The truth of the path is mainly equivalent to the primordial wisdom that directly realizes emptiness. The essence of this primordial wisdom is its utter purity, which is to be understood as complete purification. It is utterly pure in the sense that the defilements of the mental poisons and their remaining imprints are eliminated and no longer present.

The veil of the hindrances to knowledge mainly consists of the following three aspects: the first is the fact that the so-called three circles (Tib. *'khor gsum*) or complexes, that is, actor, object, and action, are perceived as something truly existent. This is the coarse aspect of the obstructions to knowledge. A subtler aspect is the fact that the three complexes are perceived in terms of their characteristics. The third aspect consists of the fact that the three complexes appear as two. This perception of mere duality as such is the subtlest aspect of the veil of the hindrances to knowledge.

Thus the truth of the path is primordial wisdom, which is free from the veil of the hindrances to knowledge. The "brilliant light rays of the direct knowledge of all aspects" are this primordial wisdom that directly realizes the true nature of all phenomena, or in other words, the absolute truth.

Annotation 8:

A conceptual understanding is any worldly understanding that perceives the relative.

The three poisons are desire, aversion, and mental blindness.

When speaking of the two truths comprising complete purification, the term "complete purification" refers to the following: Two parts are to be distinguished: that of complete purification (Tib. *rnam byang phyogs*) and that of the mental poisons (Tib. *nyon mongs phyogs*). The first part includes the fruit of the process of purification, which is the state of utter purity from any defilement, as well as the means to bring about this purification. In the same way, the latter part includes the veils or obscurations as well as their causes.

Annotation 9:

The term "freedom from attachment" covers three aspects: the means that frees one from attachment, the basis to be freed from attachment, and the state of freedom from attachment.

When one speaks of the two types of purity, the first type is the utter purity of the nature, which is to say that the nature of mind, or the element, the sugatagarbha, has been free from all defilements such as the mental poisons and so on since beginningless time. From the viewpoint of the essence, gold contained in ore is also pure gold. Corresponding to this example, the nature of mind is completely pure. The second type of purity is freedom from the adventitious defilements. This is comparable to the purity achieved through processing the ore and removing the dross. Once the dross is completely removed there are two types of purity, the first being the purity that is also present while gold is contained in ore, and the second being the purity achieved through the complete removal of the dross.

Annotation 10:
When speaking of self-aware primordial wisdom present during meditation, this is to be understood as follows: "meditation" here refers to
a condition of balanced equipoise in which one directly dwells within
the true state (Skt. *dharmatā*), or in other words, within emptiness, the
nature of mind, which is the absolute truth or reality.

The term "self-aware" is also part of the terminology of the Chittamatra system (the Mind-Only School), yet is used there in another
meaning. The system of the Chittamatra speaks of a self-aware consciousness. While the consciousnesses of the five senses focus outwards and perceive outer objects, the mental sense-consciousness focuses inwards and experiences by itself its own essence (Tib. *rang gi
ngo bo rang gis myong ba*). In the system to which the *Uttara Tantra Shastra*
belongs, however, the term "self-aware" denotes a realization that is
self-sprung, by means of which the true state, the nature of mind, is
realized directly, free from the duality of perceived and perceiver.

A worldly understanding is the understanding of an ordinary being.
This is any understanding that does not directly realize emptiness.

Synonyms of the term "suchness" (Tib. *de bzhin nyid*) are the terms
"true state" (Tib. *chos nyid*), "emptiness" (Tib. *stong pa nyid*), "dharmadhatu" (Tib. *chos kyi dbyings*), or "absolute truth" (Tib. *don dam pa'i
bden pa*).

Annotation 11:
When one has directly realized emptiness, one does not fall back to
the level of the smaller vehicles. Since a bodhisattva, that is, a noble
one, an heir of the Buddha (Tib. *rgyal sras*), has this realization, one
speaks of the bodhisattvas who do not fall back.

By the phrase "their own minds have directly revealed themselves
as being by nature clear light and functioning as the antidote ... ," the
following is expressed: In the context explained here, "one's own mind"
is equivalent to the nature of mind or to the way the relative mind
truly exists. This is the true state of the mind, which is the inseparable
union of emptiness and clear light. It can be said to be an antidote
since it is only the mind in terms of its true existence or state that
counteracts the illusory appearances or the appearance of duality (Tib.
gnyis snang).

The fact that it has directly revealed itself (Tib. *mngon sum du gyur
pa*), or in other words, that it is realized as it is, means the following:
Two kinds of realization, direct realization (Tib. *mngon sum*) and inferred

realization (Tib. *rjes dpag*), are to be distinguished. These terms are also used within the teachings on valid cognition (Tib. *tshad ma*). Generally speaking, the teachings on valid cognition represent "that which makes the mind free from being confused and deluded." In this context all inferences and deductions taking place on the basis of symbols, characteristics, and logical reasonings are inferred valid cognitions (Tib. *rjes dpag mtshan ma*). A realization taking place without the support of these is a direct valid cognition (Tib. *mngon sum tshad ma*). Simply because it is in front of us, a flower, for instance, is perceived directly by means of the sense consciousness of the eye. This seeing, which is to say the sense consciousness perceiving the flower, is called direct valid cognition. If one makes inferences about the flower and finds that it is empty or does not exist as a self, the understanding perceiving it in such a way is an inferred valid cognition, since this understanding had to be derived. Put briefly, there are two ways of realizing any phenomenon: an inferred and a direct realization. The first takes place on the basis of symbols, characteristics, and logical reasonings. In the context of the second, the object is realized directly, without any obscuration and just as it appears.

When the statement that the mind has revealed itself as being by nature clear light is seen in the light of the Shäntong or Mahamudra views, it is equivalent to the direct or immediate realization of the nature of mind, or of the way the mind truly exists. The point at which one faces the nature of mind, the inseparable union of emptiness and clear light in which all conceptual elaboration has finally subsided, is called direct realization.

The statement that the essence of the mental poisons has been free from arising since beginningless time refers to the following: The term "arising" means that something is by nature existent, truly existent, by its individual characteristics existent, and so on. Freedom from arising is therefore equivalent to the fact that the subject matter in question is not truly existent and so on.

Generally speaking, we all can notice that the mental poisons arise within us. Yet, this arising is but a relative one. It only comes about as a dependent origination, due to the meeting of causes and conditions. In truth the mental poisons are free from arising. This can be shown by the example of dream. While dreaming, all kinds of images arise. Whatever arises comes about interdependently as an illusory appearance. In truth these appearances are free from arising. Whatever appears during a dream does not exist, not even in the form of a single atom. Arising as something adventitious and being able to be removed like mud in water or clouds in the sky, the mental poisons are not truly existent. Their essence has been free from arising since beginningless time. When one dreams, for example, and the appearances in this dream are seen differently as friend and enemy, aversion in view of the enemy and affection and desire in view of the friend will arise. These mental poisons are free from arising; they do not truly exist. Since the object is free from arising, the subject perceiving it is also free from arising, or in other words, not truly existent. In this sense one should reflect thoroughly. While one has a dream containing the duality of friend and enemy, and while as a reaction desire and aversion arise, the objects, that is, friend and enemy, do not truly exist. While friend and enemy do not truly exist, at the same time they form the basis for the arising of the mental poisons. These arise fleetingly and do not have an arising in terms of being truly existent. When the perceived object does not truly exist, it is not permissible to state that the perceiving subject is truly existent.

When reflecting in this way, in my opinion the Chittamatra view constitutes a very deep approach for a beginner. The view of the Madhyamaka, for instance, is not directly realized until the first bodhisattva level is reached. Its realization will be attained when, on the path of junction, a view is cultivated that corresponds to that of the Chittamatra system. This has been stated by the omniscient Pema Karpo and others in many scriptural passages. When, while traveling the path of junction, one believes in the truth of the Madhyamaka view, but for the sake of its direct realization cultivates that of the Chittamatra during one's meditation, these two aspects will become one.

The passage "therefore the bodhisattvas truly realize the nature of every being . . ." is to be understood as follows: The nature of beings is equivalent to the way all beings truly exist. With regard to any subject matter, its way of existence (Tib. *gnas lugs, gnas tshul*) and its way of appearance (Tib. *snangs tshul*) are to be distinguished. The way in which all beings appear consists of the fact that they have the nature of an illusory appearance, which has come into existence due to the predominating influence of extraneous factors, that is, due to karma and mental poisons. We all are sentient beings. Our way of appearance is to wander about in the cycle of existence, driven by the attachment to a self. We perceive as a self what does not exist as a self, as mine what does not exist as mine, and experience manifold suffering under the sway of this perception. The fact that something that does not exist as a self is perceived as a self, and that something that does not exist as belonging to this self is perceived as belonging to this self, has the effect that the aspects "friend" and "enemy" are perceived, that "my friend" and "my enemy" come into existence. These two aspects of attachment and aversion act as the basis giving rise to the manifold forms of suffering. This is the way in which beings appear.

The way of appearance of fire, for example, is that it is hot and burning. The way of existence of fire is the fact that it is by nature empty. When one dreams of being burnt by fire, this fire appears as something that is by nature hot and burning. Yet, the true nature or way of existence of this fire is emptiness in the sense that it is free from any conceptual elaboration, or in other words, free from the three aspects of arising, abiding, and ceasing.

In the same way, the nature of all beings is the ultimate selflessness of persons and phenomena. The five skandhas do not exist as a self. Nevertheless the two aspects of perception, which contain the beliefs that the person exists as a self and that phenomena exist as a self (Tib. *gang zag gi bdag dang chos kyi bdag*), arise within us on the basis of these skandhas. When on the basis of the physical body the thoughts "I" and "mine" arise, these result in a perception taking this body as being a self in the sense that a person truly exists. When these thoughts are not present, but the body is taken to be real and perceived as being truly existent, this is an understanding containing the belief that phenomena exist as a self. Yet this body exists neither as a self of the person nor of phenomena. Taking the mind for an example, thoughts such as "my mind is uneasy," "I am unhappy," and so forth represent the fault of the belief in the existence of a self of the person. If the mind is viewed as being by nature existent, this is the belief in the existence of a self of phenomena. The mind does not exist as a self. This is the selflessness of persons. The mind is by nature not existent. This is the selflessness of phenomena. This difference should be understood well.

The ultimate selflessness of persons and phenomena is non-existence of self as taught by the Prasangika Madhyamaka. Non-existence of self is taught in gradual stages. In the view of the shravakas, for instance, it is to be understood solely as the selflessness of persons, whereas in the view of the Svatantrika Madhyamaka it denotes sheer voidness (Tib. *stong kyang*) comparable to empty space. In the view of the Prasangika Madhyamaka, non-existence of self is complete peace in the sense of complete freedom from the conceptual elaboration (Tib. *spros pa*) consisting of the appearance of duality (Tib. *gnyis snang*). This is the true state or nature of everything (Skt. *dharmatā*, Tib. *chos nyid*). With regard to the nature of mind, the two aspects "spaciousness" or "expanse" (Tib. *dbyings*) and "primordial wisdom" (Tib. *ye shes*) are to be distinguished. Spaciousness is the aspect of emptiness, primordial wisdom that of clear light. The term "peace" in the sense of freedom from conceptual elaboration refers mainly to the aspect of emptiness, synonyms of which are the terms "true state" (Tib. *chos nyid*), "dharma-dhatu" (Tib. *chos kyi dbyings*), "suchness" (Tib. *de bzhin nyid*), "absolute truth" (Tib. *don dam pa'i bden pa*), and "thatness" (Tib. *de kho na nyid*). In the Mahamudra or Maha Ati systems one speaks of "the great symbol," "the great gesture," or "the great seal" (Tib. *phyag rgya chen po*) and of "the great perfection" (Tib. *rdzogs pa chen po*), respectively.

As to peace or freedom from conceptual elaboration (Tib. *spros pa zhi ba*), two aspects are to be distinguished. The first is the fact that the object, the true state, is beyond conceptualization, and the second is the fact that the understanding realizing this object is free from conceptual elaboration.

When the object, the true state, is described as being beyond conceptualization, this means that emptiness is not equivalent to either non-existence or to sheer voidness that merely refutes this non-existence (Tib. *med dgag*), nor is it truly existent and so forth. Put briefly, it is a state of complete peace, of freedom from the extreme views holding it to be existent, to be non-existent, both existent and non-existent, or neither existent nor non-existent.

Nagarjuna has said in this context:

> Permanence, impermanence and so on, where are they in this
> state of peace?
> Emptiness, non-emptiness and so on, where are they in this
> state of peace?

The state of complete peace beyond permanence and impermanence, emptiness and non-emptiness, is called freedom from conceptual elaboration. This is the aspect of the object, or in other words, of emptiness being beyond any conceptualization.

The aspect of the understanding, the realizing subject, being free from conceptual elaboration should be understood as follows: When realizing that the object, the true state, is beyond conceptualization, the subject, the realizing understanding, attains the state of freedom from conceptualization while abiding at balance within this realization. If the object is not free from being conceptualized, accordingly the realizing subject will not attain the state of freedom from conceptual elaboration. If the object is viewed as being just empty and is realized as such, the realizing subject will reach a state of mere emptiness, in which nothing whatsoever is present. This understanding still contains an idea, or in other words, a conceptual elaboration. When the object is viewed as clarity, the subject gains a corresponding realization and perceives clarity. Similarly, the subject appears as peace, as freedom from thought and conceptual elaboration, when the object is realized as being beyond conceptualization.

The fact that the realizing understanding is free from conceptual elaboration means that all thoughts, all perceptions bound up with or tinged by conceptual grasping (Tib. *'zin pa*), are completely pacified.

In this context some followers of the Mahamudra system are of the opinion that the explanation of the two aspects of freedom from conceptual elaboration, as given in the Sutrayana system, means that one absorbs oneself into the object, the true state free from conceptual elaboration, and into the subject, the realizing understanding, separately during meditation. This is an error. The proponents of the Sutrayana say on the contrary that one first gains conviction that the object is beyond conceptualization and then absorbs the subject within this freedom from conceptual elaboration.

The system of the Mahamudra teaches that one has to absorb oneself into the nature of mind itself in such a way that one naturally dwells within it just as it appears. Some who receive this teaching without understanding the explanations given in the Sutrayana system will undergo a second error. The Pandita Atisha said:

> With regard to the fact that the true state is beyond conceptual elaboration, the realizing understanding is absorbed into a condition of freedom from conceptual elaboration.

Some who practice Mahamudra meditation misunderstand this, thinking that according to the Madhyamaka view one has to absorb the understanding into the true state, into emptiness, which is free from conceptual elaboration. On this basis they believe that the object into which one has to absorb oneself and the understanding that absorbs itself are the same and not two different aspects. They believe this, since according to the Mahamudra system absorption means to naturally abide within the nature of mind itself. This is a slight error due to misunderstanding the teachings of the Madhyamaka, according to which one gains conviction that the nature of mind is beyond conceptualization and then absorbs the realizing understanding into freedom from conceptual elaboration. This error, however, is but a misunderstanding of words. It does not mean that one necessarily errs with regard to one's own true nature as well. From the point of view of one's own realization, realization will arise from naturally abiding within the essence of mind. There are numerous examples of persons who did not know the meaning of absorption as it corresponds to the Madhyamaka view and yet directly realized Mahamudra, the nature of their own mind. This difference should also be understood well.

The system of the Madhyamaka contains many different kinds or levels of explanations on the way in which one should meditate according to this system.

It is said, for instance, in the scriptures teaching the gradual stages of meditation on the highest aspect of the knowable (Tib. *shes bya'i mchog*):

> Perceived phenomena are empty according to their very own essence (Tib. *rang rang ngo bos stong*). The perceiving mind is also emptiness; it is free from conceptual elaboration. To rest unmoved within the state of freedom from conceptual elaboration, the union of emptiness and clarity, is the main practice of the highest aspect of the knowable.

In the context of the gradual stages of meditation on the perfection of discriminative wisdom, the most excellent kind of practice is described as follows:

> One gains conviction that all perceived phenomena are empty according to their very own essence. One gains conviction that the perceiving mind is also empty, free from conceptual elaboration. Then one absorbs oneself into the state of freedom from conceptual elaboration.

Similar statements are to be found in many scriptural passages. It is important that these different kinds of explanation are understood well. Sakya Pandita remarks in this context that there is not the slightest difference between the view of freedom from conceptual elaboration as taught in the system of the Paramita Yana [the vehicle of the six perfections] and the views of the Mahamudra or Mantrayana. One should be aware that if on the level of the Mahamudra or Secret Mantrayana one develops a view that does not include freedom from conceptual elaboration as taught in the Prasangika Madhyamaka system, one holds a view that is flawed with ideas, with conceptual elaboration.

When speaking of the two types of primordial wisdom, those knowing correctly and completely, this means the following: The literal meanings of the Tibetan terms here translated as "correctly" and "completely" are "as it is" (Tib. *ji lta ba*) and "as much as there is" (Tib. *ji snyed pa*). Generally speaking, the term "correctly" refers to emptiness, to the absolute truth, while the term "completely" refers to the relative truth. Correct knowledge knows what truly is. If, for example, we dream of a burning fire, what is true about this phenomenon of fire? This fire is without the three aspects of arising, abiding, and cessation and as such is empty. What is not true about it? The burning of the fire is not true; it is an illusory appearance and comes about through delusion. The term "completely" refers to what is not true or correct, to the aspect of appearance that manifests as a variety.

The understanding that perceives what is true or correct is therefore called "primordial wisdom that knows correctly," and the understanding that perceives what is not true, the relative aspect of appearance, is called "primordial wisdom that knows completely." A buddha possesses these two kinds of primordial wisdom. His correct knowledge is the immediate seeing of emptiness. His complete knowledge extends to anything relative.

The statement "they see that the true state has always been present within beings whose state is relative" should be understood as follows: The literal meanings of the Tibetan terms translated here as "true state" and "those whose state is relative" are "nature" or "quality" (Tib. *chos nyid*) and "that which has this nature or quality" (Tib. *chos can*). In the context of the *Uttara Tantra Shastra* the first refers to the absolute aspect, to the way a subject matter truly exists, while the latter refers to the relative aspect, to the way a subject matter appears. When one dreams of fire, the state of this fire is relative. Its true state is the fact that it is free from the three aspects of arising, abiding, and ceasing. This is the true nature of fire. When speaking of beings, this refers to whoever possesses a mind (Tib. *sems can*). What these beings are in truth is the way in which their relative nature or relative state actually exists, this being their true state. The true state of beings is the nature of a perfect buddha, or in other words, the tathagatagarbha, the all-pervading dharmakaya. In the view of the Rangtong Madhyamaka this dharmakaya is solely considered as emptiness in the sense of complete freedom from conceptual elaboration. In the view of the Shāntong Madhyamaka it is the inseparable union of emptiness and clear light. In the speech of Dharma this is occasionally also called the inseparable union of spaciousness and awareness (Tib. *dbyings rig dbyer med*). The term "spaciousness" refers to the aspect of emptiness or freedom from conceptual elaboration; the term "awareness" refers to the aspect of clear light.

In the following section of the praise, the two primordial wisdoms constituting the quality of awareness are shown from the viewpoint of being liberated from the veils.

Primordial wisdom that knows correctly is freed from attachment to objects—it is free from the veil of the mental poisons. Primordial wisdom that knows completely is freed from obstructions, which is to say, freed from the veil of the hindrances to knowledge. They are called "obstructions" since one will not attain the unhindered knowledge of all relative phenomena as long as they are not removed. In order to reach the omniscient primordial wisdom that knows all phenomena, all aspects of the knowable, the veiling net of the hindrances to knowledge has to be eliminated.

The correctly realizing understanding free from the veil of the mental poisons and the completely realizing understanding free from the veil of the hindrances to knowledge are the two aspects of the discriminative wisdom beyond the worldly (Tib. *'jig rten las 'das pa'i shes rab*). By means of this discriminative wisdom, noble bodhisattvas know the utterly pure dharmadhatu, or way of existence of beings, as being by nature not truly existent. This is the absolute truth, emptiness, the buddha nature. They know furthermore that this dharmadhatu pervades the limitless number of all sentient beings. Buddha nature is called "all-pervasive" since it is present within all beings alike. As far as buddha nature goes, there is no distinction between "good beings" who have attained a precious human body and "inferior beings" such as animals and so forth. It undifferentiatedly pervades all sentient beings, no matter whether they are happy or suffer, whether they dwell in the higher or lower realms of existence.

Since they have these two types of understanding, bodhisattvas possess the completely pure vision of primordial wisdom with regard to the entire range of the knowable. Whatever is able to be an object of understanding is part of the knowable (Tib. *shes bya*), this being its characteristic. The term "vision" of primordial wisdom is here equivalent to the discriminative wisdom beyond the worldly. When it is said that this vision is completely pure, this means that it is an authentic seeing that is undistorted, free from error, and complete.

In this way the bodhisattvas have the quality of liberation. The element or the sugatagarbha is present within all beings, yet is not freed from the fetter of the veil of the mental poisons and from the net of the veil of the hindrances to knowledge. When these are removed one has attained the quality of liberation.

One may wonder whether someone who has reached the bodhisattva levels is freed from all the veils of the mental poisons and hindrances to knowledge. This is not the case. At this point the veils are partly purified. This process of purification continues while one travels through the bodhisattva levels, in a degree corresponding to each level. From the point of view that buddha nature in the state of the basis is also completely free from the mental poisons and obstructions to knowledge, and not in the slightest sullied by these, there is utter purity. From the point of view of the gradual removal of the adventitious defilements there is a continuous process of purification. This is expressed in the explanation of the fourth vajra point, where it is said: "[The element] is pure and yet has affliction. [Enlightenment] was not afflicted and yet is purified." An example for this is the fact that ore also contains pure gold, but that a second type of purity, a state of purification, is achieved through the removal of the dross.

Annotation 12:
The object to be realized is the true state, or in other words, suchness, the way all phenomena actually are. This is emptiness: the nature of mind, the element, or the sugatagarbha. The means necessary to realize this object is the primordial wisdom of the noble ones.

When the noble ones are said to perceive this object as being present just as it is, this means that they realize the element, or the way in which beings exist, as being the luminous buddha nature, the inseparable union of spaciousness and awareness or of emptiness and clear light. This is the object of perception of the primordial wisdom of the noble ones.

This object of perception is seen in a way that the noble ones do not have in common with others. This can be illustrated by a general example: Whenever we have a mental experience, this is an experience we do not have in common with others. Whatever a sentient being experiences is the experience of his or her own mind, which is not shared with anybody else. Corresponding to this example, the noble ones experience or realize the nature of their own minds, just as it is.

This realization is a vision by means of inner self-aware primordial wisdom, which is to say that it is not a seeing that focuses outwards. Contrary to that, the tathagatagarbha, the true nature of mind, is called self-aware. On the level of explanation, the object, the true state, and the subject realizing this true state are both to be understood as self-sprung primordial wisdom (Tib. *rang byung gi ye shes*). During meditation these self-sprung primordial wisdoms are simultaneously realized as peace, as being free from conceptual elaboration. While receiving explanations, one gains the understanding that the object, the true state, as well as the realizing subject, are self-sprung primordial wisdom. During meditation, when a condition is reached in which all conceptualization containing the duality of subject and object has subsided and come to peace, perception proves to be self-aware. It proves furthermore to be "seeing itself by itself" or to be "self-seeing according to its own essence." The two aspects of perception, an object that is seen and a seeing subject, are no longer present. When an ordinary being first hears that "self-aware" is equivalent to "seeing itself by itself," this statement is a mere thought, since it is only during meditation that the object, the true state, proves to be self-aware. On this level, the term "self-aware" means that the conceptual elaboration that contains subject and object, a perceived object and a perceiving mind, is completely appeased, that both aspects manifest as self-sprung primordial wisdom, and that one dwells within this condition of self-sprung primordial wisdom wherever it manifests, in its very own place (Tib. *rang sar du gnas pa*). When the system of the Chittamatra speaks of "self-aware," this means that the consciousness experiences itself by itself. Self-awareness in this context is therefore equivalent to the self-experience of the consciousness (Tib. *rnam shes rang myong*).

When it is said that the state of beings is relative or, literally speaking, that they are those who have a particular state or nature (Tib. *chos can*), this means that all beings have a true state (Tib. *chos nyid*), which is the dharmadhatu, the buddha nature, or the tathagatagarbha. This dharmadhatu pervades all beings no matter how many there are, which is to say that it is undifferentiatedly present within all beings, in those of low or high rank, in those who are good or evil alike. Here, the term "dharmadhatu" is equivalent to inseparable spaciousness and awareness or inseparable spaciousness and primordial wisdom (Tib. *dbyings dang ye shes dbyer med pa*). This inseparable union of spaciousness and primordial wisdom is the buddha nature, the tathagatagarbha. In the view presented by the *Madhyamakavatara* (Tib. *dbu ma la 'jug pa*) the dharmadhatu is to be understood exclusively as freedom from conceptual elaboration. The aspect of primordial wisdom is not explained there. This difference should be understood well.

The object of perception of the noble ones is the fact that the dharmadhatu or buddha nature is all-pervasively present within all sentient beings. This means that their perception first focuses on the state or nature of sentient beings and that in this way the true state is perceived. The perception focused on the entirety of beings, on all those who have this state, is the aspect of the primordial wisdom that knows completely.

Generally speaking, the aspects of correct and complete knowledge refer to the knowledge of a buddha. In this context the realization of emptiness, the fact that the absolute truth is seen, is called correct knowledge. The realization of each and every aspect that is part of the relative is called complete knowledge. Noble bodhisattvas do not have a realization equaling the correct and complete knowledge of a buddha. Merely the same terms are being used here. Noble bodhisattvas master correct and complete knowledge to a certain extent, corresponding to the level they have reached, yet their realization does not cover all the fields and kinds of the knowable. When a bodhisattva realizes the absolute truth, this is a realization free from the veil that hinders this very realization. What is realized at this point is the fact that the true state of a sentient being is peace. This is the correct knowledge of a bodhisattva. From this knowledge the recognition results that this peace, which is the true state of a sentient being, pervades all, no matter how many there are. This is the complete knowledge of a bodhisattva. The realization of a buddha means that he directly sees the nature of all phenomena. This is his correct knowledge. He has complete knowledge from the point of view that he sees the entire range of the knowable, all phenomena in all their aspects, in a completely unobscured way. As opposed to that, the passage explained here only refers to a being or to beings respectively. When the nature of one's own mind is realized directly, the power of this realization leads one to see that all sentient beings are the same in that their true state is equally peace; one realizes that the true state that has been realized pervades them all. In other words, there are two objects of realization. The nature of one's own mind is realized directly. From this realization a second is deduced. The first object of realization is the true state of beings, which is peace. From this viewpoint there is correct knowledge.

The second object of realization is the fact that not a single being is exempted from this true state, that it pervades them all. From this viewpoint there is complete knowledge.

When it is stated that bodhisattvas see these objects of realization in a way that they do not have in common with others, this means they have command of a knowledge unequaled by that of an ordinary being, a shravaka, or a pratyekabuddha. In the view presented by the *Madhyamakavatara* and similar scriptures, the three kinds of noble ones, that is, shravaka arhats, pratyekabuddha arhats, and bodhisattvas who have reached the bhumis, are considered as being on the same level. In this view the noble shravakas and pratyekabuddhas have also realized emptiness. Yet, when talking about emptiness in this context, this refers only to the aspect of spaciousness (Tib. *dbyings*), to freedom from conceptual elaboration. In the context of the *Uttara Tantra Shastra* the object of realization is buddha nature, the tathagatagarbha, being the inseparable union of spaciousness and awareness. This is very difficult to understand. With this understanding bodhisattvas have a realization that they do not hold in common with shravaka and pratyekabuddha arhats. For bodhisattvas who have reached the bodhisattva levels, different names are used. They are also called "those who have understanding" (Tib. *blo ldan*), "the heirs of the Victorious One" (Tib. *rgyal sras*), or "shoot of the Victorious One" (Tib. *rgyal ba'i nyu gu*). The noble bodhisattvas are more excellent than the shravakas and pratyekabuddhas since they excel these in understanding.

When one speaks of the inner primordial wisdom, this means that noble bodhisattvas realize the nature of their own minds, the sugatagarbha, independently from extraneous conditions, by means of self-sprung primordial wisdom. This realization takes place in such a way that the conceptual elaboration, containing the duality of an object realized and a realizing subject, has come to complete peace. Through the power of inner realization there is correct and complete knowledge. Since noble bodhisattvas have directly realized the nature of their own minds, they possess the inner realization. Through the power of this realization they see that the true state of a sentient being is peace. This is correct knowledge. Subsequently they see that this peace pervades all beings without exception. This is complete knowledge. These three aspects are the quality of awareness.

Noble bodhisattvas are purified from the two veils of attachment and obstruction, which is to say, from the veils of the mental poisons and hindrances to knowledge. With regard to both veils, a coarse, a subtler, and an extremely subtle aspect are distinguished. Having reached the first bodhisattva level, one is purified from the gross aspects of the veils of the mental poisons and hindrances to knowledge. The coarse aspect of the veil of the hindrances to knowledge is the belief in true existence. The two subtler aspects, that is, the perception of characteristics and the appearance of duality as such, are to be removed gradually while traveling the bodhisattva levels. The quality of being unsurpassable means that noble bodhisattvas are freed from inferior views, from the understanding derived from the lesser vehicles. These are the three aspects of the quality of liberation.

Annotation 13:

The vision of primordial wisdom that knows completely arises from the first bodhisattva level onwards, since at the time when one reaches this level the meaning of the true state is seen directly.

Annotation 14:

One speaks of the path beyond the worldly or the path of the noble ones, since bodhisattvas who have reached the bodhisattva levels have a realization that is beyond the stage of an ordinary being. They see the dharmadhatu in a way that they do not have in common with others, that is, with ordinary beings, shravakas, and pratyekabuddhas, just as it is, by means of self-aware or self-sprung primordial wisdom. When this dharmadhatu is called "by nature undefiled," this means that the defilements cannot touch the essence of mind at all, that the essence of mind is free from pollution. This undefiled basis is the element, the buddha nature, or sugatagarbha, which pervades all beings without exception. The fact that bodhisattvas realize this, is called complete knowledge.

There are two ways of explaining complete knowledge. In the section commented here it is described as the realization that the dharmadhatu pervades all knowable things. In this case the dharmadhatu is to be understood as emptiness in the sense of complete freedom from conceptual elaboration, as it is explained in the Rangtong Madhyamaka system. When exclusively viewed as emptiness or as being beyond conceptual elaboration, the dharmadhatu pervades everything, all sentient beings as well as all things. When viewed in the light of the Shäntong Madhyamaka, the dharmadhatu is the inseparable union of spaciousness and awareness. This is the nature of mind or the way the mind truly exists. As such it does not pervade outer objects.

An ephemeral primordial wisdom is to be understood as a temporary or provisional one, such as that of shravakas and pratyekabuddhas who only see the selflessness of persons. In comparison with such provisional primordial wisdom, the bodhisattvas' primordial wisdom knowing correctly and completely is of extreme purity. From the viewpoint of the primordial wisdom of a buddha, however, this is not the case. From this perspective the primordial wisdom of a bodhisattva who has reached the first bodhisattva level is similar to the new moon, whereas the realization of a buddha is like the full moon. A buddha and a bodhisattva are equal as far as the realization of the meaning of the dharmata or the true state is concerned, but there is a great difference in terms of the power or ability of their understanding, in terms of its clarity and expandedness.

When it is said that the primordial wisdom of bodhisattvas is free from the veils of the mental poisons and hindrances to knowledge, this does not mean that a bodhisattva is free from all these veils without any remainder. Utter purification from the veils is not achieved until the level of buddhahood is reached. When a bodhisattva attains the first bodhisattva level he has freed himself from the veils that obstruct the direct realization of the true state, which is to say, he is free from veils during meditation while one-pointedly abiding within the true state itself, seeing the buddha nature. This can be compared to the way in which the sense consciousness of the eye is unobscured and free from veils when it perceives a flower just as it appears. In other words, the primordial wisdom of a bodhisattva is a selective or individual perception and understanding. It is not comparable to the primordial wisdom of a buddha, which covers all aspects without exception.

This is due to the fact that a bodhisattva who has reached the first bhumi has purified the veils to a certain extent. Taking the veil of the hindrances to knowledge as an example, a coarse, a subtler, and a very subtle aspect are distinguished. The attainment of the bodhisattva levels is equivalent to the moment in which emptiness is seen directly, in such a way that there is not only a passing experience but an immediate realization that cannot be lost. This realization takes place when the coarse aspect of the veil of the hindrances to knowledge, that is, the belief in true existence, is abandoned. As long as one holds things to be truly existent, one cannot realize emptiness. Once one has attained this realization and thereby the first bodhisattva level, the subtler and very subtle aspects of the veil of the hindrances to knowledge, which are the perceptional grasping of characteristics and of duality as such, are to be given up gradually while traveling the nine levels above.

There are three different explanations as to the way in which the veils are gradually abandoned. Two of these hold that the main part of the veil of the mental poisons and the coarse aspect of the veil of the hindrances to knowledge are abandoned when the bodhisattva levels are reached. According to the third it is only the coarse aspect of the veil of the mental poisons that is eliminated at this point. The subtler aspects of this veil are gradually purified until the seventh bodhisattva level is reached; the purification from the veil of the hindrances to knowledge only starts when the eighth level is attained. This is the explanation of the Gelugpa tradition, when the Prasangika Madhyamaka system is presented. There are further differences according to the Svatantrika Madhyamaka system.

Annotation 15:
During their last existence those who follow the pratyekabuddha vehicle concentrate exclusively on the twelve links of interdependent origination. Relying on this means as their sole support they endeavor to attain the fruit on their own. While traveling the path of training, pratyekabuddhas rely on numerous spiritual friends. Their last existence is the one in which they attain the state of a pratyekabuddha arhat. During this last existence they absorb themselves in their own interdependent origination without the help of a spiritual friend and reflect how this interdependent origination is to be reversed. Through their investigation of interdependence they realize that ignorance gives rise to karmic activity, which in its turn gives rise to birth up to aging and death, that in this way the entirety of samsara comes about. This leads to the understanding that death and old age have ceased when birth is ceased, that birth has ceased when karmic activity is ceased and that karmic activity has ceased when ignorance is ceased. While reflecting on the way in which this dependent origination is gradually reversed, they come to realize what ignorance means. When they are able to see and understand ignorance, they realize that ignorance is by nature not truly existent. They realize the profound meaning of interdependence and thus attain the fruit they have been striving for.

Annotation 16:
Dharma in terms of teaching comprises all the teachings of the great and lesser vehicles. When speaking of abandoning, two aspects are to be distinguished. These are abandonment by means of an antidote, and a natural process of abandonment taking place through attaining

the ultimate fruit. The veils of the mental poisons and hindrances to knowledge are to be abandoned by means of an antidote suitable to each, respectively. As far as the Dharma in terms of teaching is concerned, no antidote is needed. It is abandoned in a natural way by attaining the ultimate fruit. Once this fruit is attained, it is no longer necessary to rely on teachings, just as a boat is no longer needed once one has reached the far bank of the river.

The two aspects of Dharma in terms of realization are the truth of the path, being the means freeing one from attachment, and the truth of cessation, which constitutes freedom from attachment. The path of training consists of four aspects: the paths of accumulation, junction, seeing, and meditation. The realization of those who travel the path of training is fleeting, since it undergoes a continuous development and progresses from one stage to the next. While following the path of junction, for instance, one meditates on emptiness in such a way that one has a view or an opinion of it. One attributes a certain meaning to emptiness. Once one goes beyond this stage during which emptiness is realized as a complete non-presence of anything and so on, and realizes emptiness directly, the preceding meditation proves to be a changeable phenomenon. During the path of accumulation one meditates on suffering and impermanence, and realizes these to be facts. During the path of junction one sees them in the light of emptiness. When emptiness is realized directly, suffering and impermanence do not truly exist. In this way realization changes on the path of training, developing gradually from one stage to the next.

The truths of cessation of bodhisattvas who travel the path of training up to the tenth bodhisattva level and of arhats of the lesser vehicles are not an ultimate refuge since they do not constitute the ultimate quality. In other words, they do not embody the true ultimate fruit, since the ultimate quality is not realized. A refuge that does not embody the ultimate quality is not suited to be an ultimate refuge.

To a respective extent, the Sanghas of arhats of the lesser vehicles and of bodhisattvas who have attained the bodhisattva levels have not yet purified the subtle parts of the veils, and are therefore bound up with the fear of these veils. They have not reached the state of utter fearlessness, which is the state of a buddha. Until this is achieved, the members of these Sanghas themselves take refuge in the Buddha. Therefore they are also not an ultimate refuge.

In truth, only a buddha who is purified from the two veils and the corresponding remaining imprints, and whose understanding is expanded to cover the highest object of knowledge, is the ultimate refuge of all sentient beings without exception. When the commentary speaks of the completion of freedom from desire and attachment, this refers to freedom from the two veils. Only a buddha is ultimately free from the two veils of the mental poisons and hindrances to knowledge, while arhats and noble bodhisattvas are freed from these veils to a certain extent, corresponding to the respective level they have reached. Only when a member of the Sangha reaches the level of buddhahood has he attained his ultimate fruit, having become a buddha himself.

A buddha is an inexhaustible refuge since he is free from death. He is a permanent refuge since he is free from birth. He is an immutable or unchanging refuge since he is free from aging. He is the absolute or true refuge since he is not fleeting or unsteady, and therefore is unfailing.

Annotation 17:

In the phase of ordinary beings the dharmadhatu is completely veiled by the net of the mental poisons. In this phase, while not freed from the covering of the mental poisons to even the slightest extent, the dharmadhatu is called "the element," "the tathagatagarbha," or "the sugatagarbha." This is described in the fourth vajra point.

Through cultivating the path of the Great Vehicle, this sugatagarbha is completely and utterly freed from all the veils of the mental poisons and hindrances to knowledge, which are present in the phase of an ordinary being. This is possible since these veils are adventitious, which is to say that they are not defilements by nature and do not truly exist. When, for instance, gold contained in ore is totally freed from the dross surrounding it, the phase in which the gold was contained in ore has changed into another. Nevertheless the nature of this gold has not changed. Due to the fact that the dross was removed, the state of the gold has been completely transformed. On the basis of this transformation the pure gold is obtained.

When speaking of the dharmakaya, two aspects are distinguished. These are the dharmakaya that is by nature pure and the dharmakaya that has the two types of purity, which in addition to the first type of purity is also freed from the adventitious defilements. The nature of mind that is within all beings, whether they are good or evil, is the dharmakaya by nature pure. When this primordial dharmakaya is purified from all the adventitious defilements, a second type of purity has joined the first. On the basis of the purity of the nature of mind, which is present from the very beginning, the purification from the adventitious defilements has been completed. This results from the fact that two types of purity are present, the first being the primordial purity of the nature and the second being the purification from all obscuration. When this second purity in terms of freedom from all defilements without exception is achieved, one has reached the state endowed with twofold purity. This is the true dharmakaya. This true or ultimate dharmakaya is suchness, which is free from pollution. This is equivalent to enlightenment, which is described in the fifth vajra point.

The sixth vajra point describes the buddha qualities. Suchness when freed from any pollution is the dharmakaya possessing the two types of purity. Linked with this dharmakaya are the powers and so on, the qualities of a buddha, consisting of the fruits of freedom and of complete maturation.

When speaking of a link or connection, two kinds are to be distinguished. The first is a link in the sense that the same essence or nature is present. The second is a link in the sense of one giving rise to another, or in other words, a link in terms of cause and fruit. The first kind of connection means that with regard to the same essence or nature different aspects are present. The link between the buddha qualities and the dharmakaya is to be understood in this light. Considering the connection of fire and smoke, this is a link in terms of cause and fruit, as the first gives rise to the latter. Yet, on the basis of the essence or the nature, there is no connection. The connection of father and son is a link in that one thing has arisen from another—the son has arisen from the father. Between aspects such as compoundedness and impermanence there is a link in the sense of having the same essence or nature. A flower, for instance, is compounded by causes and conditions, and it is impermanent, undergoing a progressive process of destruction taking place from instant to instant. When first hearing this, one tends to think that these are different things. Nevertheless the two aspects of compoundedness and impermanence have the same essence or nature on the basis of the flower. Of the two types of connection described here, the link between the dharmakaya and the buddha qualities is to be understood in the sense of there being no difference with regard to their essence (Tib. *ngo bo la dbye ba med pa'i 'brel ba*).

The seventh vajra point describes buddha activity. The deeds of a buddha bringing benefit and welfare to sentient beings are called "activity." With regard to this term two aspects are distinguished: the activity of the object of action and the activity of the actor. This means that not only the actor possesses his proper power or capacity, but so does the object of action. The capacity of the object of action is to be understood as follows: In all sentient beings buddha nature or the tathagatagarbha is present. This constitutes the capacity enabling sentient beings to develop faith in the Three Jewels, compassion for others, and so on. This is the power, or the activity, of beings who are the object of action. The power of the actor consists of the fact that due to the inherent ability of the buddha qualities there is the capacity to accomplish the benefit of beings. This is the activity of the actor.

The last four vajra points, that is, the element or the tathagatagarbha, enlightenment, the qualities, and buddha activity, are the cause and the conditions giving rise to the Three Jewels as their fruit. In this context the tathagatagarbha constitutes the cause. Enlightenment, the qualities, and buddha activity are the necessary conditions. The primary cause for the growth of a flower is the seed. Earth, water, warmth, wind, space, and so on are the necessary conditions. Without these conditions a flower will never grow, although the seed may be present. Only due to the meeting of the cause with the necessary conditions does the growth of the flower take place. The cause for an individual to reach the state of buddhahood is his or her own buddha nature. The necessary conditions are enlightenment, or in other words, the Buddha, his qualities, and his activity.

The way the Three Jewels, constituting the fruit, arise from this cause and these three conditions is inconceivable, even to noble shravakas and pratyekabuddhas and to noble ones who have reached the bodhisattva levels. Here the term "inconceivable" means "inconceivable by way of direct realization." By way of inference or deduction the four vajra points and their link with the Three Jewels are conceivable. It is, for instance, possible to study them or reflect upon them. When speaking of realization, two kinds are distinguished. These are inferred valid realization and direct valid realization. As long as one has not realized emptiness directly, one has an inferred valid perception of it. This becomes redundant when emptiness is realized directly. Through this direct realization one reaches the first bodhisattva level. The true condition of this realization, such as it is, is inconceivable to ordinary beings. They can only conceive of it by means of deduction. Noble ones who have reached the bodhisattva levels have direct realization, but not the ultimate one. This is inconceivable to them.

The object realized directly, just as it appears, is the true state (Skt. *dharmatā*, Tib. *chos nyid*). This is equivalent to emptiness, which in this context is to be understood mainly as the buddha nature, the tathagatagarbha. The capacity to perceive this true state arises from the first bodhisattva level onwards. Yet only a buddha possesses the ultimate primordial wisdom directly seeing the true state in everything. This ultimate realization is exclusively the object of perception of buddhas. Shravaka and pratyekabuddha arhats and noble bodhisattvas are capable of direct realization, each to a respective extent. They are not yet capable of ultimate realization. To explain this, Nagarjuna has taken the moon as an example. Arhats of the lesser vehicles and bodhisattvas who have reached the bodhisattva levels see a new moon, while buddhas see the full moon in its utter brightness.

Annotation 18:

The element is inconceivable to ordinary beings since on one hand the nature or the way of existence of mind has always been completely pure, and yet on the other hand during the impure phase it has the mental poisons, which form on the basis of adventitious defilements. This seems to be a contradiction. It is not, since the defilements are merely adventitious and cannot touch the inherent purity of the nature of mind. The fundamental defilement is the veil that comes about through delusion, through mistaking illusory appearance. It is called "adventitious," since on one hand it arises from causes and conditions and on the other hand it is able to be removed. Its more active aspect consists of the mental poisons such as desire, hatred, and so on. They are called "afflictions," since they darken and disturb the mind by destroying its peace and torturing it. In a dream, for instance, illusory appearances will occur. On the basis of these appearances one develops desire, hatred, and so on. When these mental poisons gain strength and grow, suffering arises. The mental poisons contain the nature of suffering and are therefore an affliction.

Enlightenment is inconceivable to ordinary beings since on one hand mind exists in such a way that it is by essence always free from defilement, and since on the other hand the purification from the defilements has been newly added through the cultivation of the path. This also sounds like a contradiction. It is only a seeming one, as even when the defilements are present, they cannot touch the nature of mind. The nature of mind does not have the slightest fault. Gold contained in ore is also pure gold. In the stage when it is not purified from the surrounding dross it does not have the slightest fault either.

The buddha qualities are inconceivable, since on one hand during the phase of an ordinary being the tathagatagarbha also exists in the true state, which is completely indivisible, and yet on the other hand it does not become apparent until the state of buddhahood is reached. These statements also seem contradictory. The absolute qualities are the qualities of the dharmakaya. When the true state is said to be completely indivisible, this means that the basis tathagatagarbha, the path tathagatagarbha, and the fruit tathagatagarbha are equally native to it and that it comprises all these aspects. The fact that the power of the qualities does not unfold before buddhahood is reached can also be explained by the example of gold. Even while contained in ore, gold possesses the luster native to pure gold. Yet as long as it is not purified from the surrounding dross, this luster cannot shine forth.

Buddha activity is inconceivable to ordinary beings, since on one hand a buddha fulfils the wishes of the disciples in correspondence with their respective capacities and does so spontaneously and without deliberate effort, whereas on the other hand he is completely free from thought and ambition. This also seems to be a contradiction. That this is not the case will be shown at a later stage, when buddha activity is explained by means of nine examples in its own chapter.

The capacities of the disciples vary depending upon whether they have the shravaka disposition, the pratyekabuddha disposition, or the disposition to the Mahayana. If, for example, one has the shravaka disposition, one is capable of following the Shravakayana and of gaining the state of a shravaka arhat as one's fruit, on the basis of the practice of the shravaka teachings. (For the explanation of the term "disposition" see also Part Four, note 1.)

When it is stated that a buddha is free from thought when unfolding activity, this means the following: The general characteristic of a thought is the fact that an object and a name or term are combined and perceived together as if they were just one thing. This perception is called "thought" or "concept." When, for example, a flower is in front of us, the sense consciousness of the eye sees or perceives this object directly, just as it is. When on top of this direct perception the object is given a name and perceived in terms of this name, this is a thought, a conceptual perception. In this context two different things, that is, the object and a term, are linked into just one thing and perceived as such, although the link thus created is completely arbitrary. There is not the slightest need or reason for this particular sense-object to be called "a flower." Nevertheless this name is attached to it in such a way that, merely upon seeing it, it is perceived in those terms.

Annotation 19:

All objects of knowledge are contained within the last four vajra points, which are the element or the tathagatagarbha, enlightenment, qualities, and buddha activity. Of these, the tathagatagarbha, or suchness bound up with pollution, is what is to be realized. During the time in which suchness is present in such a way that it is obscured by the defilements, the whole of samsara is contained in this state. Samsara consists of the mental poisons and karma, which give rise to the skandhas, the elements, and the entrances. These mental poisons in their turn are the defilements causing the obscuration of suchness or the tathagatagarbha. For this reason it is said to comprise all objects of knowledge.

When this tathagatagarbha is freed from all adventitious stains of delusion without any remainder, these stains having been removed by means of the discriminative wisdom realizing the non-existence of a self, this is enlightenment, the very essence of realization.

Linked with enlightenment, in the sense that there is one and the same essence, are the sixty-four qualities of freedom and complete maturation, which are thus the attributes of realization.

Realization holds power, which is buddha activity. This means that a buddha has not only attained ultimate realization himself, but causes the other disciples to realize their buddha nature, or sugatagarbha, as well. Thus his activity is the means or method to bring about the realization of the other disciples.

The tathagatagarbha bound up with pollution, as it is described in the fourth vajra point, is the cause or the basis to be purified. This is because the Three Rare and Sublime Jewels arise when this buddha nature is purified from the obscuration of all the adventitious defilements without exception. Once an individual has purified the defilements hindering the direct realization of the tathagatagarbha, and thus immediately sees his own buddha nature, he has become a member of the Sangha of noble ones. Due to the power of the direct realization of the sugatagarbha, the mind of a member of the Noble Sangha is immersed in the truth of cessation and the truth of the path. The truth of cessation is freedom from defilements. The truth of the path is the realization freeing one from defilements. These truths are the two aspects of the sacred Dharma in terms of realization. Once a member of the Noble Sangha has finalized the practice of this Dharma, he has himself turned into a buddha. Therefore the three Rare and Sublime Jewels arise from the fact that the buddha nature is purified from all pollution without any remainder.

The remaining three vajra points, that is, enlightenment, the qualities, and the activity of buddhahood, are the conditions bringing about the purification from the adventitious defilements. This is comparable to the way in which gold is freed from the surrounding dross. The action of removing the dross is the necessary condition to obtain the pure gold.

Annotation 20:
The fact that the dharmakaya is all-embracing can be compared to the way in which light diffuses and embraces everything within its reach. The dharmakaya pervades all phenomena as, for example, butter pervades milk, in the sense that all milk can be turned into butter.

Samsara is equivalent to conditioned existence, the nature of which is suffering. When going beyond the suffering of samsara one has reached the state of nirvana. Samsara and nirvana are the same in that with regard to their true state or suchness, there is not the slightest differentiation. There are not two different types of suchness, one of samsara and another of nirvana. The dharmadhatu, or emptiness, is by nature utterly pure. It never suffers the slightest impairment through the veils obscuring it until buddhahood is reached. These veils in their turn are able to be removed. When gold, for example, is contained in ore, the gold itself is completely pure. Its essence is not touched by the surrounding dross. The dross in its turn constitutes a defilement that is removable up to the point where not the slightest trace is left. The nature of beings is called the disposition of the Tathagata or the disposition to buddhahood (Tib. *sangs rgyas kyi rigs*), since it holds the power or ability to become a real buddha who possesses the two types of purity. This is comparable to the way in which the seed will inevitably become a flower once it meets with the necessary conditions.

The quotation from Lodän Sherab points out that the three reasons why the tathagatagarbha can be said to be present within all sentient beings refer to three different aspects, these being the fruit, the nature, and the cause. According to his view the first reason refers to the dharmakaya being the real Tathagata. The nature of beings is not the Tathagata. It is merely named after it. The difference between the real subject itself and a subject that is named after it is to be understood as follows. Taking the term "lion" as an example, this can be used as the name of the real subject itself and as a name attached to another subject respectively. When the animal himself is called "lion," this is the real name. When an individual who has great strength and power is called "lion," this is an attached or imputed name given for the reason that this individual wields great power as does a lion. Similar to this example, beings do not have the dharmakaya possessing the two types of purity, that is, the inherent purity of the nature and the additional purity that has come about through the total purification from all the veils. Yet beings are able to attain this dharmakaya, which is the real Buddha or Tathagata. Therefore the dharmakaya is explained as being all-pervasive. In the view presented by Lodän Sherab, the dharmakaya is to be understood as that which has the two types of purity, whereas suchness is equivalent to emptiness. This suchness is the nature of both a buddha and beings because, when considered from the aspect of the utter purity of the nature, the tathagatagarbha is present without any differentiation within a buddha and beings alike.

According to this view, the disposition to buddhahood is the real nature of beings. Being the cause of the Buddha, or Tathagata, it has been given the name of the fruit.

In short, according to Lodän Sherab, the nature of a buddha is the dharmakaya, the nature of beings is the disposition to buddhahood, and suchness, which is equivalent to emptiness, is the nature of both a buddha and beings, pervading them undifferentiatedly.

In the quote from the words of the Buddha ["since buddha wisdom is always present within the assembly of beings..."] it is the primordial wisdom of a buddha that pervades all beings. "The undefiled nature" refers to the dharmakaya, and "freedom from duality" refers to suchness or the true state. In this context, Jamgön Kongtrül the Great clarifies that the above words of the Buddha, which are contained in the version of the root text he comments, neither appear in all the translations of the root text nor in every commentary, especially not in those of his time. Yet he points out that these words have been quoted, explained, and commented by many eminent scholars. Golo was a great translator; Karma Könchön and Rongtön were both great scholars. The latter belonged to the Sakya school. The Jonangpas, that is, Dolpopa, Taranatha and others, were the first to establish the Shäntong view. Dolpopa Sherab Gyaltsen, also known as Künchen Dolpo Sangjä, is especially famous and revered for his giving the practice of the Kalachakra Tantra, which belongs to the Vajrayana system. (For further information in English, see S.K. Hookham, *The Buddha Within* [Albany: State University of New York Press, 1991], pp. 135-136, and index, pp. 387, 394.)

Annotation 21:

Here in this section, what is to be purified, that is, the tathagatagarbha, and the path or means to purify it are explained together.

(1) As far as its very essence is concerned, a precious wish-fulfilling gem is free from any defilement. When the sky is obscured by clouds, these clouds have arisen as something fleeting: they are but an adventitious obscuration that does not touch the nature of the sky itself. The sky is by nature completely pure. When water is mixed with mud and the like, this does not affect the purity of the water. The water itself is by nature completely pure and has never been defiled in any way. These three are examples for the fact that the tathagatagarbha or the dharmadhatu is by nature utterly pure and never touched by the slightest defilement. Here the dharmadhatu is to be understood as being equivalent to the way the mind truly exists, which is the inseparable union of spaciousness and awareness or of emptiness and clear light. When viewed in the light of the Rangtong Madhyamaka, the dharmadhatu is nothing but emptiness in the sense of freedom from conceptual elaboration, whereas in the Shäntong and Mahamudra views it is spaciousness-awareness inseparable. On the basis of sheer emptiness it could not become the cause for the attainment of buddhahood. The fact that the dharmadhatu is the inseparable union of spaciousness and awareness or of emptiness and clear light constitutes the reason why the fruit, the level of buddhahood, can be reached. Thus the power allowing the arising of the primordial wisdom and the kayas of a buddha is present. For this reason the view of the dharmadhatu being the inseparable union of spaciousness and awareness plays a very prominent part in the Shäntong Madhyamaka and Mahamudra traditions.

When it is said that the dharmadhatu is by nature always free from the stains of the mental poisons, this explains the way in which the essence is by nature utterly pure and at no time affected by the slightest fault, though adventitious defilements are temporarily present, until the state of buddhahood is reached. This is expressed above (B.II.2.2. 1.3) where the fourth vajra point is described as being inconceivable, by stating: "[The element] is pure and yet has affliction." Even while it is present the pollution of the veils cannot touch its essence. The essence itself has been utterly pure since beginningless time. The way it is pure is to be understood by means of the three examples of a precious jewel, the sky, and water. The essence of a jewel itself is free from any defilement, the essence of water itself is free from mud, and the essence of the sky itself is free from clouds. Thus they are by nature completely pure.

It is very important to understand that there is not the slightest pollution as far as the essence is concerned, that defilements, though present, cannot touch the essence. In the light of this view, the Mahamudra and Maha Ati traditions speak of "freedom from bondage and liberation." On the basis of this complete purity of the essence, the view of "purity and equality" is introduced on the level of the secret Mantrayana. The reason why one can speak of the purity and equality of all phenomena is the fact that no stain has ever impaired their essence, that this essence has been completely pure since beginningless time, as it is taught in the *Uttara Tantra Shastra*. Once this fact is understood well, one will be able to understand the view of purity and equality or of "utter purity" (Tib. *dag pa rab 'byams*) as taught in the system of the secret Mantrayana. In order to gain the understanding that the essence is completely pure, one should reflect on the process of dreaming: No matter how many impure appearances arise during dream, this impurity does not have the slightest substance in the sphere of the mind; the impure things do not really exist in any way. When reflecting in this way, first understanding, then certainty, and finally firm conviction, will arise. As long as individuals like us do not thoroughly reflect by means of suitable examples, as for instance dreaming, appearances are viewed as being different in that there is the duality of pure and impure appearances. There is perception of a multitude of pure and impure things, of a beautiful flower, revulsive filth, and so on. This is not worthwhile to reflect upon. Such perception is present in the phase in which understanding is polluted by the belief in true existence and all appearances are perceived in the light of this understanding. From the viewpoint of correct valid cognition this phase can be illustrated by means of the example of drunkenness. It is a state marked by confusion and delusion, this delusion being due to the predominating influence of the belief in true existence. When reflecting upon the dream appearances, one will understand that their essence is pure. Once one has gained a firm conviction of the complete purity of the essence, one is able to develop an equal conviction of the teachings of the Vajrayana. On this basis one will find it easy to practice these teachings, whereas not understanding the purity of the essence one will have difficulties in gaining conviction of the Vajrayana level of teachings and will develop doubts with regard to the view of utter purity as presented there.

(2) Although the essence is by nature completely pure like the sky and so on, and thus free from bondage and liberation, there are adventitious defilements that have to be removed. The method by which these adventitious defilements are purified is the cause of the accomplishment of the fruit. This cause is fourfold.

The first cause is devotion towards the Mahayana Dharma. This is because in the view of the Mahayana, the basis to be purified is the element, the sugatagarbha. On this basis the defilements to be removed are ultimately purified up to their very end. Contrary to this, in the view of the shravakas, for instance, the basis to be purified is not the sugatagarbha. Accordingly, the followers of this vehicle do not rely on the ultimate means to purify the adventitious stains. Since the teachings of the Mahayana are the only ones to provide the means to purify all defilements preventing the direct manifestation of the sugatagarbha, devotion towards the Mahayana Dharma is needed as the unsurpassable means of purification.

The second purifying cause is highest discriminative wisdom, which realizes the non-existence of a self. There are many other kinds of discriminative wisdom among worldly beings. Higher than these is the discriminative wisdom realizing the non-existence of a self. This wisdom arises on the basis of the sacred Dharma. The highest discriminative wisdom is the one not only realizing the selflessness of persons, but realizing the selflessness of both persons and phenomena. This arises on the basis of the Mahayana Dharma.

The third purifying cause is limitless samadhi endowed with bliss, or in other words, having the nature of bliss.

The fourth purifying cause is great compassion focusing on beings as its object or point of reference. It utters itself in the wish: "If only all sentient beings were free from their suffering up to its very end!" There are three types of compassion, as they are described for instance in the *Madhyamakavatara* (Tib. *dbu ma la 'jug pa*). The first is compassion focusing on beings as its object. The second is compassion focusing on the [impermanent] nature of beings and things, and the third is compassion free from any focus. This last-mentioned type of compassion is what mainly needs to be given rise to, once one has realized emptiness. This is stated in many passages, as for example in the *Supplication for the Realization of Mahamudra* (Tib. *phyag chen smon lam*) by the Third Karmapa, Rangjung Dorjé, where it is said:

> The nature of beings is always buddha. Yet, not realizing this they wander through the endless cycle of existence. For all beings in their boundless suffering, may unbearable compassion be born in our streams of being.
>
> Even as the skillful activity of unbearable compassion unfolds without hindrance, may at the same time the meaning of its empty essence nakedly shine forth. Inseparable from this supreme unerring path of union may we meditate at all times, day and night.

These three types of compassion will arise gradually. As a beginner, one first has to give rise to compassion focusing on beings as its object. Once one realizes the impermanent nature of beings and phenomena, understanding that all compounded phenomena are impermanent in that they undergo a process of destruction taking place from instant to instant, compassion focusing on the nature arises. Finally, the realization of the emptiness of all phenomena gives rise to compassion free from any focus. As far as the purification of the defilements is concerned, this last-mentioned type of compassion is the most efficient means. Until compassion free from any focus has arisen, compassion towards sentient beings is still flawed by attachment in terms of the belief in their true existence. Once one realizes that beings do not truly exist and yet feels compassion for them, this is the most excellent type of compassion.

The realization resulting from these four purifying causes is enlightenment. This is the fruit achieved once the adventitious defilements are completely purified, as described in the fifth vajra point.

Annotation 22:
Of the three types of individuals mentioned in the commentary, those who desire existence are beings who have the cut-off disposition and beings who have great desire and are completely immersed in the cycle of existence. Those who desire freedom from existence are tirthikas, shravakas, and pratyekabuddhas. Those who desire neither existence nor freedom from existence are not specifically mentioned in the commentary. This refers to bodhisattvas who abide in neither of the extremes of cyclic existence or of the individual peace that is the fruit of the small vehicles. The term "tirthika" (Tib. *mu stegs pa*) is here used as a general name and refers to the proponents of the various non-Buddhist tenet systems. The Tibetan term *mu stegs pa* is sometimes translated as "heretic," which has a strongly negative connotation. Jamgön Kongtrül the Great, who holds an unbiased view, has clarified in his *Treasury of Knowledge* (Tib. *shes bya kun khyab*) that it refers to

proponents of tenets who have not quite entered the path to liberation and whose conduct is not altogether conducive to this aim, but who are very near to it and will eventually reach it. The term *mu* literally means "edge" or "boundary" and the term *stegs* means "support" or "platform." Based on these literal meanings, Jamgön Kongtrül the Great points out that *mu* refers to the view and *stegs* refers to the conduct. Thus he explains that the term *mu stegs pa* denotes individuals whose view is not altogether in correspondence with the truth but is at the very edge of a correct view, and whose conduct is not quite the right support but also very near to proper conduct.

Annotation 23:
Discriminative wisdom realizing the way everything exists is equivalent to discriminative wisdom realizing the non-existence of a self, or in other words, emptiness.

There are many different kinds of samadhi, many hundreds of thousands, such as the samadhi of earth, of water, of fire, of red, yellow, and so on. Whatever object of perception one focuses upon during meditation will eventually result in an according samadhi. The meditation on many different objects serves as a means to strengthen one's power of concentration and one's mental capacity. When gaining mastery over samadhi, any object one meditates on becomes limitless and one is able to actually transform oneself into this object. When practicing, for instance, the samadhi of water, one meditates upon everything as being of the nature of water, until it directly manifests in the appearance of water. When Jetsün Milarepa had gained mastery over this particular samadhi, he was able to transform his physical form into water and was seen by others as a pond into which they threw pebbles. The term "treasury of space" refers to the fact that when true samadhi is developed and mastered, one has the power to prevent the exhaustion of any material goods that other beings need to dispel their poverty. Accounts of this capacity are to be found in the life stories of many eminent lamas and realized beings, as it is, for example, described in the Bible that Jesus was able to feed a great multitude with just five loaves of bread and two fish.

The terms "samadhi" and "meditative stability" (Tib. *bsam gtan*) are being used synonymously here. They refer to a state in which the mind rests one-pointedly, in peace. The literal meaning of the word *bsam* is "reflection" and the meaning of *gtan* is "stable." Thus *bsam gtan* is defined as the mind abiding stably focused on a wholesome object.

Annotation 24:

"The absolute expanse" is equivalent to the element or the sugata-garbha. It has two particular features in that it can be considered in terms of fruit and function. The fruit consists of four perfect qualities: "True purity" refers to the fact that buddha nature in terms of the fruit is beyond the extremes of purity and impurity. "True self" refers to the fact that all conceptual elaborations in terms of the existence of a self and the non-existence of a self have been completely stilled and come to peace. "True happiness" denotes the fact that it is beyond the extremes of happiness and suffering, and "true permanence" stands for the fact that all conceptual elaboration in terms of permanence and impermanence is completely pacified.

The fact that the sugatagarbha is present within all sentient beings is not without effect. Buddha nature has a function inducing weariness of the suffering of samsara, a longing for nirvana, which is peace in that it is free from this suffering, and finally devotion towards this aim. The Tibetan equivalent for the Sanskrit term "nirvana" is *mya ngan las 'das pa*. The term *mya ngan* means "misery" or "affliction" and the term *las 'das pa* means "beyond." Thus "nirvana" is a state free from or beyond any torment and pain.

Annotation 25:

The fruit is achieved through applying the four causes, that is, devotion, discriminative wisdom, meditative stability, and compassion, and thus purifying the adventitious defilements. This fruit has four aspects. These are true purity, true self, true happiness, and true permanence. The dharmakaya has always been utterly pure. Nevertheless the children entertain four wrong beliefs with regard to this dharma-kaya, or in other words, with regard to the nature of all phenomena. The term "child" (Tib. *byis pa*) is used in two different ways. On one hand it is used for someone who is very young of age as opposed to an older person, and on the other hand it is used for someone who is very ignorant and foolish as opposed to someone who is capable and skilled in both learning and practice. Here the term "child" is to be understood in the latter meaning. It stands for a deeply ignorant person who does not understand the nature of phenomena at all. When an image appears in a mirror such a person will think that it is real and hold it to be truly existent. A child in that sense is deluded in that he or she takes things that do not truly exist as being truly existent and thus turns reality upside down. This delusion consists of four wrong perceptions: Impure things are mistakenly perceived as being pure. Suffering is mistakenly perceived as happiness. What does not exist as a self is mistakenly perceived as an existing self to which one is strongly attached. Finally, that which is impermanent is mistakenly perceived and clung to as being permanent.

When following the Shravakayana one applies four antidotes to counteract these four wrong beliefs. To remedy the perception of something impure as being pure, one meditates on the fact that one's own body and others' bodies are impure. As a remedy for the wrong concept consisting of the attachment to a truly existing self, one meditates on the non-existence of a self. To remedy the attachment that takes suffering to be happiness, one meditates on the fact that the entirety of samsara is of the nature of suffering. As a remedy for the perception of permanence, one meditates on impermanence. Thus according to the shravaka tradition the four remedies for the four wrong concepts of the children are the meditations on impurity, non-existence of self, suffering, and impermanence.

Yet, in the light of the ultimate nature of phenomena these four remedies of the shravaka tradition imply a fault as well. Though through the recognition of impurity, non-existence of a self, suffering, and impermanence one achieves the reversal of the four wrong concepts held by the children, these recognitions do not correspond to the ultimate nature of phenomena and thus represent in their turn wrong concepts of a subtler kind. If, for instance, while dreaming one sees the attractive physical appearance of a man or woman and develops attachment, viewing this body as being pure, this belief is wrong. If one reflects upon it as being impure and meditates accordingly, so that finally it actually appears as an impure phenomenon, this is a wrong vision as well. The dream appearances of one's own and others' bodies, no matter how they may be, are beyond the extremes of both purity and impurity. They represent a state of peace in terms of freedom from any conceptual elaboration. They are spacious and relaxed, movements of clear light, which is the mind itself. They are in the state of emptiness, beyond purity and dirt. This emptiness is not an emptiness in terms of "non-existent," as is a rabbit horn, nor is it nothing at all like sky. It is a state of utter peace, of complete freedom from any conceptual elaboration. This is experienced as relaxation and spaciousness within clear light, which is the nature of the mind itself.

While one applies the methods of the Shravakayana and reverses the four beliefs of the worldly beings by means of the four antidotes taught in this system, one will develop an attachment to these remedies. When, for instance, following the shravaka tradition one meditates upon the impurity of one's own body and that of others, one will gradually develop the actual consciousness realizing them as being impure and dirty. Once this consciousness has arisen, in consequence there will be attachment to this concept of impurity. At that stage one has to practice meditation until this attachment does not arise at all any more. In the tradition of the Mahayana the four aspects of the true purity of the dharmakaya and so on act as the remedies for the four kinds of attachment that form by applying the four methods of the Shravakayana.

While worldly beings perceive the body as being pure, shravakas counteract this perception through the meditation on impurity. The fruit is beyond both these extremes. It is beyond purity and impurity and thus constitutes the perfection of true purity.

Worldly beings take what does not exist as a self for an existing self and are attached to this self. In the shravaka tradition one counteracts this belief in an existing self through meditating on the non-existence of a self, yet only in terms of sheer voidness. These concepts, and mainly the latter one, are purified by the understanding that the fruit is a state of peace, of complete freedom from the conceptual elaboration of an existing self or of the non-existence of a self. Thus it is the perfection of true self.

Worldly beings are attached to happiness and mistake suffering for happiness. Shravakas counteract this belief by means of the understanding that all feelings of ordinary happiness are in fact suffering. Thus they meditate on the entirety of samsara as being of the nature of suffering. In the tradition of the Mahayana one gains the understanding that the fruit is beyond any extreme, that it is beyond both happiness and suffering and as such free from all conceptual elaboration. Thus it is the perfection of true happiness.

Worldly beings take what is impermanent as being permanent and are attached to permanence. In the shravaka tradition one recognizes and contemplates the fact that whatever appears to be permanent undergoes a process of destruction taking place from instant to instant and thus is of an impermanent nature. In doing so one develops attachment holding the very subtle aspect of impermanence to be real or truly existent. In order to reverse this attachment one has to meditate as taught in the Mahayana tradition. One has to understand that while permanence does not exist, impermanence, which is merely its contrary or opposite, cannot exist either. Light cannot exist without darkness and darkness cannot exist without light. If there is no light in this world, darkness will not appear. If there is no darkness, there will be no light. The same is true of hearing and sound. Without sound there is no hearing. Without hearing there is no sound. These can only exist together in that they mutually presuppose each other. One has to understand that the fruit is beyond this mutual implication, being beyond permanence and impermanence and thus constituting the perfection of true permanence.

In short, in the state of children the dharmakaya is obscured by four wrong beliefs. Once these have been reversed by means of the four antidotes as taught in the shravaka tradition, four kinds of attachment have formed, which in their turn obscure the true state of the dharmakaya. The obscuration caused by the four antidotes of the shravaka tradition has to be removed subsequently by the understanding that the dharmakaya is true purity, true self, true happiness, and true permanence. The means leading to the perfection of these four qualities are the four causes mentioned above, which are outstanding devotion, highest discriminative wisdom, meditative stability, and compassion.

Annotation 26:

The term "perfection of true self" is to be understood as follows: The tirthikas, such as different Hindu traditions and so on, hold the belief of there being a self or atman that is eternal (Tib. *rtag pa*), unique (Tib. *gcig*), and independent (Tib. *rang dbang*). This self or atman is called "true self." The shravakas and so on remedy this belief by the meditation on the non-existence of a self. They meditate that everything does not exist as a self at all, that everything is nothing but sheer voidness. The belief in the existence of an eternal, unique, and independent self is a wrong concept and perception. While the recognition that everything is utterly non-existent constitutes a valid remedy for this wrong perception of the tirthikas, it is in its turn also distorted in that it does not correspond to the ultimate nature of everything either. The ultimate nature of everything is a state of peace completely beyond the conceptual elaboration in terms of the existence of a self or the non-existence of a self. If, for instance, while dreaming one thinks in terms of "self" and "I," attachment to one's body will arise born from the belief in an existing self. This is a mistaken reaction based on a deluded concept. If, while dreaming, one thinks that a self does not exist at all and therefore takes this body to be nothing but empty, this is also a deluded thought. In truth it is beyond any of these conceptual elaborations. There is a great difference between "true self" as taught in the Hindu traditions and as taught in the Mahayana system. In the first sense the term "true self" denotes a self that is eternal, unique, and independent. "True self" as taught in the *Uttara Tantra Shastra* is equivalent to the state of peace in terms of complete freedom from any conceptual elaboration. This state of peace has only been given the name of "true self." There is a mere similarity in terms. The Mahayana system does not hold the view of an eternal, unique, and independent self. Between light and darkness, for instance, there is only a similarity inasmuch as they are both things (Skt. *bhāva*, Tib. *dngos po*) fulfilling a function. Apart from that they contradict each other; there is not the slightest similarity.

Arhats who have reached the fruit of the lesser vehicles still have subtle skandhas, or in other words, a body of mental nature. These skandhas are due to the fact that arhats still have an undefiled type of karma resulting from the mental poisons, which consist of the remaining imprints of ignorance. When the state of an arhat is reached, ignorance itself is eliminated. Nevertheless the remaining influence of ignorance, which constitutes a very subtle obscuration, is still present and needs to be abandoned. When these subtle remaining imprints of ignorance are called "mental poisons," this is merely an imputed name. Arhats have ceased all mental poisons, and the remaining imprints of ignorance are in fact a subtler part of the veil of the hindrances to knowledge.

When Dolpopa states that the absolute expanse is spontaneously present, this refers to the fact that the qualities of buddhahood have been spontaneously present since beginningless time. In the Shäntong tradition the faults are viewed as being adventitious and the qualities are viewed as being spontaneously present, whereas in the Rangtong tradition the faults are also held to be adventitious, while the qualities are to be newly attained.

Annotation 27:

The literal meaning of the Sanskrit term "skandha" (Tib. *phung po*) is "heap." [This term arose from the fact that, when the Buddha explained the skandhas, he heaped up various grains into five piles to represent the categories of impermanent phenomena.] The five skandhas represent all impermanent phenomena, those of the personal continuum as well as those of the external world.

Those who are dominated by great desire are beings who are attached to and crave for the happiness of existence. They believe that the five skandhas are an existing self or entity and perceive them accordingly. Thus they fall into the extreme of existence. The only means to cut this belief in the existence of a self and the wrong perception resulting from it is the discriminative wisdom realizing that neither a self of the person nor of phenomena exist. As long as this wisdom is not present, one cannot cut the attachment to a self.

One speaks of "dormant tendencies" (Tib. *bag la nyal*) as opposed to something that directly manifests. At the time, for example, when strong faith or great love arises, feelings of anger and the like are potentially present in a dormant state. When one gets angry, this changes into a direct manifestation.

Shravakas and pratyekabuddhas are mainly concerned about their own suffering and therefore strive to free themselves from this suffering and to attain a state of peace for themselves. Thus they fall into the extreme of mere individual peace. The means to remedy this limited motivation is great compassion uttering itself in the wish that all sentient beings without exception may be free from all their suffering.

When thoroughly cultivating these two means, one does not abide in any extreme. Discriminative wisdom realizing emptiness prevents one from abiding in the extreme of existence. Inspired by great compassion, one will not strive to attain a state of mere peace. Thus one will eventually reach the non-abiding nirvana, which is the ultimate fruit.

Annotation 28:

The fact that an individual is able to feel weary of the suffering of samsara and to develop longing for the attainment of the state of liberation is considered as being due to the presence of the disposition to buddhahood. Without this disposition these feelings would not arise. This refers to the fact that the mind is not just the power of this body of flesh and blood, but constitutes a particular force.

Generally speaking, any human being, although he has not developed love as taught in the Dharma, is able to feel love and compassion for another. Furthermore, the mind will undergo changes and manifest a great number of different expressions. At one time one gives rise to love, at another time it does not arise. Even towards a friend whom one loves, one may suddenly get angry. At that time love is no longer present. These changes could not take place if the mind was simply the power of this body of flesh and blood. If that was the case, whatever had arisen would be there to stay. Once love had arisen, anger could not arise. Once anger had arisen, love could not arise.

The fact that the mind undergoes these changes is the sign that the mind constitutes a particular power, which is not the power of this body but comes from previous lives. The body depends on this particular power. When a person is mentally unhappy, his body is not able to be happy. It does not have an independent force of its own.

As long as the disposition to buddhahood is not awakened, an understanding of what is to be adopted and what is to be rejected will not arise. The awakening of the disposition can be illustrated by the following example: while a pig likes to dwell in mud and filth and cares little about a flower garden, a human being finds filth revulsive and delights in a beautiful garden. Once this pig has been reborn as a human being its attitude will have changed. It will no longer delight in filth and mud, but prefer the flower garden.

Annotation 29:
Whereas according to the Rangtong view the qualities in terms of the fruit are something that is developed and newly attained, the Shāntong view holds that the qualities in terms of the cause and the qualities in terms of the fruit are equally inherent to the element or the buddha nature. According to this view the three aspects of the tathagatagarbha in terms of basis, path, and fruit are only distinguished from the viewpoint of the purification from the adventitious stains of delusion. The buddha nature itself does not change, and the qualities that become apparent, once all the adventitious stains have been completely removed, are inseparable from it and have always been present. This can be understood by means of the example of muddy water. It contains the qualities in terms of the cause as well as those in terms of the fruit. Water containing mud of itself has the power to become clear, in that the mud will settle by itself once the water rests unmoved. These are the qualities in terms of the cause. While water is muddy, it will not show a clear reflection of the moon, whereas once the mud has settled by itself and the water has become clear, the reflection of the moon will appear extremely clearly. These are the qualities in terms of the fruit. Both types of quality are equally inherent to the water, even while it is muddy.

The qualities in terms of the cause are devotion towards the Mahayana Dharma, discriminative wisdom, samadhi, and compassion. They are called causes since they bring about the removal of the adventitious stains. The qualities in terms of the fruit are the first five kinds of clairvoyance, unpolluted primordial wisdom, and the fact that the abandonment of these adventitious stains has been completed.

There are six kinds of clairvoyance: The first five are the clairvoyance of divine sight, of divine hearing, of knowing the minds of others, of knowing death and birth, and of remembering previous lives.

"Unpolluted primordial wisdom" here refers to the two aspects of primordial wisdom: knowing correctly and knowing completely.

The statement that the qualities in terms of the fruit are inseparable refers to the fact that there is only a difference in terms of aspects. They all have one and the same basis, or essence, which in itself is completely indivisible. This essence is the buddha nature.

Annotation 30:

The seven properties of no-more-learning, that is, the first five kinds of clairvoyance, unpolluted primordial wisdom, and abandonment free from defilement, correspond to the level of a buddha.

Annotation 31:

The topic "manifestation" refers to the fact that with regard to suchness three phases are to be discerned. The first phase is that of an ordinary being who has not directly realized the meaning of emptiness. The second phase is that of a noble bodhisattva who has directly realized the nature of the mind, or truth. The third phase is that of a perfect buddha who has eliminated the two veils along with all their remaining imprints without any exception, who has perfected the two aspects of abandonment and realization. These three phases are called the suchness of an ordinary being, the suchness of a noble one, and the suchness of a perfect buddha. In this context it is important to understand that these three "types of suchness" are just three different aspects in terms of its manifestation in three different phases. As far as the essence is concerned there is not the slightest differentiation. Suchness itself is indivisible.

"The Omniscient One who Directly Sees Thatness" is an epithet of the Buddha. A buddha is called "omniscient" since he possesses the unhindered knowledge of all aspects of the knowable. The direct vision of thatness (Tib. *de kho na nyid*) is synonymous with the vision of reality as it is, with the direct realization of emptiness, of the absolute truth, of the dharmadhatu or the sugatagarbha.

A being is called "fortunate" (Tib. *skal pa dang ldan pa*) when he has the karmic fortune or gift enabling him to practice the Dharma. The term "fortune" (Tib. *skal pa*) is equivalent to the frame of mind and the ability of a person. If, for instance, one wants to practice the teachings of the secret Mantrayana, one needs the respective karmic fortune or gift that consists of faith and pure vision. Without these one can study those teachings but will not be able to put them into practice.

"The Victorious One" is another epithet of the Buddha. The common explanation why this term is used is the fact that a buddha has been victorious through overcoming the four maras or demons (Tib. *bdud*). (See also Part Four, note three.)

Annotation 32:
Through the topic "manifestation" the following is explained: Although in terms of the essence, suchness cannot be divided, there is a division into three different kinds due to the different individuals who are its basis. Therefore the classification presented is only a classification by means of the basis. As to space itself, for instance, there are no different kinds, nevertheless there is an eastern, a western, a southern, and a northern space, when space is viewed from the basis of the earth. Likewise, there is an inner and an outer space on the basis of a house and so on. Without such bases space cannot be divided at all. Corresponding to this example, the dharmadhatu is classified into three kinds, that is, into the unpurified suchness, the partly purified and partly unpurified suchness, and the completely purified suchness, on the basis of three respective types of individuals.

When it is said that suchness manifests in the phase of a buddha in an unperverted way and as freedom from any conceptual elaboration, this refers to the following: In this phase the ordinary concept-bound mind (Tib. *sems*) is no longer present, but has been replaced by primordial wisdom (Tib. *ye shes*). The ordinary mind is characterized by the fact that there is the appearance of duality through the perception of an outer object by a perceiving inner subject or consciousness. In the phase of a buddha, the mind is equivalent to primordial wisdom. Thus it is unperverted, which is to say that it is free from any delusion. The different ways in which understanding will manifest can be shown by the example of dreaming: The understanding present while one recognizes that one is dreaming, and the understanding present while one does not recognize the dream for what it is, are not the same. There are two different ways of manifestation.

The terms "conceptual elaboration" (Tib. *spros pa*) and "freedom from conceptual elaboration" (Tib. *spros med*) are to be understood as follows: All thoughts (Tib. *rtog pa*) are conceptual elaborations. These elaborations are of two kinds: those of the perceiving subject and those of the object perceived. The thoughts that constitute the perceiving subject are conceptual elaborations. By means of these thoughts the conceptualization of the perceived object will come about. When, for instance, while dreaming one thinks "this is fire," "this is water," etc., or "this is pure," "this is dirty," and so on, these thoughts are conceptual elaborations of the perceiving subject. Accordingly there are "water," "fire," "friend," "enemy," etc., a multitude of conceptualized outward appearances. Once the conceptual elaboration of the perceiving subject has arisen, the elaboration of the object will arise in the same measure. There is an interdependent origination in terms of the initial thought forming the support and the perceived object being supported by this thought. This is best understood by the example of dream. To body and speech themselves, thoughts do not arise, yet with regard to body and speech, perceiving thoughts will occur. All thoughts arise either on the basis of body or speech. Thoughts such as "my body," "my head," "my legs," "my hands," and so on arise on the basis of the body. Thoughts such as "this is good," "this is bad," "this is pure," "this is dirty," "this is a friend," "this is an enemy," and so on arise on the basis of terms, the expression of speech. All thoughts that arise on the basis of the body and the ones that arise on the basis of speech equally occur in connection with names. Thus all thoughts arise on the basis of terms and are therefore just nominal. Freedom from conceptual elaboration is the state of peace in which all thoughts have subsided.

Annotation 33:

The unpurified phase corresponds to the tathagatagarbha in terms of the basis (Tib. *gzhi de gshegs snying po*). The partly unpurified and partly purified phase corresponds to the tathagatagarbha in terms of the path (Tib. *lam de gshegs snying po*), and the utterly purified phase corresponds to the tathagatagarbha in terms of the fruit (Tib. *'bras bu de gshegs snying po*).

When it is said that during the partly unpurified and partly purified phase buddha nature is purified to a certain degree, this means the following: Once the buddha nature is purified from all the defilements that are to be abandoned on the paths of seeing and meditation, the level of the fruit, the state of buddhahood, is reached. A bodhisattva has not attained this fruit, but is purified from these defilements to a certain degree, corresponding to the level he has reached. When, for instance, the first bodhisattva level is attained, one is purified from the veil to be abandoned through seeing. When one has reached the second or third bodhisattva level, one is purified from the veil to be abandoned through seeing; in addition to that, one is purified from the coarse aspect of the defilements to be abandoned through meditation, to a degree corresponding to each of these levels.

One may wonder why buddha nature, although it pervades all sentient beings, is expressed by the three different names of "being," "bodhisattva," and "tathagata." This is due to a different degree of purification from the adventitious stains of delusion. The true state itself is not of different kinds. Nevertheless there is a difference concerning the individuals who are the basis of this true state or buddha nature: There are those who have not purified the adventitious stains at all, those who have purified them to a respective degree, and finally those who have completely purified all defilements without exception. These three different types of individuals are explained by means of the aforementioned three names.

Annotation 34:
This section clarifies that as far as the essence is concerned there is not the slightest difference between the three aspects of the basis tathagatagarbha, the path tathagatagarbha, and the fruit tathagatagarbha. This is the view of the Shäntong Madhyamaka. If one understands it well, one will find it easy to understand the teachings on Mahamudra. These teachings also introduce the three aspects of basis, path, and fruit. In this context one speaks of basis Mahamudra, path Mahamudra, and fruit Mahamudra, the essence of which is considered as being inseparable. The fact that the essence is unchanging has been shown in detail by means of the examples of the sky, of water containing mud, and of gold. The different phases of basis, path, and fruit as they are explained in this section are presented from the viewpoint of there being a difference only in the degree of purification from the adventitious defilements. With regard to the essence itself, to the tathagatagarbha, there is not the slightest difference. When the system of the Rangtong Madhyamaka speaks of the essence being undifferentiated, this essence is synonymous with emptiness, with freedom from conceptual elaboration. It does not refer to the inseparable union of spaciousness and primordial wisdom, as is the case in the Shäntong Madhyamaka system.

Annotation 35:

Space is characterized by being empty and providing an opportunity. Space is empty in that it is nothing at all, and it provides an opportunity in that it does not constitute the slightest obstruction and thus allows the appearance of any visible object. The quality of the dharmadhatu is peace in the sense of freedom from all conceptual elaboration.

Annotation 36:

The characteristic of a thing (Tib. *dngos po*) is the power to fulfill a function (Tib. *don byed pa'i nus pa*).

Annotation 37:

When it is stated that the skandhas, the elements, and the sense faculties are bound up with pollution (Tib. *zag bcas*), this refers to the fact that they are subject to arising and disintegration.

Annotation 38:

The skandhas are said to attract suffering (Tib. *nye bar len pa dang bcas pa*) since they come into existence due to the predominating influence of the karma and mental poisons of previous existences. Since former actions and mental poisons are the source of the skandhas, from the mere presence of these skandhas suffering will ensue. A human being, for instance, will invariably experience suffering by the mere fact that he or she has a physical body.

Improper conceptual activity (Tib. *tshul bzhin ma yin pa'i yid la byed pa*) is equivalent to wrong or perverted thoughts, such as taking something that is impure to be pure, something that does not exist as a self to be an existing self, something that is impermanent to be permanent, suffering to be happiness, and so on.

Annotation 39:

The view expressed in this and the following section is very similar to the view as it is presented in the Mahamudra system. When the nature of mind is described as being the luminous dharmadhatu (Tib. *od gsal chos kyi dbyings*), this is to say that the nature of mind is not just empty, but has the aspect of clarity as well. The term "luminosity" or "clear light" (Tib. *od gsal*) refers to this aspect of clarity, whereas the term "dharmadhatu" refers to the aspect of emptiness. Thus the nature of mind is the inseparable union of emptiness and clear light (Tib. *gsal stong dbyer med*). This nature of mind is similar to space, which provides the basis for all things but in itself has not come into existence on the basis of a cause, and is thus uncreated. Likewise the nature of mind does not depend upon productive causes (Tib. *nyer len gyi rgyu*), nor on simultaneously active conditions (Tib. *lhan cig byed pa'i rkyen*). The productive cause of a flower, for example, is the seed. The simultaneously active conditions befriending and furthering its growth are earth, water, warmth, and so forth. Since the nature of mind is not dependent upon causes and conditions and therefore also not dependent upon a gathering of these, it is free from an initial arising. If there is no initial arising due to a gathering of causes and conditions, there is also no final cessation, nor an abiding in the meantime. Thus the nature of mind is free from arising, abiding, and ceasing, which are the three properties of anything created.

Annotation 40:
Bodhisattvas who have reached the bodhisattva levels have directly realized thatness, or the nature of the tathagatagarbha. As long as one is an ordinary being, one only realizes this nature by way of deduction. Thus one's meditation is tinged by a concept of it. When emptiness is realized directly, one has reached a state of freedom from the obscuration of thoughts. Emptiness is not an object for thoughts and concepts. It is realized immediately, just as it appears, in a state of freedom from conceptual elaboration in which all thoughts have subsided. Even now, for example, people like us will have meditative experiences connected with thoughts, and at times we will have experiences that are free from thought. These thought-free experiences, however, are not very subtle. At our stage a very subtle thought-free understanding will only occur while we are sleeping or, sometimes, while our mind is immersed in great bliss. Nevertheless, for the time being our mind is a coarse, conceptual one that constantly focuses outwards and conceptually perceives a conceptualized object. In this state one does not know experience that is free from thought. Within direct realization of emptiness there is neither conceptual perception nor a conceptualized object. It is nakedly realized, just as it appears.

Due to their direct realization of emptiness, bodhisattvas have developed great compassion for all those sentient beings who have not yet gained this realization and must therefore undergo an immeasurable amount of suffering. This can be understood by means of the example of dreaming: If someone dreams that he is burnt by fire, he knows the suffering connected with this experience. Once he recognizes it to be a dream appearance, no matter how often he dreams of being burnt by fire, he will no longer feel the slightest suffering. Yet, when seeing others who have the same dream but do not recognize that they are dreaming, his own experience of suffering and his recognition of its being just a dream will generate compassion for these other beings. If at the time when one has recognized that one is dreaming and thus does not experience any suffering oneself, one sees one's friends or one's own father and mother dreaming that they are caught in a fire and, not recognizing their dream for what it is, being helplessly delivered to their suffering, one will give rise to heartfelt compassion for them. In this way the bodhisattvas have great compassion for all those beings who in their state of unknowing are bound to the cycle of existence and the suffering it involves.

Once one has directly realized buddha nature, one is free from karma and the mental poisons and thus free from birth, which comes about through their predominating influence. Being free from birth, one is also free from death, sickness, and aging, which occur as a consequence of birth. Thus one is free from the process of disintegration starting with birth and ending with death. One is not subject to any change. Though through their direct realization of buddha nature they are freed from birth and so on, bodhisattvas are fully activated and alert because of the power of their great love and compassion. Therefore they demonstrate birth, sickness, aging, and death and appear to the vision of others as if they were subject to disintegration and change.

In this context, one's own vision (Tib. *rang snang*) and the vision of others (Tib. *gzhan snang*) are to be distinguished. From the viewpoint of their own vision, the bodhisattvas do not have real skandhas in terms of the individual characteristic of the skandhas (Tib. *rang mtshan par med pa*). They appear in the form of skandhas to the vision of others. In order to understand this, one can look into the question of what kind of body is possessed by a person of whom one dreams. The body of this dream person does not have the individual characteristic of an outer physical body. It appears in the likeness of it. It appears as an enemy or friend, and one can see it experience suffering and misery. As shown by this example, bodhisattvas, once they have directly realized emptiness, do not have real skandhas themselves, but demonstrate real skandhas to the other beings. Though changeless, they show themselves to the vision of others as if they were actually changing. Although they are not subject to this process, they show themselves as if they were born, falling ill, aging, and finally dying, in order to help all ordinary beings gain the realization they themselves have attained.

The main force enabling bodhisattvas to take birth in an existence corresponding to their intention is the power of their former wishing prayers for the benefit of others. Even while a bodhisattva is still an ordinary being, and throughout the time that he travels the bodhisattva path, a very important means for his future ability to accomplish the benefit of beings is his vast and sincere wishing prayers. These will contain the wish that he may gain this future ability and be only of help to others. An example is the *Wishing Prayer for Entering the Bodhisattva's Path* by Shantideva, in which he prays that he may transform into food for the hungry, into clothes for the naked, into a bridge for wanderers who are stuck by turbulent water, and so on. In short, wishing prayers such as these are the cause that will lead one to gain the power to dispel the suffering of beings.

Annotation 41:

"The four means of attraction" (Tib. *bsdu ba'i dngos po bzhi*) are the giving of desired material necessities (Tib. *mkho ba sbyin pa*), speaking agreeably (Tib. *snyan par smra ba*), teaching in accordance with the benefit of the worldly beings (Tib. *'jig rten don mthun pa*), and conduct that is of benefit to the disciples (Tib. *gdul bya'i don la spyod pa*). Once one has become a bodhisattva who dwells on the bodhisattva levels, one makes use of the four means to gather beings into an assembly and thus help them to reach realization themselves. The first means of attraction is the giving of material things that a disciple needs or desires. The second is the fact that a bodhisattva knows what will make each individual sentient being happy. Thus he will speak to them in friendly words, he will sing, tell stories, and do whatever makes sentient beings feel warm and cozy. The third is the fact that a bodhisattva knows which of the teachings of the smaller or greater vehicles will be of benefit to each individual being. Due to this knowledge, he will teach them accordingly. The fourth is the fact that a bodhisattva's conduct will always be in accordance with the respective level of teaching he gives.

Annotation 42:

A bodhisattva who dwells on the eighth bhumi has attained the level of non-returning in that he will not fall back to a stage in which one perceives in terms of characteristics during the post-meditative phase. Such a bodhisattva has completely abandoned the conceptual elaboration consisting of the perception of objects in terms of their characteristics, such as "this is a flower," "this is white," "this is red," and so on.

Annotation 43:

Bodhisattvas who dwell on the tenth bodhisattva level are called "those who have reached the last existence," since the next step in the career of such a bodhisattva is the attainment of buddhahood.

When it is said that these bodhisattvas are free from all thoughts and ideation, having eliminated these in the process of a complete transformation of state (Tib. *ngas yongs su gyur pa*), this means that the ordinary consciousness has been transformed into primordial wisdom. Through this transformation all concepts are also transformed and thereby relinquished.

A bodhisattva who has reached the tenth bhumi is capable of emanating an almost unimaginably great number of form kayas, of physical bodies, which are illusory appearances (Tib. *sprul pa*). A small amount of this capacity is first attained when one reaches the first bodhisattva level, and it will grow gradually throughout the following levels. On the first bodhisattva level one is able to emanate a hundred illusory physical bodies, on the second level one is able to emanate a thousand, and so forth. (For further information see Hopkins, *Meditation on Emptiness,* p. 100.) These emanations, however, are not equivalent to the sambhogakaya and nirmanakaya of a buddha.

A bodhisattva who dwells on the tenth bodhisattva level appears to the disciples as an ordinary being, but is of a different nature. His or her very nature is the accomplishment of the welfare of all sentient beings.

Annotation 44:

Dolpopa Sangjä, the founder of the Jonangpa school, has written a famous commentary on the *Uttara Tantra Shastra.* The present commentary by Jamgön Kongtrül the Great is partly based upon Dolpopa's work, representing a greatly expanded version. Thus their mode of explaining the meaning of the root text is very similar. The Third Karmapa Rangjung Dorjé has written a summary of this meaning. While according to Dolpopa and Jamgön Kongtrül the Great the root text does not differentiate between the qualities of a bodhisattva who dwells on the ninth bodhisattva level and those of a bodhisattva who has reached the tenth bodhisattva level, the Third Karmapa Rangjung Dorjé interprets the three stanzas starting with "By the power of their former [prayers]..." slightly differently. In his opinion the first two describe the qualities of a bodhisattva who dwells on the ninth bodhisattva level, while the last stanza starting with "Always [acting] spontaneously and without obstruction..." describes the qualities of a bodhisattva who has reached the tenth bodhisattva level.

Annotation 45:
When one has reached the highest state of a shravaka arhat, one is an arhat without remainder. This refers to the fact that at this point even the subtle remainders of the skandhas have been overcome. In this state the stream of being is cut. There is no activity whatsoever and therefore no possibility to bring about the benefit of beings. Such an arhat abides in a state of extinction similar to an extinguished fire or stagnant water. Once the stream of being is cut there will be no further birth. One has reached the nirvana equivalent to mere peace. Even in the expanse of this nirvana without remainder the dharmakaya possesses inexhaustible and immeasurable qualities and is therefore permanent. When one attains the dharmakaya, one possesses these qualities. While the shravaka and pratyekabuddha arhats who are without any remainder of skandhas are like an extinguished fire and their streams of being are cut, a buddha does not cut the stream of being. In the expanse of the nirvana without remainder he also has the thirty-two qualities of the dharmakaya. Arising on the basis of these qualities are the form kayas, which have the quality of being uninterrupted in appearance. They are the means that bring about the benefit of all sentient beings.

When someone who follows the Shravakayana or Pratyekabuddhayana reaches the nirvana without remainder, any remainder of skandhas is merely extinct and has gone into nothingness, whereas someone who follows the bodhisattva path and employs the specific means of the Vajrayana will realize emptiness directly and thereby attain the form kaya of emptiness. Through the immediate vision of emptiness, the ordinary body, which is of the nature of flesh and blood, is transformed into the nature of light and one attains what is called "the rainbow body." On the level of buddhahood all skandhas are utterly purified and the form kaya of emptiness is finally achieved.

Annotation 46:

As has been explained before, arhats have a birth in a body of mental nature. In consequence they undergo a subtle process of falling sick and aging, until they finally die in a way inconceivable to an ordinary being. This is because they have not yet overcome the very subtle obscuration consisting of the remaining imprints of ignorance. The dharmakaya is even free from these types of birth, death, sickness, and aging.

Annotation 47:

The tathagatagarbha (Tib. *de bzhin gshegs pa'i snying po*, lit. "essence or heart of a tathagata") in the utterly purified phase is the dharmakaya of all buddhas. With respect to the classification in terms of the three kayas, the dharmakaya of all buddhas is considered to be of one and the same essence. Of the form kayas, which manifest on the basis of this dharmakaya, the sambhogakaya is considered to be one and the same, whereas the nirmanakaya is considered as being of different kinds. This different manifestation comes about due to the wishing prayers uttered by a buddha while traveling the bodhisattva path.

The tathagatagarbha in the utterly purified phase is also the Tathagata. The term "Tathagata" (Tib. *de bzhin gshegs pa*), an epithet of the Buddha, can be explained as follows. *De bzhin* is short for *de bzhin nyid* (Skt. *tathatā*, suchness) and *gshegs pa* is a honorific term meaning "the One who has gone." Thus the Tathagata can be described as the One who has traveled the path of suchness, of the true state (Skt. *dharmatā*, Tib. *chos nyid*), or in other words, the One who has relied on the path of suchness that abides in neither of the extremes of existence and peace, and thus has truly gone to great enlightenment. An equivalent for the term "Tathagata" is the term "Sugata" (Tib. *bde bar gshegs pa*). Accordingly the tathagatagarbha is also called the sugatagarbha (Tib. *bde bar gshegs pa'i snying po*). The Tibetan term *bde ba* means "happiness" or "bliss." The term *bde bar* is an adverb and means "comfortably." Thus a buddha is called the Sugata, since he or she can be described as the One who has relied on the bodhisattva vehicle, which constitutes a comfortable path, and thus has gone to the fruit, the level of perfect buddhahood, which is bliss.

The tathagatagarbha in the utterly purified phase is the noble truth, since it is the truth of cessation of all noble ones.

It is also the absolute nirvana. Only the state of buddhahood constitutes the ultimate nirvana, whereas the nirvana reached by shravaka and pratyekabuddha arhats is a limited and temporary one.

The dharmakaya of all buddhas, the Tathagata, the noble truth, and the absolute nirvana are but synonymous terms, being just different aspects that have the same essence.

Furthermore, the ten powers and so on, that is, the thirty-two qualities of the dharmakaya, are also completely inseparable from the dharmakaya itself. In terms of essence there is no differentiation.

For these reasons there is no actual or true nirvana except for perfect buddhahood.

Annotation 48:

"Emptiness endowed with all supreme aspects" (Tib. *rnam kun mchog ldan stong pa nyid*) is a name for the true nature of mind, or the way the mind truly exists, which is the inseparable union of emptiness and clear light. The emptiness of all outer objects, such as forms, sounds, odors, tastes, tangible objects, and so forth, is called "emptiness endowed with the aspect of matter" (Tib. *bem po rnam bcas kyi stong pa nyid*).

Annotation 49:

The painter who is the only one to know how to paint the head of the king stands for discriminative wisdom fully and thoroughly discriminating all phenomena. His having gone abroad and the painting staying unfinished signifies the fact that without this discriminative wisdom, by means of the first five perfections alone, it is impossible to accomplish the direct manifestation of the dharmakaya. This direct manifestation of the dharmakaya, or in other words, of emptiness endowed with all the supreme aspects of means, corresponds to the well-painted image of the king being fully perfected.

Annotation 50:

What is to be understood by primordial wisdom and discriminative wisdom is explained slightly differently in the Rangtong and Shäntong systems.

(1) According to the Rangtong view, there is a relationship between these in terms of cause and fruit. Discriminative wisdom is considered as being the cause and primordial wisdom as being the fruit. In

this view discriminative wisdom is equivalent to the three discriminative wisdoms arising from learning, reflection, and meditation (Tib. *thos bsam sgom byung gi shes rab*). According to the Rangtong tradition, ordinary beings do not possess primordial wisdom. This is only true of noble ones, of bodhisattvas who have reached the bodhisattva levels. In this context two aspects are distinguished: primordial wisdom present during meditation and the one present in the post-meditative phase (Tib. *mnyam bzhag gi ye shes dang rjes thob kyi ye shes*). Once emptiness is no longer a passing experience but realized directly, one has reached the first bodhisattva level by means of this direct realization. From this moment onwards, the two primordial wisdoms are present. The primordial wisdom present during meditation is the one that realizes emptiness. It manifests while a noble bodhisattva rests in meditative equipoise, one-pointedly within emptiness itself. The wisdom present in the post-meditative phase is wisdom that realizes all phenomena as being mere appearances, as being dream-like or like magical illusions. This wisdom manifests whenever a noble bodhisattva does not dwell in meditation.

(2) According to the Shäntong tradition, primordial wisdom is what is to be realized and discriminative wisdom is the means to realize it.

In this view, discriminative wisdom is of two kinds, these being the discriminative wisdom focusing outwards and the one focusing inwards. Generally speaking, discriminative wisdom is the ability to individually discriminate each and every object. This ability in its aspect of focusing outwards is also native to ordinary beings. In the Shäntong view, discriminative wisdom constitutes the ability to discern all relative phenomena, each individually, and to know them for what they are. While the relative phenomena are examined by means of discriminative wisdom, their way of existence and their way of appearance are understood. It is seen that they are empty, lacking inherent existence, that they do not truly exist and yet appear on a relative level like a dream image or a magical illusion.

In the Shäntong view, primordial wisdom is considered as being within all sentient beings. This is because in this view it is no other than the mind itself in terms of its true existence. The essence of mind is emptiness and its nature is clear light. These two aspects being inseparable, primordial wisdom is equivalent to the inseparable union of emptiness and clear light, or of spaciousness and awareness. With regard to this primordial wisdom three aspects are distinguished: those of the basis, path, and fruit. The primordial wisdom present within all beings needs to be realized in order to reveal itself immediately or directly. This realization has to take place in such a way that primordial wisdom itself recognizes its own face (Tib. *ye shes rang ngor shes pa*). The primordial wisdom present from the very beginning within the stream of being, which is the true nature of the minds of all sentient beings, the inseparable union of emptiness and clear light, is called the basis primordial wisdom and also "ever-present wisdom" or "ever-present dharmakaya." The phase in which this nature of mind is initially realized and during which this realization is cultivated is called the path primordial wisdom. At the time when all the adventitious stains of delusion are eliminated, this inseparable union of emptiness and clear light is called the fruit primordial wisdom.

(3) The view of Mahamudra is very similar to the Shāntong view. In this context one speaks of basis Mahamudra, path Mahamudra, and fruit Mahamudra. Once the primordial wisdom present since the very beginning, which in this context is called "the joint manifestation of emptiness and clear light," sees its face through discriminative wisdom having become self-liberated, the realization of Mahamudra has become immediate.

Annotation 51:

(1) The topic "essence" shows enlightenment as possessing two aspects of purity. The term "sphere" refers to the dharmadhatu being concept-free or free from any mental elaboration. The second type of purity marks the difference between an ordinary and a fully enlightened being. In the foregoing chapter the inconceivability of buddha nature was described by the words: "[The buddha element] is pure and yet has affliction." While the nature of mind is primordially pure, it is obscured by the adventitious stains of the mental poisons and hindrances to knowledge in the state of an ordinary being. A second type of purity needs to be achieved—this consists of the elimination of all these veils. Once total purification has joined the ever-present purity of the nature of mind, there is the enlightenment of a buddha endowed with twofold purity.

(2) The cause bringing about this twofold purity is described as the practice of the path of the meditative and post-meditative phases. These consist of two types of primordial wisdom, which are "utterly non-conceptualizing wisdom in meditation" and "wisdom thoroughly discriminating all knowable objects in post-meditation" (Tib. *mnyam bzhag rnam par mi rtog pa'i ye shes dang rjes thob shes bya rnam par 'byed pa'i ye*

shes). While abiding in total pacification of any mental elaboration one will eventually come to feel the nature of mind itself, which is the union of spaciousness and awareness. When during meditation one dwells evenly balanced and one-pointedly immersed in this nature of mind, there will be insight called "utterly non-conceptualizing wisdom in meditation." This means that there is primordial wisdom that is not bound up with or does not involve any concept. By the power of this thought-free wisdom, there is "the wisdom thoroughly discriminating all knowable objects in post-meditation." While not meditating, all phenomena are seen in their ultimate and relative aspects. Ultimately they are seen as being by nature not truly existent, as being luminous emptiness, and at the same time their way of appearance is known. On the relative level all phenomena are seen as being dreamlike or like a magical illusion. This means that in post-meditation a firm and invincible certainty of knowing the absolute and relative truths will arise. Taking these two primordial wisdoms as one's path, one will attain twofold purity, which is the essence of ultimate enlightenment.

Moving towards this aim, a noble bodhisattva will abide in the indivisible union of spaciousness and awareness while resting in meditative equipoise, and thereafter gather the accumulation of merit to the vastest possible extent. This accumulation is carried out while knowing that it is ultimately empty and relatively illusory, like a dream or a magical illusion. In the language of the Dharma there are various ways of expressing this. Here non-conceptualizing wisdom and wisdom discriminating each and every phenomenon are described as the causes of buddhahood.

(3) Through relying on the path of these two primordial wisdoms one attains the fruit, which is freedom from the two veils of the mental poisons and hindrances to knowledge. The topics "essence" and "fruit" are partly similar in meaning, but emphasize different aspects. While the first describes enlightenment as a state of utter purity, the second stresses the fact that there is freedom from the pollution of the two veils.

(4) Through eliminating both veils—the mental poisons and hindrances to knowledge—a function unfolds, which is the accomplishment of the benefit of oneself and others. Without achieving benefit for oneself, one is not able to achieve the benefit of others. Though a bodhisattva mainly concentrates on bringing about the good of others and will not do so with his or her sake in mind, still one's own benefit or enlightenment has to come first. Otherwise one lacks the power

necessary to achieve the benefit of others, just as someone who does not know English himself could not communicate in this language with others.

(5) The basis for the fulfillment of the two benefits is provided by those buddha qualities that are the thirty-two qualities of the dharma-kaya. These are called "inconceivable" since they are very hard to fathom and an ordinary being cannot understand them as they truly are.

(6) Enlightenment manifests in terms of the three kayas, which are the svabhavikakaya or dharmakaya, the sambhogakaya, and the nirmanakaya. The term "sambhogakaya" (Tib. *longs spyod rdzogs pa'i sku*) literally means "body of perfect enjoyment" and is explained as the kaya perfectly enjoying the Dharma of the Great Vehicle. The disciples of the sambhogakaya are the bodhisattvas who dwell on one of the ten bhumis. To them it manifests visibly as the five buddha families and so forth, teaching the Dharma by means of different aspects, such as ornaments, gestures, and so on, without needing to express the instructions in words. The term "nirmanakaya" (Tib. *sprul pa'i sku*) literally means "emanation body" or "body of illusory appearance." It teaches the ordinary beings by manifesting in various illusory appearances corresponding to their different kinds. To a human a nirmanakaya appears in human form, to a god in god's form, to an animal in animal form, and so on.

Generally speaking, when explained in accordance with the Shāntong view, the three kayas are to be understood as follows: The joint manifestation of the realization of the essence and of liberated primordial wisdom of awareness is called dharmakaya (Tib. *snying rtogs dang rig pa'i ye shes sgrol ba zung 'jug chos kyi sku*). The form kayas manifest without moving away or being apart from this dharmakaya. The aspect appearing to bodhisattvas of the ten bhumis in the form of signs and symbols is called the sambhogakaya, and the aspect appearing to ordinary beings in accordance with their aspirations, manifesting a reflection of buddhahood in whichever form appropriate, is called the nirmanakaya.

When buddhahood is presented in terms of five kayas, two further aspects are distinguished, which are called "the kaya of actual enlightenment" and "the vajra kaya" (Tib. *mngon par byang chub pa'i sku dang rdo rje sku*). The first refers to the fact that the realization of the three kayas does not involve any pride. When, on the path of training, we think of "reaching enlightenment," we will believe that someone who has achieved this feat will feel extremely capable and special. In truth, though, the actual reaching of enlightenment does not entail any such notion. The vajra kaya denotes the fact that buddhahood is indivisible and that the three kayas, therefore, are of one and the same essence.

(7) Buddhahood is permanent in that the dharmakaya is as unchanging as space and the form kayas are uninterrupted in appearance as long as sentient beings exist.

(8) When the first bodhisattva level is reached, the dharmakaya or the dharmata, the true state of everything, is realized directly and an ordinary being becomes a noble bodhisattva. Until this realization has taken place the final ultimate truth is inconceivable.

Annotation 52:

In the teachings pertaining to the middling turning of the wheel of Dharma, all the direct instructions on emptiness contain the definitive meaning (Skt. *nitārtha*, Tib. *nges don*), whereas anything else is relative and conveys a provisional statement (Skt. *neyārtha*, Tib. *drang don*) leading up to the absolute truth, the direct vision of emptiness. Literally *drang ba* means "leading towards." In the Shäntong view, which the Buddha taught during his third turning of the wheel of Dharma, the definitive meaning as presented by the second turning is not the final and ultimate one. Definitively true are the teachings on the nature of mind clearly showing it as the indivisible union of spaciousness and awareness. (For the meaning of "nitartha" and "neyartha" see Part Four, note 10.)

Annotation 53:

As shown above (annotation 51) the enlightenment of a buddha comes about through two types of primordial wisdom. When one attains the utterly non-conceptualizing wisdom of meditation, the wisdom thoroughly discriminating all knowable objects in post-meditation will arise as well. Jetsün Milarepa, for instance, directly realized Mahamudra through the utterly non-conceptualizing wisdom of meditation. On the basis of this realization his mind became totally clear as to all phenomena, and in post-meditation he knew and remembered everything without having to rely on books. The Buddha himself has said that when firm realization of his words is achieved, full clarity of mind with regard to any relative phenomenon will be present simultaneously. In the light of the two types of primordial wisdom one will know all phenomena as being ultimately empty and like a dream appearance or a magical illusion on the relative level. Someone who has this vision will carry out any action, such as being generous, making offerings, and so forth, with the perception of discriminative wisdom not focused on the three spheres, or wheels, of subject, object, and action.

Luminous clarity, or clear light, is inseparable from the nature of primordial wisdom. This means that the qualities of enlightenment are inseparable from those of the basis, which is the nature of mind. They are of one and the same essence. If there was no clarity in the state of the basis, there could not be the realization of clarity when attaining the fruit. In the Shäntong view the true nature of mind is the inseparable union of emptiness and clarity. Once it has been freed from all the adventitious defilements, the realization of clarity will come about. If, as according to the Rangtong view, the basis did not hold any clarity, primordial wisdom would be something that newly arises. If this was the case, it would come about on the basis of causes and conditions. As such it would be created, and being created it would not last and would finally be destroyed. Furthermore, if the nature of mind was solely empty, there could not be the inseparable union of spaciousness and primordial wisdom in the state of the fruit. Spaciousness is equivalent to emptiness. If spaciousness and awareness or clarity were not already inseparable in the state of the basis, they could not become inseparable in the state of the fruit.

Annotation 54:
When it is said that the dharmakaya is indivisibly manifest in the nature of all sentient beings, this means the following:

The only difference between the inseparable union of spaciousness and awareness, which is the nature of the minds of all sentient beings, and this union being endowed with twofold purity is the fact that the latter is free from all the adventitious stains, while the former is still obscured by these. The essence of the true state of mind is naturally pure, and with regard to this aspect there is not the slightest difference between an ordinary and an enlightened being. The empty sphere of space, for instance, is the same in all empty vessels. Nevertheless, a difference comes about due to the different kinds of vessels. Space itself is not of different kinds and without there being different kinds of vessels there will not be different kinds of space. Once the vessel is broken, the space around it and the space within will become inseparable. In the same way, the dharmakaya is indivisibly manifest in the nature of all sentient beings. Both the dharmakaya and the nature of the minds of beings are the inseparable union of spaciousness and awareness. As to their essence there is no difference. For this reason, basis, path, and fruit are undifferentiated according to the terminology of the Shäntong and Mahamudra traditions. Though basis tathagatagarbha, path tathagatagarbha, and fruit tathagatagarbha are no different in essence, still the adventitious stains need to be abandoned in order to attain the fruit. In this respect, there is a difference, which is expressed in the lines: "All sentient beings are buddha but obscured by adventitious stains." As has been said before, this can be understood by means of the example of gold when still contained in ore and when totally freed from all the surrounding dross. As far as the purity of the gold is concerned, there is no difference in both cases. Nevertheless, it will appear as if it has changed once all the dross is removed.

There is only a seeming change, though, and the inseparable union of spaciousness and awareness within all sentient beings will reveal itself as the ever-present dharmakaya, once freed from all its adventitious veils. The nature of beings and the dharmakaya will merge and prove to be inseparable. This is shown in the *Mahayanasutralamkara* (Tib. *mdo sde rgyan*) and similar scriptures by means of many examples. As was said before, space only appears as a variety due to vessels of various shape. Similarly, all small and great rivers on this planet finally flow into the great ocean. Each takes its individual course through an individual country and has its individual name, but the moment it reaches the sea, its waters become inseparable from the ocean. Thus all water is the same. When many thousands of different butterlamps are burning in one place, each gives off its light and yet all these lights merge and become inseparable.

When it is said that the dharmakaya has spontaneously possessed all the properties of a buddha since beginningless time, this means that the qualities of buddhahood are not something newly attained. If they were, they would be conditioned. The empty nature of mind is not brought about by causes and conditions, and thus is uncreated and spontaneously present. If this was to be joined by newly arising—and therefore conditioned—qualities, these qualities could never become inseparable from the true state of the mind, which is emptiness present since the very beginning.

Annotation 55:
The statement that the stains obscuring the pure nature of mind have not been truly existent since beginningless time can be understood by the example of dream. When one dreams of being burnt by fire or

carried away by a flood, this fire and water have never existed in any way. If during a dream attachment towards pleasant objects and aversion towards unpleasant objects arise, these objects of attachment and aversion have had no existence since the very beginning. Therefore, the mental poisons based upon these objects are also not existent in the light of the ultimate truth. They come into the mind as something fleeting and adventitious, like clouds in the sky.

While all faults are adventitious, the qualities are spontaneously present. In the Shäntong view, all faults are self-empty (Tib. *rang stong*), while the qualities are not empty of their own essence. They are other-empty (Tib. *gzhan stong*). This is to say that the nature of mind is empty of all faults, of everything foreign to it, but it is not empty of the spontaneously present qualities, of everything native to it. As it is stated in the section explaining the tathagatagarbha (B.II.2.2.2.1.3.5.2):

> The element is empty of the adventitious [stains],
> which are featured by their total separateness.
> But it is not empty of the matchless properties,
> which are featured by their total inseparability.

While dreaming of being burnt by fire, carried away by water, and so forth, all these outer faults that arise when the mind focuses outwards will prove to be adventitious once the dream is recognized. They come and go. Yet while this happens, the nature of mind, the inseparable union of spaciousness and awareness, does not undergo any change. Based upon this fact, the practice of the secret Mantrayana unfolds its power. If the true state of mind was not the inseparable union of spaciousness and awareness, what benefit could arise from the meditation on a yidam deity? If there was no coexistence of the body having an impure nature and the mind being inherently pure, there would not be the slightest benefit in meditating on any deity. Since the mind in terms of its true existence is spaciousness and awareness inseparable, the meditation on the pure form of a yidam deity will purify the impure appearance and perception of the physical body. Then the true deity, which is this spaciousness and awareness inseparable, will reveal itself and become immediately apparent. All yidam practices, such as meditating on Avalokiteshvara, Amitabha, Vajravarahi, and so forth, singly serve the purpose of purifying this impure appearance that the physical body seems to be. When the true deity is the inseparable union of spaciousness and awareness, the meditation on a deity being visualized in its likeness has the power to lead one to the achievement and realization of the true deity, of the nature of mind. If spaciousness and awareness inseparable was not present in the impure phase already, if everything was nothing at all or mere emptiness, and if both faults and qualities were like space, one could not attain any quality.

The faults consist of the veils of the mental poisons and hindrances to knowledge, the former being the obstacle to liberation and the latter the obstacle to omniscience. When one has attained the level of a shravaka or pratyekabuddha arhat, one has only purified the veil of the mental poisons and thereby reached liberation to the extent of being liberated from the cycle of existence. One has not yet attained the state of omniscience. In order to reach that state as well, one must abandon the veil of the hindrances to knowledge.

Annotation 56:

Generally speaking, correct realization or "realizing as it is" (Tib. *ji lta ba rtogs pa*) refers to the direct understanding of emptiness; complete realization or "realizing as much as there is" (Tib. *ji snyed pa rtogs pa*) refers to all relative appearances. In the explanations pertaining to the Shäntong system, ultimate correct realization is direct understanding of the inseparable union of spaciousness and awareness, and complete realization is direct understanding of all relative, artificial appearances.

The three realms are the desire realm, the realm of form, and the formless realm. Primordial wisdom, which is completely free from ideation, acts as the remedy for the mental poisons of the three realms, or in other words, for the concepts entertained by the beings of these realms. As for the term "concept" or "thought," the veils of the mental poisons and hindrances to knowledge, when put concisely, are nothing but concepts. While the veil of the hindrances to knowledge consists of very subtle kinds of concepts, the veil of the mental poisons constitutes the very coarse types. If, for instance, desire arises on the basis of something pleasant, and aversion comes up on the basis of something unpleasant that is viewed as being hostile, these are very gross and rough concepts and a sentient being with these reactions has a coarse mind. The veil of the hindrances to knowledge has three aspects in terms of progressively subtler concepts. The first is holding on to true existence (Tib. *bden par 'dzin pa*), the second is holding on to characteristics (Tib. *mtshan mar 'dzin pa*), and the third is the appearance of duality (Tib. *gnyis snang*). Towards the last-mentioned aspect people like us will develop an extremely subtle concept, whereas a bodhisattva who dwells on the tenth bhumi will perceive the mere appearance of duality as such without conceptualizing it any further. Here again the dream example is helpful to develop an understanding. What will happen if during a dream one realizes that one is dreaming? When one recognizes one's dream for what it is, appearance will be there but holding on to its true existence will be ended. Then the power of direct recognition will arise. Similarly, bodhisattvas who dwell on one of the ten bodhisattva levels have realized the meaning of emptiness. Not leaving it at this initial realization but cultivating it to ever subtler levels, one will gain a respectively firm ability that, having become unshakable, will lead one to attain the state of a buddha.

Primordial wisdom completely free from ideation is to be understood as thought-free primordial wisdom or primordial wisdom released from any thought or concept. It can be explained, for instance, through the teachings on valid cognition. In this context four types of valid cognition are distinguished: direct valid cognition of the senses (Tib. *dbang po mngon sum tshad ma*), direct valid cognition of intellect (Tib. *jid mngon sum tshad ma*), self-aware direct valid cognition (Tib. *rang rig tshad ma*), and direct valid cognition in yoga or in meditation endowed with bliss (Tib. *rnal 'byor mngon sum tshad ma*). The last-mentioned is described as "knowing, which arising from meditation, is free from mental elaboration and undeluded." The term "knowing" is to be understood as being equivalent to primordial wisdom. Through cultivating the knowing or primordial wisdom which arising from meditation is free from mental elaboration and undeluded to its final unlimited extent, one will reach the level of buddhahood.

The term "cultivation" or "meditation" (Tib. *sgom pa*) is defined as follows: Once direct realization of the true nature is reached, one leaves the mind unwaveringly within this realization without giving rise to distraction and thus purifies one's stream of being. In the traditions of Mahamudra and the Mantrayana it is appropriate to apply this cultivation in all daily activities and any form of conduct. Especially when one has attained a good realization of Mahamudra, one has the power to meditate on the meaning of Mahamudra while carrying out any work or activity. Since the ultimate true nature of Mahamudra is the inseparable union of spaciousness and awareness, one will be able to work and act within this vision of spaciousness and awareness inseparable. If, as in the Rangtong system, the true nature of Mahamudra is viewed as being merely empty, one will meditate evenly balanced in mere emptiness and the consciousnesses of the six senses will cease.

According to this tradition, the consciousness of all outer appearances, such as the eyes seeing form, the ears hearing sound and so on, must be stopped, whereupon one has to meditate one-pointedly on emptiness. According to the Mahamudra tradition, one has to gain the ability to meditate in everyday life while carrying out any kind of activity. This is what is meant by the inseparable union of spaciousness and awareness or of emptiness and clarity. The presence or non-presence of emptiness and clarity inseparable leads to different types of meditation. The difference is mainly marked by the aspect of clarity, by the question whether the nature of mind is viewed as holding clear light or not.

In his song for Rechungpa on turning daily behavior into a practice, Jetsün Milarepa said:

> At times I eat, and while eating I meditate.
> When meditating while eating and eating,
> I know eating and drinking to be a ritual feast.
> These instructions I have, while others have not.

> At times I sleep, and while sleeping I meditate.
> When meditating while sleeping and sleeping,
> mental blindness shines forth as clear light.
> These instructions I have, while others have not.

Once one understands well the view of the Mantrayana, and especially that of Mahamudra, one will be able to meditate in connection with any form of conduct and any mental poison that arises. At the time when the mental poisons are extremely coarse, one will purify one's mental poisons by means of the mental poisons themselves. This is the principle of Mantrayana practice. One has to purify desire on the basis of one's desire, anger on the basis of one's anger, and so on. The term "secret Mantrayana" is used since it contains these deep and subtle methods of purification.

Though, generally speaking, this is not the time to explain the secret Mantrayana, a short introduction is given here since the Shäntong view leads up to the secret Mantrayana. The *Mahayana Uttara Tantra,* which itself belongs to the Sutrayana level of teaching, is a shastra building a bridge between sutra and tantra, since the views presented by the Shäntong and Mantrayana systems are almost identical. On the basis of the essence of mind being the inseparable union of spaciousness and awareness, the ultimate nature of mind is explained as emptiness and bliss inseparable on the level of the secret Mantrayana. The aspect of clarity or clear light is experienced as bliss and the aspect of spaciousness is identical to emptiness. Without viewing the mind as the inseparable union of spaciousness and awareness the experience of the inseparable union of emptiness and bliss will not arise. "Inseparable" means that the essence is undifferentiated and not able to be divided.

Annotation 57:

"Calm abiding" (Skt. *śamatha*, Tib. *zhi gnas*) and "special or vivid insight" (Skt. *vipaśyanā*, Tib. *lhag mthong*) are defined as follows: "Calm abiding" means that all movements of the mind towards the outside are totally appeased or stilled and one abides one-pointedly focused on the virtuous or authentic object. "Vivid insight" means that within this state of calm abiding, or in other words, while the mind is free from thought, the authentic object is truly and individually discerned or analyzed. On the level of an ordinary being these two aspects of meditation are developed. This is not yet qualified special insight (Tib. *lhag mthong mtshan nyid pa*), which in the Mahayana tradition is defined as direct realization of emptiness. With this realization, qualified special insight arises in one's own stream of being. This is the path of seeing whereby one reaches the first bodhisattva level and goes beyond that of an ordinary being.

The two benefits are benefit for oneself (Tib. *rang don*) and benefit for others (Tib. *gzhan don*). Through abandoning the veils of the mental poisons and hindrances to knowledge without leaving a trace, one achieves final ultimate benefit for oneself, and final ultimate realization provides the benefit of others. Without the vision of supreme realization one is not able to truly benefit other sentient beings. "Ultimate" (Tib. *mthar phyin pa*) means that there is nothing beyond or further. The bodhisattvas who dwell on the ten bhumis, for instance, achieve their own benefit and that of others to a certain respective extent, but only a buddha embodies the final ultimate perfection of the two benefits. The same is true of nirvana, the state beyond the cycle of existence or beyond torment and pain. A shravaka or pratyekabuddha arhat has only reached nirvana from the viewpoint of the coarse defilements being eliminated. Similarly, someone who attains the bodhisattva levels within the direct realization of emptiness has only gone beyond samsara from the viewpoint of this coarse level. With respect to the extremely subtle defilements, an arhat or a noble bodhisattva is not yet beyond the cycle of existence. In order to reach the ultimate nirvana one must attain the state of buddhahood. As is said above in the explanations of the tathagatagarbha (B.II.2.2.2.1.2.2. 8.2.3.2.2): "One will therefore not attain nirvana without attaining the state of buddhahood."

When it is said that a buddha teaches in accordance with the disciples' streams of being, this means that he teaches in accordance with their different temperaments, aspirations, wishes, mental capacities, and dispositions.

Annotation 58:

When it is said that true buddhahood is of an uncompounded nature, this means that it is not compounded due to causes and conditions. The Tibetan term here translated as "nature" is *chos can*. It is widely used in the context of the teachings on valid cognition (see above, annotation 11) and its literal translation is "that which has or is qualified by a property." Here the term *chos can* is to be understood as being equivalent to the Tibetan term *rang bzhin*, which means "nature" in the sense of something unable to be separated from a particular phenomenon.

The nature of something compounded by causes and conditions can be understood, for instance, from the teachings on impermanence, where the samsaric condition is described as follows:

> All those who are born have the property of dying.
> All those who desire each other have the property of getting
> separated.
> All things that were gathered have the property of getting
> exhausted.

We are born from causes and conditions and thus have the property of dying. Death cannot be separated from our nature and we will have to die sooner or later. Nevertheless, truly mastering the practice of the creation and completion phases of the Vajrayana, one can attain deathlessness. If one knows all appearances to be of mental nature, illusory manifestations of the mind, and thus realizes the meaning of the inseparable union of spaciousness and awareness or of Mahamudra, which is unborn clear light, one attains the power of becoming deathless. As Jetsün Milarepa said in one of his songs to Pachig Dhampa Sangjä:

> Within unborn mind there is supreme immortality.
> The characteristics of being born and dying are liberated of
> themselves.
> How happy I am in the firm vision of the highest view!

Generally speaking, first one needs to understand that everyone who is born is of the nature of dying. To think: "I am still young and will not die as yet" is of no benefit. One will surely die and it can happen any time. Yet, if one practices the sacred Dharma well, and especially if one manages to carry out the practices of the Vajrayana in the proper fashion, one can be liberated from death and go beyond dying. Padmasambhava, for instance, attained an immortal body, and the disciples of Milarepa known as "the three sons and four daughters," Rechungpa and so on, did not die. Their bodies became like rainbows and they departed into the pure fields. This is called "the great transmigration in rainbow body" (Tib. *'ja' lus 'pho ba chen po*). There were very many in Tibet who attained the kaya of great transmigration in rainbow body. A person who departs from the world in this way will leave hair and fingernails behind, while his or her body will transform and become rainbow-like, thus vanishing from the earth. In order to achieve this, one does not have to be a very learned or important person. Anyone who receives the special oral instructions and puts them into practice as it should be can become a siddha (Tib. *grub thob*), an accomplished being.

One should therefore apply the means to go beyond having the property of dying and to accomplish deathlessness, the kaya of immortality (Tib. *'chi med kyi sku*). Only the Vajrayana holds these means, whereas the vehicle of characteristics (Tib. *mtshan nyid kyi theg pa*) does not. Nevertheless, one needs it as a basis. In the context of the vehicle of characteristics, or in the course of the second turning of the wheel of Dharma, the two truths and the meaning of their equality are presented. If one does not understand this thoroughly, one will not understand the meaning of purity and equality (Tib. *dag pa dang mnyam pa'i don*), which forms the basis of any Vajrayana practice. As long as this view is not understood well and is not truly adopted, the meditation on a deity, though it constitutes the heart of Vajrayana practice, will seem very easy and will become equally shallow. Any small child could do it, once he or she was taught what to visualize: "Oh yes, there is a body with one head, two arms, and two legs, and there is also a flower in the left hand . . ." With this approach one might wonder why the recognition of the absence of a personal self as taught in the Shravakayana is so much more difficult and why the Vajrayana is called "secret." To be able to practice the Vajrayana one needs the ultimate view. This is the inseparable truth of purity and equality (Tib. *dag mnyam bden pa dbyer med*), meaning that all appearances that could possibly occur are equal in their state of utter purity (Tib. *dag pa rab 'byams*). One needs to develop unshakable certainty that all phenomena are equally pure and inseparable in their nature of purity, since otherwise doubts will arise. One day one will meditate very well with pure faith, but the next day it will be gone and one will wonder what one is doing. In this way, one's diligence, discriminative wisdom, and faith will deteriorate. Once one has developed firm conviction of one's own inner view, there will be no doubt, and one's diligence, wisdom, and faith, not getting weakened, will ever increase and lead one to the state of a siddha. What this means can be seen from the biographies of saintly beings such as Tilo, Naro, Marpa, Mila, and so forth.

In Tibet some among those who attained great transmigration in rainbow body mainly worked during their lives, as for instance cutting "Om Mani Peme Hung" in stones. The Vajrayana holds instructions on how to combine work with meditation. Someone who really understands these deep instructions will manage to meditate while working and carrying out everyday activities. This is a sign that practice is profound. Lacking profundity, one's meditation will go away while one is working, and while meditating one will not be able to engage in any kind of conduct. Yet, once one has acquired the necessary skill, both one's work and the innermost heart of Dharma will go well. One will benefit the truth, benefit sentient beings, and benefit oneself. In my view this aspect is especially important nowadays, as the manners and customs on this earth have changed. The way to benefit sentient beings best is not the same as it was at the time of the Buddha or of Jetsün Milarepa. When in those days a practitioner of Dharma renounced the world and stayed in the wilderness to meditate, people liked that very much and developed great faith. Thus this form of practice was extremely beneficial for other beings as well.

The Buddha and his following of bhikshus, for instance, gave up all worldly activities. Yet, in order to communicate with people and to give them the opportunity to gather virtue, they went into the cities and begged for alms. Then the people, before eating themselves, would offer food to the Buddha and his many thousands of monks, and would dedicate their own food to Buddha, Dharma, and Sangha. In this way their faith and supplications were greatly strengthened. At the time when Jetsün Milarepa appeared, people greatly admired anyone who withdrew into a cave to dedicate his life to meditation, and felt deep devotion towards such a person. Therefore, a single man such as Milarepa, by meditating in the wilderness, would attract an extremely large number of disciples who would follow his example, and there would be many sponsors who would joyfully sustain this lifestyle. Thus it was very good for everyone.

Times have changed, though, and the present situation is different. When in our time someone decides to follow the ancient examples in the literal sense and gives up all work in order to meditate solely, he or she will be considered a very bad and useless person. One will be called "work-shy" or "sluggard" and no one will have respect, let alone any faith. Yet, if on the contrary one works very hard and efficiently in everyday life, and at the same time manages to practice the Dharma, this is in my opinion very good for oneself and will become an equally good example to others. Working hard will increase one's own capacity of diligence, and being seen to combine work with the practice of Dharma will arouse faith in one's fellow beings. In this way one will manage to benefit others and oneself as well.

With respect to the manners and customs of the world in these days, it is therefore extremely good to learn how to meditate while one is working. If there were no such instructions, this would be very difficult. Nowadays many people think: "In order to practice as the Buddha taught I have to give up all worldly activities. Since this is not possible, I cannot practice Dharma. Therefore, a new style of Buddhism must be found." This is not true. The Buddha taught gradually in three turnings of the wheel of Dharma. Following the system of the Shravaka-yana, which belongs to the first turning of the wheel of Dharma, one has to abandon all worldly activities. In the teachings of the Great Vehicle, and especially in the context of the Mantrayana, the Buddha has taught how it is possible to practice while being engaged in any worldly activity. Thus we do not have to invent anything new, but are able to practice as the Buddha taught in our modern days as well.

When it is said that buddhahood is equivalent to one's own benefit being finally perfected, one may wonder whether a buddha desires personal welfare and strives for this aim. There is no such intention. Even while being a bodhisattva, a buddha never had any egoistic motives but solely strove to bring about the benefit of others. Yet in doing so one naturally achieves best possible benefit for oneself.

When the text speaks of a saintly person with karmic fortune whose sense faculties have become supreme, this refers to a bodhisattva who has reached the bhumis. The sense faculties of someone who attains the first bodhisattva level undergo a transformation of state, thereby acquiring specific qualities. In the state of an ordinary being, for instance, the eyes only perceive visible things but are shut to sound, and the nose only grasps smell but cannot experience taste or touch, and so on. On the path of seeing, though, the senses become utterly pure and the single sense-faculty of the eye can perceive all sensory objects at the same time. The consciousness behind the visual faculty of a bodhisattva is able to grasp every form, sound, odor, taste, and touch occurring in the ten directions simultaneously. This and many other qualities of the senses are attained once the first bhumi is reached.

Annotation 59:
When it is said that manifold sensory objects are perceived as being merely relative (Tib. *kun rzob tsam du*) or merely nominal (Tib. *tha snyad tsam du*), this is to be understood as follows: The various appearances arising in a dream, for instance, such as visible things, sounds, odors, tastes, and different kinds of touch, are not really there. They only exist relatively or nominally. Yet when the mind is deluded during the dream phase, these merely relatively existent sense-objects will seem [to be] real and be perceived accordingly. When while dreaming one recognizes that one is dreaming, one will know that whatever one perceives is only a dream appearance and does not really exist. Still, as long as one does not wake up from sleep, appearances will arise, but to the perception of someone who recognizes them for what they are they will only have a relative or nominal existence. There will be the perception of mere appearance (Tib. *snang tsam du*). Similarly, in ultimate truth all phenomena are luminous emptiness free from any mental elaboration; nevertheless, appearance is there, but only in terms of mere appearance, in terms of something relative or nominal. We practice the Dharma in order to exhaust all impure appearances, all delusions of impurity. As long as we have not managed to do so, these impure appearances will be there. Once all delusion of impurity has been exhausted, everything will shine forth as pure physical form and the appearance of primordial wisdom (Tib. *dag pa'i sku dang ye shes kyi snang bar shar ba*). The way in which this actually takes place is very difficult to understand and people like us, lacking the actual realization, can only imagine it slightly through inference.

When it is said that pure vision comes about through the power or on the basis of having previously gathered the accumulations, this refers to the time when one has followed the path of training and accumulated merit in enacting the bodhisattva conduct. This power or ability will therefore be of different kinds.

The elements are of four kinds: earth, water, fire, and air. "Being made from the elements" means that there are many phenomena in terms of visible things, sounds, odors, tastes, and different kinds of touch, all of which are made from or composed by these elements. As opposed to that, the form kayas are not made from the elements. They are not of the nature of these. The form kayas are the sambhogakaya and the nirmanakaya, and one may wonder whether they are other than the dharmakaya. They are not, since the dharmakaya itself holds power or ability (Tib. *nus pa*), a multitude of qualities and types of activity.

Generally speaking, "a noble one" (Tib. *'phags pa*) is anyone who has transcended the level of an ordinary being. "A great noble one" is someone who has reached the pure bodhisattva levels—the eighth up to the tenth, inclusively. (See also Part Four, note 5.)

Suppleness (Tib. *shin sbyangs*) means that both body and mind have become extremely malleable, so that during meditation one does not experience any physical discomfort no matter what hardships one undergoes in order to practice the Dharma, and the mind is able to meditate on any subject. When this is reached, one's meditation will go well, whereas until then one will feel physical pain and the body will not be spacious and relaxed. The mind will not keep its focus, but will wander and not rest evenly. Once one has attained physical and mental suppleness, one should not listen too much to other people regarding the proper way to meditate. Otherwise another fault would arise. When, unlike before, the body is continuously relaxed and spacious during meditation, and the mind has a strong aspect of lucidity, managing to meditate on anything without thinking, this is samadhi itself manifesting naturally and spontaneously (Tib. *ting nge 'dzin de kar rang*). Then one will attain the fruit of samadhi, which is the touch (Tib. *reg bya*) or experience of bliss arising from physical and mental malleability. This touch is not comparable to contact felt by the body. It is attained through samadhi and arises of its own force, so that body and mind are pervaded by bliss. This is not the same as the bliss practiced in the Mantrayana, but is the bliss of shamatha or calm abiding. Once the mind is fully settled and abides unwaveringly, bliss will arise in body and mind.

Generally speaking, this is a sign that the true nature of mind is the inseparable union of clarity and emptiness. When resting within this inseparable union of clarity and emptiness, bliss will arise in the mind and by the power of this mental bliss the body will become blissful as well. Especially on the level of the secret Mantrayana, one needs this quality, since according to this system, realization is equivalent to the direct revelation or actualization of the inseparable union of emptiness and bliss. Leading up to this view of bliss-emptiness inseparable is the view of the Shäntong system, in which the final ultimate truth is the inseparable union of spaciousness and awareness. If the final ultimate truth is considered as being merely empty, one will absorb oneself into a condition of total absence of thought and the mind will gain an according experience. In this state of just empty emptiness (Tib. *stong pa stong kyang*), no bliss will arise. By knowing the ultimate nature of the mind as being the inseparable union of spaciousness and awareness, one will rest within this spaciousness and awareness inseparable during meditation, and when true samadhi is attained, mind and body will be filled with bliss. With this basis one will understand the view of the true nature of mind being jointly manifest bliss-emptiness as taught in the Vajrayana or secret Mantrayana.

The phrase "the mode of the Dharma that is deep according to its own essence" (Tib. *rang gi ngo bo nyid kyis*) means that it is by nature deep, as a butterlamp is by nature radiant.

"The intelligence that analyzes the absolute" (Tib. *don dam dpyod byed kyi rig pa*) is equivalent to the intelligence or awareness analyzing emptiness. Mainly there are five kinds of intelligence, which are analyzing the essence, the cause, the fruit, both cause and fruit, and mere appearance. They are called "the Five Great Established Meanings" (Tib. *gtan thsigs chen po lnga*). What is referred to here is the fifth, of which Jamgön Kongtrül the Great has said in his *Treasury of Knowledge* that analyzing or discerning mere appearance is the established meaning of interdependent origination (Tib. *snang tsam la dpyod pa rten 'byung gi gtan thsigs*) in that mere appearance is the appearance of interdependence. Elsewhere, in other traditions, the fifth aspect of awareness is also called "the established meaning of the King of Awareness" (Tib. *rig pa'i rgyal po'i gtan thsigs*).

The term translated here as "goodness" is *dge legs*, which consists of the words "virtue" (*dge ba*) and "definitive good" (*nges legs*). This means that the Sugata provides benefit both temporarily and ultimately. Temporarily it is experienced as bliss, and ultimately it constitutes the cause through which one attains the fruit, the level of buddhahood.

The term *dbang 'byor* can also be explained as *dbang po'i 'byor pa,* which means "the treasure or wealth of the senses." This refers to the fact that the sense faculties of a bodhisattva undergo a complete change of state once emptiness is seen directly, and thereby acquire a great multitude of qualities. As was said before, the single sense-faculty of the eye of a noble bodhisattva, for instance, can perceive all visible things, sounds, odors, tastes, and forms of touch simultaneously. These qualified senses are beyond the ordinary sense-faculties and the sense-objects they experience are extremely subtle. The bodhisattvas who dwell on the ten bhumis perceive forms, sounds, odors, tastes, and contacts that are beyond the elements and all phenomena consisting of them. They appear through the power or creative ability of the dharmakaya. Thus the tathagata, though it is free from any reason generating a fruit, generates all goodness, displaying the illusory appearance of mandalas, the reflection of the sambhogakaya, and teaching Dharma by means of signs and symbols. All these appearances are not made from the elements and are seen by noble bodhisattvas whose sense faculties have been transformed through the path of seeing.

Annotation 60:

Of the five paths, the first four, which are the paths of accumulation, junction, seeing, and meditation, constitute the path of training (Tib. *slob lam*). The fifth is the path of no more training (Tib. *mi slob pa'i lam*).

The two aspects of ultimate abandonment and realization, which are presented here as the vimuktikaya (Tib. *rnam par grol ba'i sku,* "the body of complete liberation") and the dharmakaya (Tib. *chos sku,* "the body of qualities") are also called the svabhavikakaya (Tib. *ngo bo nyid kyi sku,* "the essence body") and the jnana dharmakaya (Tib. *ye shes chos kyi sku,* "the body of the quality of primordial wisdom").

When it is said that both the vimuktikaya and the dharmakaya are uncreated or uncompounded (Tib. *'dus ma byas*), this means that they are not made from causes and conditions. Anything made from causes and conditions is a created or compounded phenomenon (Tib. *'du byed*) and defined as follows:

> All compounded phenomena have the quality of being destroyed.
> All compounded phenomena have the quality of being impermanent.
> All compounded phenomena have the quality of being unreliable.

In the terminology of the teachings on valid cognition, created and uncreated phenomena have two opposite characteristics: "Being wont to arise, cease, and abide are the three characteristics of the created. Not being wont to arise, cease, and abide are the three characteristics of the uncreated" (Tib. *skye 'gag gnas gsum rung ba 'du byed kyi mtshan nyid / skye 'gag gnas gsum mi rung ba 'dus ma byas kyi mtshan nyid*). Ultimately buddhahood is truly uncreated in that it is beyond both the extremes of createdness and uncreatedness. This is to be understood in the sense as, for instance, the dharmakaya is described as being "true self" in the section explaining the tathagatagarbha (B.II.2.2.2.1.2.2. 2.2.1.2): "It is true self since all conceptual elaboration in terms of self and non-self is totally stilled." In the Shäntong view, ultimate buddhahood is already present in the state of the basis, and will reveal itself once all the pollution caused by the veils of the mental poisons and hindrances to knowledge is abandoned without leaving a trace. If it was to be newly attained and arose from something created, there would be no reason for it to become uncreated later. Having to be newly attained, it would be compounded, and being compounded it would have the quality of being unreliable, impermanent, and subject to destruction. Viewed ultimately, though, buddha is no other than the nature of mind when purified from all the adventitious stains. The nature of mind being clarity-emptiness or space-awareness inseparable, nothing else or further needs to be achieved.

Annotation 61:

Meditative equipoise (Tib. *snyoms 'jug*) is equivalent to samadhi. The obstacles to samadhi are mainly of two kinds: agitation (Tib. *rgod pa*) and dullness (Tib. *'bying ba*). The first means that the mind is scattered and wanders towards the outside, engaging, for instance, in thoughts about past, future, or present doings. Dullness means that the mind, though it is not distracted by outer objects but stays within, lacks the aspect of lucidity and its focus is not clear. Another fault is called *rmugs pa* in Tibetan, which might be translated as "stupor," and is very similar to dullness. It means that the mind is very dense and hazy. Since these are mental states, they are difficult to describe exactly.

Annotation 62:

The noble ones who have a wisdom body are those bodhisattvas who dwell on one of the three pure bhumis. The noble ones below are the bodhisattvas who dwell on one of the seven impure bhumis and the shravaka and pratyekabuddha arhats.

Annotation 63:

The absolute buddha (Tib. *don dam pa'i sangs rgyas*) is the dharma-kaya, whereas the sambhogakaya and the nirmanakaya are the relative buddha (Tib. *kun rzob kyi sangs rgyas*), since the form kayas appear to the sense faculties and consciousnesses of the disciples as something conceivable in terms of perceived and perceiver (Tib. *yul dang yul can gyi rnam pa snang ba*).

Annotation 64:

The characteristic of being unperverted (Tib. *phyin ci ma log pa'i mtshan nyid*) is not dwelling in either of the extremes of assertion and denial or of overstatement (Tib. *sgro 'dogs*, lit. "decorating with feathers") and understatement (Tib. *skur 'debs*, lit. "casting abuse"), respectively. Claiming something that does not exist to be existent is an overstatement and claiming something that exists to be not existent is an understatement. If one said, for instance, that a human being has horns, this would be a [false] assertion, and if one said that a human being does not have two legs, this would be a [false] denial. Similarly, if one claimed that the mind was the power of flesh and blood, this would be an overstatement, since there are reasons to refute this assertion. The clear and aware essence of the mind could not arise from a gathering of flesh and blood. If, on the contrary, one claimed that the mind did not have intelligence, this would be an understatement, since the mind is able to understand many things even without requiring any study.

A reasoner (Tib. *rtog ge pa*) is someone who is very skilled in reasoning and argumentation (Tib. *rtog ge ba*), which generally means establishing or defining all phenomena by means of proofs and logical conclusions. Thus the insight derived from reasoning (Tib. *rtog ge ba'i rig pa*) consists mainly of very good and pure thoughts. The dharma-dhatu is not an object for reasoning. Its nature of clarity has always been beyond the reach of any such thoughts. In order to realize it one has to meditate, as it is only to be experienced through the power of meditative equipoise. This marks a main difference between the Rangtong and Shäntong systems. According to the Shäntong view, anything defined by means of proofs and logical conclusions (Tib. *rtags dang gtan thsigs*) is the field of experience of thinking, to which the final ultimate meaning is not accessible at all. Whatever is able to be grasped by thought is part of the relative, which is self-empty in that it is empty according to its own essence (Tib. *rang rang gis ngo bo'i stong pa*) or empty of an existing essence. As such all aspects of the relative can be shown by means of logical reasoning. The ultimate object of experience, the true nature of mind, is empty of the adventitious stains that are other than it, but not empty of qualities that are native to it. It is spaciousness and awareness inseparable. This can neither be shown nor experienced by those means, but needs to be realized in yoga while dwelling evenly balanced within spaciousness-awareness itself. If one tried to establish the experience of clear light by means of logical reasoning, one would be immersed in thoughts. While thinking, there is no way to experience it. The true nature of mind is only to be realized through valid cognition in yoga (see above, annotation 56), which, arising from meditation, is free from mental elaboration and undeluded. When freedom from mental elaboration and from delusion has arisen, the ultimate truth reveals itself and becomes immediately apparent.

When it is said that a tathagata never rises from the dharmata, this means that the vision and understanding of the true state of everything is uninterruptedly present throughout all meditative and post-meditative phases.

Annotation 65:
The three methods of teaching employed by a supreme nirmanakaya can be understood from the way Buddha Shakyamuni trained his disciples gradually. First he provided the means for a worldly being to gain access to the path of individual release resulting in the nirvana in terms of pacification of all suffering. Towards this aim he taught the Four Noble Truths, saying:

> Monks! One must understand suffering.
> One must abandon its origination.
> One must actualize its cessation and rely on the causal path.

To those who had entered the path of release and generated firm conviction with respect to the Dharma, he granted the teachings of the Great Vehicle in order to mature them thoroughly. In this context he started by giving instructions that were easy to understand, and then proceeded to ever profounder levels. In terms of the two emptinesses, for instance, he first explained the relative level from the viewpoint of self-emptiness, whereupon he elucidated the ultimate level as being spaciousness-awareness inseparable from the viewpoint of emptiness of other. Finally, in the course of the teachings pertaining to the secret Mantrayana, he expounded the unchanging realization of a buddha as being the realization of the utter purity of all appearances that could possibly occur (Tib. *snang srid dag pa rab 'byams*). He gave these teachings in many gradual stages, explaining the view, meditation, and action in the light of the Vajrayana system throughout four or six classes of tantras. Thus the Buddha taught in gradual stages, refining his instructions ever further up to the most sublime level. To those who were ready he granted prophecy as to their future enlightenment, predicting at what time, in what place, by what name and so forth they would reach buddhahood. This process can be compared to the way in which one cultivates a flower. First one will employ the means to make it grow, then the ones to make it ripen, and finally those to prevent it from decaying.

Annotation 66:
Self-awareness (Tib. *rang rig*) means that the duality of an object to be aware of and of an aware consciousness is not present (Tib. *rig bya dang rig byed gnyis med pa*). Through abiding within spaciousness-awareness inseparable itself, one frees oneself from the two veils along with their remaining imprints. When this freedom is achieved, there is individually discerning self-awareness, which is equivalent to ultimate direct realization in yoga.

Annotation 67:
When the union of means and discriminative wisdom (Tib. *thabs dang shes rab zung du 'brel ba*) is explained on the sutra level, means or method is equivalent to the practice of great compassion and so forth, and discriminative wisdom is equivalent to the wisdom realizing the nonexistence of a self and so on. On the level of the Mantrayana it is to be understood as the joint manifestation of bliss and emptiness in that means is equivalent to great bliss and discriminative wisdom to emptiness.

The Tibetan translation of the Sanskrit term "yogi" is "naljorpa" (*rnal 'byor pa*) and can be explained as follows. The word *rnal ma* is synonymous with the words *gzhi* and *ngo thog*, and thus means "basic, fundamental state" or "real, actual condition." The word *'byor ba*, which means "to stick or adhere to," is the intransitive form of *sbyor ba*, which means "to fasten together" or "to apply." *Rnal 'byor*, or "yoga" as it is called in Sanskrit, is therefore generally defined as "applying primordial wisdom to the meaning of the basic state" (Tib. *rnal ma'i don la ye shes sbyor ba*); a *rnal 'byor pa* is someone who adheres to this application. The content of yoga in view and practice differs according to the progressive levels of the Buddha's teaching.

In the Sutra tradition, yoga is "applying primordial wisdom to the meaning of the dharmata, which is the real condition of everything" (Tib. *rnal ma chos nyid kyi don la ye shes sbyor ba*).

In the Rangtong system one has applied primordial wisdom to the meaning of the basic state when one has realized the meaning of freedom from conceptual elaboration. This realization is reached once the nature of all phenomena is seen as their being empty of an existing essence, or literally speaking, self-empty according to their own essence (Tib. *rnal ma chos thams cad rang bzhin rang rang ngo bos stong pa'i spros pa dang bral ba'i don rtogs pa*).

According to the Mahamudra tradition one applies primordial wisdom to the inseparable union of spaciousness and awareness itself (Tib. *dbyings rig dbyer med kyi rang du ye shes sbyor ba*). This means that primordial wisdom is no other than spaciousness-awareness inseparable. Apart from that there has never been any primordial wisdom. There is no external realizing subject that could be applied. Once one has gained the capacity of resting in this very union of spaciousness and awareness, it itself holds the power to appease all the adventitious veils.

When one practices according to the tradition of the secret Mantrayana, primordial wisdom is applied to the inseparable union of bliss and emptiness itself (Tib. *bde stong byer med kyi rang du ye shes sbyor ba*). This is done by applying primordial wisdom to the meaning of purity and equality being inseparable (Tib. *dag mnyam byer med kyi don la ye shes sbyor ba*) or by applying primordial wisdom from within the understanding of purity and equality (Tib. *dag pa dang mnyam pa nyid kyi nang nas ye shes sbyor ba*). For someone who has gained the realization of the unsurpassable ultimate view of the Mantrayana, there is not the slightest impurity. When people like us, who are bound to an understanding perceiving the truth of the relative, hear this statement, they will not believe their ears and it will not enter their minds. At our present stage we mainly experience the worldly deluded mind that perceives duality, having "valid cognition" based upon terms and names. Yet, when taking the dream as a basis of one's reflection, any impure appearance that may arise does not exist in terms of impure matter. Whatever is there while dreaming is spaciousness-awareness inseparable. If there was not the inseparable union of spaciousness and awareness, no dream could ever occur.

Following the view of the highest tantra, one applies primordial wisdom to utter or universal purity (Tib. *dag pa rab 'byams la ye shes sbyor ba*), whereby one will eventually dwell within bliss-emptiness inseparable. This is the highest view and practice as it accords with the Annuttarayoga Tantra. Within the system of the Mantrayana the Buddha taught four classes of tantras: Kriya, Charya, Yoga, and Annuttara-yoga or Mahayoga Tantra. These are practiced gradually, and in their course view and meditation are refined ever further up to the ultimate level. In Kriya Tantra, for instance, there is the duality of purity and impurity and a lot of emphasis is given to creating purity in every respect. Nevertheless, when practicing the highest Tantra, the understanding of the utter purity of all appearances that might possibly occur is indispensable. One has to apply primordial wisdom to this true state of everything. There is no such wisdom to be imported from elsewhere. The understanding of utter purity is the application of primordial wisdom. When doing so, one is a yogi who will equally understand and experience the inseparable union of bliss and emptiness. An ultimate yogi is a buddha.

Annotation 68:

The way in which a supreme nirmanakaya unfolds activity without moving from meditative equipoise within the dharmakaya can be illustrated by the modern example of television: a single person who is recorded in a studio will be seen by many people on a multitude of screens without this person moving away from the studio at all.

Annotation 69:

The three vehicles referred to here are the Shravakayana, Pratyeka-buddhayana, and Mahayana.

Annotation 70:

When the dharmakaya, sambhogakaya, and nirmanakaya are described as being permanent in terms of nature (Tib. *rang bzhin gyi rtag pa*), of uninterruptedness (Tib. *rgyun mi 'chad pa'i rtag pa*), and of continuity (Tib. *rgyun gyi rtag pa*) respectively, this means the following: The dharmakaya has always been unchanging according to its own essence. The essence of the sambhogakaya is not permanence in terms of being unchanging but it uninterruptedly appears to the pure disciples, the bodhisattvas dwelling on the ten bhumis. A supreme nirmanakaya cuts the stream of his physical existence, but from the time of having reached buddhahood onwards he will display manifold different illusory appearances as they are fit to train all sentient beings. Thus there is continuity of appearance.

Annotation 71:

When it is said that the great enlightenment of a buddha does not consist of existence or peace (Tib. *srid bzi ma bsdus pa*), this means that it is not contained in samsara and nirvana, since the state of buddhahood does not dwell in either of the extremes of existence and peace. Shravaka and pratyekabuddha arhats, for instance, have attained a state of mere peace and abide within this peace itself. When doing so, the continuity necessary to bring about the benefit of beings is cut. Thus their state consists of peace in terms of extinction. As opposed to that, a buddha neither adheres to existence nor peace. By means of great discriminative wisdom he knows the nature of existence as being free from arising and thus does not abide in samsara. At the same time, by means of great compassion, he brings about the benefit of beings and thus does not abide in a nirvana limited to pacification. Conduct carried out through the power and force of great compassion is like a magical illusion, and in the chapter on buddha activity is described as being free from any deliberate effort. To gain an impression, an ordinary being should reflect upon the question of how someone would act in a dream while realizing that he is dreaming. Buddha activity is conduct in terms of mere appearance.

Annotation 72:

According to the Shäntong view the ultimate dharmakaya is to be understood as spaciousness and awareness inseparable, in which all illusory appearances along with their remaining imprints are totally uprooted and exhausted. The visible kayas are said to be relative, since they become an object of perception for the sense faculties of sentient beings. Anything perceived by the sense faculties of beings, such as forms, sounds, and so on, is a relative appearance. A buddha has to rely on these relative appearances in order to bring about the benefit of beings, since the ultimate truth, the total pacification of whatever illusion, is not a field of experience for the sense faculties. Thus a buddha benefits all sentient beings within the frame of their faculty of perception. He does so on the basis of the relative form kayas, which are the power or ability of the dharmakaya.

Annotation 73:

A supreme nirmanakaya in all his beautiful signs and marks is only seen by a sentient being who has purified the veil of negative karma, whereas to someone whose mind is still obscured by former very negative actions he may appear in a very ordinary or even revulsive form, just as the clear reflection of the moon is only seen in unpolluted water. Once one has reached the bodhisattva levels one is able to open manifold doors of samadhi and to see the sambhogakaya. This capacity increases while traveling through the bhumis, and the supreme sambhogakaya is only seen by bodhisattvas who dwell on the tenth bhumi.

Annotation 74:

The path that definitively reveals release (Tib. *nges 'byin gyi lam*) consists of the path of seeing, in the course of which truth is seen as it is, for the first time, and of the paths above, that is, the paths of meditation and of no more learning.

When it is said that sentient beings are fully sustained or supported (Tib. *yongs su 'dzin pa*) by buddha activity, this can be understood by the way in which a spiritual friend will support his or her disciples in any way, refining their minds by teaching them what to adopt and abandon and guiding them onto the authentic path towards total release.

Annotation 75:

The ultimate dharmakaya is uncreated in that it is beyond both the extremes of createdness and uncreatedness as explained above (annotation 60).

Annotation 76:

The three types of miraculous display refer to the aspects of body, speech, and mind. "Displaying the miraculous effects of teaching the Dharma" represents buddha mind bestowing blessing and thereby awakening realization.

Annotation 77:

What Karma Thrinläpa says is that the drum sounding the Dharma can be heard by beings on earth who have the conducive karmic imprints, since this drum has arisen due to the blessings of the buddhas and the former virtue of the gods.

Annotation 78:

When it is said that the extremely subtle and profound teaching of the Buddha does not reach the ears of all the disciples, this means that the teaching of the Buddha is heard and understood in accordance with an individual's karmic fortune and tendencies formerly acquired. Thus someone with the shravaka disposition, for instance, would not grasp the Buddha's words when he gave the instructions pertaining to the second or third turnings of the Wheel of Dharma. For this reason the followers of the Shravakayana and Pratyekabuddhayana claim that the Mahayana and Vajrayana teachings do not originate from the Buddha.

Annotation 79:

In the *Madhyamakavatara* (Tib. *dbu ma la 'jug pa*) by Chandrakirti, three types of compassion (Tib. *snying rje*) are described: compassion focusing on sentient beings (Tib. *sems can la dmigs pa'i snying rje*), compassion focusing on the nature (Tib. *chos la dmigs pa'i snying rje*), and compassion free from focus (Tib. *dmigs pa med pa'i snying rje*). The first type is compassion as it is developed by an ordinary being. It still goes along with the perception of duality and with attachment in terms of the belief that sentient beings truly exist. The second type is compassion that arises in recognition of their impermanent nature, while the third type is the compassion of a noble bodhisattva who has realized that sentient beings do not truly exist. All these three types of compassion, however, are given rise to by means of progressively subtler thoughts. As opposed to that, the great compassion (Tib. *thugs rje chen po*) of a buddha manifests without any thought or deliberate effort, since upon reaching buddhahood one undergoes a complete transformation of state (Tib. *gnas yongs su gyur pa*).

Annotation 80:

A buddha is the ground of everything that is best within the world and beyond it, since he has given the teachings of the three vehicles—the Shravakayana, Pratyekabuddhayana, and Mahayana. The latter again divides into the vehicle of characteristics and into the secret Mantrayana, which offers innumerable individual paths to liberation. If one practices these teachings, one will attain the best possible achievement within the world and beyond it. If, for instance, one meditates on patience as it accords with the Buddha's words and cultivates this practice, one will temporarily achieve the happiness consisting of the appeasement of anger and hatred. Ultimately one will attain the level of a perfect buddha, as patience is one of the six perfections, which will lead one beyond one's ordinary perception and thoughts. Thus, through the power of practicing one teaching of the Buddha, such as patience, one will attain the best possible goodness in the world and beyond. Furthermore, having experienced the truth of one teaching through the result of one's own practice, one will believe in the validity of all the teachings of the Buddha and will be a living example and source of inspiration even to those who have no connection with Dharma at all. Likewise, if following the Mahayana tradition one has cultivated love and compassion, and resulting from that has developed a genuinely benevolent heart towards all sentient beings, one will be convinced of the truth of the Buddha's words and will take them to heart in their entirety. Thus one will temporarily harvest happiness through the practice of virtue, through everything beneficial for oneself and all others, and ultimately achieve the level of buddhahood.

The best possible goodness to be achieved within the desire realm is mainly a very agreeable and pure sensation through the five doors of sense-perception, which comes about through the practice of virtue. Bad and hurtful visible form, sound, smell, taste, and touch are the main obstacles for a being of the desire realm to experience the goodness it can provide. The causes for the best possible achievement within the realm of form are the four levels of meditative stability and the four immeasurable contemplations—the cultivation of limitless love, compassion, joy, and equanimity. When one has developed the latter four, one will attain a rebirth comparable to that of Brahma, the lord of the gods. The best possible achievement within the formless realm consists of the modes of resting evenly in meditative equipoise. These are the experiences of boundless space (Tib. *nam mkha' mtha' yas skye mched*), of boundless consciousness (Tib. *rnam shes mtha' yas skye mched*), of nothingness itself (Tib. *ci yang med pa'i skye mched*), and of conscious non-conscious intuition (Tib. *'du shes med 'du shes med min skye mched*).

Annotation 81:
The intrinsic and general characteristics of all phenomena (Tib. *rang dang spyi'i mtshan nyid*) are to be understood as follows: Whatever is accessible to the five sense-faculties of the eyes, ears, nose, tongue, and body, and whatever appears as their object of perception, is an intrinsic characteristic. As to a general explanation, all phenomena that become an object of thought are included in the term "general characteristic." The appearance of every form, sound, smell, taste, and touch that is unmixed with thought and yet experienced as other than oneself is the intrinsic characteristic (Tib. *rang mtshan*) of a thing. This

is direct experience of the senses not entangled in thoughts. Whatever appears to and is recognized by thought is a general characteristic (Tib. *spyi'i mtshan*).

"Knowing all synonymous names" means that one and the same thing is expressed differently by many varying verbal expressions, which are all known without exception. For a buddha, for instance, many epithets are used. The term "buddha" itself means "being awakened, since the veils of the mental poisons and the hindrances to knowledge along with their remaining imprints are exhausted." Apart from that, a buddha is called by the names of "the Victor," "the Sugata," "the Bhagavan," "the Tathagata," and many others. The fact that all phenomena are by nature not existent is also expressed as "not truly existent," "non-existent according to its own essence," "not existent in terms of being attained as form," "not existent in terms of its basic nature," "not existent in terms of how it is viewed," and so forth. Though one meaning is intended, manifold terms are used. "Emptiness" is also called "the absolute truth," "thatness," "suchness," "dharmadhatu," "the unborn," "space of the appeasement of all mental elaboration," "the great middle," "the great gesture," "the great perfection," "the perfection of discriminative wisdom," and so on. Thus many synonyms are used for one thing.

PART FOUR

Translator's Notes

Note 1:

With regard to the disposition of a tathagata or the disposition to buddhahood five aspects are distinguished:

    (1) the cut-off disposition
    (2) the uncertain disposition
    (3) the shravaka disposition
    (4) the pratyekabuddha disposition
    (5) the disposition to the Mahayana.

(1) Those with the cut-off disposition have the following six characteristics: They do not feel the slightest weariness of the suffering of samsara. They do not have the slightest faith, modesty, or compassion, and they do not feel the slightest remorse. [The term "cut-off disposition" is used as it refers to sentient beings who are totally cut off or estranged from their true nature, not feeling its basic goodness, warmth, and light at all.]

(2) Those with the uncertain disposition depend upon conditions: When they rely on a spiritual friend who is a shravaka, or have friends who are shravakas, or see the shravaka sutras and thereupon develop faith in the shravaka view, their disposition turns into the shravaka disposition and they themselves really become shravakas. This is equally true when they rely on a spiritual friend who is a pratyekabuddha, etc., or when they rely on a spiritual friend who is a follower of the Mahayana, etc.

(3) Those with the shravaka disposition are characterized by the fact that they are afraid of samsara, that they have faith in the quality of nirvana, that they strive for its attainment, and that they have but little compassion.

(4) Those with the pratyekabuddha disposition have the following six characteristics: They are afraid of samsara. They have faith in the quality of nirvana and strive to attain it. They have but little compassion. They are very proud. They keep their teacher secret and delight in dwelling in solitude.

(5) The disposition to the Mahayana is thoroughly presented by means of the following six points, which are (a) types, (b) essence, (c) synonyms, (d) the reason why it surpasses the other dispositions, (e) manifestation, and (f) signs.

(a) The disposition to the Mahayana is of two types, these being the naturally present disposition and the disposition accomplished through correct cultivation.

(b) The essence of the naturally present disposition consists of the fact that it constitutes the power giving rise to the buddha qualities, that it has been present within beings since beginningless time, and that all sentient beings have attained it in terms of their true state.

The essence of the disposition accomplished through correct cultivation consists of the fact that it constitutes the power giving rise to the buddha qualities, that it unfolds through the former practice of the roots of virtue, and that it is the cause of the sambhogakaya and the nirmanakaya.

(c) Synonyms of the term "disposition" are the terms "seed," "element," "nature," and "essence."

(d) The reason why it surpasses the other dispositions: The two dispositions to become a shravaka or a pratyekabuddha are lesser, since they turn into a completely purified disposition by the mere purification of the veil of the mental poisons. The disposition to the Mahayana is most excellent, since it turns into a completely purified disposition through the purification of both the veils of the mental poisons and hindrances to knowledge.

(e) The disposition to the Mahayana has two ways of manifestation, which are the awakened and the unawakened disposition. In the case of the awakened disposition, the actual manifestation of the fruit is present and the signs are apparent. In the case of the unawakened disposition the actual manifestation of the fruit is not present and the signs are not apparent.

There are four conditions obstructing the awakening of the disposition. These are a birth in unfavorable circumstances, the non-presence of remaining imprints, the entertainment of wrong views, and the fault that consists of the presence of the veils.

There are two conditions conducive to the awakening of the disposition: an outer and an inner. The outer condition is the fact that the sacred Dharma is taught, and the inner condition is conceptual activity that corresponds to reality or truth.

(f) The signs of the disposition to the Mahayana, or in other words, the signs of a bodhisattva, are the following: Body, speech, and mind are naturally gentle without there being the need of applying an antidote. Deceit and hypocrisy are very minute and there is love for sentient beings. Love for sentient beings is the primary sign of a bodhisattva.

The above explanations are taken from the chapter "The Cause is the Sugatagarbha" of the text *Jewel Ornament of Liberation* (Tib. *dam chos yid bzhin nor bu thar pa rin po che'i rgyan*) by the Noble Gampopa.

There are three English translations of this work: Herbert Guenther, *The Jewel Ornament of Liberation* (London: Rider & Company, 1959); Ken and Katia Holmes, *Gems of Dharma, Jewels of Freedom* (Forres: Altea, 1995); and Khenpo Konchog Gyaltsen Rinpoche *The Jewel Ornament of Liberation* (Ithaca: Snow Lion Publications, 1998).

Note 2:
For further information on non-Buddhist tenets see, for example, Hopkins, *Meditation on Emptiness*, pp. 186, 317-333.

Note 3:
Generally speaking the term "demon" (Skt. *māra*, Tib. *bdud*) refers to various difficulties and obstacles met by a person who endeavors to practice the teachings of the Buddha. The "four demons" are the demon of the skandhas (Skt. *skandha-māra*, Tib. *phung po'i bdud*), the demon of the mental poisons (Skt. *kleśa-māra*, Tib. *nyon mongs pa'i bdud*), the demon of the lord of death (Skt. *mṛtyu-māra*, Tib. *'chi bdag gi bdud*), and the demon of the divine child (Skt. *devaputra-māra*, Tib. *lha'i bu'i bdud*). The first consists of the fact that one mistakenly believes the five skandhas to be an existing self. The second consists of the fact that one is overcome and steered by the mental poisons. The third represents death, which interrupts one's practice of Dharma unless one has learned how to make the process of dying a part of it. The fourth represents the seduction that can be induced by the bliss experienced during meditation, as long as one is still on the level of the god realms within samsara.

Note 4:
(1) The five skandhas or aggregates (Tib. *phung po*) are forms (Skt. *rūpa*, Tib. *gzugs*), feelings (Skt. *vedanā*, Tib. *tshor ba*), discriminations (Skt. *saṃjñā*, Tib. *'du shes*), compositional factors (Skt. *saṃskāra*, Tib. *'du byed*), and consciousnesses (Skt. *vijñāna*, Tib. *rnam shes*).

(2) The eighteen elements or constituents (Skt. *dhātu*, Tib. *khams*) consist of the six sense-objects, the six sense-faculties, and the six sense-consciousnesses.

The six sense-objects are forms, sounds, odors, tastes, tangible objects, and phenomena.

The six sense-faculties are the eye sense-faculty, the ear sense-faculty, the nose sense-faculty, the tongue sense-faculty, the body sense-faculty, and the mind sense-faculty.

The six sense-consciousnesses are the eye-consciousness, the ear-consciousness, the nose-consciousness, the tongue-consciousness, the body-consciousness, and the mental consciousness.

(3) The twelve entrances or sources (Skt. *āyatana*, Tib. *skye mched*) consist of the six sense-objects and the six sense-faculties, as mentioned above.

(For further information see, for example, Hopkins, *Meditation on Emptiness*, p. 271-274.)

Note 5:

On one hand the ten bodhisattva levels (Skt. *bhūmi*, Tib. *byang chub sems dpa'i sa bcu*) are related to the ten perfections (Skt. *pāramitā*, Tib. *pha rol tu phyin pa*), which are successively accomplished while one travels these levels. On the other hand they are related to the gradual process of purification during which the two veils of the mental poisons and hindrances to knowledge are eliminated. They are called:

    (1) Supremely Joyful
    (2) Stainless
    (3) Luminous
    (4) Radiant
    (5) Very Difficult to Overcome
    (6) Directly Manifest
    (7) Gone Afar
    (8) Immovable
    (9) Excellent Understanding
    (10) Cloud of Dharma.

These names can be explained as follows:

(1) The first bodhisattva level corresponds to the path of seeing. It is called "Supremely Joyful" since it is on the path of seeing that for the first time the nature of mind is realized directly and as it is. This realization is not just an experience, but is lasting and will not fade. It contains the certainty of henceforth wielding the ability to be of true benefit to all fellow beings. The dawning of this certainty is accompanied by great joy. The path of seeing, through which the first bodhisattva level is reached, contains the far-reaching transformation of an ordinary being into a bodhisattva. At this level the perfection of giving is achieved.

(2) On the second bodhisattva level, ethics reach their perfection. Through this attainment the conduct of a bodhisattva who dwells on

this level has become utterly pure. Since there are no faults of behaviors whatsoever, the second bhumi is called "the Stainless."

(3) "Luminous," the name of the third bodhisattva level, refers to an experience arising to a bodhisattva who dwells on this level during the post-meditative phase. At this time a copper-colored glow is seen, which is due to the fact that primordial wisdom shines through the phenomena perceived. In the system of the Sutrayana this experience is not developed, whereas in the Vajrayana system it is cultivated until gradually the streams of rainbow-colored light in which the deities appear are seen. On the third bodhisattva level the perfection of patience is achieved.

(4) The fourth bodhisattva level is called "the Radiant," since at this stage the copper-colored light, which is seen for the first time on the third bodhisattva level, gains an extraordinary intensity. The Sutrayana system of teachings does not contain any further explanation, whereas in the Vajrayana teachings this light is described extensively in terms of ten stages covering all the colors of the rainbow. On the fourth bhumi diligence is perfected.

(5) On the fifth bodhisattva level the perfection of meditative stability is attained. Its name "Very Difficult to Overcome" can be explained in two ways. On one hand it is difficult to purify the veils that obscure the nature of the mind at this point. On the other hand it is difficult to incite the disciples' effort towards serious discipline and practice.

(6) The sixth bodhisattva level is called "Directly Manifest" since a bodhisattva who dwells on this level has gained the ability of directly seeing the illusory nature of samsara. Samsara and nirvana are seen to be one and the same. There is no longer the slightest difference between them. On the sixth bodhisattva level discriminative wisdom reaches perfection.

(7) "Gone Afar," the name of the seventh bodhisattva level, can also be explained from two angles. On one hand it refers to the fact that the seventh bodhisattva level represents a state of development higher than that of a shravaka or pratyekabudbha arhat. When the Buddha sends forth light rays from his forehead to awaken these arhats from the state of extinction in which they abide, thus causing them to gain access to the Mahayana path, they take up this path at the beginning of the seventh bodhisattva level. On the other hand the name refers to the fact that during the seventh bodhisattva level the conceptual elaboration consisting of the perception of characteristics is completely abandoned,

and that a bodhisattva on this level goes beyond this obscuration. On the seventh bhumi the perfection of means is achieved.

(8) The eighth bodhisattva level is called "the Immovable" since a bodhisattva who dwells on this level is neither shaken by the concept that thoughts are present nor by the concept that no thoughts are present. On the eighth bhumi the perfection of wishing prayers is accomplished.

(9) The ninth bodhisattva level is called "Excellent Understanding" since a bodhisattva who dwells on this level has gained the capacity of seeing all phenomena that are objects of knowledge, as well as their true state, in an all-embracing way. On the ninth level power is perfected.

(10) The name of the tenth bodhisattva level is "Cloud of Dharma" since a bodhisattva who dwells on this level conveys the sacred Dharma to beings in a way that is spontaneous and free from any deliberate effort. This is similar to the sky in which rain clouds gather and release their abundant waters spontaneously and without effort onto the earth, where the rain provides for a good harvest. On the tenth bodhisattva level the perfection of primordial wisdom is achieved.

The ten bodhisattva levels represent progressive stages of purification from the two veils, which are the veils of the mental poisons and hindrances to knowledge.

(1) The two veils are defined as follows:

(a) The veil of the mental poisons (Skt. *kleśāvaraṇa*, Tib. *nyon mongs pa'i sgrib pa*) consists of the primary mental poisons, which are desire, hatred, and mental blindness, and of the secondary defilements stemming from these. The literal meaning of the Tibetan term *nyon mongs* is "affliction." This term is used since the arising of the mental poisons causes suffering and torment to the mind. The way in which the mental poisons arise can be illustrated by the example of dreaming. Suppose one dreams of friends and enemies. A dream has a nature that is illusory and the dream-appearances do not truly exist. In spite of this, desire and aversion will arise when facing a friend and an enemy respectively, as long as one does not recognize that one is dreaming. This example shows that it is the affliction of ignorance that constitutes the cause for the arising of all the other mental poisons.

The three primary mental poisons are eliminated by means of the following methods: Ignorance is abandoned by means of discriminative wisdom realizing the non-existence of a self. Aversion and hatred are eliminated by means of love and compassion. With regard to the abandonment of desire, different methods are used within the systems of the three vehicles. When following the shravaka path, desire is eliminated by means of its antidote. This is the meditation on revulsiveness, in the course of which one absorbs oneself into the fact that objects, which appear to be pleasant and are therefore desired, are in truth revulsive and thus undesirable. In the system of the path of the Mahayana, desire is abandoned by referring it back to emptiness and thus transforming it into this emptiness. Within the system of the Vajrayana desire itself is made use of as the means to overcome it.

(b) The veil of the hindrances to knowledge (Skt. *jñeyāvaraṇa*, Tib. *shes bya'i sgrib pa*) consists mainly of the fixation resulting from the fact that the so-called three circles or complexes, that is, subject, object, and their interaction, are taken to be truly existent. A subtler aspect of the veil of the hindrances to knowledge consists of the fixation upon characteristics. This is to say, a perception that is freed from the belief in true existence is present, but it conceptually identifies an object of perception by means of its characteristics, which are simultaneously labelled by a name. The subtlest aspect of the veil of the hindrances to knowledge is called "the appearance of duality as such." This means perception is no longer ruled by the belief in the true existence of the perceived object nor by the concepts of its characteristics, but identifies a mere "appearance as two" (Tib. *gnyis su snang ba*). These three types of hindrances to knowledge can also be illustrated by means of the example of dreaming. Suppose one dreams of giving a gift to somebody else. As long as one does not recognize that one is dreaming, one takes oneself (the giver), the other person (the receiver of the gift), and the action of giving to be truly existent. This action is virtuous since it springs from a good motivation. It cannot be said to be utterly pure, though, since the belief in the true existence of subject, object, and their interaction obscures the way of existence of these three aspects, which is the fact that they are empty of an existing essence. As soon as one recognizes that one is dreaming, the belief in the true existence of the giver, the receiver, and the action of giving is no longer present. What is present in the state of this realization is merely the perception of the appearance of these aspects, the characteristics of which are identified by a name. They appear as relative phenomena and are realized for what they are, as something empty by its very essence. Once the fixation on the conceptualized characteristics of phenomena is abandoned as well, there is nothing more than a mere "appearance as two," which is completely free from any further ideation.

(2) The relation of the ten bodhisattva levels to the gradual removal of the veils is as follows: All beings who have not realized the way of

existence of phenomena, who have not realized that phenomena are empty according to their essence, are infested by the fixation consisting of the belief in their true existence. This fixation is eliminated by direct realization of emptiness. Through this realization, by which the veil of the mental poisons and the coarse aspect of the veil of the hindrances to knowledge are removed, an ordinary being reaches the first bodhisattva level and becomes a noble bodhisattva. From the first up to the seventh bodhisattva level inclusively, the belief in the true existence of phenomena is no longer present. What is present is the subtler aspect of the fixation upon characteristics. For this reason these stages are also called the "impure bodhisattva levels." From the eighth up to the tenth bodhisattva level inclusively, the fixation upon characteristics is also overcome and no longer present. At this stage there is merely the appearance of duality as such, not accompanied by any fixation or concept. The last three are therefore called "the pure bodhisattva levels." At the time when a bodhisattva leaves the tenth bodhisattva level, this subtlest aspect of the veil of the hindrances to knowledge is also eliminated and the state of buddhahood is reached. This implies complete freedom from any concept whatsoever. It is the state of a tathagata, a vast and open space, which is by essence empty and by nature clear light in a completely indivisible way.

The division into the ten bodhisattva levels is therefore only due to a respective degree of purification from the two veils. With regard to the nature of mind itself, which has been utterly pure since beginningless time, there are no different stages. This nature of mind is always the same, just as, for instance, the new moon and the full moon are equally the moon, and there is no difference between these as far as the moon itself is concerned.

(The above is a rendering of oral teachings by Khenpo Tsultrim Gyamtso Rinpoche. They were given while he explained the *Jewel Ornament of Liberation* by Jetsün Gampopa in the spring of 1978, in La Poujade, France, and in the course of his explanations of this present text in the summer of 1979 in Karma Zöpa Ling, Langwedel, Germany. For further information see, for example, Hopkins, *Meditation on Emptiness,* especially pp. 96-109, 255-271, 296-304.)

Note 6:

The ten kinds of mastery are (1) mastery of life (Tib. *tshe la dbang ba*), (2) mastery of mind (Tib. *sems la dbang ba*), (3) mastery of necessaries (Tib. *yo byad la dbang ba*), (4) mastery of karma (Tib. *las la dbang ba*), (5) mastery of birth (Tib. *skye la dbang ba*), (6) mastery of intentions (Tib. *mos pa la dbang ba*), (7) mastery of wishing prayers (Tib. *smon lam la dbang ba*), (8) mastery of miraculous powers (Tib. *rdzu 'phrul la dbang ba*), (9) mastery of primordial wisdom (Tib. *ye shes la dbang ba*), and (10) mastery of Dharma (Tib. *chos la dbang ba*).

(1) Mastery of life is the capacity to live as long as one wishes.

(2) Mastery of mind is the capacity to rest in samadhi just as one wishes. Thus it is complete mastery of meditation.

(3) Mastery of necessaries is the capacity to cause an immeasurable rain of precious goods to fall onto beings.

(4) Mastery of karma is the capacity to transform the karma of other beings. A bodhisattva who has reached the tenth bodhisattva level is able to transform negative karma, the result of which would have to be experienced in a certain realm, in a certain place, as a certain being, as a certain type of birth, and at a certain time, into another karma that will result in a rebirth in the higher realms of existence.

(5) Mastery of birth means that such a bodhisattva is able to take birth in the realm of desire without leaving the state of meditative stability in which he is dwelling and without this state suffering the slightest deterioration. Although he is born there, he is not polluted by its faults.

(6) Mastery of intentions is the capacity to transform earth and so on into water and so on, just as one wishes.

(7) Mastery of wishing prayers is the capacity to utter wishing prayers that bring about the best possible benefit of others and to accomplish the fulfillment of these prayers.

(8) Mastery of miraculous powers is the capacity to demonstrate powerful miracles in order to awaken aspiration towards the Dharma in beings.

(9) Mastery of primordial wisdom is supreme and ultimate knowledge with respect to all phenomena, to their meaning and definition, and with respect to one's own courage. The former means that a bodhisattva who dwells on the tenth bodhisattva level knows the absolute and the relative truths. The latter refers to his capacity of fearlessly teaching the Dharma in every aspect and to any assembly.

(10) Mastery of Dharma means that a bodhisattva who has reached the tenth bodhisattva level is able to transmit the teachings of the sutras and so forth to all sentient beings by using the linguistic instruments, such as words, terms, names, and so on, in such a way that in manner and amount they correspond exactly to the respective mental capacity

of each individual being. In doing so he is able to satisfy the minds of different beings through one single teaching, which is heard simultaneously in their respective native languages.

(The foregoing explanation is taken from the chapter "The Necessary Condition is the Spiritual Friend" of the *Jewel Ornament of Liberation* by Jetsün Gampopa.)

Note 7:

The Dharma in terms of instruction consists of the words of the Buddha, which he expounded in twelve different ways called "the twelve branches of the supreme speech of the Buddha" (Tib. *gsung rab yan lag bcu gnyis*). They consist of the sections of discourses (Tib. *mdo sde'i sde*), of songs (Tib. *dbyangs kyis bsnyad pa'i sde*), of prophecies (Tib. *lung du bstan pa'i sde*), of poetry (Tib. *tshigs su bcad pa'i sde*), of commitments (Tib. *chad du brjod pa'i sde*), of stories (Tib. *gleng gzhi'i sde*), of expressing realization (Tib. *rtogs pa brzod pa'i sde*), of history (Tib. *de lta bu byung ba'i sde*), of expounding the lineage of great beings (Tib. *skyes pa rabs kyi sde*), of full and complete explanation (Tib. *shin tu rgyas pa'i sde*), of relating the wondrous deeds of saintly beings (Tib. *rmad du byung ba'i sde*), and of reàsonings (Tib. *gtan la 'bab pa'i sde*).

Yet, the actual teaching of the Buddha is the Dharma in terms of realization. That is whatever genuine experience has dawned within one's own stream of being through practicing the actual meaning of the words of the Buddha, through cultivating the qualities resulting from the three trainings and from the developing and perfecting stages [of the Vajrayana system], respectively.

(The above is taken from *Clarifying Suchness: A Fool's Note on the Developing and the Perfecting Stages* [Tib. *bskyed rdzogs kyi zin bris blun gtam de nyid gsal ba bzhugs so*] by Dzogchenpa Shönnu Yeshe Dorje, who is also known by the name Do Khyentse Rinpoche.)

Note 8:

Karma Thrinläpa lived in the late fifteenth/early sixteenth century and was an eminent teacher belonging to the Sakya school. He was the main disciple of Rongtön, though his root teacher was the Seventh Karmapa Chötrag Gyatso. Later Karma Thrinläpa himself became the teacher of the Eighth Karmapa Mikyö Dorjé.

The comparison with the noise of the rabbit is an allusion to the tale of the rabbit who, when a fruit (or branch) fell on his head, thought that this was a sign that the world was coming to an end. He ran off into the forest to tell everybody and thus initially caused a wild panic.

Note 9:

The four continents are Videha in the east, which is white and semicircular; Jambudvipa in the south, which is blue and trapezoidal; Godaniya in the west, which is red and round; and Uttara-Kuru in the north, which is green and square.

The seven possessions of a Chakravartin are the following:

(1) The thousand-spoked wheel made of gold from the river Jambud.

(2) The eight-sided wish-fulfilling gem, which is bright as the rays of the sun and can be seen to shine from a distance of several yojanas.

(3) The beautiful queen possessing the thirty-two marks of feminine perfection.

(4) The minister who excels in both physique and intelligence and who can find treasures buried underground.

(5) The golden-necklaced white elephant with his seven steadfast limbs, who can carry the Chakravartin anywhere.

(6) The excellent horse colored like a peacock's neck, who can circle the four continents in an instant.

(7) The mighty general possessing the sixty-four special skills.

The above is taken from *The Torch of Certainty* (Tib. *gnes don sgron me*) by Jamgön Kongtrül, translated by Judith Hanson (Boston and London: Shambala Publications, 1994). For further information see there pp. 97-104.

Note 10:

The thirty-seven dharmas conducive to enlightenment (Skt. *bodhipakṣikadharmas*, Tib. *byang chub kyi phyogs dang mthun pa'i chos*) constitute the path to be traveled by a yogi and divide into seven sections:

(1) The first section consists of the four aspects of the development of mindfulness (Skt. *smṛtyupasthāna*, Tib. *dran pa nye bar bzhag pa bzhi*), which are mindfulness with respect to the body, emotions, thoughts, and phenomena. The four kinds of mindfulness are cultivated on the small path of accumulation. They consist of the meditations on impermanence, suffering, emptiness, and on the fact that one's own body, thoughts, emotions, and the other inner phenomena do not exist as a self. A bodhisattva would extend his or her meditation to embrace the bodies, thoughts, and so forth of all other beings as well.

(2) The second section consists of the four aspects of thorough abandonment (Skt. *samyakprahāṇa*, Tib. *yang dag par spong ba bzhi*): abandoning mental poisons that have already arisen, not giving rise to mental poisons that have not yet arisen, generating pure dharmas that have not yet been generated, and increasing pure dharmas that have

already been generated. The four kinds of thorough abandonment are cultivated on the middling path of accumulation. They are called "thorough" since their practice is suited to lead one to buddhahood, provided they are supplemented by the aspiration of wanting to reach supreme enlightenment in order to become able to benefit all sentient beings. The development of pure dharmas or virtues is also called an "abandonment," since in order to develop any virtue its respective contrary needs to be abandoned.

(3) The third section consists of the four supports of miraculous powers (Skt. *ṛddhipāda*, Tib. *rdzu 'phrul gyi rkang pa bzhi*), which are the samadhis of longing (Skt. *chanda*, Tib. *'dun pa*), of diligence (Skt. *vīrya*, Tib. *brtson 'grus*), of intention (Skt. *citta*, Tib. *sems*), and of discrimination (Skt. *mimāṃsa*, Tib. *dpyod pa*). They are called "supports" since they are the prerequisites for a manifestation coming about miraculously. They are cultivated on the great path of accumulation.

(4) The fourth section consists of the five capacities (Skt. *indriya*, Tib. *dbang po lnga*), which are faith (Skt. *śraddhā*, Tib. *dad pa*), diligence (Skt. *vīrya*, Tib. *brtson 'grus*), mindfulness (Skt. *smṛti*, Tib. *dran pa*), samadhi (Tib. *ting nge 'dzin*), and discriminative wisdom (Skt. *prajñā*, Tib. *shes rab*). They are attained on the levels "heat" and "peak" of the path of junction.

(5) The fifth section consists of the five powers (Skt. *bala*, Tib. *stobs lnga*), which are faith, diligence, mindfulness, samadhi, and discriminative wisdom (see above) as they are attained on the levels "forbearance" and "highest mundane dharma" of the path of junction.

(6) The sixth section consists of the seven branches of enlightenment (Skt. *bodhyaṅga*, Tib. *byang chub kyi yan lag bdun*), which are mindfulness (Skt. *smṛti*, Tib. *dran pa*), discrimination of phenomena (Skt. *dharmapravicaya*, Tib. *chos rnam par 'byed pa yang dag*), diligence (Skt. *vīrya*, Tib. *brtson 'grus*), joy (Skt. *prīti*, Tib. *dga' ba yang dag*), suppleness (Skt. *praśrabdhi*, Tib. *shin tu sbyangs pa yang dag*), samadhi (Tib. *ting nge 'dzin*), and equanimity (Skt. *upekṣa*, Tib. *btang snyoms yang dag*). These are accomplished on the path of seeing.

(7) The seventh section consists of the noble eightfold path (Skt. *āryamārgāṅga*, Tib. *'phags pa'i lam yan lag brgyad*) the branches of which are right view (Skt. *samyagdṛṣṭī*, Tib. *yang dag pa'i lta ba*), right thought (Skt. *samyaksaṃkalpa*, Tib. *yang dag pa'i rtog pa*), right speech (Skt. *samyagvac*, Tib. *yang dag pa'i ngag*), right action (Skt. *samyakkarmānta*, Tib. *yang dag pa'i las kyi mtha'*), right livelihood (Skt. *samyagājīva*, Tib.

yang dag pa'i tsho ba), right effort (Skt. *samyagvyāyāma*, Tib. *yang dag pa'i rtsol ba*), right mindfulness (Skt. *samyaksmṛti*, Tib. *yang dag pa'i dran pa*), and right concentration (Skt. *samyaksamādhi*, Tib. *yang dag pa'i ting nge 'dzin*). They are attained on the path of meditation.

When arhathood is reached, all the thirty-seven dharmas conducive to enlightenment are accomplished.

(The above is taken from the eighteenth chapter of the *Jewel Ornament of Liberation* [Tib. *dam chos yid bzhin nor bu thar pa rin po che'i rgyan*] by the Noble Gampopa, teaching the five paths. For further information see, for example, Hopkins, *Meditation on Emptiness*, pp. 205, 206).

Note 11:
As a general guideline for a practitioner to take to heart, the Buddha advised that one should rely on four principles rather than upon four others. This advice is as follows:

> Rather than on the words rely on the meaning.
> Rather than on personalities rely on Dharma.
> Rather than on any relative truth rely on the ultimate truth.
> Rather than on the provisional rely on the definitive meaning.

As for the last statement there are, generally speaking, two ways in which the Buddha taught and in which his teachings are therefore presented. The first is called "neyartha" in Sanskrit (Tib. *drang don*), which can be translated as "provisional meaning" or "meaning requiring interpretation." This refers to teachings that are given for a specific purpose and are not identical to truth itself: they are meant to lead one gradually to the understanding of the actual truth. This does not mean that these teachings are false. They are true but not totally so. They are valid to a certain extent and on the relative level. One might call them a half-truth that will guide one into truth as it actually is. The Buddha has described these teachings by means of the following example:

Suppose there is a house with many children inside and this house is abundantly filled with all kinds of beautiful toys and very attractive pleasurable things. Then you suddenly see that the house has caught fire and will go up in flames any time. So you call the children: "Come out! Come out! Quickly! The house is burning!" Yet, being so immersed in their toys and pleasures they will not listen. All these playthings are far too exciting to be left behind and the children do not realize the danger. Therefore you have to decoy them and shout: "There are so many wonderful toys out here, much more and far nicer ones than in the house! You should come outside and have a look!" Hearing that, the children become curious and run from the house. There may not be any toys outside but the children are saved from the fire!

This illustrates what is to be understood by the teachings conveying the provisional meaning: in a way one is not telling the full truth, but this is done for a purpose that otherwise would not be achieved. Then again it cannot be said to be totally untrue. One may not have any toys out there but it is possible to find and provide some later. Since the children did not die, they are still able to play. If they had died, there would be no other chance for them to enjoy any toy. A statement that was not totally truthful at the time saved their lives and thus provided a future opportunity. For this reason it is called a provisional truth. All the teachings expressing the relative level are contained in this aspect. The second is called "nitartha" in Sanskrit (Tib. *nges don*). This can be translated as "definitive meaning." It refers to those teachings that directly express the truth, the ultimate level, the way everything really is.

(The above is an explanation by Ringu Tulku Rinpoche, as given 1997 in Theksum Tashi Chöling, Hamburg.)

Note 12:

Rahu (Tib. *sgra gcan*) is the name of a planet that, according to Chinese and Brahminical astrology, exercises malignant influences on the destinies of mankind. It is especially known for its being at enmity with the sun and the moon on which it takes continuous vengeance by swallowing them and thus causing eclipses.

Note 13:

The four essentials of partnership (Tib. *bsdu ba'i dngos po bzhi*) are: giving the necessities of life (Tib. *mkho ba sbyin pa*), speaking in an agreeable and conciliatory way (Tib. *snyan par smra ba*), acting in accordance with the manners and customs of the world (Tib. *'jig rten don mthun pa*), and fulfilling the benefit of the disciples (Tib. *gdul bya'i don la spyod pa*).

Note 14:

Generally speaking, ten sciences (Tib. *rig gnas bcu*) are distinguished of which five are higher and five are minor. The latter are the sciences of healing or medicine (Tib. *gso ba rig pa*), of words or language (Tib. *sgra rig pa*), of valid cognition (Tib. *tshad ma rig pa*), of dialectics (Tib.

gtan tshig rig pa), and of mechanical crafts (Tib. *bzo rig pa*). The five higher sciences referred to here consist of the knowledge of the inner meaning of the three pitakas (Tib. *nang don sde snod gsum rig pa*). The three pitakas are the vinayapitaka, the abhidharmapitaka, and the sutrapitaka; these comprise all the teachings of the Buddha.

Dedication

May the merit resulting from the work with this text contribute in the greatest possible measure to the temporary and ultimate welfare of all sentient beings.